Failure of Intelligence

Failure of Intelligence

The Decline and Fall of the CIA

Melvin A. Goodman

ROWMAN & LITTLEFIELD PUBLISHERS, INC.
Lanham • Boulder • New York • Toronto • Plymouth, UK

To Lini and our magical grandchildren:
Alex, James, Julia, Matthew, and Willa

ROWMAN & LITTLEFIELD PUBLISHERS, INC.

Published in the United States of America
by Rowman & Littlefield Publishers, Inc.
A wholly owned subsidiary of The Rowman & Littlefield Publishing Group, Inc.
4501 Forbes Boulevard, Suite 200, Lanham, Maryland 20706
www.rowmanlittlefield.com

Estover Road
Plymouth PL6 7PY
United Kingdom

British Library Cataloguing in Publication Information Available

Library of Congress Cataloging-in-Publication Data

Goodman, Melvin A. (Melvin Allan), 1938-
    Failure of intelligence : the decline and fall of the CIA / Melvin A. Goodman.
    p. cm.
    Includes bibliographical references and index.
    ISBN-13: 978-0-7425-5110-7 (cloth : alk. paper)
    ISBN-10: 0-7425-5110-5 (cloth : alk. paper)
    1. United States. Central Intelligence Agency. 2. Intelligence service—United States.
    3. United States—Politics and government—2001- I. Title.
    JK468.I6G663 2008
    327.1273—dc22   2007032794

Printed in the United States of America

⊚™ The paper used in this publication meets the minimum requirements of American
National Standard for Information Sciences—Permanence of Paper for Printed Library
Materials, ANSI/NISO Z39.48-1992.

Contents

Contents

1

The Central Intelligence Agency: Organizing for Intelligence

The time has arrived for a serious review of the CIA's role in our national security community. Strategic intelligence failures over the past twenty years have undermined the Agency's ability to perform its most important mission: providing our policymakers with objective, independent analysis of the international challenges we face. Recent failures include the lack of strategic warning of the collapse of the Soviet Union and of the 9/11 attacks and the corruption of intelligence to support the Bush administration's war against Iraq. These failures have made the CIA vulnerable to further encroachment on its independence by the policy community and the military. The CIA, moreover, no longer knows how to provide truth to power and lacks the courage to do so. The CIA costs the nation more than $5 billion annually and the entire intelligence community spends more than $50 billion. The limited changes that have taken place since 9/11 have not improved this enterprise; indeed, they may have weakened it. Until we understand the reasons for past failures, the nexus between intelligence and policy, and the need for an intelligence agency independent of policymakers, it will be difficult to get genuine reform. This book is devoted to informing such a discussion and developing a reform agenda.

Sixty years ago, President Harry S. Truman created the CIA to prevent another surprise attack, such as Pearl Harbor in 1941, and to deal with the Soviet threat in the wake of the Second World War. As in 1947–1948, when the CIA was created, the United States now faces an international environment that has been entirely recast. The threats are new, and the institutions created to fight the cold war, particularly the intelligence agencies, must be redesigned. If steps are not taken to improve the intelligence community, particularly the CIA, we can expect more terrorist attacks without warning and greater proliferation of nuclear technology to Third World states and nonstate actors, the greatest threat facing the United States. The failure of the CIA to learn the hard lessons of failures regarding the collapse of the Soviet Union, the terror attacks of 9/11, and the pre-Iraq War collapse of analytic tradecraft does not augur well for the future of intelligence in the United States. The greatest intelligence scandal in American history was the corruption of intelligence used to go to war against Iraq. This failure has already cost several hundred thousand Iraqi lives and nearly thirty thousand American fatalities and casualties.

Credible and incisive intelligence is essential to the national security of the nation. In Joseph Conrad's novel, *The Secret Agent* (1907), there is a minor character, an anarchist called the professor, whom no one dares to touch because he has wired himself to a powerful bomb. The novel ends with a view of the mad professor walking like a "pest in the street full of men." This grotesque vision, familiar to many in Israel, Iraq, Colombia, Lebanon, and Great Britain is now a clear and present danger to America. This vision brings home to us that, in the long run, law enforcement agencies and local police will win the campaign against terrorism. They will rely on intelligence collected and analyzed by a reformed intelligence community and a rebuilt CIA. The Iraq War has demonstrated that the blunt use of military force merely creates more terrorists than it can eliminate. Understanding the challenge and dealing with the threat requires objective and balanced intelligence.

Objective and independent intelligence is needed to assess the nature of geopolitical threats, which too often become exaggerated in a partisan political environment. Whether it was international communism in the 1950s or international terrorism in the 1980s, the threat of the Soviet Union during the worst days of the cold war, or the fear of Islamic extremism today, intelligence must put the threat in perspective in order to support the formulation of a clear-eyed and rational national security policy. If nothing else, objective intelligence should enable policymakers to challenge today's polemicists and alarmists and deal with the real threats to our national security. As the great journalist from Baltimore, H. L. Mencken, warned decades ago: "The whole aim of practical politics is to keep the populace alarmed—and hence clamorous to be led to safety—by menacing it with an endless series of hobgoblins, all of them imaginary." Our threats have not always been imaginary, but the portrayal of them has often been terribly exaggerated, such as the distorted view of a dysfunctional Soviet Union portrayed as ten-feet tall in the 1980s or the depiction of regional actors such as North Korea, Iraq, and Iran joined in an "axis of evil." The most damaging of these exaggerations was the Bush administration's drum-beat of fear concerning Iraq's fictional arsenal of weapons of mass destruction in the run-up to the Iraq War. Currently, President Bush is justifying our presence in Iraq to "make sure that the terrorists do not follow us home." Professional and independent intelligence analysis would have given the lie to these campaigns.

* * *

The National Security Act of 1947 created the CIA and the National Security Council, the Department of Defense, and the Air Force (as a separate military service). The United States was aware of the need for a central intelligence agency from the time of the surprise attack on Pearl Harbor on December 7, 1941, which led directly to the postwar interest in premonitory intelligence. The congressional hearings on the establishment of a central intelligence agency turned on concerns about Pearl Harbor and what had gone wrong on December 7, 1941. Pearl Harbor created the groundwork for the creation of the CIA and was the catalyst that overwhelmed the American opposition to a permanent intelligence organization in peacetime, which had been engrained in the American political culture since the time of the Founding Fathers. But Pearl Harbor alone could not override this opposition. The sinister role of Joseph Stalin and the unpredictability of the Soviet Union also played major roles.

Prior to the attack at Pearl Harbor, the United States had collected sufficient intelligence to anticipate and drastically limit the damage of the Japanese air and naval forces. The intelligence services of the U.S. Army and Navy had broken the Japanese diplomatic and military codes and, as a result, were aware of Japanese plans to attack British and Dutch targets in Southeast Asia. The evidence of imminent Japanese attacks against American targets was not as precise, but, nevertheless, the United States was aware as early as November 19, 1941 that the Japanese foreign ministry had sent a coded message ("East wind rain") that pointed to a decision to go to war. Several days later, intercepted Japanese communications traffic ("MAGIC") indicated that Foreign Minister Togo had ordered the ambassador in Washington to settle negotiations by November 29 because "after that, things are going to happen automatically."

During this period, the Japanese Navy changed its ship call signs, which pointed to the possibility of confrontation, and on December 2, the foreign ministry ordered its embassy in Washington to destroy its codes, ciphers, and classified documents, another indication of war. Japanese aircraft carriers and submarines were out of port and their exact location had been lost to the United States; there were reports that Japanese naval air units were practicing simulated torpedo attacks against ships in harbors in southern Japan. U.S. military intelligence was also aware of Japanese agents in Hawaii collecting intelligence on military facilities at Pearl Harbor and Clark Field;

U.S. ambassador Joseph Grew reported that his Peruvian counterpart had learned that Japan was planning a "surprise attack against Pearl Harbor with all their strength and emphasizing all their equipment" if relations between the United States and Japan worsened.[1] Like the 9/11 tragedy of 2001, there had been sufficient collection of intelligence prior to Pearl Harbor to provide strategic warning of the attack. And like 9/11, the problem was inadequate distribution of intelligence and mediocre analysis of collected intelligence.

With the beginning of the cold war, U.S. policymakers wanted an independent intelligence agency that could assess not only the capabilities, but the intentions of the key threat, the Soviet Union, in order to prevent miscalculations. Soon after the end of World War II, Prime Minister Winston Churchill warned President Harry Truman that an "Iron Curtain" had descended across Europe, and that the United States and England could not drop their military guard. Truman's first director of the Central Intelligence Group (CIG) was his friend and advisor, Rear Admiral Sidney Souers, who also become the first director of the CIA. Truman playfully dubbed Souers his "director of centralized snooping," and conferred upon him a "black coat, black hat, and wooden dagger."[2] Souers, well aware of the opposition to his new organization, did his best not to foster misgivings or animosity toward the CIA.

In view of the traditional American opposition to creating a secret intelligence agency in a democratic society, the surprise attack at Pearl Harbor was not sufficient to explain the creation of the CIA. Without the concerns about the Soviet Union and its paranoid leader, Stalin, and without the fear of a cold war, it is hard to imagine a consensus to allow the creation of a secret agency that was perceived as a challenge, if not a threat, to the powers of the Pentagon and the Federal Bureau of Investigation (FBI). Just as the FBI opposed the creation of the CIA, fearing a rival in clandestine collection and counterintelligence, the Department of State (DoS) and the new Department of Defense (DoD) did not want a rival agency, such as the CIA, preparing its own political and military assessments.[3]

Policy departments, such as the DoS and DoD, could not be trusted to assess the Soviet or Chinese threat or calculate their intentions without a policy bias. The CIA was created as an independent agency within the Executive Office of the President in 1947 to prevent such bias. It would advise the National Security Council on intelligence matters, evaluate intelligence on national security matters, and perform "other such functions and duties" related to intelligence.[4] The reference to other functions presumably covered clandestine collection of intelligence and covert action, but President Truman's primary concern and focus was the need for central and independent intelligence analysis for the policy community and the distribution of this analysis to the entire national security community. He wanted an independent agency to inform the White House of international developments, but had concerns that a powerful agency could lead to an "American Gestapo." The urgent needs of the development of the cold war convinced him to forget his concerns and endorse a CIA.

In its first five years, the CIA had to deal with sensitive intelligence issues that had a huge impact on policy, such as the Iron Curtain in Central Europe, atomic testing in the Soviet Union, the communist revolution in China, and the start of the Korean War. The first tasking directives of both the CIG and the CIA dealt with gathering intelligence on the Soviet Union and making sure that U.S. policymakers understood the intentions of the Soviet leaders and the capabilities of the Soviet Red Army. The Truman administration and the American people were willing to overlook concerns about the CIA because of its mission against the Soviet Union, just as today the United States appears willing to justify CIA crimes in the name of the fight against terrorism. America had decided in the 1950s to fight "fire with fire" in the cold war, and fifty years later claimed the need to fight "fire with fire" in the so-called war against terror, thus fostering a climate that permitted abuses of power.

There was resistance to the creation of the CIA from the outset, particularly from Secretary of State Dean Acheson, FBI director J. Edgar Hoover, and the Pentagon's senior military officers. Acheson warned President Truman that "neither he, the National Security Council, nor anyone else would be in a position to know what it was doing or to control it."[5] Hoover's opposition was simply one of bureaucratic politics; he vehemently opposed any agency that rivaled his own FBI in the fields of intelligence collection and counterintelligence. He campaigned against maintaining the OSS in peacetime, arguing that it would become an "American Gestapo." Several months after the war ended, the OSS was abolished and a small intelligence organization, the Strategic Services Unit (SSU), was created in the War Department. The Pentagon embraced the SSU because it wanted to dominate the intelligence business, realizing that intelligence analysis was essential to making the case for the Pentagon's budget and for threat perception. The Pentagon did not want to share these responsibilities with a civilian agency. The policymakers who opposed the creation of the CIA were right about the threat the Agency would represent to their narrow parochial interests.

Admiral Souers realized that his most important mission was to establish an elite body of experts from the military and civilian agencies in order to produce credible strategic intelligence. It was not until the outbreak of the Korean War in 1950, which was a major intelligence failure, that there was recognition of the need to build a professional analytic cadre for current intelligence and the production of NIEs. The misreading of events on the Korean peninsula prior to the North Korean invasion of the South in 1950 was costly in terms of blood and treasure and contributed to President Truman's decision not to run for reelection in 1952.

The North Korean leadership had convinced Soviet and Chinese leaders to support its decision to invade South Korea because of an assumption that the United States had drawn its defense perimeter in North Asia without incorporating the Korean peninsula. Such a decision seemed to be reflected in the remarks of Secretary of State Acheson, who gave a speech to the Council on Foreign Relations in April 1950 that omitted Korea from U.S. security interests in the region. The CIA did not understand the impact of Acheson's remarks; it traditionally pays insufficient attention to U.S. statements on foreign nations and foreign policy. It also failed to understand that North Korean leader Kim Il Sung was pressing for war against South Korea, and he had to persuade China and the Soviet Union to provide the weapons and the wherewithal to give Kim the confidence to attack.

The U.S. preoccupation with the Korean War from 1950 to 1953 permitted the CIA to take on additional activities in the fields of clandestine collection of intelligence and covert action, without adverse reaction from the rest of the national security community or from Congress. As a result, somewhat ironically, covert action emerged as the key facet of the Agency and had great impact on national policy. Two key early covert actions were the overthrow of the popularly elected Mohammed Mossadegh government in Iran in 1953 and the Jacobo Arbenz Guzman government in Guatemala. Mossadegh and Arbenz were heroes to the deprived classes of Iran and Guatemala, respectively, and both pursued leftist policies that were anathema to the Eisenhower administration. As with other covert actions, the president approved the overthrow of Mossadegh and Arbenz. U.S. interests would have been far better served over the long term if these populists had been left in power.

At the start, it was not clear whether the CIA would be able to produce its own finished intelligence as opposed to simply correlating the information of other agencies and departments. Since the State Department did very few intelligence estimates and assessments and the Pentagon frequently resorted to worst-case assessments to justify greater defense spending, a consensus developed to permit the CIA to play a greater role in the collection and production of intelligence. The first important office created in the field of intelligence analysis in 1948 was the Office of Scientific Intelligence, which concentrated on nuclear-related issues. Gradually, CIA analysts began to receive special clearances on particular issues and from this group, grew an office of analysts who concentrated on current intelligence on the Soviet Union.

This new group had many analytic failures in the immediate aftermath of World War II; these failures included the inability to provide warning of the communist takeover of Czechoslovakia, Tito's departure from the Soviet Bloc, the collapse of the Nationalist government in China, the timing of the first Soviet atomic test, the Greek civil war, and the outbreak of the Korean War. The intelligence failure regarding testing was particularly embarrassing to the CIA because the intelligence that would have allowed strategic warning of Soviet testing was available but not circulated to the appropriate CIA offices. These failures led to demands for bolstering the intelligence capabilities of the CIA and for creating a special unit to concentrate on the production of NIEs. After the start of the Korean War, the CIA received a new director, Lieutenant General Walter Bedell Smith, who was more high-powered and competent than his one-star military predecessors; he immediately moved to improve intelligence analysis. He abolished the Office of Research and Evaluation and replaced it with the Office of National Estimates (ONE) to produce national estimates; the Office of Research and Reports (ORR) to do basic research; and the Office of Current Intelligence (OCI) to produce intelligence analysis on fast-moving events, resembling the wire service reporting of the Associated Press or United Press International. The triad of current, estimative, and historical intelligence was the key to competitive analysis and methodologies; the decline in estimative and historical capabilities has significantly weakened the capability of the CIA to provide strategic intelligence.

The Agency's most important intelligence requirement was the production of estimates and assessments tracking Soviet political and military interests, particularly any Politburo decisions that could lead to a confrontation or challenge with the United States. It was particularly important to understand the scope and lethality of Soviet strategic capabilities, particularly Moscow's nuclear capabilities. The urgent need for military intelligence led to the development of intelligence collection platforms that included reconnaissance flights and naval incursions into Soviet territorial waters as well as tunnels burrowed into East Berlin to tap into Soviet military cable lines. General Curtis LeMay, head of the Strategic Air Command, revealed that in the 1950s he authorized many penetrating reconnaissance overflights, including a demonstration flight over the Vladivostok defense region without political authorization.[6] Sophisticated technical systems including the rapid development of the high altitude U-2 reconnaissance aircraft, which the Soviets could track but not interdict, and the SR-71 (nicknamed *Blackbird*) that could fly 2,100 miles an hour and, with aerial refueling, had global range. Satellite photography was the most important method for producing intelligence imagery, which eventually became the key to arms control and disarmament agreements in the 1970s and 1980s. The CIA, from the beginning, was at the center of this triumph in American technology.

There was great concern throughout the government with the role of covert action and where to place the responsibility for covert action. No one rushed forward to claim the bureaucratic entity that would be responsible for "dirty tricks." In wartime, Secretary of Defense James Forrestal believed the Pentagon should be responsible for the conduct of covert action, but he did not want it placed in the Pentagon in peacetime. The CIA leadership itself was opposed to having responsibility for covert action, believing that the clandestine function would ultimately taint the intelligence product, a prescient observation. Many of the key policymakers feared the CIA would not be accountable for covert action. These fears led to Senator Frank Church (D-Idaho) accusing the Agency in the 1970s with being a "rogue elephant out of control." Church eventually learned through his own hearings, however, there was no "rogue elephant." The White House actually had inspired and approved all CIA covert action.

Interestingly, it was the late George Kennan, the father of containment, who made the strongest case within the State Department for the creation of a CIA as well as the ultimate placement of responsibility for covert action in the CIA's directorate of operations (DO). Kennan was the first member of the Foreign Service to warn of the Soviet threat, and he drafted national security memorandum NSC 10/2 on June 18, 1948, creating the Office of Special Projects to counter the "vicious covert activities of the USSR."[7] The office was quickly renamed the Office of Policy Coordination (OPC), which was far more benign sounding, but it was responsible for "sabotage, antisabotage . . . subversion against hostile states, including assistance to underground resistance groups, and support of indigenous anticommunist elements in threatened countries of the free world."[8] OPC was soon attached to the CIA, but responsibility for initiating covert action rested with Kennan, the head of State's Policy Planning Staff. Kennan himself soon developed second thoughts about covert action and the conduct of containment, realizing that the Soviet Union was not about to invade Western Europe. But it was too late. Many émigrés were recruited for the clandestine work of espionage, according to one of the CIA's leading Soviet experts. "It was a visceral business of using any bastard as long as he was anticommunist," said Harry Rositzke.[9] The CIA and covert action were off and running, with U.S. operatives playing key roles in electing anticommunist governments in Western Europe and participating in coups d'etat against Iran and Guatemala in the 1950s.

Official CIA materials present both Iran and Guatemala as "unblemished successes." Although each was a tactical success, each was a strategic disaster. The "success" of returning the Shah to Iran continues to bedevil U.S.–Iranian relations more than fifty years after he was installed on the throne by the United States and Britain. The intelligence services of the two countries had conspired in 1953 to overthrow Iran's elected Prime Minister Mohammad Mossadeq, who planned to nationalize its oil industry, which represented

Britain's largest single overseas investment. The operation was led by a grandson of President Theodore Roosevelt, Kermit Roosevelt, who was described as a "courteous, soft-spoken Easterner with impeccable social connections," and by George Kennedy Young, son of a poor Scottish grocer and recipient of a graduate degree from Yale University. Roosevelt and Young handpicked General Fazlollah Zahedi to succeed Mossadegh and covertly funneled $5 million to the new regime several days after the successful coup.[10] The CIA recruited Iranians to pose as communists to harass Iran's religious leaders and even to bomb a cleric's home to turn the country's Islamic community against the Mossadegh government.

The Shah was recruited to sign "royal decrees" that had been drafted by the CIA to transfer power to his government, although the U.S. and British intelligence services were prepared to go ahead with the plan regardless of whether the Shah cooperated. When the Shah showed signs of losing his nerve, the CIA recruited his twin sister, Princess Ashraf Pahlevi, and General H. Norman Schwarzkopf, the father of the 1991 Desert Storm commander, to bolster the Shah's confidence. Nevertheless, the Shah fled the country as soon as riots broke out. When the coup succeeded several days later, the Shah was returned from the Excelsior Hotel in Rome and given his own $5 million grant from the CIA. When the riots were not followed by immediate success for the coup plot, however, CIA director Dulles cabled Roosevelt to leave the country. But the Iranian goons hired by the CIA were successful; therefore, Roosevelt remained in the country and it was Mossadegh who fled. The CIA's success in Iran allowed Standard Oil of New Jersey to enter the country, ending the British oil monopoly.

"Success" in Guatemala, like Iran, was marked by inept performances on the part of the Western intelligence agencies, and was bloodier and more costly over the long run. The army's reign of terror in Guatemala lasted for decades, with the deaths of hundreds of thousands of the indigenous population. The CIA's assassination activity in Guatemala, more than any other experience, led to CIA director William Colby's decision to support a ban on assassination activity in the 1970s. The country was a virtual colony of the United Fruit Company, whose monopoly had existed since the 1930s with the help of John Foster Dulles, a lawyer with Sullivan and Cromwell, the most prestigious international law firm in the United States. U.S. concerns about the success of the communists were highly exaggerated, particularly in view of the fact that the Guatemalan Communist Party had fewer than two hundred active members.

Like Iran in 1953, the United States had destabilized a democratically elected government in Guatemala, and like Iraq in 2003, the United States resorted to force without any plan to stabilize conditions there. The Guatemalan operation was not well planned, but the CIA benefited from the fact that Jacobo Arbenz Guzman and the entire Guatemalan army panicked and collapsed. Just as Mossadegh was targeted for wanting to nationalize the British oil holdings in Iran, Arbenz was vulnerable because he wanted to appropriate the holdings of the United Fruit Company. Assistant Secretary of State John Moors Cabot owned stock in United Fruit and his brother, Thomas, had served as president of the company. UN ambassador Henry Cabot Lodge was a United Fruit stockholder and had defended the company while serving as a U.S. senator. Walter Bedell Smith, the undersecretary of state and former CIA director, also served on the company's board of directors.

Guatemala represented no national security risk to the United States and was in no position to threaten its tiny neighbors. Its small army was totally disorganized and inept, and various military juntas vied for power in Guatemala before Castillo Armas consolidated power in 1954. The Eisenhower administration had to raise the bogus threat of Soviet influence in Guatemala in order to justify its actions, which was similar to later U.S. operations in Cuba, Nicaragua, and Grenada. The CIA created a small pirate air force to bomb Arbenz into submission, and then recruited soldiers of fortune to pilot the aircraft. Armas and the CIA also worked together to develop sabotage teams that performed assassinations against so-called leftist supporters of Arbenz. Officially the CIA maintains that "no covert plan involving assassinations of Guatemalans was ever approved or implemented," although the unofficial records of those involved in Guatemala maintain that assassinations were attempted.[11]

The ease of tactical success in Iran and Guatemala led directly to the hubris to create a "quick-fix" plan to remove Fidel Castro, which revolved around the landing at the Bay of Pigs. This was ultimately termed the "perfect failure" by the Inspector General of the CIA. A modest plan under President Eisenhower involving the infiltration of a limited number of Cuban exiles to create an underground resistance against Castro morphed into a larger landing force with anticipated support from the U.S. Air Force under President John F. Kennedy. Virtually the same cast of CIA characters responsible for the events in Guatemala was responsible for the planning of the Bay of Pigs. And in both events, Guatemala and Cuba, CIA officials lied to Presidents Eisenhower and Kennedy about the full nature of the operations, the risks, and likely losses.

The events in Iran and Guatemala in 1953 unfortunately convinced the Eisenhower administration to consolidate the ascendancy of covert action over clandestine collection and intelligence analysis at the CIA. President Eisenhower was looking for ways to cut the defense budget in the wake of the Korean War, and Secretary of State Dulles and his brother, CIA director

Allen Dulles, believed covert action was a way to conduct warfare on the cheap. Eisenhower and the Dulles brothers liked the fact that the CIA was small and elite and provided the president with plausible denial. They created an executive-branch panel under General Jimmy Doolittle ostensibly to examine clandestine operations as an instrument of foreign policy. Its real mission, however, was to give the CIA an official mandate for the conduct of covert action, leading CIA director Dulles to remark that the intelligence officers at the CIA had more influence in the United States than in any other country in the world.[12] The mandate could not have been clearer:

> It is now clear that we are facing an implacable enemy whose avowed objective is world domination by whatever means and at whatever cost. *There are no rules in such a game. Hitherto acceptable norms of human conduct do not apply.* If the United States is to survive, longstanding American concepts of "fair play" must be reconsidered. We must develop effective espionage and counterespionage services and must learn to subvert, sabotage, and destroy our enemies by more clever, more sophisticated means than those used against us. *It may become necessary that the American people be made acquainted with, understand, and support this fundamentally repugnant philosophy.*[13] (Emphasis added.)

From 1954 to 1976, when the Congressional oversight committees were created, the Senate and House had no particular interest or genuine picture of the extent of CIA's covert action.

The Soviet threat absorbed the overwhelming majority of CIA personnel and funds during the cold war, but the Agency's haphazard collection and analysis led to the misreading of Soviet signals on the global competition. The CIA exaggerated the Soviet role in North Korea's decision to invade South Korea in 1950, expected a Soviet invasion of Poland in 1980, and missed the decline and disarray in Moscow in the 1980s. The CIA failed to anticipate the Soviet use of force against Hungary in 1956, when the Western powers were weakened by the British–French decision to invade Egypt, and in Czechoslovakia in 1968, when the CIA believed that President Lyndon Johnson's willingness to begin strategic arms reduction talks with the Kremlin would prevent Moscow's use of force in Eastern Europe. The CIA provided some warning of the Soviet invasion of Afghanistan in 1979, although President Jimmy Carter, like Johnson before him, believed imminent disarmament negotiations with the United States would dissuade the Kremlin from resorting to force.

The CIA's failures were not limited to the Soviet problem. The Agency often failed to understand the relations between the client states and allies of the United States and the Soviet Union over a fifty-year period. The Israeli preemptive attack that started the 1967 Six-Day War caught the Johnson administration and the CIA off guard. The Israeli decision to preempt against Egypt was a suprise, particularly because there was no intelligence evidence that Egypt was actually planning an attack against Israel. The United States and the CIA failed to anticipate the Khomeini revolution in Iran in 1979 and the fall of the Shah, as well as the Iraqi invasions of Iran in 1980 and Kuwait in 1990. The failure to anticipate the introduction of Soviet missiles in Cuba created a serious crisis in 1962, and the failure to monitor Indian nuclear testing in 1998 led to the defeat of the Comprehensive Test Ban Treaty in the U.S. Senate. The lack of strategic warning in all of these examples created serious problems for U.S. administrations.

Preoccupation with the Soviet threat in the 1980s led the CIA to ignore the rise of radical Islamic movements in the Middle East. The CIA was consumed with the risk of sectarian violence that could lead to possible confrontation between the Soviet Union and the United States and, as a result, assumed all violence and terrorism in the Middle East in the 1970s and 1980s was controlled by Moscow. CIA was particularly slow to respond to Islamic terrorism organizations, particularly al Qaeda, convinced that such organizations could not operate without the backing of an aggressive state actor, such as Iraq or Iran. Similar miscalculations were made by U.S. administrations and the CIA in the 1980s and 1990s, when the United States failed to calculate the impact of its military actions on various insurgent and terrorist organizations, particularly Islamic fundamentalist groups, which believed the United States was pursuing an imperial policy in the Third World (e.g., Afghanistan, Angola, Mozambique, Nicaragua, and Somalia) against indigenous interests.

U.S. counterterrorism was often cited to justify Islamic terrorism. The United States has not appreciated the impact of the role of the CIA in supporting military adventures in southern Africa, the Horn of Africa, and the Middle East that has created an Islamic fundamentalist backlash against the presence of the United States and the CIA in Africa and the Middle East. At the same time, the CIA's failure to understand the origins and true nature of nonstate Islamic terrorism ultimately led to the intelligence failure of 2001. The CIA underestimated the threat of nonstate actors who did not require support from major or even minor states.

INTELLIGENCE ORGANIZATION

The function of intelligence is to provide policymakers with the most complete and objective strategic analysis possible to ensure that policy decisions are well-informed. Strategic intelligence must have a long-range focus and not be simply premonitory; it must address both capabilities and intentions of the most likely threats to national security, and it must incorporate political, economic, and military aspects of international relations. Policymakers require strategic intelligence, historical context, and current intelligence and, as a result, the CIA initially organized intelligence around an Office of National Estimates, a Special Research Staff, and an Office of Current Intelligence. Currently, current intelligence drives the work of the directorate of intelligence; there is very little historical production, and there has been a serious decline in the value and immediacy of NIEs.

There is a natural tension between policymakers and intelligence analysts. Most policymakers prefer that intelligence supports their favored policies. This tension has been evident to some degree in virtually all U.S. administrations and, on various occasions, has led to flawed or biased intelligence. This was less apparent in the CIA's first three decades, but beginning with the Casey era in 1981 and the role of the deputy director for intelligence (DDI), Robert M. Gates, there was greater pressure from the highest levels of the Agency to politicize or tailor the finished product. William Casey and Gates made a decision in the early 1980s to provide the Reagan administration with intelligence justification for hostile relations with the Soviet Union and unprecedented peacetime defense spending. Twenty years later, CIA director George Tenet and his deputy, John McLaughlin, decided to provide the Bush administration with the intelligence to justify the use of force against Iraq.

Nearly all of the intelligence failures of the CIA stemmed from political and cultural bias, politicization, or flawed assumptions. Bias was a major factor in the failure to anticipate the surprise Egyptian–Syrian attack against Israeli in 1973 (the October War). The CIA and the Israeli Mossad intelligence organization simply underestimated the Arabs and never believed that Egyptians and Syrians could cooperate at the highest level of war or that they would have the courage to take on a strong Israeli force. Flawed assumptions were the source of the failure to provide warning of the 9/11 attacks in 2001. The CIA did not believe that the al Qaeda organization would attack the United States *inside* the United States, and the FBI did not believe that al Qaeda even had the organization in the United States to do so. Prior to the creation of the CIA, the greatest U.S. intelligence failure was the Japanese attack at Pearl Harbor in 1941, when cultural bias and flawed assumptions contributed to a devastating attack on U.S. naval power in the Pacific. Just as the CIA underestimated the Egyptian–Syrian alliance in 1973, U.S. military intelligence totally underestimated the power and potential of the Japanese military and believed that Pearl Harbor was outside Japan's range.

Politicization of intelligence is most likely when a specific policy itself becomes flawed or has failed, and political pressure is placed on the intelligence community to shape the finished intelligence product to the policy agenda. Failure in Vietnam led to pressure to suppress the actual number of Viet Cong insurgents in South Vietnam. The decision to significantly increase defense spending against the Soviet Union in the 1980s led to pressure on the CIA to create the picture of a Soviet threat that was ten feet tall. Politicization was the key factor in the failure to chart the decline of the Soviet Union in the 1980s, culminating in the demise of the Soviet Union in 1991. The Reagan administration would not accept any sign of Soviet weakness or constraint, and CIA director Casey and deputy director for intelligence Gates cooperated to provide intelligence that presented the Russian Bear as threatening and warlike. The decision to go to war against Iraq in 2003 led to White House and Defense Department pressure on the CIA to tailor intelligence on weapons of mass destruction and so-called links between Iraq and the al Qaeda organization.

Origins of Current Intelligence

In the aftermath of World War II, when the Office of Strategic Services was disbanded, several branches of the OSS were distributed to other agencies of government. Many critics of the OSS emphasized that the Office had far more analytical success than operational ones, so there was no great interest in providing an initial operational mandate to the CIA. The counterintelligence branch was given to the War Department as the Strategic Services Unit, and the Research and Analysis Branch was placed in the Department of State. Many of the analysts of the Research and Analysis Branch moved to the CIA in 1947, providing the core of the new agency's analytic infrastructure as the Office of Reports and Estimates (ORE). This office concentrated on daily intelligence summaries for President Truman as well as National Intelligence Estimates (NIEs) based on the intelligence collection of the Department of State and the military services. The ORE also took responsibility for basic economic and geographic research, but initially deferred to the Department of State and the Pentagon on political and military areas. The CIA also inherited from the wartime Manhattan Project to build nuclear weapons a capability to provide intelligence on foreign atomic energy matters.

Originally, the Office of Research and Estimates (ORE) was responsible for CIA analysis. ORE concentrated on economic analysis throughout the 1950s and gradually became the authoritative voice within the expanding intelligence community for economic intelligence. The CIA and the State Department reached an agreement in 1951, giving ORE responsibility for economic research and analysis on the Soviet Union and the Soviet Bloc. Many analysts transferred from State to CIA and, with the threat of a purge of the State Department because of the anticommunist campaign of Senator Joseph McCarthy (R-Wisconsin), more State Department experts found their way to the CIA, where they received the bureaucratic protection that Secretary of State Dulles refused to provide. A leading academic economist, Max Millikan, was recruited from the Massachusetts Institute of Technology to head ORE, and he conducted an extensive recruiting program to make sure that ORE's economic analysts were capable of standing up to their counterparts at academic institutes and think-tanks.

The Office of Current Intelligence (OCI) was created in 1951 to produce intelligence analysis on fast-moving events. In many ways, it resembled the wire service reporting of the Associated Press or United Press International. I joined OCI in 1966 as a Soviet analyst in an office that was organized on regional lines. The office was responsible for production of the President's Daily Brief (PDB), which was briefed to the president, key members of the cabinet, and the national security advisor five or six times a week. The Office also prepared the National Intelligence Digest (NID), which was sent electronically to thousands of intelligence officials and policymakers at home and abroad.

OCI took on greater importance in the 1960s, particularly with the interest of the Kennedy administration in political intelligence. Kennedy's complaints about receiving redundant and duplicative information led OCI to create the President's Intelligence Checklist, which became known as the PICL, pronounced "pickle." The checklist was eventually renamed the President's Daily Brief (PDB), which provided daily up-to-date intelligence information to the White House, key members of the cabinet, and the national security advisor. The president was an avid reader of intelligence and wanted a small document—rarely more than five to six pages—he could fit into his breast pocket and carry around. He wanted it in the "president's language and not officialese," according to the senior White House military aide, Major General Chester Clifton.[14] The PDB explained developing crises and exploited the intelligence collection of the entire national security community. It made OCI a heady place to work because analysts, even junior ones, were often writing directly for the president of the United States. The secret and covert operations of the directorate of operations (DO) were the center of gravity for many a member of the intelligence community, but the production of current intelligence reports and NIEs were the center of gravity as far as most analysts were concerned.

OCI was abolished in 1979, when the deputy director of intelligence, John McMahon, decided to organize intelligence on regional lines (Europe and Russia, Asia, Middle East, Africa, and South America) instead of functional lines (political, economic, and military) with the hope of generating more multidisciplinary analysis. The reorganization failed as the larger number of military analysts dominated the smaller number of political and economic analysts. Subsequently, somewhat ironically, the CIA abandoned key areas of military analysis, such as order of battle intelligence. This caused a decline in the influence of CIA intelligence, particularly in comparison with the Defense Intelligence Agency. The failure to track the decline of the Soviet Union in the 1980s pointed to the DI's inability to conduct multidisciplinary analysis.

With the absence of OCI, the PDB became the major driver of all current intelligence. It also drives the daily calendar of the newly created director of national intelligence (DNI). A typical PDB or "notebook" often runs to thirty pages in length, according to John Negroponte, the first DNI. It contains "assessments of emerging problems or enduring challenges, results of long-term research, NIC estimates," and even "open-source reporting, as well as occasional analysis that challenges conventional wisdom on critical issues."[15] Far too much attention and energy is given to a product having limited utility for the president of the United States and, if the DNI is spending most of his day working on a product for the president that deals with current intelligence, then it is not possible for him to address the essential demands of strategic intelligence and intelligence reform.

Origins of National Intelligence Estimates

In abolishing ORE in 1951, the new CIA director, General Walter Bedell Smith, created an elite Office of National Estimates (ONE) under Harvard Professor William Langer, a senior OSS analyst during World War II. ONE consisted of two major offices, an upper tier known as the Board of National Estimates (BNE), composed of senior government and academic officials, and an Estimates Staff to draft NIEs. When I arrived at the CIA in 1966, the BNE was facetiously referred to as the "College of Cardinals" because of its expertise and arrogance. The dozen or so board members drove the assumptions and the conclusions of the NIEs; the estimates themselves were written by the Estimates Staff, under the leadership of Ray Cline who worked for Langer in the OSS. The staff wrote the first drafts of the estimates and were responsible for coordinating their work with other intelligence agencies.

ONE was created at the CIA in 1950 as a result of the Agency's failure to provide strategic warning of the Korean War. General Smith's first move for the new office of estimates in 1952 was to summon Professor Langer from the history department at Harvard University to set up and recruit for the elite office. Langer was the perfect choice, having run the OSS's Office of Reports and Analysis during World War II. Under Langer, ONE immediately became the elite stone in the intelligence mosaic, starting out as a part of the DI but ultimately achieving a special status as an independent fiefdom that reported directly to the CIA director. ONE's elite status and the independent line to the director and deputy director of the CIA was resented throughout the DI, but it served to create a corporate headquarters for finished intelligence within the intelligence community. Its mission was to go beyond the instant analysis of OCI and provide assessments of the intentions and capabilities of the country's leading threats.

Langer's BNE included a dozen luminaries from academe, the State Department, the military, and private enterprise to produce coordinated NIEs. In the late 1960s and early 1970s, Ambassador Llewellyn Thompson, who provided important policy advice to President Kennedy during the Cuban missile crisis, served on the board. ONE did excellent work in this period on Soviet strategic capabilities, arms control and disarmament, and the Middle East. CIA director Smith made sure that ONE was the focal point of the CIA's analysis from the start, and it remained so until it was abolished in 1973 by CIA director James Schlesinger, who wanted to end ONE's dominance and independence.

Langer and his successor, Yale professor Sherman Kent, were keen analysts in their own right and merciless in criticizing the work of their colleagues. Both Langer and Kent were independent, tenacious, and tough-minded. They made sure that analysts "told it like it was," even if the conclusions of the estimates were not consistent with favored policy.[16] Kent emphasized that he wanted intelligence delivered with the "bark on," no matter how unpopular the message was to policymakers. Bob Gates turned that approach on its head in the 1980s and tried hard to anticipate the views of policymakers in order to pander to their needs. Unlike Kent, Gates consistently told his analysts to make sure never to "stick your finger in the eye of the policymaker."

Sadly, Kent's shoes have never been filled, and his strictures about the danger of intelligence analysts getting too close to policymakers have been ignored. Kent understood the need for tension between policymakers and intelligence analysts, and never believed that the intelligence community should be part of the policy "team." Much of the intelligence damage in the run-up to the Iraq War was due to the DI believing that it was actually "serving" the White House in preparing its assessments on Iraqi WMD. Langer and Kent did not see themselves as "serving" the White House, but "informing" the White House.

ONE was backed by a small staff of area specialists responsible for preparing initial draft estimates and integrating a wide range of contributions from the intelligence community. The staffers also reviewed the intelligence assessments of other members of the intelligence community, and were essentially available as consultants for many less experienced intelligence analysts. They represented a white male bastion from the Ivy League that didn't recruit its first female analyst until 1970, when Helene Boatner, the daughter of Korean War hero General Haydon Boatner, was recruited to analyze developments in the Middle East. The first African American arrived in the 1990s. By the time I entered the CIA in 1966, from Indiana University, there had clearly been a geographic and cultural shift from the Ivy League to the Big Ten. Currently, the leading U.S. university sending recruits to the CIA just happens to be Texas A&M, where former CIA director Gates was president until December 2006, when he became secretary of defense.

ONE military estimates were among the most important documents the office produced; they were particularly helpful in assessing the intentions and capabilities of the Soviet Union and China, and challenging the worst-case assessments of the Pentagon and the Joint Chiefs of Staff that were designed to justify greater defense spending. Initially, the estimates provided net assessments, evaluating Soviet military capabilities against the military power of the United States. By measuring Soviet forces against U.S. and Western forces, there was a greater sense of the ability to counter and match the Red Army. Pressure from the Pentagon in the 1960s ended the concept of net assessments and made Soviet military forces appear to be far more threatening than they actually were. In the 1980s, Casey and Gates made sure that the CIA would measure the production cost of Soviet weaponry in dollars, instead of rubles, making these weapons systems far more expensive then they actually were.

The NIEs in the 1950s and early 1960s effectively placed Soviet military power into perspective, but worst-case estimates in the 1980s exaggerated Soviet military power. Initially, the estimates provided the fodder that defeated the worst-case assessments that created the "bomber gap" alarm in the mid-1950s and the "missile gap" alarm of the late 1950s and early 1960s. From the creation of the CIA in 1947 to the dissolution of the Soviet Union in 1991, the Soviet military never introduced a new strategic weapon to its inventory that had not been analyzed in the NIEs. This was one of the greatest successes of U.S. intelligence during the cold war. CIA estimates on the Soviet military in general were particularly influential regarding decisions on U.S. defense programs. The strategic and national intelligence of the CIA proved to be far more accurate than the military intelligence from the Pentagon and tended to be one of the most accurate guides to Soviet strategic thinking.

The golden age of ONE and the production of objective and balanced NIEs ended in 1973, when CIA director Schlesinger abolished the Office of National Estimates and created the National Intelligence Council (NIC). Schlesinger wanted to make the board and its staffers less independent and more responsive to the policy demands of the White House and the NSC. The NIC has been a far less expert group and far less independent than ONE. Throughout this period, all intelligence agencies participated in refining and coordinating the NIEs, with the United States Intelligence Board vetting the final draft of the estimates since 1958.

The National Intelligence Officers (NIOs) who replaced the members of the Intelligence Board have been far less serious and far less respected than their predecessors, and too many of them (Fritz Ermarth, Graham Fuller, Robert Gates, Larry Gershwin, the late George Kolt, Paul Pillar, and Robert Walpole) have willingly done the bidding of their policy masters. There were few serious examples of politicized estimates in the period from 1952 to 1973, although there were occasions when CIA director Helms didn't take an NIE to the White House when it candidly assessed the losing battle in Vietnam. The institutionalized politicization of the NIEs began in the 1980s, under Casey and Gates, particularly on the Soviet political and military estimates, the Soviet Union and terrorism, and a controversial estimate on Iran in 1985 that created the intelligence justification for the illegal policy of Iran-Contra. In 2002, the CIA and the NIC were responsible for the infamous NIE and the unclassified White Paper on Iraqi WMD. In December 2004, the Intelligence Reform Act created the Director of National Intelligence to centralize the production of finished intelligence and to end the CIA's dominance of the process.

The development of modern satellite and aerial reconnaissance systems led to a quantum leap in the collection of intelligence and the need for new analytic techniques for overhead photography. The DI already had a small office of imagery analysis, but in 1961, the intelligence community created the joint CIA–Pentagon National Photographic Interpretation Center (NPIC) to deal with the new information. A year later, NPIC and the Office of Imagery Analysis had a great success with the discovery of medium- and short-range Soviet missiles being deployed in Cuba. A month earlier, in September 1962, ONE had predicted the Kremlin would not put Soviet–American relations at risk with the installation of such missiles, but imagery provided a certainty that clandestine sources could never provide and, as a result, President Kennedy had two weeks of strategic warning to prepare his response to Moscow's deployment of missiles in Cuba. The role of CIA's imagery analysts and a key clandestine asset, Colonel Oleg Penkovsky, gave Kennedy the time and the context to develop a diplomatic strategy to avoid hostilities with the Soviet Union and to gain the withdrawal of the Soviet missiles. Penkovsky was central to the task of understanding the weakness and limitations of the Soviet military, particularly its strategic deficiencies. The role of a high-ranking ONE officer on loan from the Department of State, Ambassador Llewellyn Thompson, who favored a diplomatic solution to the crisis, was instrumental in avoiding a possible military confrontation, although he has never received the full credit he deserved.

The intelligence collected from the U-2 reconnaissance aircraft and the Corona photographic satellite also gave CIA analysts the necessary material to resolve the so-called bomber and missile gaps of the 1950s and 1960s. President Eisenhower had an intuitive sense that the military had grossly exaggerated Soviet strategic capabilities, and he was right. President Kennedy was less sophisticated than his predecessor and quite vulnerable to the worst-case estimates of the Pentagon. He campaigned against Vice President Richard Nixon on the basis of a nonexistent missile gap, and he refused to drop his charges against the Eisenhower administration even after receiving sensitive CIA briefings that put the lie to the so-called gap.

The ability of the CIA to calibrate the strength of the Soviet military arsenal more accurately than their military competition gave the Agency more stature within the community, which permitted the CIA to play a major role in providing support for arms control and disarmament agreements throughout the 1970s and 1980s. During that period, CIA directors were particularly innovative in providing bureaucratic solutions to important analytic problems. In the early 1960s, CIA director John McCone formed the Directorate of Science and Technology, which was responsible for both the collection and analysis of intelligence. In 1967, CIA director Helms created the Office of Strategic Research to conduct military research and to widen the aperture of analysis beyond its concentration on Soviet matters. In the 1970s, a new Office of Weapons Intelligence was created to deal with all weapons-related issues. A crucial aspect of all disarmament treaties was the capability of the United States to monitor Soviet compliance, and the CIA played the central role in this activity.

Origins of Research

The inability of the CIA to provide good intelligence to the Eisenhower administration on the policies and intentions of Joseph Stalin, as well as early signs of differences between the Soviet Union and China, led the DI to permit a small group of Soviet analysts in OCI to study the Soviet hierarchy as well as international communism as a movement. This group started with several analysts; there were never more than a dozen analysts in this group, and they initially began Project CAESAR in 1952 to study all available intelligence on the Soviet leadership. The consumers for their work included the analysts and operatives of the CIA, as well as key officials in the State Department and NSA.

In 1956, the director of OCI, Ray Cline, established a small research staff designated as the Sino–Soviet Studies Group (SSSG) to continue the CAESAR project and to begin two new research endeavors: Project POLO was designed to study the Chinese Communist leadership, and ESAU was launched in 1959 to examine the Sino–Soviet relationship. In 1963, this group morphed into the Special Research Staff (SRS) that reported directly to the deputy director for intelligence, Ray Cline, who devoted much of his career to fostering analytical research. Cline was particularly impressed with the work of the research staff in developing evidence of a Sino–Soviet dispute, which attracted "furious" opposition within the CIA and the intelligence community and great skepticism from policymakers.[17] SRS prepared lengthy historical studies or special projects without the burden of deadlines and policy constraints, and gained in prestige as a result of reporting directly to the DDI and attracting an audience for their work on the Sino–Soviet dispute. In addition to useful work on the Soviet Union, Walter (Bud) Southard took on a major managing role within SRS and brought his own expertise on Chinese leadership to the staff. This work, which initially focused on the politics and policies of Washington's two major challenges—the Soviet Union and China— represented some of the most prescient and useful work of the DI. These assessments provided a standard for research in the fields of government, academia, and the think-tank community.

The best work of SRS took place in the late 1950s and early 1960s when senior analysts Harry Gelman from Columbia University and Arthur Cohen from the University of Chicago did a series of studies on the Sino–Soviet rift, which was not acknowledged by most American policymakers and academicians until years later. The group prepared four major studies in 1960 that noted the development of Sino–Soviet discord, including Soviet criticism of China's commune and Great Leap Forward; Mao's willingness to take risks in relations with the West; and Chinese criticism of the Soviet use of force against demonstrations in East Germany, Poland, and Hungary. These studies ultimately provided the intelligence justification for a major shift in policy during the first years of the Nixon administration to try to exploit the rift between Moscow and Beijing and improve Washington's relations with both capitals. The SRS also did groundbreaking work on China's economy, politics in Indonesia, and politics in the Kremlin. When I joined OCI in 1966, it was customary to prepare new analysts for their assignments by having them read the most recent studies of the SRS. There was no research in the academic community that compared with the products of the SRS. The work of this group established the fact that the best way to get good intelligence is to recruit good analysts and then give them enough time and independence to pursue their work. Since the SRS papers were considered "working papers," they did not require formal coordination within the DI or other agencies within the intelligence community, which is another way to encourage out-of-the-box thinking.

CIA director Schlesinger, however, was not content to allow the Agency's analysts to pursue their craft. He ended the separation of intelligence production into estimative, historical, and current intelligence in 1973, when he centralized intelligence production and abolished two of the three major analytical centers. Schlesinger wanted to control the intelligence sent to the White House and the NSC, and the best way to do so was to end the competition in the DI and to centralize intelligence production. The end of this competition seriously harmed the reputation and the intelligence production of the CIA. On the other hand, Schlesinger's paranoia regarding the CIA led him to demand what the Agency was keeping from him. He directed every employee to report every instance of activity that might be outside the Agency's charter, the so-called "family jewels," that were finally declassified and published in 2007, fifteen years after a Freedom of Information Act request.

Like Porter Goss, who had a mandate from President George W. Bush to get the CIA to conform to the policy lines of the White House, Schlesinger arrived at the CIA in 1973 with a mandate to ensure support for the policies of the Nixon White House. Schlesinger told the Soviet analysts of the directorate of intelligence that they were "to stop screwing Richard Nixon." Schlesinger quickly abolished ONE and SRS, which were the most independent departments within the DI and the hardest to control. ONE was replaced by a group of NIOs, who were appointed by the director of CIA and were beholden to the director. They took over the function of producing and managing national intelligence estimates. Under Admiral Turner, the NIOs were organized into a National Intelligence Council, and under Bill Casey, the NIC was placed under the deputy for intelligence, Bob Gates, ensuring that Gates would be the political filter for all intelligence produced at the CIA.

Schlesinger's politicization of analysis touched off a series of bureaucratic maneuvers over the next ten years that created a great deal of confusion and malaise within the organization. Some of the best analysts left the directorate and the CIA during this period, and there was a definite decline in the level of expertise and professionalism within the organization. What was left of ONE and SRS was folded into a new Office of Political Research (OPR) in 1973, to stand alongside the military analysis of OSR, the economic analysis of OER, and the political analysis of OCI. CIA historians praise the reorganization as a return to the "model first pioneered by the OSS's Regional and Analysis Branch in World War II," but it did not lead to improved strategic intelligence or to greater multidisciplinary studies.[18] Three years later, George H.W. Bush abolished OPR and what was left of OCI and created a single Office of Regional and Political Analysis, which merely extended the period of bureaucratic turbulence within the DI.

In the early 1980s, CIA director Casey and his deputy director for intelligence, John McMahon, a CIA veteran but a novice in the field of political intelligence, abolished OSR, OER, and OPA in order to create geographic offices. Geographic offices replaced functional ones with all Soviet analysts regardless of their specializations placed in the Office of Soviet Analysis (SOVA), which was moved ten miles away from CIA headquarters to Vienna, Virginia, immediately creating a serious problem for morale and logistics. The director of OSR, a military expert, was named head of SOVA, and there was a definite decline in the political and economic work of the organization. The new structure was supposed to be more capable of producing multidisciplinary intelligence, but there was little capability to manage and produce such analysis. Indeed, one of the reasons for the failure of the CIA to track the decline and fall of the Soviet Union was the inability to compare the political, economic, and military evidence of the disarray in the Soviet Union. The politicization of the intelligence by CIA director Casey and his deputy Gates was the major reason for the failure.

The politicization of intelligence or the systematic slanting of intelligence collection and analysis to serve policy interests became institutionalized during Casey's tenure as CIA director from 1981 to 1987. Casey brought to the CIA a strong policy agenda that marked the Soviet Union as an "evil empire," responsible for the world's problems and particularly intent on destroying the West. He was a political appointee of the Reagan administration that wanted to end détente and arms control, create more active anti-Soviet policies in the Third World, and double defense spending in order to "rollback" the Soviet threat. Casey was well served by Bob Gates, a career intelligence official, who was a special assistant to Casey in 1981, his deputy director intelligence in 1982, and eventually the deputy director of the CIA in 1985. Gates knew how the intelligence process worked and how to ensure its responsiveness to Casey's policy interests. In several years, Gates successfully used policies of reorganization and personnel management to assume direct control over all CIA intelligence analysis and to bolster reporting that emphasized the Soviet threat and inhibit analysis that emphasized Moscow's serious economic problems and worsening international position. As a result, Gates and the CIA failed to predict the dramatic changes in Soviet policy in the 1980s. The bias built into CIA reporting during the Casey/Gates years undermined the Agency's ability to produce quality intelligence long after the death of Casey in 1987 and the end of Gates' stewardship of CIA in 1993. Many of the managers and analysts responsible for the politicization of intelligence prior to the war in Iraq were products of the Casey/Gates years. The issue of politicization of intelligence is not widely understood, but the problems created by flawed intelligence are significant enough to require serious and concentrated attention.

INTELLIGENCE NEEDS FOR THE TWENTY-FIRST CENTURY

The central question in the world of intelligence is what kind of intelligence system is essential for U.S. security in an age of terrorism and appropriate to our democratic system? We have learned from the 9/11 terrorist attacks, the run-up to the war in Iraq, and the Bush administration's misuse of the intelligence community that the current system is dysfunctional in terms of our needs in support of policy and corrupt in terms of our democracy. Internationally, the CIA has created secret prisons in Europe and Asia, conducted torture and abuse in U.S. military facilities as well as its own prisons, conducted the rendering of innocent civilians in violation of international law, and created serious diplomatic problems with our friends around the world. At home, the CIA has protected those individuals who should be accountable for the 9/11 intelligence failures, failed to brief the appropriate congressional oversight committees and the Department of Justice, and provided tainted intelligence to the president of the United States as well as senior policymakers. The recommendations of the 9/11 Commission failed to address these problems and the Intelligence Reorganization Act of December 2004 made a bad situation worse, creating an office for the Director of National Intelligence that further centralized the production of intelligence. A major overhaul is needed in order to provide trenchant intelligence analysis to policymakers on the key issues of the day, as well as to convince an international audience that the U.S. intelligence community reflects our democratic ideals.

KEY ISSUES

Iran and the Nuclear Threat

Iran could eventually pose a ballistic missile threat to the United States but, like the North Korean situation, the 1998 Rumsfeld Commission and the NIEs of 1999 and 2000 have exaggerated the threat. Iran, hoping to challenge the supremacy of U.S. forces in the region, has been trying to develop an advanced ballistic missile capability since the early 1970s in order to establish regional influence. This goal has become more compelling for Iran in recent years due to the 150,000 American troops in Iraq and the 12,000 American troops in Afghanistan, and the role of U.S. special operations forces in Iran. The great inaccuracy of Iran's missiles thus far points to a terror weapon and not a weapon that could threaten U.S. interests.

The absence of diplomatic relations between the United States and Iran makes it extremely difficult for the CIA to collect clandestine intelligence in

Iran. The State Department–CIA connection is intimate according to General William Odom; thus the absence of a U.S. embassy removes the most traditional and prevalent arrangement for clandestine collection. The absence of diplomatic relations also compromises the most effective tool for learning about and reaching out to a revolutionary society. The United States needs to expand contacts with Iran's younger generation, particularly its influential technocrats, in order to correct the impressions formed by earlier contacts with the United States and the U.S. relationship with the Shah, but the U.S. policy of nonrecognition limits such contacts. CIA efforts to recruit Iranian assets overseas have been very unsuccessful.

Continued speculation in the United States about a possible military attack against Iran's nuclear facilities, including the possible use of tactical nuclear weapons in such an attack, also contributes to the worsening of ties between the United States and Iran, as well as the Iranian consensus for continuing their nuclear program. The role of the Pentagon and CIA in conducting special operations in Iran has led the government in Tehran to arrest U.S. citizens and even challenge the British Navy on the high seas in the Persian Gulf. The possible use of force against Iran creates the same kind of pressure on intelligence analysts that took place in the run-up to war with Iraq in 2002–2003, which led to highly politicized intelligence.

India–Pakistan and the Problem of Proliferation

On July 18, 2005, the United States and India signed a joint statement for broad nuclear cooperation, which will require the U.S. Congress to grant special exceptions to U.S. nonproliferation law. These exceptions will create new intelligence problems in the field of counterproliferation because they will allow the United States and third countries to sell nuclear materials and reactors to India. Current law and international export rules bar trade with states, such as India, that have not signed the Nonproliferation Treaty (NPT) and do not accept comprehensive international safeguards. The NPT also forbids the United States from assisting another country's nuclear weapons program "in any way." The tense relations that exist between India and Pakistan, both nonsigners of the NPT, add to the political and military intelligence challenges that exist in South Asia. The failure of the joint statement to address the need for facility-specific safeguards on a broad list of current and future civil Indian nuclear facilities and material as well as a cutoff of Indian fissile material production for weapons add to this list of challenges. Thus far, India has only permitted "voluntary" IAEA safeguards on its civil nuclear facilities, a practice now limited to only the five NPT nuclear-weapon states (United States, Russia, United Kingdom, France, and China).

Various aspects of the joint U.S.–Indian statement, which were not sufficiently addressed, add to the intelligence problems. The United States and India have not agreed on those Indian nuclear facilities to be declared military ones, and those to be declared civilian and subject to IAEA safeguards. The United States might allow India to keep significant amounts of its existing spent fuel from its nuclear power reactors free of IAEA safeguards, and is not seeking to impose restrictions on India's use of India-origin fuel. These concessions to India will create verification problems for the U.S. intelligence community, and will contribute to the difficulty of making sure Iran adheres to all aspects of the NPT and agrees to forswear its own uranium enrichment facilities.

Closer U.S.–Indian relations have led to closer Sino–Pakistani relations and a tougher policy environment for the United States in Pakistan. The Musharraf government in Islamabad has been more restrictive of the U.S. presence in Pakistan and less restrictive of the Taliban and al Qaeda presence in Pakistan. As a result, there has been an increased threat to the Afghan government in Kabul, which complicates U.S. policy in Southwest Asia and creates a more difficult environment for intelligence collection.

Intelligence and Counterproliferation

The CIA had a key role in discovering and disrupting the international nuclear proliferation network of Pakistani physicist Abdul Qadeer Khan's illegal activities. President Bush, in a speech in October 2005, credited the CIA with "exposing and disrupting" the major black market operation in nuclear technology by A. Q. Khan, who is considered the father of Pakistan's nuclear weapons program. In fact, the CIA had collected sufficient intelligence on Pakistan's nuclear activities and the vital role of A. Q. Khan long before he began providing nuclear secrets to Iran, Libya, and North Korea. The CIA analysts who discovered this information, Richard Barlow and Peter Dixon, learned in the mid-1980s that Pakistan was buying restricted nuclear technology from the United States and Europe, and Barlow even "unmasked a coordinated attempt by the U.S. intelligence community" to suppress information on these activities.[19] The reward for Barlow and Dixon, whose research revealed illegal Pakistani activities, was to lose their jobs as analysts at the CIA and to defend themselves from CIA charges that they were unreliable analysts.

The Iraqi Civil War

The civil war in Iraq is complicating both the military and intelligence objectives in Iraq and making it far more difficult to plan for the withdrawal of military forces and a reduction of the huge diplomatic and intelligence presence.

State Department foreign service officers and CIA clandestine operatives are providing a steady stream of "ground truth" cables that describe the worsening situation in Iraq, but they are not receiving the support of their own bureaucracies, let alone a readership at the White House and the NSC. As violence from the civil war continues to grow, the United States has contributed to the problem by training and arming Iraqi police and army units that are infiltrated by Shiia militia units. President Bush's mantra for these units is "when they stand up, we'll stand down," but it is more likely that the very arms and training that they are receiving from U.S. personnel will eventually be used against U.S. targets.

The motto in the entrance to the CIA headquarters building in Langley, Virginia, is the biblical inscription that "the truth will set you free," and the mission of the Agency's Center for the Study of Intelligence is to assemble the best minds and bring them to bear on the most critical challenges to the Agency and the Intelligence Community. But if the CIA is unwilling to tell truth to power, which was certainly the case in the run-up to the Iraq War and during the decline and fall of the Soviet Union, then these inscriptions quickly become irrelevant. The CIA should have reexamined its missions and capabilities in the wake of the Soviet collapse, in view of the Soviet Union as the Agency's raison d'etre since its founding. But there were few evolutionary and adaptive changes in the early 1990s and certainly no examples of radical restructuring since then. Agency analysts are not equipped to deal with the radical social, cultural, and economic stresses around the world, particularly in the Islamic arena, and were caught looking the wrong way in 2005, when a Palestinian election produced a striking victory for Hamas and a stinging defeat for Fatah. Islamic analysts throughout the Middle East and Southwest Asia were not surprised; CIA analysts were shocked and presumably mortified. If the Agency cannot track and monitor the relatively open Palestinian community, then what are its chances of successes in the more opaque environments that exist in Iran and Pakistan, where there are strategic challenges to the interests of the United States? The religious and secular ingredients of the political movements in these areas, including the terrorist movements, pose particular problems for the policy and intelligence communities of the United States. The absence of diplomatic relations with Iran and North Korea adds to the problem of clandestine collection of intelligence. Religious and ethnic extremism require a more open and aggressive research environment than the one that exists at the CIA, as well as experts in demographics and sociology that have not been attracted to CIA recruitment efforts.

Strategic intelligence has been in decline at the CIA over the past three decades, dating back to the disestablishment of the Special Research Staff and the staff of the Office of National Estimates in 1973 by Director Schlesinger, who saw no need for strategic intelligence. The CIA will always have the resources to count ships and tanks, but it will be more difficult to find the expertise to understand the goals and perspectives of ethnic minorities in the former Soviet space or the leaders of the complex Islamic religious community. If the intelligence oversight committees commissioned an in-house study of the regional and linguistic expertise in the CIA's directorate of intelligence, they would be stunned by the dearth of analysts who speak the language of the countries they analyze or have spent any considerable time in-country.

The CIA has serious demographic problems and there is no easy fix for any of them. First of all, Agency analysts and operatives are extremely young and inexperienced, with very little experience in key positions and very little seniority in most fields. Nearly half of the workforce has arrived at the CIA since 9/11, which creates a difficult training problem for the new hires as well as for the experienced analysts and operatives who must train them. In the new group, more than 60 percent are under the age of thirty, and 85 percent are under the age of forty. In other words, the CIA has done an extremely poor job of attracting individuals with serious overseas and substantive experience. This is due in part to exaggerated security concerns, as those individuals who have traveled and lived overseas have a difficult time with the polygraph and various security examinations. The cumbersome security hurdles also take a year to complete, and there are many people who cannot put themselves on hold for that period of time. The paranoia of the operational environment has unnecessarily complicated the task of hiring experienced analysts. The CIA has put great emphasis into hiring people with military experience, but can manage to attract few who have served with the military. The associate deputy director of intelligence, Michael J. Morrell, has described the Agency as a "doubled-humped camel," with most employees having less than five years experience or more than fifteen.[20] When the State Department encountered a similar problem ten years ago, it developed sophisticated recruitment techniques with the assistance of public relations and advertising agencies. The CIA may be doing the same, but it is not having commensurate success.

The Agency has known for the past several decades that it can track the "who" and "what" in many of the key countries around the world, but that it is deficient in responding to the "why" and the "how." The list of tactical intelligence failures speaks to this problem, including the Korean War, the Chinese intervention in the Korean War, Soviet nuclear testing, Soviet invasion of Hungary and Czechoslovakia, the October War of 1973, the fall of the Shah in 1979, the Iraqi invasion of Iran and Kuwait, the Tienanmen Square uprising and the Chinese willingness to use force, Indian nuclear testing in 1998, and a series of terrorist attacks between the 1993 bombing of the World

Trade Center and the 9/11 disaster in 2001. We have become accustomed to the charge of the CIA failure to "connect the dots" prior to 9/11. In many of these cases, there were ample intelligence collections to prevent failure, but the lack of rigor and imagination in connecting the dots and creating a multidisciplinary environment for analytical research have prevented success.

The original organization of the DI into current, estimative, and research intelligence produced some of the best analysis in the history of the CIA. It is important for any intelligence organization to have creative tension within its ranks, since truth is elusive and no single office should have a monopoly on intelligence analysis. The CIA benefited from having all its analysts in the three core disciplines compete for success, along with the analytical division of the Foreign Broadcasting Information Service. It is noteworthy that two CIA directors, Jim Schlesinger and Bob Gates, resented the independence of these analytical groups and were responsible for abolishing the estimative and historical groups as well as the propaganda analysis. Schlesinger and Gates also failed to encourage analysts to consult with experts outside the CIA, both in academia and elsewhere in the intelligence community. The increased centralization of intelligence analysis and the greater military control of the intelligence community and the CIA certainly do not augur well for future success.

What is needed is a return to the structure that existed in the early days of the CIA that divided the production of intelligence into current, long-term strategic, and estimative intelligence, affording three different methodologies to compete with each other. Such a system would decentralization intelligence production as opposed to the centralization in the current model that offers insufficient competitive analysis. It is the competitive process that ensures challenges to assumptions, offers obstacles to politicization of intelligence, and guarantees alternative analysis to national security problems. It is also essential to protect a small cadre of analysts to do long-term analysis so that the constant demands of current intelligence do not prevent retrospective views of intelligence collection and alternative methodologies for strategic intelligence. Such a group could have prevented the intelligence failures that marked the dissolution of the Soviet Union, the 9/11 terrorist attacks, and the decision to go to war against Iraq.

2

Crimes of the Central Intelligence Agency

In the history of nations, the influence of spying has been generally exaggerated. It is true that the secret services of states have played exciting underhand roles throughout modern history. But the clandestine achievements of secret agents amounts to gathering precious fragments of information that may or may not confirm but that does not formulate already existing diplomatic and strategic policies.

—John Lukacs, *The End of the 20th Century and the End of the Modern Age*

The United States must not adopt the tactics of the enemy. Each time we do so, each time the means we use are wrong, our inner strength, the strength that makes us free, is lessened.

—Senator Frank Church (D-Idaho), 1976

The salient lesson that I learned out of Iran-Contra was that other parts of the intelligence community can cause controversy, but it seems like the clandestine service is the only part that can cause real trouble.

—Robert M. Gates, 1991[1]

The CIA has committed every crime there is except rape.

—General Walter Bedell Smith, former DCI

The clandestine operations of the CIA—both covert action and, to a lesser extent, clandestine collection of intelligence—grew out of threats to our security during the cold war. The sudden and unexpected collapse of the Warsaw Pact in 1990 and the Soviet Union in 1991 suggested that Washington's intelligence and policy communities had exaggerated the power and influence of the Soviet Bloc, and had invested too much treasure in countering the Soviet threat. The perception of the Soviet threat was used to justify criminal activities of the CIA, with policymakers arguing that there were no rules in any contest with "an implacable enemy whose avowed objective is world domination by whatever means and whatever cost."[2] Today the threat of terrorism is used to accomplish similar objectives, with war crimes being committed in Iraq and Afghanistan.

The term "covert action" is a peculiarly American invention; it does not appear in the lexicons of other intelligence services. Nor does the term appear in the National Security Act of 1947, which created the CIA, the Department of Defense, and the National Security Council. Covert action, in the U.S. intelligence lexicon, refers to a secret operation to influence governments, events, organizations, or persons in support of a foreign policy in a manner that is not attributable to the United States. These actions may include political, economic, propagandistic, or paramilitary activities. Just as the cold war was used to justify the most egregious activities in the 1950s and 1960s, now the Global War on Terrorism (GWOT) has become the justification for another wave of illegal CIA activities, particularly in the wake of U.S. wars in Afghanistan in 2001 and Iraq in 2003, that have lasted longer than either World War I or World War II.

All postwar presidents have used the CIA for illegal covert actions. Within months of its creation, the CIA was engaged in sensitive covert actions in Western Europe, influencing democratic elections in Italy and France. At the direction of the National Security Council and the urging of Secretary of State George C. Marshall and Policy Planning chief George F. Kennan, the CIA provided funds to the Christian Democratic Party and to anticommunist trade unions in Italy in order to prevent a communist victory in the 1948 presidential elections. The CIA helped to fund similar campaigns in France and Japan, with "black bag" payments usually concealed from the U.S. ambassadors.[3]

The early election successes in Europe led to even wider use (and misuse) of covert action, including assassination plots against Fidel Castro and Patrice Lumumba, the disastrous Bay of Pigs invasion in 1961, which damaged the presidency of John F. Kennedy, and the illegal use of funds in the Iran-Contra scandal of the 1980s, which hurt the administration of Ronald Reagan. Presidents Dwight Eisenhower, Richard Nixon, and Jimmy Carter considered covert action a major instrument of policy and mounted major U.S. initiatives in Iran in 1953, Chile in 1973, and Afghanistan in 1980, respectively. In Iran and Chile, the United States took illegal actions against democratically elected governments; in Afghanistan, the United States sponsored activities that unexpectedly led to the emergence of the anti-Western Taliban government in

Kabul and the beginnings of anti-Western terrorist organizations in major Afghan cities. The covert operation in Iran included the harassment of religious figures and the bombing of their homes in order to turn them against the government of Premier Mohammad Mossadeq. Presidents Lyndon Johnson and Bill Clinton also resorted to covert actions, but were far more suspicious of the CIA than most of their White House peers.

For nearly forty-five years, clandestine operations played a major role in the collection of intelligence in the Soviet Union and Eastern Europe in support of U.S. policy against Moscow. Covert action captured the imagination of the CIA's political masters in the White House and Congress and, according to former CIA director Robert M. Gates, these actions were the CIA's "heart and soul."[4] All major covert actions were conducted on orders from the White House, according to congressional investigations, included those headed by Senator Frank Church (D-Idaho) and Representative Otis Pike (D-New York) in the mid-1970s. These investigations followed revelations of CIA participation in assassination plots against leaders in the Third World, as well as in illegal activities in the United States against the Vietnam antiwar movement.

Today, we must consider whether clandestine operations should play the same prominent role in U.S. foreign policy. The end of the cold war and the collapse of the Soviet Union in 1991, and the declaration of the Global War on Terrorism (GWOT) in 2001 clearly demand a reexamination of covert action. Covert action and even clandestine collection can seriously damage U.S. bilateral relations and are often at odds with U.S. values. Over the past ten years, CIA officers have been embroiled in public accusations of spying by such friendly nations as France, Germany, India, Italy, and Japan, and CIA officials concede that the "tradecraft" of their agents in recent years has been less than professional. The failure to detect Indian nuclear testing in 1998 was linked to the inept performance of the CIA in New Delhi, and the U.S. bombing of a pharmaceutical factory in Sudan in the same year raised serious questions about the methodology of clandestine collection of intelligence used to justify military force. Ironically, Sudan was one of the few countries willing to help the Clinton administration arrest Osama bin Laden. European officials and politicians are calling for a major examination of their relations with the U.S. intelligence community because of the rendering of terrorism suspects from their nations to Islamic countries that routinely conduct torture as part of their interrogation techniques. German and Italian courts have subpoenaed CIA officials in connection with illegal renditions that have taken place in their countries.

Covert action remains a dangerously unregulated activity. There are no political and ethical guidelines delineating when to engage in covert action, although previous covert actions have harmed U.S. strategic interests. At various times, such criminals as Panama's General Manuel Noriega, Guatemala's Colonel Julio Alpirez, Peru's intelligence chief Vladimiro Montesinos, and Chile's General Manuel Contreras have been on the CIA payroll. Although President Bush, like every other president since Gerald Ford, has signed an executive order banning political assassination, exceptions have been made in the covert pursuit of Iraqi president Saddam Hussein and former Afghanistan prime minister Gulbuddin Hekmatyar, both of whom received significant U.S. assistance in the 1980s.

A LEGACY OF THE COLD WAR

Covert action was a major aspect of U.S. policy for containing the Soviet Union. These actions may have been responsible for a small part of the CIA's budget, but from the installation of the Shah of Iran in 1953 to the Bay of Pigs in 1961, as well as the Iran-Contra operation in Nicaragua and Iran in the 1980s, they have caused the United States and the CIA great embarrassment. The role of CIA officers in the torture and even deaths of terrorism suspects and the extraordinary renditions of other suspects have raised additional questions about the legality of CIA activities in the global war on terrorism.

Any discussion of clandestine operations must recognize the incompatibility of covert action and the American democratic political process. Although the initial use of covert action was designed to buttress democratic elements in postwar Europe and to serve U.S. national interests, Hodding Carter III argued in a dissenting opinion to a Twentieth-Century Fund report in 1992 that "covert action is by definition outside the ambit of democracy."[5] In an age of terrorist activity, it is unlikely that the United States will entirely abandon covert action, but our democratic principles compel us to define the boundaries that should be placed around covert action, to determine what should and should not be attempted, and to ensure that there is careful, continuous control over it. Unlike the 1970s, when the Senate and House intelligence committees tried to place political limits on the conduct of covert action, these committees have neglected their oversight functions since the collapse of the Soviet Union. As a general principle, covert action, like military action, should be applied as a last resort, only when vital security interests cannot be achieved in any other way.

It is easy to justify the use of covert action in wartime, but we must decide whether the capacity to conduct covert action in peacetime should continue. The House intelligence committee reported in 1996 that, in the clandestine services, "Hundreds of employees on a daily basis are directed to break extremely serious laws in countries around the world in the face of frequently sophisticated efforts by foreign governments to catch them."[6] It went on to state, "A safe estimate is that several hundred times every day (easily 100,000 times a year) officers from the directorate of operations (DO) engage in highly illegal activities (according to foreign law) that not only risk political embarrassment to the United States, but also endanger the freedom if not lives of the participating foreign nations and, more than occasionally, of the clandestine officer himself."

Recent congressional reports on intelligence reform indicate, however, that the foreign policy establishment is unwilling to tackle serious reform of clandestine operations.[7] Despite recent problems and scandals in the clandestine services, the reports introduce no new thinking on clandestine operations. In fact, they endorse increased spending for covert action and a global presence for the National Clandestine Services, formerly the directorate of operations. Despite the misuse of fabricated and fallacious intelligence from clandestine sources in order to make the case for war against Iraq, there is no discussion of the need to reform the clandestine collection of intelligence to guard against misinformation and disinformation in the national security process.

The need for radical reform is compelling. Under three former directors of central intelligence (William Webster, Robert Gates, and James Woolsey), the CIA provided "intelligence" to several presidents that the DO had wittingly obtained from Soviet double agents put in place by the KGB.[8] Instead of acknowledging that they had lost their most important spies in the Soviet Union in the mid-1980s and were recruiting only double agents, the DO and the director of central intelligence (DCI) knowingly provided tainted information to the White House during the final years of the cold war without informing Presidents Reagan, Bush, or Clinton. Similarly, in the run-up to the Iraq War in the winter of 2002–2003, the CIA provided false information to President George W. Bush on weapons of mass destruction, which was ostensibly the reason why the United States went to war against Iraq. When the CIA misleads the White House, it is time start over.

THE ORIGINS OF COVERT ACTION

The laws authorizing the establishment of the CIA—the National Security Act of 1947 and the Central Intelligence Act of 1949—make no mention of covert action, paramilitary or secret operations, or special operations, all euphemisms for secret warfare. The first director of central intelligence, Rear Admiral Roscoe H. Hillenkoetter, resisted clandestine operations because he was convinced, from his wartime experience, that the Agency could not effectively engage in both information-gathering (the CIA's major mission) and covert action. The CIA's general counsel, moreover, believed that clandestine operations were illegal and that Congress had not intended to grant such authority.

It was the State Department that insisted in 1948 on the need for political and psychological warfare in response to Moscow's efforts to unsettle the European governments. The coup d'etat in Czechoslovakia and the Berlin blockade in 1948 led to war jitters in Washington, with the late George Kennan, the head of policy planning at the State Department, making the first proposal to create a CIA bureau to run covert operations.[9] The bureau, according to Kennan, would report to the Department of Defense in wartime and to the State Department in times of peace. Nearly sixty years later, Secretary of Defense Donald Rumsfeld successfully led a behind-the-scenes effort to return the Pentagon to the covert operations game and to share power for these operations with the CIA.

The CIA in fact, began to conduct covert actions in 1947, but received its mandate for such actions only in 1954, from an executive-branch panel charged with examining clandestine operations as an instrument of foreign policy. President Eisenhower was looking for ways to cut the defense budget, and Secretary of State Dulles believed that covert action was a way to conduct warfare on the cheap. The panel, under the leadership of General Jimmy Doolittle, concluded there were

no rules in such a game. Hitherto acceptable norms of human conduct do not apply. The United States had to learn to subvert, sabotage and destroy our enemies by more clever, more sophisticated means than those used against us. It may become necessary that the American people be made acquainted with, understand, and support this fundamentally repugnant philosophy.[10]

The use of covert action, which the Doolittle panel endorsed, is questionable, both morally and politically. Covert action, which became a staple of U.S. intelligence, contradicts American values and detracts from the message that the United States functions more openly than other nations; this is particularly the case when we take actions abroad that would be neither tolerated nor legal in this country. Most of these actions raise moral and humanitarian questions that tarnish our quest for international stability. Key third-world countries and leaders today, traditionally the primary targets of covert action, are far less vulnerable to U.S. manipulation than in the past, and our allies in Europe and Asia have grown increasingly impatient with the intrusive presence of clandestine officers in their countries. We must therefore address where, when, and whether covert actions are still necessary. We must ask whether their supposed benefits outweigh their many costs.

The CIA destroyed numerous files that would have provided information on other covert actions, such as in Iran, thus depriving America of a clear record of U.S. activities abroad. The successful overthrow of Jacobo Arbenz Guzman in 1954 (as well as the Mossadegh regime in Iran in 1953) led to the decision to overthrow Fidel Castro in 1961, the so-called "perfect failure" at the Bay of Pigs.[11] Sympathetic accounts of CIA covert action actually describe the Iran and Guatemala operations as "unblemished triumphs," although the conventional wisdom in the wake of the corrupt reign of the Shah Mohammed Reza Pahlavi in Iran and the horror of the reign of terror against the indigenous Indians for decades in Guatemala teaches a far different lesson.

COVERT "SUCCESSES"

Covert action has had its successes in terms of meeting U.S. foreign policy objectives, particularly during the worst days of the cold war, when the CIA initiated Radio Free Europe and Radio Liberty to bring information to the heavily censored environment of the Soviet Union and Eastern Europe. The CIA provided material assistance to Western European trade unions and political parties that were struggling against well-financed communist counterparts. The CIA published books and magazines for the member states of the Warsaw Pact and, with support and guidance from the State Department, developed programs to support democratic regimes in these countries. When democratic regimes finally emerged in the former states of the Warsaw Pact in 1990 and 1991, the CIA had justification to boast of its achievement in keeping the hopes of democratic governance alive behind the Iron Curtain for more than forty years.

The CIA also mounted covert actions against governments or parties the United States sought to contain, which provided short-term benefits in terms of U.S. policy objectives:

- In 1982, the CIA began a major program, in close coordination with the Vatican, to destabilize the Communist government in Poland and support Solidarity, the trade-union movement that opposed that government. The CIA smuggled portable radio and video transmitters to Solidarity through the AFL-CIO's American Institute for Free Labor Development, and created a fund for the legal defense of arrested Solidarity leaders and for fines imposed on illegal publications.[12]

- In 1983, the CIA engaged in unusual cooperation with the government of Iran to crush the underground Communist Tudeh party. Using information from a KGB defector, Vladimir Kuzichkin, the United States supplied Iran with information that was used to destroy the Tudeh and the Soviet intelligence network in that country.[13]
- In 1989, after the Chinese crackdown at Tiananmen Square, CIA officers conducted a clandestine rescue of some of the most important pro-democracy leaders. With the support of Ambassador James Lilley, a former CIA chief of station in Beijing, the CIA smuggled out students, dissidents, and intellectuals who formed the nucleus of the Chinese democracy movement in exile.[14]
- In 1991, during the Persian Gulf War, the CIA, in conjunction with Polish intelligence, mounted an operation to get U.S. diplomats out of Iraq.[15] A decade earlier, the CIA mounted a similar operation in Iran during the hostage crisis to get U.S. diplomats out of Tehran, with the assistance of Canada.
- The CIA's clandestine services also played a major role in the capture of the Cuban revolutionary Che Guevara, the international terrorist Carlos, and Abimael Guzman, the head of Sendero Luminoso (Shining Path) in Peru, which led to a decline in terrorism and insurgency in Latin America and the Middle East. With the support of foreign liaison intelligence services, the CIA—and not the U.S. military—has been responsible for rounding up two thousand al Qaeda suspects and sympathizers.

The CIA played a major role in Afghanistan in the wake of the 9/11 attacks, assisting the Afghan opposition and overthrowing the Islamist Taliban regime in the fall of 2001.[16] Prior to 9/11, the CIA had deployed teams to the Panjshir Valley of northern Afghanistan to meet with various tribal warlords, particularly with Ahmed Shah Masood, the head of the Northern Alliance. The CIA's Northern Afghanistan Liaison Team (NALT) and the Tajik-led Northern Alliance were responsible for the defeat of the Taliban regime by early December. Bin Laden and other top al Qaeda leaders escaped, although senior CIA operatives believe that if the CIA team had adequate assistance from the military forces of Army General Tommy Franks, their escape could have been prevented.[17] There is no doubt that the CIA was particularly quick in getting forces on the ground on Afghanistan, whereas the Pentagon was caught totally off guard and had great difficulty in getting "boots on the ground." The Defense Intelligence Agency (DIA) prepared a paper in October 2001 that concluded "Northern Alliance forces are incapable of overcoming Taliban resistance in northern Afghanistan" and "will not capture the capital of Kabul before winter arrives."[18] Secretary of Defense Rumsfeld widely circulated the flawed DIA paper.

AND COVERT FAILURES

More often than not, however, covert actions have not been beneficial, and even supposedly short-term policy successes have become long-term failures or liabilities. In Iran, which did not pose any challenge to U.S. national interests in the 1950s, the intense unpopularity of the Shah, whom the CIA had helped return to power in 1953, led to the Islamic revolution of 1979. Major covert actions in Laos and Vietnam failed to alter the results of fighting in Southeast Asia. Interventions in Angola and Mozambique had no beneficial effect on conflicts in southern Africa. Covert actions in Nicaragua and El Salvador in the 1980s increased the violence in Central America and brought great embarrassment to the United States. The excessive reliance on covert action by the Reagan administration in the 1980s contributed to the formation of radical Islamic terrorist groups that targeted the United States and its overseas military facilities.

As a result, it is reasonable to presume that CIA support for revolutionary and counterrevolutionary violence throughout the Third World contributed to the spread of revolutionary activity, including terrorism, against the interests of the United States and the West over the past ten to fifteen years. U.S. covert support for the apartheid regime in South Africa, the Contras in Nicaragua, and the anti-Soviet forces in Afghanistan certainly led to increased violence in these regions.

- In Guatemala, Central America's most brutal regime was installed in 1954 with the help of a CIA-backed coup. The country was dominated by its repressive military for the next forty years. Governments documents show that in 1990, Colonel Julio Roberto Alpirez, a CIA informer, was involved in the cover-up of the murder of Michael Devine, an American citizen, and that in 1992 he helped cover up the murder of Efrain Bamaca Velasquez, a Guatemalan insurgent who was married to Jennifer Harbury, an American citizen. In 1997, the CIA released a small batch of records on the 1954 military coup in Guatemala, but it has declassified practically nothing on the Guatemalan security forces, which have killed an estimated 200,000 Guatemalans since the coup. The Agency trained and supported some of these forces, along with similarly abusive internal security organizations in Nicaragua, Honduras, and El Salvador.[19] Such episodes undermined the credibility of the CIA and raised questions about its judgment and objectivity.
- In Honduras, government officials risked their lives to prosecute some two dozen military men involved in a death squad that killed at least 184 people in the early 1980s. The death squad grew out of collaboration

between the CIA and the Honduran military. Recently declassified CIA documents "linked Honduran military personnel to death-squad activities."[20] These documents confirm that the CIA (and U.S. ambassador John Negroponte) knew that the Honduran military committed systematic human-rights abuses in the 1980s, but that the Agency continued to collaborate with its Honduran partners and misled Congress about the abuses. The CIA was closely involved in the formation and training of the notorious Battalion 316, and CIA officers had exclusive access to all the secret detention centers in Honduras.[21] Ambassador Negroponte participated in the cover-up of the crimes in Honduras and his predecessor (Jack Binns) was removed from his post for refusing to do so. Binns was sent off to Arizona in retirement; Negroponte became U.S. Ambassador to the United Nations and Iraq, the nation's first intelligence czar in 2004, and currently serves as deputy secretary of state.

- Bob Gates, former DCI and now secretary of defense, termed support to the Mujahideen fighting the Soviets in Afghanistan the CIA's "greatest success," but today Afghanistan is a country of death and misery; weaponry supplied to the Mujahideen by the CIA has fueled conflicts in the Balkans and Africa, and rebels trained by the CIA have been involved in terrorist actions against the United States.[22] Agency-backed Mujahideen equipped with surface-to-air Stinger missiles worsened the situation facing Soviet leaders, but the Kremlin's decision to withdraw from Afghanistan was made before the arrival of the missiles.[23] In 1994, the CIA had to begin a $65 million covert effort to buy back the Stingers, which in the hands of the Mujahideen had become a long-term security and terrorist problem, just as many U.S. officials had warned in the 1980s.[24]

  Much of the CIA weaponry went to fundamentalist Gulbuddin Hekmatyar, one of the most anti-Western of the resistance leaders, Sheikh Omar Abdul-Rahman, who was imprisoned in New York for seditious conspiracy to wage a "war of urban terrorism against the United States, and Muhammad Shawqui Islambuli, the older brother of the assassin of Anwar Sadat. The terrorist network has targeted Saudi Arabia, Egypt, and Pakistan—Washington's most pivotal Islamic allies in the region—and has claimed responsibility for the first terrorist attack in Saudi Arabia and some of the worst attacks in Pakistan. Osama bin Laden, who has led terrorist attacks against U.S. installations in the Persian Gulf and North Africa, indirectly received CIA support that went to Afghanistan in the 1980s.

- Many of the most spectacular CIA failures occurred during the Kennedy administration, when the Agency misread or ignored the likely effects of its actions on target nations. The nadir of the CIA's covert actions was the Bay of Pigs invasion of Cuba in 1961, when high-level ignorance of Fidel Castro's popularity led the CIA to launch its ill-fated paramilitary operation. Even if the operation had gone flawlessly, it would not have dislodged Castro. In the wake of the failure of the Bay of Pigs, Cubans who received CIA training conducted their own freelance anti-Castro operations. Several Cubans, initially trained by the CIA for covert action against their home country, were involved in the break-in of the Democratic National Committee's offices in the Watergate complex ten years later.[25]

In 1998, after thirty-six years of secrecy, the CIA finally released its Inspector General's report on the Bay of Pigs, a startling and brutally honest inquest on the Agency's greatest fiasco.[26] The Agency had destroyed nearly every copy of the report except for those of the director of central intelligence, the Inspector General, and the records center. The report put the blame squarely on what it described as "arrogance, ignorance, and incompetence" within the CIA, found that the Agency was shot through with deadly self-deception, and described its secret operations as "ludicrous or tragic or both." Since plausible denial is the *sine qua non* of covert action, it is noteworthy that the report concluded that in the Bay of Pigs "plausible denial was a pathetic illusion," and argued that the Pentagon should conduct future paramilitary operations.

- Revelations of assassination plots in Cuba, the Congo, the Dominican Republic, and Vietnam in the early 1960s—at the direction of the Eisenhower and Kennedy administrations—finally led to a ban on CIA political assassinations in the mid-1970s. Nevertheless, covert action in Ethiopia in the early 1980s, according to Ambassador David Korn, led to the deaths of many people, including some who were entirely innocent and extraneous to the CIA's attempt to overthrow the government of Mengistu Haile Mariam. The recipients of CIA antiterrorist training in Lebanon set off a car bomb that killed eighty innocent people in Beirut. In 1984, the CIA displayed its contempt for the ban on assassination when it produced a manual for the Contras that discussed "neutralizing" officials in Nicaragua.[27]
- In addition to covert action against regimes identified by the Agency as dictatorial or subversive, there have been actions against identified neutrals, such as Indonesia, and democracies, such as Chile. In the late 1950s, the CIA, reflecting the Eisenhower administration's intolerance of neutrals, tried to unseat President Sukarno of Indonesia. In 1970, it tried to prevent the election of Salvador Allende, a leftist, as president of Chile. After Allende's election, the CIA moved to subvert his government. There was no justification for these actions in terms of American

national security or national interest. Henry Kissinger, President Nixon's national security advisor, facetiously described Chile as a "dagger pointed at the heart of Antarctica," but he did not "see why the United States should stand by and let Chile go communist merely due to the stupidity of its own people."[28]

Kissinger's efforts against Chile were particularly outrageous, involving bribes to members of the Chilean congress in order to allow the Christian Democratic president, Eduardo Frei, to seek reelection in violation of the country's constitution. Kissinger authorized covert propaganda to convince Chile's congress that the economy would be ruined if Frei were not reelected. He also authorized the introduction of two dozen CIA-sponsored journalists from around the world to produce stories hostile to Allende, the Marxist candidate. The instructions from the president and the national security advisor to Richard Helms, head of the CIA, were explicit, allowing Helms to say that "if I ever carried a marshal's baton in my knapsack out of the Oval Office, it was that day."[29]

Frei and his Christian Democrats wanted no part of Kissinger's chicanery; they were less afraid of an Allende victory than of a covert scheme to trample the electoral process. The commander-in-chief of the Chilean army, General Rene Schenider, also wanted to protect Chile's democracy and was opposed to the idea of a military coup, which Kissinger favored. But Kissinger had no qualms about interfering with the democratic electoral process. The CIA provided money and machine guns to right-wing renegades who were to kidnap and kill Schneider, but others got to Schneider before the CIA-sponsored groups. The general was killed two days before the congress voted Allende into office.

Far too often, paramilitary aid from the CIA has carried with it substantial danger for the recipients. The CIA established covert relations with the Kurds in northern Iraq, the Bay of Pigs invaders, and the Meo tribesmen in Laos, only to abandon them when U.S. policy changed. The CIA encouraged rebellion among Hungarian freedom fighters in the mid-1950s, but the United States did nothing when the Hungarian revolution began in 1956. The U.S.-backed Contra War against Nicaragua's Sandinista government and the CIA support for the National Union for the Total Independence of Angola (UNITA) in Angola in the 1980s raised the level of violence in both nations, with CIA officials in Central America and Africa keeping sensitive information from the Congress and U.S. ambassadors.

The CIA, moreover, was aware of the efforts of the Nicaraguan Contras to traffic drugs in the United States. According to declassified CIA studies, the CIA worked with twenty-four Nicaraguan rebels and their supporters during the 1980s despite knowledge that they were trafficking in drugs.[30] As early as 1981, the CIA knew that the Contra leadership "had decided to engage in drug trafficking to the United States to raise funds for its activities." The leader of the Contra group was Enrique Bermudez, whom the CIA had picked to run the military operations of the Contra organization. DCI Casey made no attempt to report these activities to the Justice Department, as required by law, and eventually obtained a waiver from Justice to provide a "legal basis" for his illegalities. Casey also ordered the Drug Enforcement Administration "not to make any inquiries" regarding the airfield in El Salvador that was being used as an arms-for-drugs transshipment point. CIA director Tenet and CIA lawyers also received protection from the Justice Department for the conduct of torture and abuse against so-called enemy combatants rounded up in Iraq and Afghanistan, until the Detainee Bill of September 2006 placed some unspecified limits on CIA conduct.

The most violent CIA operation in Central America took place in Guatemala, where Agency operatives helped to organize a Guatamalan "K" group that carried out political assassinations in the 1950s. CIA officials, as well as U.S. ambassadors in Central America, were also witting of the "death squad" activities of paramilitary groups in El Salvador, Honduras, and Nicaragua. When U.S. ambassadors Robert White, Jack Binns, and Anthony Quainton reported this activity to the State Department, Secretary of State Alexander Haig ordered them to stop reporting on the subject. All three disobeyed Haig, and all three were replaced. Binns' successor in Honduras was Negroponte, who was more than willing to go along with the cover-up.

The use of covert action as a quick fix for American foreign policy to deal with foreign leaders perceived as hostile or nation-states seen as renegades causing strategic problems for the United States. U.S. interests would have been far better served if Arbenz, Mossadegh, and Allende had remained in power in Guatemala, Iran, and Chile, respectively. The U.S. signal to permit the overthrow of Ngo Dinh Diem in South Vietnam ultimately meant that there would not be a stable government in Saigon to serve as a U.S. ally. We are currently experiencing in Iraq the problem that has bedeviled U.S. interests in the Third World since the end of World War II: the use of military power and covert action without any plan for reconstruction and stabilization, which compromises U.S. interests and creates chaos in the target country. A National Intelligence Estimate in 2006, for example, concluded that the Iraq War led to enhanced recruitment of terrorists and greater terrorism against U.S. interests.

Finally, the use of violence in the Third World has to be examined in the context of the post-cold war landscape, particularly the funding and training of armed groups to conduct low-level counterrevolutionary or counterinsurgency struggles. U.S. support for groups that resorted to violence in Indochina, South America, Africa, and Afghanistan cannot be dissociated from nonstate organizations that resort to terrorism. Mahmood Mamdani, a cultural anthropologist at Columbia University, reminds us that the best known CIA-trained terrorist is, of course, Osama bin Laden.[31] Mamdani argues that terrorism is the defining characteristic of the last phase of the cold war, and that U.S. support for such proto-terrorist organizations as UNITA and RENAMO (the Mozambiquian National Resistance) contributed to the rise of terrorism in the 1980s and 1990s. UNITA and RENAMO were armed and trained by the South African Defense Force, which received cooperation from the CIA. U.S. support for the Contras in Nicaragua and the Mujahideen in Afghanistan has also created problems for U.S. strategic interests.

Support for covert action in one area often compromises U.S. strategic objectives in other areas. The need to channel arms to the Mujahideen through Pakistan meant that the United States ignored Pakistan's nuclear weapons program in the 1980s. During that period, Casey and Gates kept sensitive intelligence dealing with Pakistan's nuclear program from the Senate Select Committee on Intelligence. More recently, the CIA repressed intelligence that cast doubt on Iraqi programs on WMD, which differed from the efforts of the Bush administration to cite Iraqi WMD to justify use of force.

Finally, the United States and the CIA used the cover of the United Nations and the United Nations Special Commission (UNSCOM) to conduct secret operations against Iraqi military communications. The United States had consistently denied Iraqi charges that it was exploiting UN inspections for the purposes of American espionage against Saddam Hussein, but CIA operatives infiltrated the UN inspection teams. The UN effort, which did not authorize or benefit from U.S. surveillance, was designed to gather information on Iraq's suspected nuclear, chemical, and biological weapons programs, but the CIA program was not aimed at Iraqi WMD. According to Scott Ritter, a former UN weapons inpector, CIA operatives penetrated Iraqi communications in order to bring down Hussein's regime, a covert action sanctioned by the U.S. Congress in the Iraqi Liberation Act.[32] This exploitation of the United Nations doomed further inspection efforts in Iraq and undercut the credibility of multilateral inspections around the world. The CIA thus made a liar out of the White House, which denied the use of covert action to undermine the Iraqi government, and a truth-teller out of Saddam Hussein, who cited the CIA's espionage as a reason to deny UN inspectors reentry into Iraq in 1998.

Ironically, the CIA and its intelligence collection failed miserably in the essential task of monitoring and verifying Iraqi WMD. Conversely, UNSCOM and the International Atomic Energy Agency did an excellent job of tracking the WMD and of demonstrating that Iraq had not reconstituted its nuclear programs. Unlike the CIA, the UN inspectors immediately recognized the documents on so-called Iraqi attempts to garner uranium from Niger as a fabrication. The UN also used excellent tradecraft to expose the poor clandestine reporting that was speciously used to make the case that there were links between Saddam Hussein and bin Laden. UN inspections, indeed, became a model of how to conduct international inspections as a way to reduce opportunities for proliferation of WMD. Meanwhile, the CIA found itself in its worse intelligence scandal because its analysis ostensibly became the justification for the White House's case to go to war against Iraq.

THE WAR ON TERROR AND WAR CRIMES

The tactical campaign against al Qaeda and its affiliates represents the largest covert action in the history of the CIA, involving the abduction of suspects on the territory of friendly nations, such as Italy; the use of Europe as a stopover point for the transport or "rendition" of suspects to Asian and Middle Eastern countries, where torture is routinely employed to extract confessions; and the use of torture by CIA and contract interrogators in secret CIA prisons in Afghanistan, Thailand, and East Europe. The CIA has employed such clumsy tradecraft in some of these renditions that an Italian judge issued arrest warrants for twenty-five CIA operatives in December 2005 for the illegal abduction and rendering of an Egyptian cleric in Milan in 2003. The cleric was tortured and abused repeatedly in Egyptian jails and, as a result, even former Italian prime minister Silvio Berlusconi, a U.S. ally in the war in Iraq, criticized U.S. policies.

The CIA's counterterrorist activities have taken place without sufficient debate or dialogue in Congress or within the national security community. Congress appears to want to know nothing or very little about the CIA's counterterrorist campaign, which is reminiscent of the 1950s and 1960s when Congress gave the Agency carte blanche in its campaign against the Soviet Union. Indeed, the Congressional oversight process has proven to be dysfunctional in the CIA's war against terrorism.

The most serious CIA crimes have been the most recent ones, during the occupation of Afghanistan and Iraq following the 9/11 attacks. CIA officials and contract employees were directly involved in the murder of several Afghan and Iraqi prisoners, but the Bush administration prepared legal memoranda giving the CIA (referred to in these memoranda as "other governmental agencies") legal immunity against prosecution for the use of techniques that amounted to torture.[33] Government lawyers at the Department of Justice and the Pentagon know the Uniformed Code of Military Justice restricts the conduct of U.S. military officers in the prisons in Afghanistan, Guantanamo, and Afghanistan, but CIA officials are only bound by the U.S. anti-terror statute, which was weakened by memoranda from the Bush administration. In his confirmation hearings for the position of Attorney General, Alberto Gonzales acknowledged that the presidential order directing that prisoners be treated in compliance with the Geneva Conventions did not apply to the CIA or other nonmilitary agencies.

The operative language in these memoranda stated, "Physical pain amounting to torture must be equivalent in intensity to the pain accompanying serious physical injury, such as organ failure, impairment of bodily functions, or even death. For purely mental pain or suffering to amount to torture . . . it must result in significant psychological harm of significant duration, e.g., lasting for months or even years." In other words, U.S. anti-torture statutes would not prohibit cruel and inhuman punishment that fell short of this definition. This formulation justified the CIA's use of such extreme techniques as "waterboarding," in which a prisoner is strapped upside down to a board and immersed in water to simulate drowning. This technique was used to interrogate Khalid Sheikh Mohammed, the planner of 9/11.

Key spokesmen for the Bush administration, particularly Vice President Dick Cheney and former secretary of defense Donald Rumsfeld, were not concerned that use of force to establish democracy in the Middle East ultimately will be judged by the moral example of U.S. practices and procedures in the region. Moreover, the United States and the CIA are creating a process that serves to attract more terrorists and insurgents to various causes in the Middle East and Southeast Asia. An American commander in Iraq described the Abu Ghraib prison as a "graduate-level training ground for the insurgency."[34] If so, then the Bush administration has sanctioned CIA measures making Iraq a magnet for violent extremists from across the Islamic world. Just as Islamic fighters were lured to Afghanistan in the 1980s to fight the Soviet occupiers, Islamic warriors are now traveling to Iraq to battle with the U.S. occupation. At the very least, the United States and the CIA are alienating friendly Islamic governments and key Islamic religious figures that are needed in any effective campaign against al Qaeda and its offshoots.

CRIMES AND MISDEMEANORS

In the wake of 9/11, the United States and the CIA have resorted to a series of illegal and immoral practices unrivaled in American history. These practices include torture and abuse; secret prisons in Europe, Asia, and the Middle East; and extraordinary renditions that involve delivering terrorist suspects to Arab intelligence services that routinely practice torture and abuse. Extraordinary rendition consists of the illegal abduction of individuals suspected of involvement in terrorism, and their arrest and transfer to a third country for interrogation, which usually involves torture and abuse. Although military lawyers have made courageous efforts to stop the immoral practices of torture and abuse in military prisons in Iraq and Afghanistan, CIA lawyers have looked for ways to justify similar practices in CIA facilities. These practices should concern all Americans who respect the U.S. Constitution, as well as the various international statutes that prohibit such practices. The Supreme Court has traditionally supported a strong oversight role for Congress in these matters, but Congressional intelligence committees have been slow to act. In the 1970s, there were bipartisan efforts to put a stop to illegal CIA behavior, but there is no bipartisan spirit at work today to limit the Agency.

The current actions of the CIA are reminiscent of the worst days of the cold war in the wake of the 1954 Doolittle Commission that gave the Agency carte blanche in the field of covert action. The CIA placed "secret prisons" in Eastern Europe, Southeast Asia, and Southwest Asia, conducted torture and abuse at these "black sites," and rendered terrorist suspects to intelligence services in Egypt, Jordan, and Morocco, where torture is practiced routinely. The CIA has its own fleet of Predators (unmanned aerial vehicles capable of firing antitank Hellfire missiles) that have killed both terrorist suspects and innocent civilians in Pakistan and Yemen, including at least one naturalized American citizen. In another aspect that is reminiscent of the worst days of the cold war in the 1950s and the 1960s, there is no indication that the appropriate congressional oversight committees are interested in these actions or that the Justice Department is investigating the crimes that have been committed.

Torture and Abuse

The CIA has engaged in abuse and torture in support of U.S. policies since the 1950s. CIA agents worked closely with death squads in El Salvador, where the organizer of the rural paramilitary and intelligence network received CIA payments and was sent on a tour of Vietnam to work with Green Berets and CIA operatives. The CIA regularly provided the El Salvadoran army with intelligence about various "suspects" who later "disappeared" or were assassinated.[35] One of the most appalling atrocities was the assassination of the Archbishop of San Salvador, Oscar Arnulfo Romero, as he said mass on March 24, 1980. U.S. Ambassador White informed Washington within two weeks that Roberto D'Aubuisson, the country's leading right-wing politician, had ordered the killing. The CIA knew who actually pulled the trigger at D'Aubuisson's order, a regular Salvadoran Army officer whose nom de guerre was Captain V, but the Agency didn't inform the intelligence committees, and Deputy Director for Intelligence Gates suppressed all intelligence on the killing. Assistant Secretary of State for Latin America Elliott Abrams called the defeat of the Salvadoran guerrillas a "fabulous achievement" for the Reagan administration, but the price was the creation of a huge military establishment in El Salvador that became an impediment to the creation of democracy. A genuine peace came much later when the administration of President George H. W. Bush changed policy from one of confrontation to encouraging negotiation with the rebels. The CIA has buried many of the truths of American policy toward Latin America in the 1980s.

Tortures and killings were far more prevalent and notorious in Guatemala, where CIA involvement began in the 1950s with the training and arming of a group of military dissidents who organized a violent coup against President Jacobo Arbenz. An on-again, off-again civil war in Guatemala lasted until a final peace accord in 1996, with tens of thousands of Arbenz supporters killed or driven from their homeland. The use of torture and "disappearances" was a routine part of a campaign of terror against the indigenous Indian population, which resulted in hundreds of thousands of deaths. The Intelligence Oversight Board concluded, in 1996, that the CIA used numerous "assets" in Guatemala that were involved in "serious human rights abuses such as torture.[36] CIA officers were closely involved with the training and equipping of the notorious Battalion 316, which kidnapped, tortured, and "disappeared" thousands of suspected "subversives, and had full access to secret detention centers where not even the Honduran police or court officials were permitted to enter."[37] The routine use of torture, abuse, and "disappearances" in Central America in the 1980s hardly differs from the world of "secret prisons," torture, and extraordinary renditions of today.

In the fall of 2004, the CIA's Inspector General completed a study of the interrogation practices that were pursued in the CIA's secret prisons and the military facilities, which confirmed that CIA officers had used techniques violating international covenants. The CIA's IG confirmed that abuse and torture had been committed; these exact words apparently were never used nor was there a reference to war crimes. Nevertheless, it is certain that war crimes were committed and this would not be the first time that CIA officers could be accused of abuse and torture. Unlike previous instances, however, the CIA was given legal protection with memoranda from the White House and the Justice Department that were prepared in the wake of the 9/11 attacks.[38] The dismissal of the Geneva Conventions as a "quaint document" and the redefining of torture itself opened up the field to CIA abuse in the prisons of

Afghanistan, Iraq, and Guantanamo. Cheney's public campaign to gain an exemption for the CIA in Senator McCain's amendment against torture provided prima facie evidence of the Agency's use of torture. CIA directors Goss and Hayden accompanied Cheney in these lobbying efforts, which violated the CIA prohibition against policy advocacy.

The Bush administration opened the door to torture and abuse by CIA and the military in February 2002, when the president decided to circumvent the Geneva Conventions, which prohibit both torture and "outrages upon personal dignity, in particular humiliating and degrading treatment." Military lawyers for all the services, including the general counsel of the U.S. Navy, Alberto J. Mora, challenged the decision to ignore the Geneva Conventions, but they were marginalized by White House lawyers, particularly from Cheney's staff. Cheney's chief of staff, David Addington, a former CIA lawyer, played a prominent role in squelching any challenge to government memoranda permitting torture, which has led to a significant number of lawyers leaving the Department of Justice. Unlike the military lawyers at the Pentagon, CIA lawyers do not oppose the use of torture and abuse, and there is no evidence of any CIA officials resigning because of war crimes.

In the process of fighting the "long war" against terrorism, the CIA has developed its own terminology, referring to "waterboarding" as an "enhanced interrogation technique" and not as torture and abuse. Serious suspects are referred to as HVTs or "high-value targets," and a major gray area now exists with CIA facilities holding terrorists for long periods of time; suspects have no legal recourse and no means of seeking release. There is no judicial process that rules on renditions or extraordinary renditions, and it is ludicrous that the CIA's Office of the General Counsel accepts disingenuous assurances against torture before turning over suspects to foreign liaison services. The CIA even has its own fleet of executive aircraft to fly suspects from country to country. In the world of post-9/11 legality, the White House and the Justice Department's Office of Legal Counsel have created a legal framework that violates international law, the Geneva Conventions, and even U.S. domestic laws against abuse. DCI Michael Hayden nominated the CIA's major defender of these practices, John Rizzo, to be general counsel of the CIA, but Senator Ron Wyden (D-OR) blocked his confirmation.

Waterboarding has a particularly ugly history. It was used by the Japanese against U.S. prisoners during World War II and by U.S. soldiers against Vietnamese prisoners during the Vietnam War. It involves pouring water on a prisoner's face, while covering his nose and mouth, in order to create the sensation of drowning. This technique was used against Khalid Sheik Mohammed, the key planner of 9/11, although a former senior intelligence official, in describing the information that Mohammed provided, said "not all of it was reliable."[39] The technique was pictured in a CIA interrogation manual from 1963, and the Agency requested permission to use waterboarding after 9/11. The Detainees Act provides retroactive legal protection to all those CIA officers who used waterboarding and other coercive interrogation techniques.

The CIA's Renditions Policy

In the mid-1980s, the CIA began the practice of "rendering" terrorist suspects from one country to another without any court hearing or extradition process. Renditions involve bringing suspected terrorists to the United States or Guantanamo; extraordinary renditions involve turning over low-level, suspected terrorists to foreign intelligence services known to torture prisoners. In those days, joint CIA and FBI teams would bring drug traffickers and terrorism suspects to the United States, where they would be read their rights, given lawyers, and then put on trial. In the wake of the 1993 attack against the World Trade Center in New York, these detentions, or "renditions," were largely replaced by a policy of "extraordinary renditions," taking suspects to a third country. The CIA decided that some suspects, mostly Islamic terrorists, should be kept out of U.S. courts for fear of jeopardizing their sources and to protect intelligence officials from other countries who did not wish to be called as witnesses.

Violence in the Balkans led to a significant increase in CIA renditions of Arab men. At least four suspected Islamists were abducted in the Balkans in 1998 and taken to Egypt. One disappeared, two were reported to have been executed, and one later alleged that he was tortured. An Islamist organization threatened retaliation for these abductions and two days later, the U.S. embassies in Tanzania and Kenya were blown up, killing 224 people. The Bush administration reviewed and renewed the presidential directive authorizing the rendition program and, after the 9/11 terrorist attacks, the number of abductions significantly increased. According to Scott Horton, an international law specialist who helped prepare a report for the New York University School of Law, as many as 150 people have been "rendered" since 2001. Most of these people have not been charged with any crime. These suspects are denied lawyers, their families do not know their whereabouts, and their detention is concealed from the international committee of the Red Cross.

We have learned a great deal about the CIA's illegal activity of extraordinary renditions over the past ten years. The specific destinations for rendered subjects include such Middle Eastern locations as Egypt, Jordan, Morocco, Saudi Arabia, Syria, and Yemen, where torture is used in interrogations, according to official documents of the U.S. Department of State. The Senate and House intelligence committees know about renditions in principle, but have made no serious effort to learn the number and location of rendered subjects. Much of what we know comes from Western journalists, particularly John Crewsden of the *Chicago Tribune,* as well as Dana Priest and Anthony Shadid of the *Washington Post,* who closely watch these activities. Now that several European countries (Italy, Germany, Spain, and Portugal) are willing to prosecute dozens of CIA agents in absentia for their actions in their countries, we will learn more.

Although it is not possible to gain official confirmation of renditions, the following examples are the most prominent:

- In September 1995, U.S. intelligence agents picked up one of Egypt's most wanted Islamic militants in Croatia and placed him on a ship in the Adriatic Sea for interrogation. He was turned over to Egyptian authorities, and his family believes he was executed in Egypt.[40]
- In 1998, U.S. agents transferred Talat Fouad Qassem, a leader of the Islamic Group, an Egyptian extremists organization, to Egypt after he was picked up in Croatia. Egyptian lawyers said he was questioned aboard a U.S. ship off the Croatian coast before he was taken to Cairo, where a military tribunal had already sentenced him to death in absentia.[41]
- In 1998, CIA officers and the Albanian police seized five members of Egyptian Islamic Jihad who were allegedly planning to bomb the U.S. embassy in Tirana. After three days of interrogation, the men were flown aboard a CIA-chartered plane to Egypt, where two of the men were put to death.[42]
- In 2001, Sweden expelled two Egyptians, who were transferred to Egypt on a Gulfstream V, a private jet presumably used by the CIA. Sweden claimed to have "diplomatic assurances" from Egypt that the two men would not be tortured but, according to Human Rights Watch, both were tortured. The Swedish Ministry of Justice confirmed that the U.S. government was involved in the transfer to Egypt.[43]
- In 2002, Indonesia transferred an Egyptian, who allegedly had worked with the "shoe-bomber" Richard Reid, to Egypt with the assistance of the CIA. Again, the transfer took place on an unmarked, U.S.-registered Gulfstream V.[44]
- In 2002, Maher Arar, a Syrian-born Canadian citizen in transit at John F. Kennedy International Airport in New York was taken into custody by the FBI, shackled, flown to Amman, Jordan, and then transferred to Syria. In Syria for nearly a year, he was tortured and kept in a shallow grave. No charges were ever filed in any of the countries involved in his transfer and he was eventually allowed to return to Canada, which conducted a public

inquiry into the circumstances of the transfer. The United States refused to take part in the inquiry, and U.S. officials have conceded that the case fits the profile of a CIA rendition.[45] The Canadians have completely cleared Arar of any wrongdoing, but he remains on the U.S. terrorist watchlist.

One of the worst examples of extraordinary renditions involved the CIA abduction of an Ethiopian living in London who was rendered and tortured in Morocco. In the case of the Ethiopian, he reportedly "confessed" to plotting with Jose Padilla, an American citizen, who had been arrested in Chicago and held incommunicado for several years. The Ethiopian was accused of plotting with Padilla to set off a "dirty bomb" in the United States. Padilla was never charged with the crime, but the Ethiopian remains in Guantanamo. The CIA also has resorted to "constructive custody" or "proxy detention" with such allies as Pakistan, Jordan, and Morocco, holding detainees at the request of the United States and giving CIA operatives free access to them.[46]

In dealing with both renditions and secret prisons, it is important to remember that the CIA is not acting on its own hook, but following instructions and procedures that have been blessed by lawyers at the White House, the NSC, and the Department of Justice. Former CIA analyst and operative Michael Scheuer is responsible for expanding the rendition program against al Qaeda in the mid-1990s, and he disingenuously maintains that there was never a covert operation that "was more closely scrutinized by the director of central intelligence, the NSC, and the congressional intelligence committees."[47] In fact, there is no indication of any scrutiny.

Scheuer is the major public defender of rendering and even torturing of rendered suspects in the hands of such nations as Egypt, Jordan, Saudi Arabia, and Syria. He credits himself with approaching Clinton administration officials for permission to conduct extraordinary renditions and was told to "do it." At the time, Scheuer was chief of the CIA's bin Laden unit, which was responsible for tracking and monitoring the activities of the al Qaeda leader. Scheuer knew that it was against U.S. law to take suspects to a country where there are "substantial grounds" for believing they will be tortured, but CIA officials argued that they received third country assurances against torture. The fact that suspects were "rendered" to countries that routinely torture criminal suspects points to the disingenuous position of the CIA and Secretary of State Rice, who maintained at a news conference in Europe on December 5, 2005 that U.S. terrorist suspects were not turned over to countries without assurances against torture.[48]

U.S. officials have admitted off the record that the government has engaged in extraordinary renditions, and the CIA's Inspector General has initiated an internal investigation into the Agency's detention and interrogation practices in Iraq.[49] The Department of Homeland Security's Inspector General announced that he would review the reasons behind the rendition of Arar to Syria, as well as the policies used by U.S. immigration officials regarding the rendering of nonimmigrants, but there has been no release of information.[50] The Defense Department and other federal agencies have refused to release records on the transfer of immigrants and nonimmigrants, prompting the ACLU to file a lawsuit in federal court.[51] In response, a federal judge ordered the government to "produce or identify" the documents regarding the transfer of detainees from Guantanamo to third parties.

Secret Prisons

In November 2005, the *Washington Post* confirmed a long-rumored story that the CIA was operating a series of at least eight secret prisons in Eastern Europe and Southeast Asia and Southwest Asia, where more than one hundred prisoners were held and, in some cases, tortured by CIA agents and contract officials.[52] Human Rights Watch confirmed that the Eastern European prisons were in Hungary, Poland, and Romania, with a former Soviet airbase in Poland serving as the largest prison facility. In addition to these eight countries that were directly involved in the prison system, the CIA was operating hundreds of flights, which included approximately one hundred flights through Germany and more than eighty flights through England. Many European nations were involved in handling these flights, including Denmark, Portugal, France, Italy, Spain, and Sweden. The European Union is conducting its own investigation of the countries involved, with the possibility of sanctions against those Eastern European countries that provided prison facilities.[53] The fact that the Bush administration would sanction these activities in such new and fragile democracies as Hungary, Poland, and Romania begs serious questions regarding the administration's emphasis on building democracies around the world. Vice President Cheney tried to obtain an exception for the CIA on the Senate's amendment to ban torture, and presidential spokesman Sean McCormack outrageously defended the policy of rendition as "one that is recognized by the international system."

The CIA has wrongfully imprisoned numerous terrorism suspects, including one German citizen for at least five months. Unlike the military prison at Guantanamo Bay, Cuba, where judicial review has led to the release of 180 prisoners, there is no tribunal or judge to check the evidence used by the CIA to arrest and hold suspects. In other words, the CIA makes a decision to capture and transfer a suspect for interrogation (the process of "rendition"), and only the

CIA is responsible for accounting for its prisoners and its errors. Dana Priest has reported that as many as three dozen individuals have been erroneously "rendered" and thus falsely imprisoned.[54] Upon learning that there was no evidence to sustain CIA charges, some of these suspects were transferred to Guantanamo, which has become a "dumping ground" for CIA mistakes, according to a counterterrorism official. Thus, the CIA has created a "gray area," where it may be holding terrorist suspects with no legal counsel and no charges for an unspecified period of time.

One of the worst examples of such false arrests involved a German citizen, Khaled Masri, who the CIA picked up in Tirana with the assistance of Albanian police. CIA officials were divided over whether to render Masri, some believing that his passport should first be verified. Cooler heads did not prevail, and Masri was handcuffed and blindfolded, drugged for a long flight, and flown to Afghanistan where he was beaten and warned: "You are here in a country where no one knows about you, in a country where there is no law. If you die, we will bury you, and no one will know."[55] Several months later, the CIA's Office of Technical Services concluded that Masri's passport was genuine, but it took two additional months of bureaucratic wrangling at the CIA and the State Department to decide on the means of releasing Masri. The CIA unceremoniously returned Masri to Albania, where he was taken to a narrow country road and told "not to look back when I started walking." Masri feared that he would be shot in the back. German prosecutors have listed twenty CIA operatives suspected in the abduction of Masri, but there have been no arrest warrants or indictments due to a lack of cooperation from the United States.

The startling discovery of the CIA's secret prisons and the terrifying accounts of false imprisonments have caused a firestorm of criticism in Europe and the United States, but no immediate change in the tactics and operations of the National Clandestine Service. Pressure from the White House, the National Security Council, and the CIA convinced the editors of the *Washington Post* to delay Priest's expose of the CIA's secret prisons, presumably giving the Agency time to close down the prisons in Poland, Hungary, and Romania. These prisons were the most controversial ones in the CIA's system, particularly because the collaboration of these Eastern European countries conflicted with their obligations of membership in the European Union. In any event, the CIA had time to move the thirty or forty prisoners to even more secret facilities in Afghanistan or Iraq.

There is every reason to believe that secret prisons still exist, that renditions and extraordinary renditions still take place, that interrogation techniques continue to violate international treaties and covenants, and that a fleet of Gulfstream aircraft still moves detainees from country to country.[56] This program is now larger than the CIA's covert actions in Central America during the cold war, which led to the killing of innocent civilians, and the programs in Afghanistan, which led to support for eventual Islamic fundamentalists, such as bin Laden. Senator John McCain (R-Arizona) successfully introduced a ban on torture and cruel and inhumane treatment of prisoners into the defense appropriations bill in December 2004, which should be a useful tool in limiting the use of torture by the military, but the CIA continues to have de facto immunity for crimes against humanity because of various Justice Department memoranda, as well as the department's lack of interest in pursuing cases of CIA abuse.

The combination of international pressure and a change in directors at the CIA led the Agency to inform its European allies that it had stopped the policy of extraordinary renditions and was looking for ways to return most of the captives at Guantanamo prison to their own countries. The debate in the United States over the release of captives has found Cheney and his chief of staff, David Addington, favoring no release, and Secretary of State Rice and Secretary of Defense Gates wanting to end renditions and secret prisons, as well as shutting down Guantanamo in order to improve the diplomatic position of the United States. Nearly three hundred prisoners have been released from Guantanamo since 2002, but another foru hundred remain with nearly one hundred of them eligible for transfer or release. The British and others have pressed for a complete closing of Guantanamo and several European parliaments have begun to investigate their own cooperation with U.S. rendition policy. In November 2006, a committee of the European Parliament condemned the complicity of European governments in the illegal detention and transportation of prisoners.

The Absence of Oversight

The virtual disappearance of congressional oversight has made the CIA largely unaccountable in its activities, which has returned the issue of covert action and espionage to the halcyon days prior to the Church Committee and the Pike Committee in the 1970s, when the CIA could do as it pleased, including assassination activities. The United States may sever its diplomatic and military relations with countries, such as Uzbekistan, that restrict human rights and conduct torture in its prisons, but the CIA presumably retains its liaison relations with the intelligence services in those countries. The congressional oversight committees need to know more about these liaison activities.

The Senate and House intelligence committees should be examining these activities, but the former Republican chairmen in both institutions, Senator Roberts and Representative Hoekstra, blocked investigations and inspections.

Similarly, the Justice Department has no interest in examining possible violations of international and domestic law, and the CIA's Inspector General has been reluctant to look under every rock. In the wake of the November 2006 election, Congressional oversight leadership has shifted to two Democrats, Senator Rockefeller and Representative Reyes, who have promised to be more aggressive in examining these matters.

The questionable legality and morality of some of these actions has led former and current members of the CIA to talk to members of the press, although they lack the whistle-blower protection that is given to other officials in the U.S. government. Unable to attract any concern at the Justice Department or from Congressional oversight committees, some of the sources for various exposes in *The New York Times* and the *Washington Post* have been current and retired officers from the CIA and the NSA. Within their respective agencies, officers from the CIA, the FBI, and the Defense Intelligence Agency have sent secret memoranda objecting to the use of torture and abuse in military and CIA interrogations, denouncing them as unethical, counterproductive, and destructive.

Former secretary of defense Rumsfeld had allies within the policy and intelligence communities in support of torture and abuse, particularly Vice President Cheney and CIA director Hayden, who lobbied for a CIA exemption in any legislation to ban torture and abuse. Hayden was careful with his public remarks, but he essentially supported the position of his predecessor, Porter Goss, who maintained that the interrogation techniques of the CIA are "unique and innovative ways, all of which are legal and none of which are torture."[57] These innovative ways include waterboarding, which creates a terrifying fear of drowning; shaking and striking detainees; severe temperature change for naked prisoners; and forcing prisoners to stand handcuffed and shackled for up to forty hours. These are the same techniques that are denounced by the State Department in its annual human rights reports and that are defined as "cruel and inhuman" in the Convention Against Torture and Other Cruel, Inhuman, and Degrading Treatment or Punishment, which the Senate ratified in 1994. Goss was at war with senior members of the National Clandestine Service on the issue of torture, and replaced the chief of the Counterterrorism Center, Robert Grenier, who objected to these loathsome techniques. Secretaries of State Powell and Rice also challenged Rumsfeld and Cheney, aware that any use of torture and abuse was weakening the rights that American soldiers could expect overseas and the ability of the United States to gain the high ground in any cooperative effort against terrorism.

On September 6, 2006, President Bush finally admitted that the United States and the CIA had sponsored a group of secret prisons and that the fourteen top al Qaeda leaders in those facilities would be transferred to Guantanamo Bay, Cuba. These leaders included the planners of the 1998 attacks on two U.S. embassies in East Africa, the October 2000 attack on the USS *Cole*, and the 2001 attack on the World Trade Center and the Pentagon. There is a great deal of international opposition to the military facility at Guantanamo, but the Bush administration helped itself, particularly in Europe, with the admission of the secret prisons and the incorporation of the prisoners into the military justice system. In the wake of the Supreme Court's *Hamdan* decision in June 2006, which struck down the military tribunals at Guantanamo as unconstitutional, the White House and the Congress were instructed to agree on a system for putting terrorism suspects for war crimes on trial. There has been no information on several hundred former prisoners who had been held at CIA secret prisons in East Europe and Southeast Asia. Whenever former CIA director Tenet is asked about CIA torture, his standard reply is "We don't do it and I'm not going to talk about it."

The Bush administration continues to insist on maintaining the CIA's secret prisons, as well as the CIA's ability to ignore the protections from abuse and torture granted to prisoners by the Geneva Conventions. Many CIA officers are opposed to the use of torture, and there are CIA officers who have referred to the "war crimes" committed by their colleagues. CIA clandestine officers have signed up for a government-reimbursed, private insurance plan that would pay their civil judgments and legal expenses if they are sued or charged with criminal wrongdoing.[58] They presumably have doubts that they can be protected by Cheney and his senior staff aid on the issue of torture and abuse, and could ultimately have to go into court or congressional inquiry without the protection of the Department of Justice. The opposition of three senior Republicans, Senators McCain, John Warner (Virginia), and Lindsay Graham (South Carolina), as well as most Democrats, to the continued use of torture and abuse is also causing CIA officers to take a second look at any behavior that violates international law and U.S. criminal statutes.

Senior CIA officers also must realize that the protection that they were afforded in a sweeping presidential directive from September 17, 2001, which authorized the CIA for the first time to capture, detain, and interrogate terrorism suspects and to create a network of secret prisons, is subject to change. Since that time, there have been serious disputes between the FBI, which favors standard interrogation procedures, and the CIA, which has resorted to the kind of torture and abuse that has led to deaths in the secret prisons and in military facilities. The only CIA employee facing justice on these issues is David Passarro, a contract employee, who was responsible for the death of a prisoner in Afghanistan. The CIA was also responsible for the torture and abuse of Abu Zubaydah, the first al Qaeda leader taken into the Agency's custody, who turned out to have no sensitive information on operational matters.

CIA lawyers and senior clandestine operatives have become particularly nervous about their interrogation practices ever since the Congress passed Senator McCain's law in late 2005 that placed new restrictions on the handling of detainees, and the congressional chairmanship passed to Democrats in the November 2006 elections. The CIA, moreover, was getting little operational intelligence from these interrogation practices, and the secret prisons were becoming an impediment to foreign liaison cooperation in Europe, where there was opposition to the illegal prisons located in East Europe. Nevertheless, Cheney and CIA director Hayden remain aggressive defenders of torture and abuse, and President Bush maintains that CIA interrogation techniques are "safe, lawful, and effective."[59] The president also has made many false claims for the intelligence gained from torture, particularly from Khalid Sheikh Mohammed. The 9/11 Commission said that the CIA learned of Mohammed's various aliases, as well as the fact that Ramzi bin al-Shibh was an accomplice in the 9/11 attacks before the attacks took place, and not from the torture of Khalid Sheikh Mohammed. Thus, there continues to be a great deal of smoke and mirrors in the claims being made on behalf of torture and abuse.

WHAT NEEDS TO BE DONE?

Despite the failures of clandestine collection of intelligence and the strategic problems associated with covert action, virtually every reform proposal, such as the Brown Commission in 1996 and the 9/11 Commission in 2004, called for more spending on human intelligence, not less, and more espionage and covert action. Then-chairman of the House intelligence committee, Representative Larry Combest (R-Texas), who was responsible for the committee's report in 1996, even favored removing the directorate of operations from the CIA and combining it with the Pentagon's defense human intelligence (HUMINT) service to create a comprehensive organization for espionage. The effect would have been an even stronger clandestine capability, more involved in domestic surveillance and less susceptible to congressional oversight.

The fact that the CIA's National Clandestine Service passed tainted intelligence to several U.S. presidents (including President Clinton) that was obtained from Soviet and Russian double agents is reason enough for a major shake-up of the clandestine corps. Recent spy scandals include flawed CIA efforts to collect intelligence in France, Germany, India, Italy, and Japan, which have some of the most important CIA contingents overseas and raise additional questions about the judgment and goals of the directorate. More recently, thanks to an aggressive reporter from the *Chicago Tribune*, John Crewsden, we have a detailed account of the bungled tradecraft of the CIA stations in Milan and Rome, which were responsible for conducting ill-advised renditions in Italy. The fact that the CIA supported military organizations throughout Central America despite the long history of their human-rights abuses and the limited value of clandestine collection in the region begs questions about current CIA practices in Venezuela, Bolivia, Nicaragua, Brazil, and Ecuador, where populist leaders have come to power or are in position to claim power. Covert actions to influence the course of events in foreign countries that are democratic, which means all the nations of Central and South America, undermines U.S. principles and should be authorized only in times of genuine national peril.

The end of the CIA's original mission as an instrument to combat the Soviet Union should have presented Congress with an opportunity to reexamine the appropriate mission for clandestine operations. The late Richard Bissell, onetime head of covert operations and the planner of the Bay of Pigs operation, conceded that there "have been many short-term tactical victories" in covert action, but "very few lasting successes." Now that covert action has become a major part of the global and continuous war against terrorism, it is particularly essential for the congressional oversight committees to examine the role and the practices of the DO in that war. CIA successes against international terrorism have stemmed primarily from information from foreign liaison intelligence services and not the clandestine operations of the CIA. The presidential finding of September 17, 2001, that permits the CIA to create paramilitary teams to hunt and kill designated individuals anywhere in the world could complicate these liaison relations. We certainly need to continue clandestine collection of intelligence on the proliferation of WMD and international terrorism, but this could be done with a smaller and more specialized operational presence abroad that focuses on key issues and does not duplicate the work of foreign service officers with the Department of State, the Department of Agriculture, and the Treasury Department. Recent CIA directors have focused clandestine collection on support for military operations, which marginalizes the role of the CIA in strategic and political intelligence.

The failure to address the problems associated with covert action has been compounded by the failure to address the problem of oversight. The intelligence oversight committees and their staffs are small in comparison with the community they monitor; they must be strengthened. The National Reconnaissance Office managed to misplace $4 billion because of obsessive secrecy and weak oversight, then failed to return the unspent funds to Congress, which the law required. Oversight of clandestine activities and intelligence analysis is deficient and should be strengthened; intelligence and operational failures must be studied. Nevertheless, the presidential commission on intelligence reform (the Brown Commission) insisted in 1996 that the Senate and

House committees have provided "rigorous and intensive oversight," and the House study introduced a new (and shocking) role for congressional oversight: that of "advocate." Then-chairman of the House intelligence committee, Representative Porter Goss (R-Florida), who became CIA director, regularly referred to himself as an "advocate" for the CIA, which totally distorts the chairman's role as a chief of oversight. As Steven Aftergood argued in *Secrecy and Government Bulletin*, any "advocacy role is fundamentally incompatible with credible oversight and is, in fact, the reduction to the absurd of the oversight mission."[60]

The problem of oversight of clandestine collection and covert action has become even more complicated with the introduction of the Pentagon into the area of intelligence collection. Former secretary of defense Rumsfeld, who was never satisfied with the CIA's clandestine collection of intelligence and favored a more aggressive military role, introduced small teams of Special Operations forces into a number of American embassies to collect intelligence and conduct covert action.[61] In view of the weak oversight role of the Senate Armed Services Committee, it will be very difficult to study these teams and their actions. Reportedly, at least a dozen of these teams are operating out of embassies in Africa, Southeast Asia, and South America under the aegis of the Special Operations Command, which was authorized to take the lead in military operations against terrorists in March 2004. The director of national intelligence, and the intelligence oversight committees have no control over the activities of these paramilitary groups. Senior embassy officers know little about these groups operating in their own countries and, in 2004, a "military liaison element" had to be withdrawn from Paraguay after some of its members were involved in the killing of an armed robber.[62] The creation of these elements will add even more chaos and disorganization to U.S. counterterrorism activities around the world.

For too long, the intelligence committees have been advocates for the CIA—particularly for the clandestine world of spies and covert action. Thus, Congress has failed to make the CIA accountable for its transgressions, and Iran-Contra demonstrated that no form of accountability was sufficient to monitor ideological zealots in the CIA and the NSC. A presidential pardon in 1992 for key CIA operatives involved in Iran-Contra meant that we never learned the extent of CIA perfidy in presidential maneuverings related to that scandal. No CIA officer has been indicted thus far in the conduct of war crimes as the White House and the Justice Department have collaborated to prevent any legal action against members of the intelligence community.

In September 2006, the Senate and House did pass a Military Commissions Act that could limit the CIA's use of torture and abuse in its overseas facilities. They did so in the wake of the Supreme Court decision involving *Hamdi v*

Rumsfeld (June 2006) when the court ruled that the president could not simply lock up anyone—even a foreign citizen—without giving him an opportunity to challenge his detention before a "neutral decision maker." The Act is terribly flawed, still stripping detainees of habeus corpus and the right of appeal, giving the president broad latitude to decide who is an enemy and which interrogation methods violate the Geneva Convention, and permitting the CIA to operate its secret prisons. It does appear, however, that the Act could lead to the end of such CIA practices as waterboarding, dousing naked prisoners with water in fifty-degree cold, and forcing shackled prisoners to stand for forty consecutive hours. According to the legislation, an interrogator could face legal action if a court finds that his techniques caused "serious" mental or physical "suffering." Courts have previously ruled that waterboarding, hypothermia, and prolonged sleep deprivation constitute torture and abuse. The three Republican legislators who fought for a ban on torture (Senators McCain, Warner, and Graham) were less aggressive in ensuring that the CIA could not resort to the techniques "clearly prohibited by the bill."[63] Thus, the Military Commissions Act is an affront to our constitutional and democratic values, and hardly the compromise that the key Republican senators claim. Hopefully, in the short run, it will give pause to the worst of the CIA knuckle-draggers and, in the long run, the bill will be termed unconstitutional by the Supreme Court or at least strengthened by the new Congress.

In a democracy, where laws are derived from broad principles of right and wrong and where those principles are protected by agreed procedures, it is not in the interest of the state to flout those procedures at home, or to associate overseas with the enemies of this nation's founding ideals. Continued CIA abuses point to the failure of the system of checks and balances in the field of national security. The intelligence committees, at the very least, should take a hard look at the British system, where espionage and clandestine collection are conducted by an organization that reports to the highest levels of the British Foreign Office. Radical reform would allow the CIA to return to President Truman's original conception of the Agency as an independent and objective interpreter of foreign events.

3

Intelligence: The Importance of Success

A popular government without popular information, or the means of acquiring it, is but a prologue to a farce or tragedy, or perhaps both. Knowledge
will forever govern ignorance, and a people who mean to be their own Gov-
ernors, must arm themselves with the power which knowledge gives.

—James Madison

So much attention has been given to intelligence failure that intelligence success has often been ignored. Sound intelligence analysis can help to form effective foreign and national security policy and to prevent foreign policy re-
versals and even disasters. The CIA did some of its best work before and
during the Vietnam War, when it told the Johnson and Nixon administrations
that the South Vietnamese government was corrupt and would not be a capable ally in the war against the North, and that the strategic bombing campaign
would fail. But the CIA also politicized intelligence on the Viet Cong, and
failed to challenge the politicized analysis from the Pentagon and the National
Security Council on the numbers of Viet Cong in South Vietnam. If the Johnson administration had been paying any attention to CIA analysis, there probably would not have been a massive troop buildup in the 1960s. President
Richard Nixon paid more attention to the intelligence on Vietnam, but was
contemptuous of CIA's assessments. President Nixon and national security advisor Henry A. Kissinger followed CIA intelligence that monitored the split
between the Soviet Union and China, and developed a strategic policy to exploit the rift and radically improve the geopolitical position of the United
States vis-à-vis Moscow and Beijing. Finally, both Democratic and Republican administrations took advantage of excellent collection and analysis from
the entire intelligence community, particularly the CIA, which gave policy

makers strategic warning on *every* strategic weapons system that the Soviet Union introduced to its arsenal. This analysis pointed the way to the SALT and ABM agreements of 1972, and ensured monitoring of a series of arms control agreements.

Successful intelligence analysis is not always well received at the White House, particularly if it doesn't corroborate a particular policy. Lyndon Johnson compared the role of the "intelligence guys" to getting a full pail of milk from one of his cows and then have the cow "swing her shit-smeared tail through that bucket of milk." According to Johnson, "that's what those intelligence guys do. You work hard and get a good program or policy going, and they swing a shit-smeared tail through it." The Johnson administration was furious with the pessimistic assessments of the CIA on the Vietnam War, which is similar to the Bush administration's dismissal of the CIA's critical views regarding the Iraq War and the prospects for American success. President Nixon was so fed up with CIA intelligence on Vietnam and Southeast that he eventually asked his national security advisor, Kissinger, "What is it those clowns out at Langley do?" The CIA's analysis on the Middle East was not welcomed at the Reagan White House, where the deployment of U.S. Marines led to a disaster in 1983. The Bush administration presumably would prefer not to recall CIA forecasts of wider turbulence and civil war in Iraq.

At one time or another, every president from Truman to George H.W. Bush had to deal with CIA analysis on the Soviet Union. Eisenhower's intuition on the phony bomber and missile gaps was helped by CIA analysis of the indispensable imagery of U-2 flights and Corona satellites in the late 1950s and early 1960s. Kennedy used CIA photo imagery on the installation of Soviet missiles in Cuba to maneuver a successful end to the Cuban missile crisis in 1962. Carter believed he was ill-served by CIA intelligence on the Soviet invasion of Afghanistan; as late as December 19, 1979, less than a week before the invasion, the CIA reported that the "pace of Soviet deployment does not suggest . . . urgent contingency."[1] The CIA's "President's Daily Brief" (PDB) had described the establishment of a military command center in southern Russia in late November, but the NSC read nothing into this indicator of war, and the CIA itself never highlighted the command center as an intelligence indicator of imminent Soviet force. President Reagan relied on his intuition in dealing with the Soviets, and paid very little attention to CIA intelligence. I was a backbencher in a strategic briefing for Reagan before the inauguration, and he didn't make a comment or ask a question. The popular notion that Clinton was not interested in intelligence was in error. The problem was that Clinton never established a personal relationship with CIA director Woolsey and, as a result, Woolsey had limited access to the White House. George W. Bush wanted the CIA to provide the intelligence justification for the invasion of Iraq, and when the CIA was slow to do so, the president and vice president looked for ways to punish the Agency. The punishment arrived in the form of CIA director Porter Goss, whose short stewardship included efforts to politicize the Agency. The establishment of the office of the director of national intelligence (DNI) in 2004 and the appointment of flag officers to lead the office of the DNI and the CIA was designed to limit the CIA's influence.

Although the CIA registered major intelligence failures in the Middle East (e.g., the October War of 1973, the fall of the Shah in 1979, the Iran–Iraq War in the 1980s, the Iraqi invasion of Kuwait in 1990, and Iraqi WMD in 2003), there were also important successes that gave the White House sufficient time to mobilize a policy response. Although the CIA did not predict the start of the Six-Day War in 1967, it informed the White House of Israeli preemption and predicted an Israeli victory within one week. There was a good deal of skepticism with the latter prediction, and Secretary of State Dean Rusk told CIA director Richard Helms, "All I can say is to remind you of the immortal words of New York Mayor Fiorello La Guardia—'If this is a mistake, it's a beaut!'"[2] On the basis of CIA intelligence, President Johnson encouraged the Israelis to avoid the use of force, but the American president was preoccupied with Vietnam, and the White House initially rejected CIA intelligence on the Israeli preemptive attack. When the Office of Current Intelligence sent an urgent memorandum to the White House describing the start of the war, national security advisor Walt Rostow returned it, claiming he had Israeli assurances they would not preempt. CIA director Helms stood by the memorandum, and it was returned to Rostow with meaningless changes. Rostow was already unhappy with CIA's intelligence on Vietnam and, as a result, was never friendly toward the Agency. The CIA's belief that the Israelis had deliberately attacked the USS *Liberty*, a naval communications ship seconded to NSA, also ran headfirst into the White House desire to avoid a contretemps with the Israeli government.

The CIA is tasked with providing early warning to the White House, and administrations are particularly grateful when they receive premonitory intelligence of newsworthy events. Thanks to a well-placed clandestine source, the CIA warned President Nixon in 1972 the Egyptians would demand the removal of most of the Soviet military advisory presence in Egypt. I wrote that piece for the PDB, and it led to a phone call from CIA director Helms who told me that Henry Kissinger had called to praise the CIA for finally scooping *The New York Times*. CIA intelligence on the Middle East in the early 1980s should have given President Reagan ample reason to pause before deploying marines in Lebanon, but his national security advisor, Marine Colonel Bob McFarlane, was committed to using U.S. forces to pull Israel's chestnuts out of the Lebanon fire that the Israeli government had created. McFarlane ignored CIA intelligence at his own peril. The CIA warned President

Bush that the use of force in Iraq could cause tremendous discontinuity in Iraq, perhaps leading to the possibility of civil war, but the White House was not listening.

The CIA's overall performance on the Soviet Union, which was central to the development and growth of the Agency, ultimately proved to be abysmal because of the inability to recognize and track the decline and ultimate fall of the Soviet Union in 1991. Nevertheless, there were episodes in economic and military analysis that pointed both to the prescience or courage of CIA analysts, as well as the ability to tell truth to power. A CIA paper warning of the Soviet Union's impending descent into economic stagnation, "Soviet Economic Problems and Prospects," was issued in 1977, setting out the reasons why the Soviet economy was in trouble and why its future was so grim. But the Agency failed to call attention to this work and abandoned this thesis in the 1980s, when CIA director Casey and his deputy director for intelligence, Gates, wanted to create a picture of Soviet power and not weakness. Thus, the CIA missed the decrepitude of the Soviet economy. The CIA couldn't block the efforts of the Reagan administration to try to stop the Siberian–West European gas pipeline, but it provided ample warning of the ineffectiveness of the proposed sanctions and embargoes. Again, Gates did his best to limit the distribution of CIA analysis. His deputy, Richard Kerr, released the final draft on the gas pipeline to the policy community in August 1982, when Gates was on vacation and out-of-town. Upon return, Gates was furious! The CIA was also first in calling attention to the problems in Soviet oil production and citing the oil problem as an element in the overall economic decline.

The Vietnam Dilemma

Although the CIA had mixed results in their analysis of Vietnam, the overall record is more positive than negative. The CIA maintained from as early as 1963 that U.S. bombing of Vietnam (no matter how unrestricted) would not hinder Hanoi's ability to carry on the war against the South and that the North Vietnamese would match every U.S. act of escalation, no matter how great the physical suffering.[3] The CIA prepared a series of studies for President Johnson, National Security Advisor Rostow, and Secretary of Defense McNamara that concluded that such bombing operations as ROLLING THUNDER, designed to complicate the enemy's war effort, had not reduced enemy operations in the South or the amount of enemy supplies moving into the South. The JASON division of the Institute for Defense Analysis, corroborated the work of the CIA and added its own pessimistic assessment of the bombing programs, which was the "most categorical rejection of bombing as a tool of our policy in Southeast Asia to be made before or since by an official or semiofficial group."[4] The Agency reports also led to Johnson's decision after the Tet offensive to curtail U.S. bombings of the North.[5]

President Johnson was never happy with the bad news from CIA intelligence analyses, but he received it and moved on. President Nixon, on the other hand, became irate with every unwanted CIA message and held it against the group of "Ivy League liberals" at Langley who "had always opposed him politically."[6] Nixon eventually forced the resignation of Richard Helms as CIA director in 1973 and appointed James Schlesinger to replace him to stop the flow of bad news and to remove the "existing regime of anti-Nixon Georgetown dilettantes and free-range liberals" who were making the president's life miserable.[7] Schlesinger lasted four months as CIA director, moving to the Pentagon in June 1973 to replace Elliott Richardson.

The Vietnam Intelligence Battlefield

The CIA was credited with the best intelligence on North Vietnam's order of battle (O/B), which is particularly telling in view of CIA director Gates' decision in 1992 to transfer the Agency's responsibility for O/B analysis to the Pentagon's DIA. In the wake of the Pentagon's criticism of the CIA for the lack of intelligence support during the Desert Storm war, Gates simply did not want to antagonize the military with CIA's assessments on such issues as O/B intelligence. At DIA, O/B analysis was subjected to the influence of military commanders with a vested interest in analysis, leading to worst-case views of a particular enemy.

The O/B problem is particularly difficult in any guerrilla/paramilitary situation because of the uncertainty in counting members of the hostile force. The United States Military Assistance Command, Vietnam (MACV) intelligence staff consistently carried lower and more optimistic numbers of the enemy military and guerrilla forces in South Vietnam. MACV estimated there were a total of 250,000 to 300,000 total forces in the South; the CIA believed there were 500,000. Most of the discrepancy was due to a higher guerrilla count on the part of the CIA, about 250,000 to 300,000, as opposed to a MACV estimate of 100,000 to 120,000 Viet Cong irregulars. The military was wedded to a lower estimate in order to substantiate their rosy estimates of North Vietnamese losses in the South. The White House similarly wanted to justify its optimistic appraisal of the military situation. But the CIA knew that the North Vietnamese and the Viet Cong were gaining strength, and the Agency was right. Unlike military intelligence, the CIA refused to accept the optimistic assessments of the South Vietnamese.

There was a basic difference between the approach of the Johnson administration and that of the current Bush administration: Johnson and his senior policymakers at the NSC and the Pentagon used the CIA to provide highly sensitive assessments of specific policy developments, especially when it appeared that a particular policy was failing, which was certainly the case in the Vietnam War. The Johnson administration actually requested NIEs on the Vietnamese situation. The Bush administration never asked the CIA on Iraqi issues, and ignored the negative assessments and estimates of the CIA, hoping to avoid any explicit or even implicit criticism of its policies. The Bush White House, for example, did not ask the CIA for a NIE on Iraqi WMD or the implications of the use of force on a country, such as Iraq, that was becoming increasingly backward both politically and economically. The chairman of the Senate intelligence committee, Senator Bob Graham (D-Florida) requested the controversial Iraqi WMD estimate in October 2002, which was highly unusual. The National Intelligence Officer for Terrorism, Paul Pillar, has noted he received no requests from the White House on international terrorism prior to the war or in the immediate aftermath for that matter.

There is an interesting similarity, however, between the roles played by former secretary of defense McNamara during the Vietnam War and former secretary of defense Rumsfeld prior to the Iraq War toward the intelligence community. Both McNamara and Rumsfeld, to paraphrase the late David Halberstam's *The Best and the Brightest*, were "can-do men in can-do societies in can-do eras." Both men made sure that the chain of command in the Joint Chiefs of Staff did not get to have an impact on the key decisions regarding troop strength and deployment. And both McNamara and Rumsfeld became major targets for critics from the left and right, with constant calls for their resignation. Pro-war critics blame them for sending insufficient forces into battle; antiwar critics blame them for their blind faith and fanaticism in driving the United States into a geopolitical quagmire. Both McNamara and Rumsfeld were forced to resign when they began to lose enthusiasm over the possibility of victory on the battlefield. In the wake of the Tet offensive in Vietnam in January 1968, McNamara began to see the war as unwinnable; he resigned in February. In October 2006, Rumsfeld wrote a memorandum to the president, detailing ideas for limiting U.S. involvement in Iraq; he resigned in November. Unlike McNamara, who appeared to be on the verge of a breakdown and left the Pentagon for the World Bank, there was no sign that Rumsfeld was suffering from any personal torment over his singular contributions to the military failure in Iraq.

McNamara and Rumsfeld served presidents who wanted to stifle dissent within their administrations. As a result, it was easy for the secretaries of defense to marginalize those who disagreed with them in any way—particularly

General Eric Shinseki in the case of Rumsfeld and General Harold Johnson in the case of McNamara. Both secretaries tried to control the intelligence on the war to make sure that dissents did not reach the White House and the NSC. McNamara's Pentagon was paranoid about intelligence estimates of the North Vietnamese, particularly Viet Cong O/B, that were more threatening than the Pentagon estimates. Rumsfeld's Pentagon was paranoid about assessments from Iraq, such as those from the CIA station chief, who disagreed with the rosy picture presented by the White House and the Pentagon. Unlike Rumsfeld, who commissioned his own intelligence to supply the analysis that the CIA would not, McNamara eventually believed that the CIA had the right answers about Vietnam and he commissioned highly classified CIA think-pieces to support his positions. Finally, both McNamara and Rumsfeld were forced to resign because they no longer believed their wars could be won.

Both the Johnson and Bush administrations ultimately ignored the intelligence community in the decision making to go to war. Decisions for war are political decisions, and intelligence rarely plays any role in the decision making. The key decisions in 1964–1965 to systematically bomb North Vietnam had no support from the intelligence supplied by CIA, the State Department, and even some military intelligence officers. As early as January 1964, the CIA warned that Hanoi would hang tough and persevere in response to U.S. bombing, matching U.S. escalation with its own escalation. It also warned prophetically that strategic bombing of the North would make South Vietnam far too dependent on the power and presence of the United States. Nearly forty years later, Arabists at the CIA and State Department were skeptical of the policy to use force in Iraq to establish a democratic regime there.

In his memoir, *In Retrospect: The Tragedy and Lessons of Vietnam*, McNamara completely distorted the warnings of the Board of National Estimates in 1964 to the Johnson administration, as well as the work of an interagency intelligence panel given to a NSC working group that same year. McNamara was aware of the warnings of the intelligence community, but blanched when he saw these "heretical thoughts on paper, which might be leaked to the press."[8] Sadly, the intelligence community under George Tenet initially had doubts about achieving success in Iraq with U.S. use of force, but it was far too passive in getting its warnings about the war to key policymakers. Tenet and John McLaughlin, like McNamara and Helms, demonstrated loyalty to the president instead of fealty to the truth.

By 1966–1967, when McNamara realized that the war could not be won, the analyses of the CIA became far more interesting to the secretary of defense. The Agency's analytical record may have been a mixed one, but the *Pentagon Papers* reveal that the CIA was far more accurate and even prescient than any other intelligence organization, with the exception of the State Department's

Bureau of Intelligence and Research (INR). By 1967–1968, CIA warnings about the ineffectiveness of U.S. bombings in North Vietnam were getting more of a hearing and presumably played some role in the decision to forego increased deployments of forces in Vietnam and even the decision of President Johnson not to seek reelection. In a private memorandum to the president in May 1967, McNamara's doubts about the war in Vietnam essentially replicated the CIA arguments over the previous four years. McNamara's defection led President Johnson to force his resignation from the Pentagon and make him head of the World Bank. Like the good sycophant, however, McNamara continued to defend the war in public and still pulled his punches forty years later.

Unlike McNamara and even Johnson, Bush and Cheney have not lost their zeal to pursue the war in Iraq and have no intention to temper their views because of the grim intelligence picture, including the picture now drawn by top military intelligence officers. As late as September 2006, Cheney told an interviewer that, if he knew then what he now knows, he would pursue the decision to go to war. Bush stated, in 2007, that the only lesson to be learned from the Vietnam War was the futility of early withdrawal. The Vietnam-era counterpart of Cheney was Walt Rostow, first as director of the State Department's Policy Planning Staff and then as national security advisor, who was the truest of the true believers and, as late as 1991, asserted that the U.S. intervention "proved beneficial to our nation and the region." Cheney is the Iraq War's cheerleader, and he was instrumental in moving former CIA director Gates into the Pentagon in December 2006 as secretary of defense. It is particularly ironic that Gates, known for his politicization of intelligence in the 1980s, is now responsible for a war that was justified on the basis of politicized intelligence.

Whenever there are differences of this magnitude between the policy and intelligence bureaucracies, students of national security policy can be sure there are vicious battles going on between intelligence analysts within the key intelligence agencies. There were prolonged battles between the Pentagon and MACV and the CIA over order of battle, with the military refusing to count Vietcong civilian supporters in any estimate of the enemy's strength. This battle reached its apogee in 1968, when it was obvious that there would be no additional troops deployed to Vietnam, and it became essential to depict increased success against enemy forces and reduced numbers of Viet Cong. Military commanders made sure that military analysts involved in the preparation of NIEs did not veer from the political line of the commanders. Similarly, there were prolonged battles between the CIA's Counterterrorism Center (CTC) and the directorate of intelligence (DI) over the nature of the sectarian violence in Iraq and the influence of foreign insurgents. The CTC was dominated by clandestine operatives who were comfortable with worst-case analysis. The analysts of the DI were more likely to call it as they saw it.

The White House typically criticizes the intelligence assessments that do not support policy lines. The CIA in the 1960s had to stand up to significant criticism from key members of the Johnson administration regarding its intelligence assessments on Vietnam. The optimistic mindset of key Johnson civilian advisors, particularly that of presidential advisors Rostow and Mc-George Bundy, led to instant criticism of CIA estimates and assessments that did not support the rhyme and verse of the administration on the likely victory in Southeast Asia. Rostow was concerned that the Agency's intelligence would compromise the White House effort to manipulate opinion and to make perceptions "coincide with specific notions, whether those notions were supportable by evidence or not."[9] The pessimistic assessments from CIA and the State Department's INR, however, had no impact on the commitment of the Kennedy and Johnson administrations. In the final analysis, it took the shock of the Tet offensive in 1968, which shattered the confidence of the president himself, as well as the nerves of the nation's opinion leaders. Prior to Tet, General William Westmoreland, the commander of U.S. forces in Vietnam, ignored intelligence assessments and assured the American people that the tide had turned. After Tet, the credibility of the Johnson administration and the Pentagon was in tatters, and the nation's political unity was broken. The Iraq War has followed a similar track in the wake of increased sectarian violence throughout the country.

The CIA's field intelligence prior to Tet was good enough to provide strategic warning of an all-out effort from the enemy to challenge U.S. forces in 1968.[10] The CIA station in Saigon had a small assessment group headed by Bob Layton from the Agency's Office of National Estimates. In November and December 1967, Layton's group filed several reports in response to requests from Rostow, which drew heavily on prisoner interrogations and captured documents and warned that "enemy special action units had been directed to engage in widespread terrorism and sabotage in South Vietnam's major cities, coordinated with military attacks on the cities from without." Layton noted that Hanoi believed that the South Vietnamese government was "corrupt, unpopular, and incapable of gaining the allegiance of the bulk of South Vietnam's population . . . and were incapable of advancing or protecting the pacification program."[11] It is easier for CIA analysts to carry unpopular messages to the White House by quoting foreign sources, rather than by providing their own analytical judgments. In this case, the assessment group added that the North Vietnamese had abandoned the strategy of a patient war of mutual attrition and would resort to a policy of an all-out offensive. This warning fell on deaf ears within the policy community.

The constant criticism of the White House of CIA assessments led CIA director Helms to withhold certain finished intelligence from distribution at the

White House and the NSC, simply because he was growing weary from the onslaught of their criticism. Helms' self-censorship included key NIEs, as well as accurate assessments of the size and capabilities of the Viet Cong forces, which the Pentagon had consciously underestimated. Helms simply had no stomach for a battle between the CIA and MACV over how many troops the enemy had in the field. The same phenomenon was at work in the run-up to the Iraq War, with CIA director Tenet starting to pull his punches in October 2002 because of constant criticism from National Security Advisor Rice and Secretary of Defense Rumsfeld.

There was also politicization at work within CIA headquarters in the 1960s. Helms had a special assistant for Vietnam matters, George Carver, who was the Agency's point of contact with the White House. The risk of close contact with the policy community, let alone the White House, is that intelligence officers become too close to the policymaker and consciously or subconsciously take on the policy arguments of a particular administration.[12] This was certainly the case with Carver, who enjoyed a high level of visibility on the seventh floor of Agency headquarters and the corridors of the NSC. Carver passed Layton's assessments to the NSC, but added a cover note stating the field assessment "should not be read as the considered opinion of this Agency" and that the assessment was "predicated on certain assumptions whose validity seems questionable from our perspective here in Washington."[13] Carver also had the support of some of the Vietnamese analysts in the DI, who did not believe that the war was going well for Hanoi. Therefore, Carver assured Rostow that North Vietnam would continue their strategy of a limited war of attrition, which contributed to the tremendous shock of the Tet offensive.

Nevertheless, members of the Johnson administration conceded in their memoirs that CIA analysis was often spot-on. Johnson himself cited Layton's work in his memoirs that were published in 1971, when he noted he "agreed heartily with one prophetic report from our Embassy in Saigon," which predicted a turning point in the war, and his concern that the communists were "going to try for a significant tactical victory."[14] Rostow also cited Layton's assessment in his own writings, noting the warning of the Tet offensive and the fact that Johnson "had been receiving regularly and following closely the piecemeal evidence on which this summation was based."[15] Several days after the North Vietnamese attacked thirty-nine of South Vietnam's forty-four provincial capitals, virtually every allied airfield, and even Saigon itself, humorist Art Buchwald had the last word, a parody of Rostow's belief that systematic U.S. bombing would "convince the North Vietnamese that it was in their economic self-interest to desist from aggression in South Vietnam." Buchwald continued:

Gen. George Custer said today in an exclusive interview with this correspondent that the Battle of Little Big Horn had just turned the corner and he could now see the light at the end of the tunnel . . . "We have the Sioux on the run . . . of course, we will have some cleaning up to do, but the Redskins are hurting badly and it will only be a matter of time before they give in."[16]

In addition to the work of Bob Layton, who provided strategic warning of a Tet-type offensive in the winter of 1967–1968, another CIA analyst—Sam Adams—did excellent research on the actual numbers of Viet Cong in South Vietnam, making it evident that military intelligence assessments of the numbers of Viet Cong were terribly underestimated and thoroughly politicized. Ironically, the CIA had conducted no centralized or systematic analysis of the Vietnamese O/B until 1967, when Secretary of Defense McNamara asked the Agency to provide periodic, independent assessments of the numbers of Viet Cong and North Vietnamese forces. McNamara did so because he was becoming scornful of the military reporting from Vietnam. McNamara began scribbling "I don't believe it" or "This is a lot of crap" on military assessments, according to Hans Heymann, one of the compilers of *The Pentagon Papers*.[17] Layton was the major supporter of Adams research on the Viet Cong O/B; thus, when Layton was reassigned to Saigon in July 1967, Adams lost his patron and no one stepped into the breach.

Adams was the model of an intelligence analyst as junkyard dog. A Harvard graduate and a gentleman farmer, he fully documented the political efforts of the White House, the U.S. embassy in Saigon, and the military command to deflate the size of the Vietnamese enemy by almost 50 percent to deceive the American people, the Congress, and the press.[18] He was a thorough and indefatigable researcher on the problem of O/B, and even his opponents agreed that he was brilliant and energetic. Adams was so thorough that he began to pick up high-powered supporters of his estimates, including George Allen, arguably the most respected Vietnamese analyst at the CIA and even Carver, the director's senior adviser on Vietnamese affairs, who eventually believed that the military should double its estimates of enemy forces simply on the basis of Adams' research. Adams' numbers also had an impact on certain military intelligence officers who were becoming increasingly skeptical of General Westmoreland's reluctance to reexamine the problem and increasingly critical of Westmoreland's low numbers.

As a result of Adams' importuning, Helms demanded a special estimate on the enemy's order of battle to establish an agreed number for the entire intelligence community. This was a particularly important turning point in the intelligence community's relations with the military because never before had a civilian intelligence agency challenged an army in the field on order of battle numbers. Helms even sent an Agency team of analysts to Saigon to try to achieve a consensus on the numbers issue when it became clear that ONE would never be able to break the stalemate between the civilian and military intelligence communities. Adams' ability to get the Agency leadership to jump through his analytical loops was unprecedented in the history of the DI.

Most CIA analysts in the DI and ONE were scornful of military intelligence in Vietnam, and there was a consensus at the Agency that the military estimates were "misleadingly low." The DI believed there were three times as many irregular forces in South Vietnam as the military counted, and two times as many overall enemy forces in South Vietnam. Senior officials at the Department of State and the Department of Defense, as well as the NSC, were well aware of these estimative differences. Unfortunately, the Agency's ONE stubbornly refused to accept Adams' higher numbers, although it agreed that military estimates were much too low.

Unfortunately, the CIA intelligence team ran up against a hard-line military intelligence team, headed by Colonel Daniel Graham, who was part of the Team A/Team B exercise a decade later to drive CIA analysis on the Soviet Union far to the right. Carver believed that the CIA group "poked gaping holes in the evidentiary basis" for the military estimates, but that MACV was "stonewalling, obviously under orders."[19] The NSC's Robert Komer and General Westmoreland had agreed that, regardless of CIA's evidence, the military would not agree to an estimate of enemy troop strength larger than 300,000. Carver cabled Helms on September 12 that the chief of military intelligence, Major General Phillip Davidson, was extremely tendentious, accusing Carver of "impugning his integrity." The MACV numbers were a "final offer," Davidson said, "not subject to discussion. We should take it or leave it."[20] The NSC and the military had an intelligence agenda and the generals held the line.

Adams had his own political agenda, believing that the correct number of Viet Cong would lead to greater U.S. troop deployments that he favored. It is unfortunate when an intelligence analyst has a policy agenda, which taints the credibility and integrity of his work. In any event, Adams wore out his welcome with CIA senior officials who were aware of Adams' policy agenda and his extreme form of policy advocacy. Adams went to great lengths to make his case, and even removed sensitive documents from the CIA that he hid on his farm in Virginia. He aired his charges in *Harper's Magazine* in 1975 and became a key source for the controversial CBS documentary that blamed General Westmoreland for the politicization of the numbers of Viet Cong. Westmoreland sued both CBS and Adams for libel, which led to the declassification of thousands of documents that substantiated Adams' claims. Westmoreland dropped his suit just before trial in exchange for a narrow CBS affirmation of his patriotism. Meanwhile, Adams incorporated the new evidence into his memoir, *War of Numbers*, which describes the politicization of intelligence at the CIA and the unwillingness of the CIA leaders to challenge the political demands of the White House and the Pentagon. Westmoreland's case was presented in *Secret of the Vietnam War*, which was written by his former intelligence chief, Philip Davidson.

The 90-minute CBS documentary, "The Uncounted Enemy: A Vietnam Deception," was produced by George Crile, with Mike Wallace as interlocutor. Their chief consultant was Adams, fourth cousin seven times removed of the second president of the United States. Adams' arguments never got a fair hearing in the print media because the journalist community accepted the arguments of the former aides to President Johnson and Adams' former bosses at the CIA, who were part of the conspiracy to keep the numbers of Viet Cong as low as possible and avoid a debate over more troops for Vietnam, on the one hand or withdrawal on the other. When Stanley Karnow dismissed the CBS show as "lousy," the journalistic community simply echoed "lousy." The print media's handling of the story of Iraqi WMD was no different, with the press helping to make the administration's case against Ambassador Joseph Wilson, who refuted assertions of Iraqi efforts to obtain uranium from Niger. My own experiences as a CIA whistle-blower suggest that contrarian views in Washington, particularly in the national security area, are easily marginalized and it is the rare journalist willing to pursue the arguments of the contrarian or to challenge the conventional wisdom. A senior *New York Times* writer, Elaine Sciolino, told me years ago that contrarians make good sources only in the short run, but journalists must rely on policymakers for long-term access and do not try to offend. This is the best explanation that I have ever received for the conventional analysis of the press corps and its reluctance to challenge high-level sources.

The Adams' memoir, which was published posthumously, is a seminal source on the bureaucratic infighting over O/B, as well as on the role of an analyst in the intelligence community.[21] It tells a tale of the deliberate undercounting by military analysts prodded by commanders who wanted to make the war effort look good, as well as prevent any debate over the need for additional troops that President Johnson would not favor. The deceptive count of the enemy was part of the strategy for leading the U.S. public down the primrose path and for the deaths of thousands of U.S. soldiers. His work begs comparison with the use of intelligence to justify the war in Iraq and the deception that is summed up by George Tenet's response to the president's request for intelligence to take to the American people to make the case for war: "Don't worry, it's a slam dunk."

In any event, the game was over when Helms decided to throw in the towel and stop bickering with the military. When he became CIA director in 1966, he was willing to send a Vietnam assessment to the president, the secretary of state, and the secretary of defense concluding, "Nothing happening to the Vietnamese Communists as of mid-1966 is bad enough to make them stop fighting."[22] But after watching the loss of influence of Secretary of Defense McNamara, United States Information Agency (USIA) director Leonard Marks (Johnson's personal lawyer for twenty-five years), and Senator George Aiken (R-Vermont) for expressing their doubts about success in Vietnam, Helms began to pull his punches for political reasons. He made no attempt to challenge Ambassador Bunker and General Westmoreland, who told the press the Viet Cong were in a bad way. Politicized NIEs went through the United States Intelligence Board, and soon articles appeared in the *Washington Daily News* and *The New York Times* proclaiming "The Enemy is Running Out of Men" and "Westmoreland is Sure of Victory."

The Vietnam Lesson

The junior analysts who arrived at the CIA in the 1960s and early 1970s were profoundly affected by the analytical warfare over Vietnam and came to various conclusions regarding the lessons of the war itself and the lessons for intelligence analysis. One school believed that the U.S. adventure in Vietnam was a human tragedy and a foreign policy disaster, and that the intelligence community should have done a better job of understanding the nationalist and anti-colonialist roots of the Vietnamese confrontation. This group realized that the Soviet Union and China had nothing to do with the struggle between North and South Vietnam, and that the war actually exposed the roots of the Sino–Soviet split, as Moscow and Beijing fought over gaining influence in Hanoi and making timely weapons deliveries to the North Vietnamese forces. Their heroes in the intelligence and operations community were Layton and Adams who took on the conventional wisdom within the intelligence community and challenged the efforts of the White House and the Pentagon to politicize much of the intelligence on Vietnam.

Opposing this group was a school of thought that highlighted the communist roots of the North Vietnamese leadership and believed that the so-called expansionist policies of the Soviet Union provided impetus to the Vietnamese revolution. This school believed that the United States was compelled to support South Vietnam because of Soviet support to the North.[23] Their heroes were Carver, who had regular access to CIA director Helms and to key policymakers at the NSC and the Pentagon, and one of their major acolytes was Bob Gates, who joined the CIA in 1966 and became the director of central intelligence in 1991. Gates and his major patron, William Casey, believed that the humiliating U.S. withdrawal gave the Soviet Union an unprecedented opportunity to exploit American weakness. They blamed the Soviet Union for every problem that the United States confronted in the Third World and, whenever possible, politicized intelligence to demonstrate that Moscow was the major force behind all acts of international terrorism around the world, including the assassination attempt against the Pope in 1981. This group totally overestimated the military and economic power of the Soviet Union and missed the central intelligence questions of the 1980s: Who was Mikhail Gorbachev and what difference would his policies have for Soviet–American relations?

The division in the analytic ranks in the wake of the Vietnam War contributed to virtually every analytical dispute from the early 1970s to the collapse of the Soviet Union in 1991. A year after the U.S. withdrawal from Vietnam, a civil war broke out in Angola, and there were policy and intelligence debates over the role of the Soviet Union and the case for American intervention. The new Ford administration feared that the Soviets were exploiting American weakness and endorsed covert arms shipments to anti-government forces in Angola. Henry Kissinger wanted to make a stand in Angola to demonstrate that the United States and the new administration, despite the retreat from Vietnam, was still capable of a military response in the spring of 1975. All of them missed the fact that Cuba and not the Soviet Union was taking the lead in Angola, which the intelligence record clearly stated. There is similar concern in Washington today that the Bush administration, in order to cover its setbacks and failures in Iraq, will strike out in another direction, such as Iran.

It would be easy to dismiss the debate over the numbers of Viet Cong as a mere food fight between the intelligence and policy communities. The sad reality was that the intelligence community, particularly the CIA and State Department's INR, warned in the 1960s and 1970s that the heavy and relentless bombing of North Vietnam and the supply trails through Laos and Cambodia would not break the will of Hanoi and would not lead to victory. To the credit of the CIA, agency analysts certainly did not tell policymakers what they wanted to hear, never said that there was light at the end of the tunnel, and never indicated that the strategy was working. Some have argued that neither the strategy of the Johnson White House nor the tactics of the Pentagon were based on estimates of overall enemy numbers. Nevertheless, the larger policy debates over the numbers of U.S. forces needed in Vietnam were based on enemy order of battle, and a better understanding of the enemy force would have forced a decision on whether to increase forces in Vietnam or to withdraw. The Johnson administration was not willing to accept either decision; therefore, it was important to policymakers to hide the real numbers in this case and thus avoid the debate and the ensuing criticism. The journalistic community was initially lined up behind the administration on the war and totally ignored what appeared to be a feckless debate over statistics concerning O/B. Secretary of Defense McNamara said the dispute was "much ado about nothing," and the press corps echoed ". . . about nothing." When President Bush was making his case for going to war against Iraq, the press, including *The New York Times* and the *Washington Post*, became a front-page echo chamber for the specious arguments of Cheney and Rumsfeld for going to war.

CIA analysis on Vietnam, which often countered the official position of both the White House and the Pentagon, led President Nixon to comment that he was "thoroughly disgusted with [the CIA's] performance on North Vietnam" and noted that "the problem is the CIA is a muscle-bound bureaucracy, which has completely paralyzed its brain."[24] Nixon wanted to know how many people could be immediately fired at the CIA simply by presidential action, and demanded that the CIA be prevented from "recruiting from any of the Ivy League schools or any other universities where either the university president or the university faculties have taken action condemning our efforts to bring the war in Vietnam to an end."[25] According to chief of staff H. R. Haldeman, Nixon said "Helms has got to go. Get rid of the clowns—cut personnel 40 percent. Its info is worthless."[26] The president learned that he could not fire CIA personnel, but he could fire Helms and replace him with Schlesinger, who upon arrival assembled the senior members of the DI on the Soviet Union to tell them that "this agency is going to stop screwing President Nixon." Helms had lied to Congressional committees on at least two occasions to protect the administration, but that wasn't good enough for Nixon.

The Nixon example was an extreme case of the kind of pressure that was placed on the intelligence community, particularly the CIA, to provide the intelligence support for policy. Often, when analysts try to stand up to this pressure, they are abandoned by their senior managers. I was not permitted to defend my intelligence assessment on Soviet involvement regarding terrorism in the early 1980s, because CIA managers were hesitant to take on the senior Soviet analyst at the NSC in the Reagan administration, the hard-line professor from Harvard University, Richard Pipes. Analysts and operational officers who opposed the use of flawed intelligence in making the case to go to war against Iraq in 2003 were ignored by their managers. In the run-up to the war in Iraq in 2002–2003, the administration demonstrated its power to get the intelligence community to back the phony arguments about Iraqi WMD and Saddam Hussein's links to al Qaeda. The pressure prior to the Iraq War was no greater than the pressure during the Vietnam War but, unlike Vietnam, CIA managers and analysts bowed to the pressure, providing a phony NIE and unclassified White Paper in October 2002 and a polemical speech for Secretary of State Powell in February 2003.

The Pentagon Papers reveal that the CIA had the best analytical record of any intelligence agency during the Vietnam War, from the mid-1950s to the mid-1970s. The Agency regularly informed the Johnson and Nixon administrations that military force alone would not win the war on the ground, that our South Vietnamese creation, the Government of the Republic of Vietnam (GVN), was not adequate to the political-military mission, that the covert presence of the Viet Cong and the North Vietnamese army in South Vietnam was terribly underestimated, that we should not underestimate the enemy's staying power, that U.S. strategic bombing would not alter the outcome of the war, and that the North Vietnamese would never be persuaded to negotiate with the United States.[27] The CIA was particularly trenchant in providing arguments against the introduction of more troops in 1963–1965, noting that the struggle was a political one that had to be won in the South by the South Vietnamese army. CIA analysis didn't change the course of the war, but it appeared to convince such latent doves as Undersecretary of State George Ball, presidential advisor Clark Clifford, Vice President Hubert Humphrey, and ultimately Secretary of Defense McNamara that U.S. policy in Vietnam was failing. In 1967–1968, Sam Adams convinced his counterparts that enemy strength in South Vietnam had been terribly undercounted, but political pressure from the White House and the Pentagon convinced Helms and the Board of National Estimates to shelve his analysis.

The Sino–Soviet Split and the CIA's Strategic Warning

Rare is the occasion when the intelligence analysis of the CIA is spot-on and the policy community is willing to heed the strategic message and pursue a policy that exploits a geopolitical vulnerability. This was the case in the CIA's exceptional analysis of the Sino–Soviet dispute in the 1960s and the Nixon administration's adoption of triangular diplomacy to exploit the burgeoning rift between the Soviet Union and China. The stars of the intelligence world were Sherman Kent, the chairman of the Board of National Estimates and Harry Gelman and Arthur Cohen of the CIA's Special Research Staff; the stars of the policy world were President Nixon and national security advisor Kissinger. In 1961, Kent prepared an analytic memorandum for a new CIA director, John McCone, that set out the key aspects of the Sino–Soviet dispute, long before anyone in the policy or academic communities supported the notion of their contentious relationship. The conventional wisdom in the 1960s was that the alliance between the Soviet Union and China was the major threat facing the United States.

Several CIA analysts knew better. Gelman, a Soviet specialist trained at Colombia University, and Cohen, a China specialist trained at the University of Chicago, wrote a series of historical studies that documented and analyzed the split between Moscow and Beijing over a series of political and military issues, particularly the unwillingness of the Soviet leadership to provide nuclear technology to Mao Tse-tung. The Soviet reason was based on simple self-interest in not allowing an unpredictable rival on its border to acquire nuclear weapons; the Chinese anger was based on their awareness that the Soviet politburo wanted to maintain China in an inferior military state. Relying on their deep understanding of Soviet and Chinese history and culture, Gelman and Cohen crafted a series of historical studies that became teaching vehicles for new analysts in the Agency's directorate of intelligence but, more importantly, guideposts for a strategic breakthrough in the foreign policy of a new administration. Actually, as early as 1954, Khrushchev warned his colleagues that "conflict between us and China is inevitable."[28]

The CIA has often been criticized for producing work that is too systematic, codified, and bureaucratic, and the Agency has produced for too many NIEs and assessments that meet such descriptions. But the work of Cohen and Gelman, which was based on all-source intelligence and code-named *Esau,* was powerful analytical work that not only connected the dots, but brought an entirely new approach to Sino–Soviet relations that many considered too optimistic and simplistic.[29] The intelligence community was too inured to the notion of a Sino–Soviet monopoly over international communism, thereby making it difficult to make room for the notion of a Sino-Soviet split, let alone the thought of a rift that the United States could exploit.

The work of Cohen and Gilman was even discredited within their own agency, particularly within the Board of National Estimates that believed there were still strong political and military ties between the two communist powers. In 1960, an NIE acknowledged there had been a "sharp increase in discord" in the Sino–Soviet relationship and that it was "not a monolith," but concluded the cohesive forces "will remain stronger than divisive forces at least through the period of this estimate [five years]."[30] The Board produced NIEs as late as November 12, 1970 that concluded there was little prospect of improvement in Sino–American relations. The policy community was also dismissive of the work of SRS, and somewhat nonplussed regarding the implications for the United States. In the early 1960s, several CIA officials briefed Ambassadors Llewellyn Thompson and Chip Bohlen on the growing nature of Sino–Soviet discord, but their response was that they were "not convinced."[31] The products of SRS were available to President Kennedy on the first day of his presidency in 1961, but there is no indication that he was prepared to act on their analysis. Nixon and Kissinger were unusual in their willingness to pursue the consequences of a Sino–Soviet rift, ignoring the conventional wisdom within their own administration.

A lesson that has not been learned at the CIA from the earlier period is that intelligence analysis thrives when the agency permits competing assessments on the same topic, encourages independent analysts who actually sign their own work, and forswears collective or group products that attract the seal of the agency but lack any analytical cachet. From the 1950s to the 1970s, the CIA had separate offices that produced current intelligence, estimative intelligence, and historical studies. These offices had their own experts and their own separate methodologies, and they were in competition with each other. Currently, the CIA pays little attention to strategic intelligence, does very little historical analysis or retrospectives, and does not have an intelligence elite that is assigned the separate task of writing NIEs. The top-heavy demands of current intelligence have driven out the demands for broad-based think-pieces and strategic analysis, and this is a real loss to the worlds of both intelligence and policy.

In the case of the Sino–Soviet dispute, CIA analysts were far out in front of their counterparts at the Department of State, Department of Defense, and even the academic community. Eventually some analysts at the DoS began to take the possibility of discord seriously and, by the late 1960s, such academic writers as William Griffith of the Massachusetts Institute of Technology and such British writers as Edward Crankshaw and Roderick MacFarquhar did so as well. When fighting broke out on the Sino–Soviet border in 1969, which was described in OCI's intelligence, the skeptics in the government and academe put aside their resistance to the heretical notions of a Sino–Soviet split.

In his memoirs, Kissinger makes no mention of the analysis of the CIA, unless it involves such failures of intelligence as the absence of warning for the October War of 1973. There is no mention of the successes of intelligence analysis during the Kissinger years at the NSC and the State Department, such as warning of the Egyptian ouster of Soviet advisors and technicians in 1972, the Syrian invasion of Jordan in 1970s, the limits of the Soviet friendship treaties with Egypt in 1971 and India in 1970, let alone the Sino–Soviet rift that provided the opening for triangular diplomacy in the first term of President Nixon. This is not unusual for secretaries of state and national security advisors, particular for Kissinger, who rarely acknowledged the acumen of others in geopolitical matters, let alone the intelligence analysts at the CIA.

The CIA had informed both the Johnson and Nixon administrations that the Vietnam War had exposed the basic differences between China and the Soviet Union on numerous security issues, not just the competition over supplying military assistance to the North Vietnamese. The CIA provided intelligence analysis to the Johnson administration detailing the difficult conditions that existed between Soviet and Chinese forces at transshipment points for Soviet assistance, but Johnson's national security advisor, Rostow, did not believe the intelligence he received. Kissinger not only believed that CIA accounts of Sino–Soviet differences, including the fighting that took place on the border in 1969, but genuinely believed that there was a chance in the near future of a Sino–Soviet war. Kissinger wanted to position the United States diplomatically before such a conflict and, just as important, wanted to exploit the Sino–Soviet rift to reopen diplomatic relations with China that were broken with the victory of the Chinese Communists in 1949.

As Nixon expected, the Soviets were frightened by the prospect of stable Sino–American relations, which would give the Chinese a free hand to concentrate their military presence on the Sino–Soviet border and ultimately make China a more formidable diplomatic, if not military, foe. At the SALT talks in Vienna in the spring of 1971, where I was the intelligence advisor to the U.S. SALT delegation, the Soviets made an unusual diplomatic foray that revealed their anxiety about the U.S. initiative. The Austrian government provided seats to the U.S. and Soviet delegations for the Vienna Opera and, during a performance of *Lucia de Lamamoor* in April 1971, only weeks after the unofficial visit of a U.S. ping-pong team to Beijing and three months before Kissinger's secret visit there, Soviet ambassador Semenov delivered a sensitive note to his counterpart, U.S. ambassador Gerald Smith.

The Soviet note to Smith, which was immediately transmitted to Kissinger over the secure CIA communications system, proposed that Washington and Moscow open talks toward the signing of a treaty of friendship and cooperation in the event of a nuclear attack against either side from a third nation. The third nation was not identified, but the Soviets were aiming their initiative at China, hoping to create the impression that Washington and Moscow had a special relationship that Beijing's diplomacy could not alter, let alone weaken. The Soviets keenly appreciated the fact that the United States and China shared a strategic concern with the power and influence of the Soviet Union, and would eventually take steps to move diplomatically against the Soviet threat. Ironically, Kissinger had advised Nelson Rockefeller in 1968, when the New York governor was running for president, to take a stand in favor of opening a dialogue with China. In the previous year, Nixon published an article in *Foreign Affairs* that pointed to his interest in improved relations with Beijing.

CIA Monitoring of Soviet Strategic Weaponry

One of the CIA's greatest successes was in the field of developing sophisticated collection technology, both spy planes and spy satellites. In the 1950s, over the protests of the Pentagon, President Dwight Eisenhower gave the CIA the managing responsibility for these projects, knowing that the military bureaucracy was far too cumbersome to take on such a difficult project within a short time frame. These projects, particularly the U-2 reconnaissance plane and the Corona spy satellite, were crucial to understanding the nature of the strategic threat and ultimately to the negotiation and ratification of a series of arms control agreements. The conservative nature of the Senate would not have permitted ratification of these agreements without the certainty from the intelligence community that these agreements could be verified. In the words of President Ronald Reagan, the name of the game was "trust, but verify."

The 1950s were an unusually unbridled environment to work in, and the CIA project manager—Richard Bissell, who would become infamous for his direction of the failed Bay of Pigs invasion—took advantage of the lack of Congressional oversight and administration controls to bring in the U-2 below budget and ahead of schedule.[32] The U-2 introduced new technology in every aspect of the project: the plane, the camera, and the film, with major roles played by Lockheed and the Polaroid Corporation. For the first time, the CIA played a major role in the development of sophisticated technology for the collection of sensitive intelligence. The U-2 gave the United States its first genuine picture of the limitations and vulnerabilities of the Soviet arsenal, particularly its air and naval bases and its bombers. The Corona satellite provided sensitive information on Soviet strategic capabilities and systems, and ultimately provided the verification and monitoring capabilities for arms control agreements, particularly SALT I and the ABM Treaty. These agreements were ratified in 1972, which coincided with the last Corona mission after 145 launches, an examination of 520 square miles of Soviet territory, images of all twenty-five ICBM complexes in the Soviet Union, and at a cost of only $850 million.[33] As Philip Taubman concluded in his masterful study of U.S. technical collection, *Secret Empire: Eisenhower, the CIA, and the Hidden Story of America's Space Espionage*, the spy satellites "played a critical role in preserving the peace, limiting defense spending, and reducing the threat of nuclear war."

Sophisticated technical collection systems, such as the U-2 and the Corona satellite, enabled a certain amount of success in anticipating the development of virtually every Soviet strategic and conventional weapons system and in calibrating the nature of the Soviet military threat. Intelligence does not do a good job of predicting political and military events, which is not surprising in view of the limitations of the social sciences, but it can and has done a good job of explaining important developments, such as the nature and configuration of the Soviet military. Forecasting political choices and predicting changes in the international system have proved to be more difficult than projecting military forces. Without sophisticated intelligence collection and analysis, however, there would have been a tendency for the Pentagon and the conservative members of both the Republican and Democratic parties to exaggerate the size and lethality of the Soviet force and to push U.S. military spending to higher levels.

It takes nearly a decade to develop and test modern weapons systems, and on many occasions, the intelligence community's sophisticated collection systems picked up new weapons in the testing and even design phase. Many of the exaggerations were due to the fact that the prototype systems picked up in early stages of technology development encountered problems in the development and production stage. The CIA also missed the serious economic and political problems in the 1980s that had a negative impact on Soviet weapons procurement.

Technical intelligence was used to address key U.S. policy questions regarding the capabilities of Soviet strategic weapons systems and how they could be used against U. S. interests. Since the Soviet Union, Eastern Europe, and China were denied areas to the United States, there was a need to develop sophisticated systems that would provide hard data on Soviet and Chinese intentions and capabilities. Traditional espionage methods were inadequate in monitoring the Soviet Bloc and China, and U.S. satellite imaging and signals intelligence collection systems became essential. New collections methods had to be accompanied by sophisticated analytical methodologies for eliciting useful information from the collection, and the CIA's Office of Scientific Intelligence, later the Directorate of Science and Technology, led the way in both collection and analysis.

The CIA also successfully monitored the technical difficulties that the Soviets experienced in the antiballistic missile program, particularly detecting, identifying, and intercepting ballistic missiles. This analysis was ignored, however, by the director and deputy director of the CIA, Bill Casey and Bob Gates, who ignored these problems in their speeches designed to justify greater U.S. spending on President Reagan's "Star Wars" program. In 1981, Casey hired a right-wing polemicist, Constantine Menges, who peddled the idea of Star Wars long before the Reagan administration adopted the scheme, when it was still known as the Strategic Defense Initiative (SDI). (Casey also made Menges the National Intelligence Officer for Latin America so that the CIA director had access to a senior intelligence officer who appeared to genuinely believe that, if the Marxists succeeded in Nicaragua, Mexico would be next.) Following President Reagan's announcement of the SDI to the National Association of Evangelicals, a minister's organization, in Orlando, Florida in March 1983, Gates made a series of speeches promoting Star Wars and politicizing CIA intelligence on Soviet strategic defense. His policy advocacy on strategic defense, a violation of the CIA's charter, was replicated in the run-up to the Iraq War, when his acolytes, including CIA deputy director McLaughlin, helped the Bush administration make the case for war.

The key to achieving the first strategic arms agreement with the Soviets in 1972 was dealing with the problems of Soviet capabilities in the area of anti-ballistic missile weapons (ABMs) and multiple independently targeted re-entry vehicles (MIRVs). The opponents of the SALT agreement argued that the Soviet surface-to-air system already constituted an ABM system and that the Soviet SS-9 had a MIRV capability that made a SALT treaty a risky proposition. Kissinger and Laird shared these two incorrect assumptions and challenged the analysts of the State Department and the Arms Control and Disarmament Agency (ACDA), who argued that the surface-to-air missile (SAM) system could not be upgraded to an ABM system and that the SS-9 was not MIRV capable. CIA analysts faced a great deal of pressure from Kissinger who wanted CIA to argue the Soviet Union already had a MIRV capability. Helms defended his analysts, and CIA documents bravely and correctly argued that the SAM system could not be upgraded to an ABM and that the SS-9 had not been MIRVed. On several occasions, when Helms ran into intense resistance from military representatives on the United States Intelligence Board that coordinated final drafts of NIEs, he would send these documents back for revision but supported the Agency's decision not to alter the substantive outcome of the estimate.

The CIA was particularly successful in analyzing and predicting some of the key aspects of Soviet strategic forces, particularly the acquisition of MIRV technology in the 1970s, when Soviet strategic forces expanded rapidly. The intelligence community predicted well in advance the MIRVing of the Soviet force, thanks to sophisticated intelligence facilities in Iran, and included in its projections estimates of the total number of weapons deployed on delivery vehicles.[35] Military intelligence grossly exaggerated the numbers of MIRVed forces. But the high and low CIA projections in the 1970s successfully bracketed the actual number of nuclear weapons in the Soviet force, with correct estimates of the numbers of MIRVs on ICBMs and the rate at which these missiles would be deployed. Nevertheless, the CIA overestimated the projected number of warheads deployed on submarine-launched ballistic missiles and underestimated the rate of MIRVing of the new force. Overall, the CIA significantly overestimated the rate of strategic force modernization, with an NIE in 1985 projecting that virtually the entire ICBM force would be replaced within ten years. Less than 10 percent of the force had been replaced by 1989, more than one third of the projection period. In the overestimates of force modernization, the CIA also exaggerated the rate of deployment and the date of initial operational capability of each weapons system. It is noteworthy that some of the CIA errors were due to an unwillingness to accept that the Soviets would actually slow some weapons programs in order to confirm to arms control limits.

The SS-9 issue was particularly important because if the Soviet ICBM was a MIRVed weapon with three warheads and these warheads could be fired independently at separate and distinct targets, then the Pentagon could argue persuasively that the USSR had a first-strike capability. Kissinger and Laird argued that the fourth version of the SS-9 was a MIRVed weapon, but the CIA did not agree. The CIA correctly termed the SS-9 a MRV weapon with maneuverable warheads that could place a cluster of explosions in a single area, and not a MIRV that could reach multiple targets. The CIA's analytic community, led by Sayre Stevens, who became the chief of the DI for his efforts, stuck to its guns, eventually persuading Kissinger of its argument, which was instrumental in negotiating the SALT Treaty two years later.

I was a member of the CIA's SALT support staff during this period and there were several meetings with Director Helms who sagely argued that the CIA could not verify Soviet adherence to a strategic weapons agreement because verification was a political judgment that only policymakers could make. The mission of the CIA, he argued, was to monitor Soviet strategic capabilities so that policymakers could make their own decisions about particular positions on arms control issues. Fortunately, Helms had the assistance of a brilliant deputy director for science and technology, Carl Duckett, who had no fears about telling truth to power. Kissinger was actually somewhat sympathetic with the position of the CIA on some of these sensitive issues, but he was hesitant to push the Pentagon too far and too fast on serious arms control issues. He believed that he could not get the Pentagon to accept both treaties on offensive and defense weapons that could lead to reduced defense spending. The huge power of the Pentagon and the military-industrial community on strategic weapons issues makes it essential to have an independent intelligence capability outside the policy community that can challenge positions taken by the DoD. The DoD can use its significant influence to determine the positions of the Defense Intelligence Agency and the military services on sensitive intelligence issues dealing with arms control and disarmament. With general officers running the office of the DNI, the CIA, the office of the undersecretary of defense for intelligence, and the National Counterterrorism Center, it will be difficult for civilian leaders of the government to obtain intelligence that has not been vetted by the senior military leadership of the Pentagon.

When the DoD and the Joint Chiefs of Staff lost the battle on ABMs and MIRVs, which eventually led to the SALT and ABM agreements of 1972, senior military officials began to press for an on-site inspection to verify any agreement, knowing that the Soviets in the 1970s were not about to allow such intrusive inspection. (Actually, if the Soviets had called our bluff, they would have learned that the Pentagon was similarly unwilling to accept an on-site inspection.) In any event, the CIA and ACDA maintained correctly that national technical means of verification, or satellite photography, would be sufficient to verify a ban on MIRV testing, as well as ABMs. Again, CIA briefers on the Hill showed a good deal of courage in lobbying for satellite inspection of the SALT and ABM agreements and, on several occasions, Kissinger personally called Helms to vent his anger at the testimony of CIA analysts before congressional committees. (Former CIA directors Casey, Gates, and Goss spent a great deal of effort to make sure that Agency briefings did not counter or compromise administration positions on sensitive issues. Gates issued constant warnings to his analysts to avoid "sticking your fingers into the eyes of policymakers.")

There are many similarities to the intelligence-policy nexus in the intelligence justification for a stronger U.S. military in the 1980s and the run-up to the Iraq War in 2003. In the run-up to war, the Bush administration took advantage of politicized intelligence, although the president was going to go to war regardless of the intelligence picture offered by the intelligence community. Similarly, the Reagan administration was going to increase the defense budget in the 1980s regardless of the intelligence presented to the White House. Even if the CIA had correctly and honestly presented the White House with a picture of constraints on the Soviet defense budget and Moscow's interest in arms control and détente, Reagan was committed to changing the nature of Soviet–American relations. He had no interest in arms control and wanted huge increases in the defense budget, the creation of a 600-ship navy, and a SDI that has resulted in an additional $100 billion in defense spending over the past twenty-five years without getting the United States any closer to a strategic defense against ballistic missiles.

The sad fact is that bad intelligence will hurt the possibility for good national security policy, but that good intelligence is no guarantee that there will be sound national security policy. If the Kennedy and Johnson administrations had been reading the CIA's estimates and assumptions on Vietnam in the 1960s, there would have good solid reasons for not resorting to force in Southeast Asia. But Kennedy was convinced of the need to check what he believed to be the actions of a Soviet proxy, and Johnson, who was never committed to the use of force in Vietnam, was insufficiently confident to push his intuition against the policy arguments of the key players of the Kennedy administration, particularly the Rostow brothers (Walt and Eugene) and the Bundy brothers (McGeorge and Bill), as well as Secretary of State Rusk and Secretary of Defense McNamara. If the Reagan administration had been reading CIA intelligence on the Middle East, presumably he would have thought twice about sending U.S. Marines into Beirut in 1983 to pull Israeli chestnuts out of a fire in Lebanon that is still raging to this day. And if the Bush administration had been reading some of the initial intelligence assessments of the CIA, then perhaps Vice President Cheney and Secretary of Defense Rumsfeld would not have talked about a cakewalk in Iraq, a U.S. presence as a liberation force, and an American withdrawal within eighteen months. Sadly, the policy process will always overrule or ignore the intelligence process, no matter how prescient and credible that intelligence is.

Intelligence analysts have good reason to be proud of much of the intelligence work on Vietnam that was part of the *Pentagon Papers*, but CIA analysts during the run-up to the Iraqi war should feel only embarrassment. CIA analysts in the 1960s and 1970s understood the strengths and weaknesses of North Vietnam, but their counterparts in the 1990s and the early 2000s totally misread the crippled and demoralized dictatorship of Saddam Hussein, the picture of WMD, and the so-called links between Saddam Hussein and al Qaeda. It is almost unbelievable that CIA missed every call that needed to be made about Saddam Hussein's Iraq. Indeed, there has probably never been a time in the history of the CIA, when its analysts were so comprehensively and significantly wrong about virtually every aspect of a key issue as was the case with Saddam Hussein's Iraq. The only exception to this disturbing record is the apparent CIA pattern of warning that U.S. troops would face significant resistance from Iraqi irregular forces employing guerrilla tactics. Policymakers were told that the irregulars would fight more fanatically than regular army forces. The fact that Tenet's CIA totally surrendered any sense of objectivity and integrity in the run-up to the Iraq War has been met with no concern from the Senate and House intelligence oversight committees adds to the intelligence disaster for American national interests.

4

Intelligence: The Consequences of Failure

Anyone concerned with national policy must have a profound interest in making sure that intelligence guides and does not follow national policy.

—Secretary of State Henry A. Kissinger, 1973

The CIA was the only agency to dissent: on the eve of the ground war, it was still telling the President that we were grossly exaggerating the damage inflicted on the Iraqis. If we'd waited to convince the CIA, we'd still be in Saudi Arabia.

—H. Norman Schwarzkopf, *It Doesn't Take a Hero*

I've asked why nobody saw it coming. It does say something about us not having a good enough pulse.

—Secretary of State Condoleezza Rice, January, 2006
(on the failure of intelligence to anticipate the
Hamas victory in the Palestinian elections)

It's tough to make predictions, especially about the future.

—Yogi Berra

There are two major types of intelligence failure: the classic failures involving inadequate or unexamined assumptions, and a failure to incorporate new information, and the politicization of intelligence, with political interference leading to corruption of intelligence production. The cases of classic intelligence failure include Pearl Harbor in December 1941, when the United States had the advantage of having deciphered Japanese diplomatic codes

89

and knowing that the Japanese government had instructed its embassy in Washington to destroy coded materials and to break relations with the United States. The surprise Egyptian–Syrian attack against Israel in October 1973 was another costly failure, with the United States failing to anticipate hostilities despite the knowledge that Soviet personnel were being evacuated from the Middle East on Soviet military air transports, a classic indicator of war. Flawed assumptions were the source of the failure to provide warning of the 9/11 attacks in 2001. The CIA did not believe al Qaeda would attack the United States at home, and the FBI did not believe al Qaeda had the organization in the United States to do so.

Political and cultural bias often plays a major role in the classic failures to anticipate major events. Cultural bias contributed to the devastating attack on U.S. naval power in the Pacific, with U.S. decision makers underestimating Japan's ability to develop the technology to reach Pearl Harbor and to modify weapons for the shallow waters there. U.S. military intelligence totally underestimated the power and potential of the Japanese military and believed that Pearl Harbor was outside Japan's range. Prior to the Egyptian–Syrian attack against Israeli in 1973, the CIA and Mossad (the Israeli intelligence organization) underestimated the Arabs and never believed Egyptians and Syrians could cooperate at the highest level of war or that they would have the courage to take on a strong Israeli force. The 9/11 failure also involved an element of cultural bias, with too many intelligence analysts (and policymakers) convinced that nonstate actors required support from nation-states to conduct significant acts of terrorism.

The politicization of intelligence led the CIA to miss the decline and fall of the Soviet Union, and to help the Bush administration make its case for war against Iraq in 2002–2003. The Reagan administration would not accept any sign of Soviet weakness or constraint, and CIA director Casey and deputy director Gates made sure intelligence analysis presented the Russian Bear as threatening and warlike. As a result, the CIA missed the radical change that Mikhail Gorbachev represented to Soviet politics and Soviet-American relations, and missed the challenges to his rule and his ultimate demise in 1991. The Iraq War has been a particular disaster for the reputation and credibility of the CIA, with the Agency providing assessments to the White House and the NSC that were not merely wrong but corrupt.

The intelligence provided in the Gorbachev era and the run-up to the Iraq War represented the failure of the CIA's moral compass. President Truman created the CIA as an intelligence agency outside the policy community to tell truth to power, provide objective and balanced intelligence to policymakers, and avoid policy advocacy. There have been pluses and minuses over the sixty-year history of the CIA, but the past twenty-five years have provided an unending cycle of failure in telling truth to power. Casey and Gates shaped intelligence to support the Reagan administration's policies toward the Soviet Union, Central America, and Southwest Asia. CIA director Tenet told President Bush that providing intelligence to the White House to make the case for war against Iraq would be a "slam dunk," the most egregious example in the history of the Agency regarding politicization. CIA director Goss used his first memorandum to all hands at the CIA to make the case for supporting the policies of the Bush administration and, in February 2006, he removed the director of the Counterterrorism Center, Robert Granier, for his opposition to the policy of extraordinary rendition and the use of "secret prisons." The moral failure is the most worrisome aspect of all because, without the willingness to tell truth to power, reform and reorganization of CIA become irrelevant.

When I locked horns with Casey and Gates on the politicization of intelligence on the Soviet Union, my immediate supervisor, Barry Lee Stevenson, ironically the current ombudsman of the CIA, would regularly stand in my doorway to sing the lyrics of a popular Kenny Rogers song, "you've got to know when to hold 'em, know when to fold 'em; know when to walk away, know when to run." Stevenson certainly knew when to fold and to run, and CIA careerists in general have learned their lessons well from the Rogers song. But there have been dissenters and contrarians, as well as whistle-blowers, and there have been analysts who were willing to fight the good fight on arms control and disarmament (Sayre Stevens), Vietnam (Sam Adams, Thaxter Goodell, and Bobby Layton), and the Soviet Union (Carolyn Ekedahl and John Hibbits). Conversely, there have been analysts who provided the intelligence that policymakers demanded on Vietnam (George Carver), Afghanistan (Fritz Ermarth), arms control (Larry Gershwin), the Middle East (Graham Fuller), the Soviet Union (Douglas MacEachin and George Kolt), and the Iraq War (Alan Foley and Paul Pillar).

The Lessons (Not) Learned

The CIA does an excellent job of collecting intelligence. Indeed, when I left graduate school at Indiana University in 1966 and arrived at the CIA, I believed that I was entering the world's greatest collection of classified materials and the greatest library on intelligence activities. I was right about the CIA as an intelligence repository, but soon learned that the CIA made no effort whatsoever to learn from their failures or from their successes for that matter. The failure to learn from past experience is particularly shocking because the CIA puts so much effort into training and education (although it fails to understand the basic difference between these two methodologies), and hires so many people out of graduate school whose original career goals placed the field of education over the field of intelligence.

CIA analysts have been criticized for failing to predict a successful coup against Nikita Khrushchev in 1964 that the Soviet leader did not anticipate. Fifteen years later, the CIA failed to anticipate a threat against the Shah of Iran that the Shah himself did not foresee. Analysts who probably could not predict the outcome of elections in their own country are held to account for failing to understand complex political developments in foreign communities. There are too many uncertainties and variables to predict American political developments that take place in a rather open environment, but critics are more than willing to lambaste American intelligence officials who have missed events in such closed societies as the Soviet Union, North Korea, and Iraq.

There is a model for lessons learned in the U.S. Army, which routinely conducts after-action reports and even established a Center for Army Lessons Learned in 1985 at Fort Leavenworth in Kansas. The Center has a small staff, but it takes advantage of teams of experts to investigate specific issues and to maintain a direct line of communication to senior military leaders to understand what needs to be examined. The studies of the Center are used in training exercises and scenarios to make sure lessons are learned. The CIA needs to emulate this example.

The Failure of Accountability

I resigned from the CIA in 1990 because of the politicization of intelligence on the Soviet Union and the promotion of those analysts who slanted intelligence. A specific case in point: in 1985, three senior analysts from the directorate of intelligence (Kay Oliver, Mary Desjeans, and Beth Seeger) produced a corrupt intelligence assessment demanded by Casey and Gates to make the case for Soviet involvement in the attempted assassination of the Pope in 1981. Two of the three analysts did not believe the Soviets were involved, yet helped to produce an intelligence assessment *in camera* for the top decision makers in the Reagan administration, including the president, vice president, and the secretary of defense.

The entire assessment was based on one uncorroborated third-hand source from Bulgarian military intelligence that Casey saw in raw form. The report had not even been selected by the directorate of operations for distribution because of its flimsy sourcing and its unsubstantiated information. More importantly, the directorate of operations (DO) and the directorate of intelligence (DI) had numerous authoritative reports that made it clear that the Soviets were not involved and had even warned their Bulgarian counterparts to avoid any involvement with terrorist organizations operating in West Europe. Many of us met with Casey and Gates to put a stop to the report, but we were completely unsuccessful.

Failure has often been accompanied by cash rewards. Graham Fuller, the author of a spurious NIE on Iran in 1985, received regular monetary awards, and the senior analysts who prepared the phony intelligence on Iraqi WMD in 2002–2003 also received regular honors. Fuller was in regular contact with a key NSC staffer, Howard Teicher, to make sure the NIE's findings were compatible with the roots of the Iran-Contra operation, designed to sell surface-to-air missiles to Iran so that profits from these sales could be channeled to the Contras in Nicaragua. Similarly, Robert Walpole, the manager of the flawed 2002 NIE on Iraqi WMD, was trying to provide a document that could be used as justification for use of force against Iraq. He was richly rewarded like many of the CIA officers who should have been held accountable for the 9/11 failure.

The Failure of Competitive Analysis

Although the CIA has done a serviceable job of providing verification and monitoring of arms control agreements, preparing strategic research on events that have already taken place, and often compiling useful and timely situation reports of ongoing crises, it is probably too much to expect the CIA or any other intelligence agency to predict the future, which is essentially the task of warnings intelligence. In this regard, the CIA is in good company because prominent global leaders have dropped the ball when it comes to providing strategic warning. In 1776, George Washington declared that the "Fate of our Country depends in all human probability, on the Exertion of a Few Weeks." In actual fact, it was another seven years before the War of Independence came to an end. In 1792, British Prime Minister Pitt justified the reduction of military expenditures by declaring "there never was a time in the history of this country when . . . we might more reasonably expect fifteen years of peace than at the present moment." Only two months later, however, the European Continent was engulfed in war and, less than a year later, Britain was involved. This began a period of almost continuous warfare for the next twenty-five years. Two days before the outbreak of World War I, the British ambassador to Berlin cabled his government that war was out of the question. And six weeks before the Russian Revolution of March 1917, Vladimir Lenin told a group of young Socialists in Switzerland, "We old people will probably not live to see the decisive battles of the coming revolution." Within a year, the decisive battles of the Russian Revolution began under Lenin's baton.

The most serious and most reversible organizational failure of the CIA's intelligence system has been the centralization of the intelligence process, which began in 1973 when CIA director Schlesinger abolished two of the three major analytical centers. Until Schlesinger's attack against the competitive intelligence offices, intelligence production was divided among the Office of Current Intelligence (OCI) in the DI, the Office of National Estimates (ONE) that reported directly to the CIA director, and the Special Research Staff (SRS) that was also housed in the DI. Casey went one step further when he made Gates the chairman of the NIC in addition to his position as deputy director for intelligence, thus putting him in charge of all CIA's finished intelligence, including NIEs, PDBs, and current intelligence. Never before had one individual wielded such authority over all the intelligence products of the DI.

Good intelligence is about warning. Warning permits policymakers to make important decisions to avoid a crisis or allow a president to be on top of a particular political situation. Conversely, bad intelligence or intelligence failure is about the absence of warning. We are all familiar with such catastrophic intelligence failures as Pearl Harbor and the 9/11 terrorist attacks, when thousands of lives were lost. However, there are so many failures of warning that it begs the question of the actual utility of current or premonitory intelligence. Soviet testing of the atomic bomb, the Korean War and China's entry into the war, the Soviet invasions of Hungary and Czechoslovakia, the October War of 1973, the fall of the Shah, Poland's imposition of martial law, the massacre at Tiananmen Square in Beijing, Iraq's invasion of Kuwait, Indian nuclear testing, the recent accumulation of thousands and thousands of missiles and rockets in the hands of Hezbollah in Lebanon were surprises to U.S. intelligence, U.S. policymakers, and the American people.

The Soviet Failure

There has always been controversy surrounding the intelligence provided to policymakers before the Cuban missile crisis of 1962. On the one hand, the CIA provided sufficient warning to President John F. Kennedy to give the White House time to use diplomacy and a naval quarantine to prevent the activation of short-range and medium-range missiles in Cuba. The timely situation reports provided by the CIA during the crisis were also invaluable, and the intelligence provided by a CIA source, Colonel Penkovsky, gave accurate accounts of Soviet military weakness. On the other hand, a month before the crisis, on September 19, 1962, the CIA produced an NIE entitled "The Military Buildup in Cuba" that stated the Soviets would be unlikely to introduce strategic offensive weapons in Cuba. Four weeks later, on October 14, 1962, there was photographic evidence of the deployment of Soviet missiles.

The CIA's reasons for assuming there would be no deployment of offensive missiles made very good sense, from an American point of view, but failed to take account of the domestic political position of Soviet leader Khrushchev, particularly the pressure from the Soviet military to match the offensive strength of its major adversary, the United States. Also, the CIA could not mention Khrushchev believed Kennedy had shown great political weakness in his handling of the Bay of Pigs crisis in 1961 and, therefore, might be intimidated by a bold Soviet move. The CIA is not permitted to assess U.S. actions that could have an impact on the actions of other nations. Ironically, the assumptions of the CIA that deemed it unlikely Moscow would deploy missiles in Cuba (e.g., Soviet fear of risk, Soviet unwillingness to confront the United States) were probably the reasons why Soviet leaders decided to capitulate to U.S. demands during the crisis. The CIA argued that Moscow did not want to provoke U.S. military intervention in Cuba; the Soviets were primarily interested in building up Fidel Castro's air defense and coastal defense capabilities against the opposition to Castro at home and abroad, and the Soviets had no interest in increasing the level of risk in Soviet–American relations.

Sometimes an experienced journalist walking the streets of Moscow can be more prescient than the entire intelligence community. CIA analysts missed the death of Soviet president Yuri Andropov in 1984, although *Washington Post* reporter Dusko Doder filed a timely warning when he noticed that Soviet television and radio had suddenly switched from jazz to classical music, a classic indicator of calamity in an authoritarian society. After walking through the city, he noticed an unusual number of lights on at midnight at the headquarters of the KGB, the Soviet secret police, and the military and defense ministries. Doder contended that these signs pointed to a "country being placed on an emergency footing," comparable to November 1982, just before Moscow announced that President Leonid Brezhnev had died.[1] Doder also noted that Andropov's son, Igor, had suddenly left his post with a Soviet delegation at a conference in Stockholm to return to Moscow. The editors at the *Washington Post* called officials at CIA, the State Department, even the White House, to garner additional information, but came up empty. The CIA presence in Moscow is an operational one and rarely houses analytical expertise. It failed to connect the dots to note the passing of the Soviet leader, but an enterprising journalist had done so and, as a result, he was investigated for having special access to Soviet information and serving as a witting or unwitting conduit for Soviet intelligence. No one at the U.S. embassy in Moscow noted these events and more than one Foreign Service officer suggested that Doder must have been "on pot." Because Doder had reached a conclusion that his intelligence counterparts could not, he was accused of being on the Soviet payroll or on drugs. A simple note of congratulations would have sufficed from the various agencies of the intelligence community.

Finally, the CIA must be accountable for failing to anticipate and monitor the decline of the Soviet Union. As late as 1989, an NIE concluded the "domestic problems of the USSR are unlikely to alter the Soviet system and the international appetites that spring from it. Just as the Soviets were withdrawing from Afghanistan, Vietnam, and the Indian Ocean, the CIA was still referring to Moscow's "international appetite." Secretary of State George P. Shultz believed that CIA analysis on the Soviet Union was "distorted by strong views about policy" that blocked any discussion of Soviet weakness. He confronted CIA director Bill Casey in 1986 and accused him of providing "bum dope" to the president; the following year, he reminded acting director Gates that the CIA was "usually wrong" about Moscow and that the Agency had dismissed Gorbachev's policies as "just another attempt to deceive us."[2] In his own memoir, Gates finally conceded that the Agency had underestimated the dramatic change of course in Soviet policy and had neither anticipated Gorbachev's retreat abroad nor the destruction of the Soviet system at home. He failed to acknowledge his role in that failure or the assistance provided by his senior advisors on Soviet matters, Ermarth, MacEachin, and Kolt, who directed the politicization of intelligence from 1981 to 1991.

Shultz's reference to "bum dope" involved virtually every aspect of the CIA's intelligence on the Soviet Union. For example, CIA economists had tracked the early stages of decline of the Soviet economy from 1976 to 1988, but Gates would not circulate assessments highlighting Soviet weakness. As a result, CIA assessments and NIEs overstated the size of the Soviet economy and underestimated the economic burden of maintaining the Soviet military. During this period, the CIA estimated the size of the Soviet economy to be nearly 60 percent that of the U.S. economy and asserted that the growth rate of personal consumption in the Soviet Union from 1951 to 1988 actually exceed that of the United States. As late as 1986, the Agency was asserting that East Germany was ahead of West Germany in per capita output; several years later West Germany "purchased" East Germany on the open market. Meanwhile, the Reagan administration used these exaggerated numbers to justify nearly $2 trillion in total defense spending in the 1980s.

The CIA was dead-wrong on the most crucial Soviet intelligence question of the 1980s: Was Gorbachev serious? The CIA missed virtually every sign of change during the Gorbachev era, beginning with the significance of his accession to power, the political impact of the appointment of Eduard Shevardnadze to foreign minister, the marginalization of former foreign minister Gromyko, and the revolution in disarmament and national security policy. The CIA's misreading of Gorbachev meant that the Agency could not anticipate any of the major events of his stewardship, including the withdrawal from Afghanistan, the retreat from the Third World, the unwillingness to intervene in the fall of the Berlin Wall in 1989, and the quick acceptance of the reunification of Germany a year later. In a scathing critique from former chairman of the Joint Chiefs of Staff Colin Powell, the CIA was described as being unable to "anticipate events much better than a layman watching television."[3] Fifteen years later, Powell accused CIA director Tenet and deputy director McLaughlin of deliberately misleading him on Iraqi WMD.

In many of these failures, moreover, the CIA had access to sufficient intelligence information in order to get it right. Prior to the October War, the NSA intercepted messages that provided strategic warning of the Soviet decision to remove its advisors and technicians from Egypt and Syria. Prior to the declaration of martial law in Poland, the CIA had the entire martial law plan from a Polish Colonel assigned to the Polish General Staff, who risked his life to obtain these sensitive documents. The Agency's senior analysts on Poland argued vehemently that the Polish military would never turn its weapons on its own people. They downplayed the authoritative documents that were passed to the CIA by the Polish source, Colonel Ryszard Kuklinski. The CIA did not recruit Kuklinski to spy for the United States; he was the classic case of a walk-in who was nearly turned away. Several years later, the Agency's senior China analysts said the Chinese would never turn their weapons on their own people prior to the massacre of innocent civilians in Tiananmen Square.

The October War Failure

It is an intelligence irony that the CIA from a distance believed, in the summer of 1973, that there were sufficient indicators of a possible war between Arab forces and Israel. The U.S. intelligence community had reported that Egypt was calling up military reservists and conducting military exercises, and that Syria was moving military forces to the Golan Heights bordering Israel. The DI informed Israeli military intelligence about these reports and pointed to the possibility of hostilities, but the Israeli response dismissed CIA's analysis as overreaction. Since Israel was on the front lines and CIA analysts had an exaggerated view of Israeli intelligence capabilities, the DI deferred to Israel and downplayed the indicators beginning to appear. Both the CIA and the Israeli Mossad were accused of the worst kind of intelligence failure, failing to anticipate the onset of military confrontation.

The indicators of war mounted. In September, the intelligence community noted Egypt was calling up military reservists and conducting military exercises, and the Egyptian army had cancelled all leaves. About the same time, Syria was moving military forces to the Golan Heights bordering Israel. These maneuvers were accompanied by the forward deployment of both Egyptian and Syrian air defenses. The Soviets were obviously concerned because they began launching extra reconnaissance satellites on October 3, three days before the war, and began ordering the evacuation of Soviet dependents and non-essential personnel from both Egypt and Syria.

In the last seventy-two hours before the war, there was frenetic activity on most fronts, enough to convince the NSA that hostilities were imminent. The NSA warning should have had some impact within the intelligence community because, most often, signals intelligence (Sigint) and communications intelligence (Comint) provide the best indicators of war. These indicators included the grounding of civilian aircraft and the closing of airports in Egypt, as well as the offensive deployment of Egyptian and Syrian forces. Ten hours before the war began on October 6, a highly placed Israeli source in Egypt reported that the attack was imminent. Of course, by then, it was too late.

The CIA and Mossad were guilty of a cultural superiority that anticipated that the Arabs would have neither the ability nor the courage to conduct an operation, particularly a joint operation, against a superior Israeli force. The Israeli failure was due to a large extent to the military dominance of the intelligence process, which inhibited independent thinking. As a result, after the October War, the major Israeli intelligence organization, Mossad, was given greater responsibility for both political and military intelligence, although civilians in the intelligence world are as vulnerable to the process of "groupthink" as their military counterparts. Military intelligence had been fooled by Egyptian President Sadat's decision to expel the Soviet military presence in June 1972, which convinced Israeli military analysts that Egypt had no military options against Israel.

The United States was guilty of the same cultural bias that compromised the ability of the Israelis to think creatively about Egyptian and Syrian intentions. Just as we found in 1941, when U.S. policymakers and intelligence analysts did not believe that the Japanese had the technological or military ability to conduct an aerial operation so far from the Japanese mainland, there were universal doubts about the prowess and sophistication of Arab military planning. Sadat's ouster of the Soviets had convinced U.S. and Israeli analysts that the military option was off the table. Both U.S. and Israeli intelligence believed that any Egyptian invasion had to be preceded by an Egyptian air attack against Israeli military targets and, without a Soviet advisory and technical presence, the Egyptians had essentially disarmed themselves. Not even the large concentration of Egyptian and Syrian troops on the Israeli borders in late September and the report of a coordinated military attack no later than 6 October (the day of the invasion) changed any intelligence assessments. The crucial piece of information arrived on October 4, when U.S. and Israeli intelligence learned that Antonov-22 aircraft had arrived in Cairo and Damascus to withdraw the families of Soviet advisors and technicians, an indicator of imminent hostilities.

President Sadat deserves great credit for creating strategic surprise in his policy to go to war against Israel. In addition to the decision to expel a large part of the Soviet presence in 1972, which convinced Israeli intelligence analysts that Egypt was in no position to use force, there were other decisions as well. The Egyptians concealed their cooperation with the Syrian armed forces that were going to take part in the October War; both sides concealed their preparations for war, and finally they concealed the exact date and time of war. Until hours before the start of *Operation Badr*, Sadat and Syrian president Hafeez Assad were able to do just that.[4] Not even the Egyptian and Syrian commanders knew when D-Day would take place; the Syrian defense minister did not learn of the date for the war's start until October 1, 1973. Just two days before the start of war, Secretary of State Kissinger met with Israeli foreign minister Abba Eban, and both men approvingly cited CIA and Mossad intelligence that there was little prospect of war.

The war had already begun when a high-level CIA officer was driving to the White House to provide an NSC meeting with assurances that there was no sign of imminent hostilities. Presidents Sadat and Assad had used classic examples of strategic deception to fool both CIA and Mossad; the U.S. and Israeli intelligence agencies had adopted flawed and inadequate assumptions that were not reexamined, let alone changed, and the cultural arrogance of both Americans and Israelis toward Arabs led to the worst intelligence failure in Israel's history. The United States and Israeli had totally underestimated the Arabs and their military forces and, ironically, the easy Israeli victory in the Six-Day War six years earlier probably preordained the intelligence failure of 1973. The CIA's underestimation of an Iraqi insurgent resistance in the wake of a U.S. invasion, and Israeli underestimation of the Hezbollah force in Lebanon in the summer of 2006 stemmed from similar cultural failures.

The Failure in Iran

The CIA's failure to provide strategic warning to the Carter administration on the political and social upheaval in Iran was a corporate failure for the Agency and contributed to President Carter's election defeat in 1980. The Iran failure was due to the CIA's inability to understand the emergence of Islamic Fundamentalism in the 1970s. The DI made no special effort to understand the movement, even though it was present in such allied states as Iran, Turkey, and Egypt. In the first year of Carter's presidency, the NSC requested the first paper to be written at the CIA on the subject of Islamic Fundamentalism. When no paper was produced, the NSC learned that the CIA had not assigned anyone to the project.[5] Only one CIA operative assigned to Tehran had a working knowledge of Farsi, and a secret agreement between Iran and the United States kept the CIA from collecting intelligence on the internal political situation. The situation was no better at the State Department, where the Bureau of Intelligence and Research (INR) lacked a full-time analyst on Iran.

The CIA was naïve about the role and capabilities of the Shah of Iran, who it placed into power in 1953. Even CIA director Helms, who ended his long government career as ambassador to Iran, did not believe that the Shah was aware of the brutality of Savak, the Iranian security and military service that was trained and indoctrinated by the CIA. In August 1978, a CIA assessment concluded that Iran was "not in a revolutionary or even a prerevolutionary situation." CIA director Turner's briefing to the president in October reaffirmed that the Shah was in full control of a powerful army, police force, and intelligence service (Savak), which were more than equal to any challenge from opposition groups."[6] As a result of these intelligence failures, President Carter traveled to Iran in 1977 and confidently declared in a toast to the Shah that "Iran is an island of stability in one of the more troubled areas of the world," which reflected the consensus within the intelligence and policy communities in Washington at that time.[7]

The emergence of violent political demonstrations in Iran in 1978 took the CIA by surprise, in view of the CIA consensus that the Shah was not threatened by opposition to his modernization policies. Violence soon spread from the holy city of Qom to the capital of Tehran, but it was the news media and not the intelligence agencies that provided the first indications of strategic warning. By the time the White House learned of its strategic problems in Iran, the degree of dissidence had made orderly transition away from the Shah's autocratic rule nearly impossible. Soon, the United States lacked any promising policy options. The situation was so bad that, in November 1978, CIA director Turner received an unusual note from the White House with instructions that only he should open the envelope. In it, was a handwritten note from President Carter, conveying his dissatisfaction with the "quality of our political intelligence" and asking for recommendations to "improve your ability to give me political information and advice."[8]

A few days later, this private and personal note was discussed in several U.S. papers, setting the stage for the accusations of "intelligence failure," when the Shah fell from power two months later. Turner knew that national security advisor Brzezinski leaked the president's note to the press in order to embarrass the CIA director. Brzezinski had no respect for Turner and was particularly upset with a CIA special assessment he received in August 1978 asserting that "Iran is not in a revolutionary or even a 'prerevolutionary' situation." A month later the Defense Intelligence Agency published an assessment stating the Shah "is expected to remain actively in power over the next ten years."[9] As a result of these intelligence memoranda, President Carter told a press conference on December 12, 1978, that he expected "the Shah to maintain power in Iran and for the present problems in Iran to be resolved." One month later, the Shah had fled from Iran and arrived in Egypt.

Probably no intelligence agency in the world has a commendable track record predicting revolutions, coups, or even electoral upsets. Nevertheless, the CIA was particularly myopic in its inability to monitor the deep political and social trends that were working against the Shah. More important than the failure to identify the opposition to the Shah was the inability to understand the growing appeal of renewed Islamic religious fundamentalism. Even those individuals outside the intelligence community who understood the problems of the Shah had no idea that he would be replaced by a 79-year-old cleric in exile in France, Ayatollah Khomeini. CIA specialists on Iran totally misunderstood the nature of the Shah's political standing, and the CIA officers in Tehran produced no significant reporting on the mounting opposition to his rule. To make matters worse, the Shah had negotiated an agreement with the CIA that permitted a large clandestine presence in Iran in return for a promise not to recruit assets among the Shah's coterie or to collect intelligence against the Shah himself. As a result, there was no CIA reporting based on sources within the religious opposition during the period from 1975–1977. The political reporting of the U.S. embassy and the CIA was totally inadequate to the task. This was a classic case of "clientitis," with the intelligence community becoming too close to the policy choices of the policymaker, and the policymakers and the diplomats having a vested interest in the continued rule of the Shah. There were no devil's advocates, no alternative theses, or no contrarian points of views; there was only unanimity and conventional wisdom.

The extreme confidence of U.S. policymakers, including the president and national security advisor Brzezinski, in the Shah's durability meant that no one was asking about the longevity of the Shah's rule and the durability of his autocracy. Policy was premised on the proposition of continued rule of the Shah, and there was a lack of imagination within the policy and intelligence communities regarding alternative U.S. policies or Iranian scenarios. There was no pressure on the Shah to bring opposition elements into his government, which would not have eased the violent opposition at this late date. Even when the CIA began to report that money was being transferred abroad and that problems were deepening in various economic sectors, there was no speculation on the implications of these actions and no concern from policymakers. Intelligence insight into the goals and expectations of opposition elements and popular attitudes toward them were completely missing from CIA reporting to the policy community. And no one in the policy or intelligence community asked whether the Shah would survive the challenge posed by various disturbances, although large-scale arms sales to Iran were very important to U.S. interests. Finally, no one on the new Senate and House intelligence committees bothered to scrutinize CIA intelligence analysis and ask for alternative explanations.

There were several instances where the media were out in front of the CIA. In April and May 1978, *The New York Times* and the *Washington Post* noted an alliance between Islamic fundamentalists and other opponents, but the CIA's *National Intelligence Daily* did not report on the existence of such an alliance until June 17, 1978.[10] The State Department's *Morning Summary* was only slightly better, identifying the factors that would work against a resolution of the crisis, although it was not until the summer of 1978 that it determined the Shah was losing his grip. State's INR lacked a full-time analyst on Iran and therefore produced no regular intelligence reporting on Iran in 1978. As late as September 1978, the DIA was predicting that the Shah was "expected to remain actively in power over the next ten years."[11]

The intelligence failure in Iran was particularly stunning because of the role of the CIA in installing the Shah of Iran in 1953 and the incestuous relationship between U.S. presidents and the Shah over a quarter century. Iran was a strategic ally of the United States for this entire period, housing monitoring facilities that tracked the Soviet strategic missile program and providing significant deliveries of oil to U.S. markets. Iran also had de facto military control over the Straits of Hormuz, the transportation route for a significant proportion of oil deliveries to U.S. allies in Western Europe, as well as Japan. The CIA trained Savak, the Iranian secret police, and cooperated with Savak to monitor the Soviet presence in Iran, according to historian Derek Leebaert. The indicators of the Shah's problems were numerous over this twenty-five-year period and the CIA managed to miss all of them, particularly the restiveness of Iran's burgeoning young population. By 1979, half the Iranian population was under sixteen and two-thirds were under thirty, but the CIA never took demographics seriously as a strategic issue. The CIA is making the same mistake regarding demographic trends in the Islamic nations of the Middle East and North Africa, where anti-Americanism is rising as a result of U.S. military occupation of Iraq. As a result, CIA analysts missed the inevitable radicalization of the Iranian population, as well as the social and cultural instability that dominated the landscape due to the youthful population; they also missed the enormous growth in the population that presented another series of political and economic pressures, as well as the increased urbanization of the population. The twin pressures of population growth and urban migration had devastating consequences.

The CIA also missed the impact of religion in Iran, where more than 90 percent of the country is Shiite Muslim, a primitive and mystic branch of Islam whose beliefs and laws are fundamentally incompatible with modern in-

dustrialized life and whose religious leaders are not capable of playing a constructive role in the modernization of society. Since the 1979 revolution in
Iran, CIA analysis has been slow to comprehend the essential backwardness
of Iranian society and culture, and CIA analysts have been far too optimistic
in anticipating the modernization and westernization of Iran. The CIA and the
intelligence community in general also underestimated the impact of Iran's
Shiite population on a postwar Iraq, where a Shiite majority would play a
dominant role in the wake of the downfall of Saddam Hussein. It is particularly ironic that the Bush administration's use of force in Iraq has enabled the
Shiites of both Iran and Iraq to assert themselves, marking a political and
strategic setback for the United States.

In addition to missing the long-term indicators of political and social upheaval in Iran, the CIA missed such short-term indicators as the growing au-
thoritarianism of the Shah's increasingly erratic leadership and corruption of
society under the Shah's leadership. The declining real income for Iran's
workers and the absence of new jobs for Iran's graduates combined to create
the perfect conditions of social discontinuity that could be exploited by such
Shiite clergy as the Ayatollah Khomeini. In the 1970s, however, both the
Nixon and Carter administrations ignored all of these indicators and proceeded to sell the Shah billions of dollars in military equipment, which contributed to the intelligence community's increased unwillingness to provide
bad news to the White House on internal conditions in Iran. Massive corruption accompanied these military sales, and the Shah's extended family was
the primary beneficiary of these dealings. Iran became particularly important
to the United States in the wake of the October War of 1973, another intelligence failure, as the Arab states moved in a direction away from the United
States and Israel, but official reporting from the embassy and the CIA station
in Tehran became less objective and realistic. The Shah believed that his oil
wealth and Iran's strategic importance made him impervious to U.S. pressure
and influence. The United States never seriously considered the importance
of democratic reform in Iran because, with its cold war mindset, it feared that
actual "democratization" would enable a Soviet takeover.

The Phony Soviet Combat Brigade in Cuba

In 1978–1979, the CIA helped to create a crisis for President Carter when it
failed to provide strategic warning about the collapse of the Shah. In 1979, the
CIA single-handedly created a crisis with the "warning" of the deployment of
a non-existent Soviet combat brigade in Cuba. This was a classic failure that
had a great deal to do with the close relationship that existed between national
security advisor Brzezinski and the CIA's NIO for the Soviet Union, Arnold

Horelick. The White House, with the 1962 Cuban missile crisis in mind, was preparing for a summit with the Soviet Union, and Brzezinski, who was paranoid about the Kremlin, feared a Soviet surprise that would catch President Carter off guard. He convinced Horelick that the surprise would be in Cuba, and a hurried review of the intelligence unearthed a report from NSA that a Soviet combat brigade had suddenly appeared in Cuba. Horelick became seized with this issue and ignored several of us who tried to persuade him that there was no such terminology as a "combat brigade," that any deployment of such a unit would have been picked up in signals intelligence at an earlier stage, and that NSA director Admiral Bobby Inman had a reputation for worst-case analysis on the problem of the Soviet Union.

This intelligence failure had huge policy implications, leading directly to the Carter administration's decision to stop its efforts to gain ratification of the SALT II treaty and ending an opportunity for a significant advance in Soviet–American relations. Even if the CIA had been right about the deteriorating political and security situation in Iran, the Carter administration could have done nothing to save the stewardship of the Shah. But, if the CIA had not falsely trumpeted the Soviet combat brigade, then SALT II would have been ratified, there would have been new life in the disarmament and arms control process, and the United States would not have squandered so much military investment at a time of Soviet military and economic decline. Senator John Glenn (D-Ohio) had been coming regularly to the CIA for briefings on the SALT II Treaty and, although once skeptical of the treaty, the briefings convinced him the treaty was in the interests of the United States and could be monitored by the CIA. The flap over the Soviet combat brigade, however, ended Glenn's support for the administration's treaty.

Everyone had a share in this intelligence disaster. First and foremost, the CIA and NSA were guilty of a terrible memory lapse, failing to search its archives and learn the so-called brigade was actually part of a Soviet military presence in Cuba agreed to during the end game of the Cuban missile crisis. McGeorge Bundy, who was national security advisor during the Cuban missile crisis, wrote an op-ed for *The New York Times* that explained the agreement to permit a Soviet military unit to remain in Cuba as a praetorian guard for Fidel Castro. Robert McNamara, who was secretary of defense during the missile crisis, testified to the Senate Armed Forces Committee in 1962 about the Soviet military presence, which perfectly explained the presence of the "combat brigade." It was a small unit, with about two thousand men, that had no connection to an airlift or sealift capability. It posed no threat to the United States, and Brzezinski and Horelick were wrong to compare the combat brigade to the missile threat in 1962, the submarine base issue in 1970, and the MIG-23 issue of 1978.

The Carter administration bungled the affair from the very beginning and then tried to use the influence of Soviet ambassador Anatoly Dobrynin to convince Soviet leader Brezhnev that the United States had made a serious mistake and was not trying to worsen bilateral relations. Dobrynin, who was ambassador to the United States from 1962 to 1986, was in Moscow at the bedside of his parents, who were being treated for terminal illnesses. Secretary of State Cyrus Vance convinced Soviet foreign minister Gromyko to return Dobrynin to Washington to resolve the mini-crisis caused by the intelligence community. Dobrynin attended the burial of his father and then left his mother's bedside to return to Washington in a mood of "anger and sorrow."[12] Dobrynin spent the next two weeks, meeting with members of Congress and the White House staff to untangle the Cuban "crisis." Quoting Marx, Dobrynin told one and all that history repeats itself, first as tragedy and then as farce.

The White House and the CIA did not understand Brezhnev had to answer to political forces as well, and that there were Soviet opponents to arms control, particularly Gromyko and KGB director Yuri Andropov, who wanted to use the Cuban flap to stop the process of SALT II. The State Department, which poorly managed the affair, privately supplied two Democratic Senators, Frank Church (Idaho) and Richard Stone (Florida), with provocative information on the so-called brigade, but provided no guidance on how to handle the information. The State Department expected these senior Senators to behave responsibly, but both were facing tough reelection battles in their states because of their support for the Panama Canal treaty and, as a result, publicly called for a Soviet withdrawal. Church, unfortunately, was also chairman of the Senate Foreign Relations Committee, which was handling the ratification of SALT II. His first words in response to the intelligence information were "That will sink SALT."[13] As a result of this brouhaha, caused by the intelligence community, SALT II was withdrawn, and Church and Stone could not save themselves in their reelection campaigns. Both lost! The intelligence community's blunder contributed to Carter's defeat the following year.

Ironically, the Soviets had such a great appreciation for the technical collection capabilities of the U.S. intelligence community that they could not believe that the so-called "combat brigade" was the result of an intelligence failure. The Kremlin was convinced that this was an example of U.S. perfidy, creating a phony military issue to worsen Soviet–American relations and to end an opportunity for the ratification of the SALT II treaty. Moscow certainly had a right to believe that somewhere in the NSC or the State Department there would be a retrieval of the 1962 document to explain the situation in 1979. In fact, the Soviets were victimized in part by their paranoid secrecy on security matters, which led the United States to engage in worst-case thinking. At the same time, however, it must be recognized that the Soviets believed that the United States trumped up threats with the Soviet Union in order to squash any opportunity for diplomatic progress, particularly at the arms control table. The brigade remained in Cuba until the collapse of the Soviet Union; Russia and Cuba announced in September 1992 that it would be withdrawn, and withdrawal was completed in July 1993. As a result of the combat brigade, it took eleven years to complete the SALT II treaty, now labeled as START I, which was ratified in 1990 during the administration of George H. W. Bush.

CIA Strategic Assessments and the Key Role of Assumptions

Until satellite photography became available in the early 1960s, the intelligence community had no direct evidence of the size of Soviet ICBM production. In view of the surprise launch of Sputnik in October 1957, there was a strong tendency to exaggerate the size of the Soviet force and to accept the wild boasting of Soviet leader Khrushchev. As a result, an NIE in 1960 stated that the "ICBM provides the USSR, for the first time, with an efficient means of delivering a heavyweight attack on the United States, and the Soviets have strong incentives to build up a substantial force."[14] This view was a key element in the notorious "missile gap" argument during the presidential campaign in 1960. Overhead photography revealed in 1961 that actual ICBM deployment was far lower than expected, but the CIA continued to predict an imminent deployment of hundreds of ICBMs. (Two decades later, the CIA learned that it had overestimated the growth in Soviet military spending, but it took five years before the Agency briefed congressional committees on the errors in intelligence reporting.)

The major error in the methodology for estimates of Soviet ICBM production and deployment was the inability to anticipate Moscow's difficulty in mastering ICBM technology, which led to significant overestimation. The CIA assumed that the nation that launched Sputnik in 1957 and started mass production of medium-range ballistic missiles in 1959 would have no difficulty in matching U.S. strategic technology. But the Soviets had great difficulty in mastering a storable propellant for their first ICBMs (the SS-6) and had to curtail its second-generation ICBMs (the SS-7 and SS-8) because of poor technical performance. It wasn't until the development of the third-generation ICBMs (the SS-9 and SS-11) in 1966 that the Soviets could finally deploy a system capable of competing with the U.S. Minuteman. The CIA also consistently overestimated the rate of Soviet modernization of their strategic forces in the 1970s and 1980s.

It is axiomatic that the CIA exaggerated the strength of the Soviet Union when there was a dearth of intelligence sources, and underestimated the Soviet threat when there was a plethora of sources. For example, the intelligence community overestimated the size of the Soviet strategic force from 1958 to 1963, when there was limited sophisticated collection against the Soviet arsenal, and underestimated the size of the force from 1964 to 1968, when there was increased overhead collection. The NIE in 1964 projected 410 to 700 ICBMs by 1970, but the actual deployment exceeded 1,300 ICBMs. Even the Air Force, which consistently estimated higher Soviet forces than the rest of the intelligence community in order to make a case on Capitol Hill for greater funding, underestimated the 1970 deployment by 400 ICBMs. The entire community concluded that it "did not believe that the USSR aims at matching the U.S. in numbers of intercontinental delivery vehicles."[15] Two years later, the Air Force (and only the Air Force within the intelligence community) concluded that the Soviets had a "determination to rise from a position of strategic inferiority to one of at least numerical parity with the U.S."

The rest of the community, however, continued to believe in the face of increasing evidence to the contrary that Soviet economic constraints ruled out another strategic competition with the United States and that the Kremlin would not engage in a massive buildup because it recognized the United States would detect and overmatch such an effort. The emphasis on economic constraints was an obvious example of mirror imaging, since there was an appreciation of U.S. constraints in such a scenario. There was another methodological mistake: the authors of the strategic estimates in the period from 1969 to 1972 made their projections without factoring in the impact of a strategic arms agreement, despite the start of SALT talks in 1969. They did not anticipate projected forces based on the proposed SALT Treaty, although the treaty appeared to be certain in 1971 and was signed in 1972. In the 1980s, the CIA failed to appreciate that serious economic constraints would have an impact on Soviet military spending and particularly strategic force modernization.

The CIA also completely dismissed the fact that Soviet leader Gorbachev had decided to reduce defense spending and to accept 50 percent cuts in Soviet strategic forces in order to present a more benign image to the West and to enhance Soviet–American relations. The intelligence community was victimized by its tendency to compartmentalize areas of specialization. The military analysts who prepared estimates on Soviet strategic forces gave insufficient attention to domestic political factors in the Kremlin, the importance of arms control to the Soviet leadership, and economic constraints. This tendency to compartmentalize also kept the CIA analytical cadre from comparing various pieces of evidences that pointed to the weakness and decline of the Soviet Union in the 1980s.

In the 1970s, the NIE authors tried to correct their mistakes by factoring in the ceiling for strategic nuclear vehicles for SALT II agreed to in Vladivostok in 1974. These projections turned out to be too low because the United States refused to ratify SALT II, and the Soviets thus refused to reduce their force to the lower limits. Projections in the 1980s were too high because the authors then assumed that, with the defeat of SALT II, the Soviets would no longer observe the ceiling of SALT I. Again, the NIE authors were in error as the Soviets remained in compliance. There is probably no better example of the role of assumptions in the writing of NIEs than the errors that occurred over the projections for Soviet strategic forces.

The errors regarding modernization revealed the CIA learned nothing from its tendency to consistently overestimate the changes in Soviet strategic forces in every NIE from 1975 to 1986. The 1985 NIE on Soviet ICBMs repeated the 1975 NIE's projections, which assumed that virtually the entire ICBM force—95 percent—would be new within ten years, even though the actual modernization rate through 1985 had been far lower—10 percent. Both the 1975 and 1985 estimates projected three new Soviet ICBMs, but two were never deployed and one (the SS-18) was delayed in the first instance, and only one of them (the SS-18 follow-on) became operational in the second instance. The modernization analysis was particularly important because modernization and procurement represented the largest share of spending on strategic forces, thus leading to an exaggerated Soviet threat, particularly the pace and scope of technological change.

The CIA also erred in assuming that the rapid Soviet missile buildup in the late 1960s would be a guide for future deployment rates. It wasn't, and the 1960s rate of deployment was never approached again. In fact, most of the Soviet ICBM force were deployed by 1970, with the Soviets concentrating on modernization of the force after 1970. The intelligence community also underestimated the impact of arms control agreements on the Soviet strategic arsenal. With the establishment of a ceiling on strategic weapons in the SALT Treaty of 1972, the key component of the arsenal was force modernization, particularly how quickly the Soviets could improve their force by changing the composition under the fixed ceilings specified in the agreements. The CIA underestimated the Soviet willingness to comply with the agreements and, therefore, forecasts overestimated the Soviet strategic threat. This argument in favor of arms control has never been fully put forward by the arms control lobby.

In areas other than ballistic missiles, the CIA had no genuine understanding of the gaps between U.S. and Soviet forces. The CIA overestimated the initial operating capability of the one new Soviet strategic bomber—the Blackjack. The first prediction was contained in the 1972 NIE, which called for a Blackjack deployment in 1978, ten years earlier than actual deployment. The emphasis on Soviet construction of nuclear-powered attack submarines did not incorporate inadequacies in Soviet antisubmarine warfare, the lack of sea-based tactical air support, and the inability to conduct naval amphibious lift to sustain long-range operations. The United States had huge advantages in all of these areas, which created an overwhelming advantage in out-of-area operations and power projection. The prediction of a Soviet aircraft carrier was purely mythological and ignored the conservative nature of the Soviet fighting force that abstained such high-risk strategies as using standard fighter and attack aircraft on naval platforms for power projection. The Soviet Union never shared the U.S. interest in power projection in the Third World and never pursued the high-risk strategies adopted by the United States. As a result, CIA predictions of a high level of activity in the Third World for the Soviet Union proved fanciful, particularly in view of the Soviet withdrawal from Afghanistan and Cam Ranh Bay, the end of Soviet naval deployments in the Indian Ocean and the Mediterranean Sea, and the general hunkering down of the entire Soviet military force. DDI Gates in the mid-1980s blocked all Agency assessments referring to Soviet weakness or restraint in the Third World (let alone Soviet retreat).

The CIA consistently maintained that the Soviets would keep pace with the modernization of NATO's theater forces, which was totally in error. The Soviets could not keep pace and their production rates fell for nearly every one of their conventional systems, in addition to falling behind in modernization. The modernization lag was due in part to the rapid decline in the economies of the Eastern European members of the Warsaw Pact that were responsible for many of the qualitative improvements in Soviet Bloc forces over the years. The CIA consistently missed the genuine gap in the force structure between NATO and the Warsaw Pact, and the intelligence community's efforts on quantitative measures of their respective forces missed the real picture of the qualitative decline that meant lesser threats and lesser mobility on the part of the Soviet Bloc forces.

THE IMPACT OF FAILURE

Intelligence failures typically have negative consequences for U.S. policy. The strategic surprise of the Soviet invasion of Czechoslovakia in 1968 forced the Johnson administration to break off negotiations with the Soviet Union for the start of strategic arms limitation talks (SALT). The failure to properly warn the Carter administration about the Soviet invasion of Afghanistan in December 1979 led to a direct setback to Soviet–American relations, including the virtual end of serious discussions to conclude a SALT II agreement.

The failure to anticipate the fall of the Shah in Iran in 1979 put the Carter administration on the defensive, and President Carter's unfortunate entanglement with Iran was the major reason for his defeat to Ronald Reagan in 1980. The incredible underestimates of the size and capabilities of the Iraqi strategic weapons programs around the time of Desert Storm in 1991 probably contributed to the overestimates of the arsenal, particularly the nuclear program, prior to the Iraq War in 2003. And the failure to anticipate and monitor five Indian nuclear tests in 1998 led to the failure to ratify the Comprehensive Test Ban Treaty in that year. Once again, controversial intelligence over the extent and immediacy of Iran's nuclear program is contributing to a tense bilateral relationship between the United States and Iran and even rumors of pending military action.

Every intelligence failure is costly, leading to increased demands for greater resources for clandestine collection of intelligence or human intelligence (HUMINT). HUMINT is far less expensive than such technical means of collection as satellite imagery or communications intercepts, and most uninitiated observers, particularly in the Congress, believe that HUMINT is a "silver bullet" in the world of intelligence collection and analysis. In fact, HUMINT is highly overestimated in its worth to finished intelligence production and to policy formulation. HUMINT is more susceptible to deception than any other means of collection, and the intelligence in the run-up to the Iraq War in 2003 is an excellent example of flawed clandestine collection and an overreliance on misinformation and unreliable sources.

One of the greatest myths in the world of clandestine collection is the belief CIA agents have great success in recruiting and running clandestine assets who supply substantial amounts of intelligence information. In fact, there are few classic recruitments in the field of clandestine collection; most useful foreign assets are walk-ins or defectors of one stripe or another who volunteer their services to the CIA and the United States. In many cases, such as the Soviet Generals Oleg Penkovsky and Major Pyotr Popov, walk-ins are often turned away by U.S. intelligence officers (as well as British intelligence officers in the case of Penkovsky) and have to return to CIA or MI-6 on several occasions to establish their worth and bonafides. Both Penkovsky and Popov were GRU (Soviet military intelligence) officers who made numerous attempts to contact U.S., British, and Canadian intelligence officers before attracting any interest from the CIA.

Penkovsky, whose information was invaluable during the Cuban missile crisis in 1962, became so desperate to contact the United States that he finally approached two American tourists on the Moskvoretsky Bridge over the Moscow River on a rainy night to ask them to deliver a packet of materials to a U.S. embassy official.[16] Penkovsky's view that Khrushchev's threatening language to the United States was not backed by an extensive arsenal of strategic weaponry was vital. It contributed to President Kennedy's decision to apply a quarantine against the Soviet navy rather than to seek an immediate military solution to the crisis. It helped that Penkovsky's views corroborated the opinions of former U.S. ambassador to the USSR, Llewellyn Thompson, who counseled the president that Khrushchev should be given the time and the opening to withdraw the missiles from Cuba.

In my twenty-four years at the CIA, there were no successful CIA or FBI recruitments of Soviet assets providing trenchant information, although there were a handful of Soviet walk-ins who provided good intelligence on Soviet weapons systems. Former CIA directors Bob Gates and Stansfield Turner have acknowledged that there were no significant recruitments of Soviet spies during their careers at the CIA, and former operational officers have conceded that spies were all walk-ins or volunteers. Dewey Clarridge, who served in the CIA in various high-level operational positions for thirty years, acknowledged that the DO "wasted a lot of emotional energy trying to recruit Soviets during the Cold War."[17] Clarridge could not recall one Soviet spy who was "spotted, developed, and recruited from scratch by a CIA case officer." Similarly, American spies for the Soviets, such as Aldrich Ames and Robert Hannsen, were walk-ins, not recruits.

Clandestine collection is rarely as useful as open source collection in most areas of the world or the reporting from Foreign Service officers and military attaches. Most political, economic, and even military reporting from open societies comes from open sources and Foreign Service Officers. As former U.S. ambassador Robert V. Keeley noted, "many FSOs could provide examples of the most extreme form of overlap by citing personal cases in which they developed very useful foreign sources of human intelligence, only to find a source drying up because he had been recruited by a CIA case officer and put on the CIA's payroll."[18] Since a much higher value is placed on clandestine collection than embassy reporting within the intelligence community, CIA reports receive higher levels of security classification and lower levels of distribution. Clandestine collection is often redundant, with the exception of collection in such arcane fields as terrorism, weapons of mass destruction, and proliferation of strategic weapons.

Reasons for Failure

When the late Les Aspin was chairman of the Oversight Subcommittee of the House Select Committee on Intelligence, he studied and identified the reasons for intelligence failure.[19] Aspin's key factors were preconceived notions, "mirror-imaging," misjudgment of strategic priorities, and political and bureaucratic pressures or politicization. Preconceived notions played a major role in the failures dealing with Pearl Harbor, the Cuban missile crisis, the October War of 1973, and the Iranian revolution of 1979. Politicization played a key role in the failure to understand the decline and fall of the Soviet Union in the 1980s and the intelligence support for going to war against Iraq in 2003.

"Mirror-imaging" was a major factor in CIA underestimates of the Soviet strategic forces, with agency analysts assuming that the Kremlin had no interest in surpassing U.S. strategic capabilities. CIA analysts exaggerated the qualitative aspects of Soviet strategic capabilities and underestimated the importance of quantitative factors in the Soviet mindset. Agency experts assumed that U.S. breakthroughs in MIRV technology would convince Soviet planners to move in the same direction. There is also a tendency within the intelligence community to overcompensate for errors by exaggerating the possibility of opposite outcomes. CIA errors in forecasting Iraqi strategic capabilities prior to the 1991 Desert Storm war probably played a role in the gross exaggeration of Iraqi WMD capabilities prior to the 2003 war.

The intelligence exaggerations that played some role in the bomber and missile gaps in the 1950s and 1960s probably played a similar role in the underestimates of Soviet strategic capabilities in the 1970s. There is also reason to believe that when the Agency had limited intelligence on a particular subject, there was a tendency to worse-case the issue, but that an overabundance of intelligence led to a more conciliatory line of thought; for example, the greater the technical intelligence on Soviet weaponry, the greater the tendency to underestimate the capabilities of such weaponry. The CIA estimate in 1962 had good reasons for arguing against the introduction of Soviet missiles into Cuba, but it never took into account the military pressure on Khrushchev to match the superiority of U.S. strategic forces and his gamble on a "quick fix" in Cuba in order to avoid another expensive missile race with the United States. U.S. lack of interest in strategic defense, civil defense, and air defense probably led to a tendency to underestimate Moscow's traditional concerns about defense based on cultural paranoia and mirror-imaging.

Politicization of Intelligence

There have been many efforts throughout the history of the CIA to slant analytical conclusions, skew estimates, and repress evidence that challenged a particular policy or point of view, which is inevitable in the battlefield that pits policymakers against intelligence officers. Politicization is most likely when a policy is flawed or failing, and political pressure is placed on the CIA to shape the finished intelligence product to support the legitimacy of the policy. Failure in Vietnam led to pressure to suppress the actual number of Viet Cong insurgents in South Vietnam; if President Johnson had to confront the action number of Viet Cong, he would have had to increase the number of American forces or withdraw them. He would not consider either option. The decision to significantly increase defense spending against the Soviet Union in the 1980s led to pressure on the CIA to create the picture of a Soviet threat that was ten feet tall. The decision to go to war against Iraq in 2002 led to White House and Defense Department pressure on the CIA to cherry-pick intelligence on WMD and links between Iraq and al Qaeda.

The systematic slanting of intelligence collection and analysis to serve policy interests became institutionalized during Casey's tenure as CIA director from 1981 to 1987. Casey brought to the CIA a strong policy agenda that marked the Soviet Union as an "evil empire" responsible for the world's problems and intent on destroying the West. He was a political appointee of the Reagan administration that wanted to end détente and arms control, create more active anti-Soviet policies in the Third World, and double defense spending in order to "rollback" the Soviet threat. Casey was well served by Gates, a career intelligence official, who was a special assistant to Casey in 1981, his DDI in 1982, and eventually the deputy director of the CIA in 1985. Gates knew how the intelligence process worked and how to ensure its responsiveness to Casey's policy interests. In several years, Gates successfully used policies of reorganization and personnel management to assume direct control over all intelligence analysis and to bolster reporting that emphasized the Soviet threat and to inhibit analysis that emphasized Moscow's serious economic problems and worsening international position. As a result, the CIA failed to predict the dramatic changes in Soviet policy in the 1980s.

Arms control and disarmament measures in the 1960s and 1970s met resistance from the Pentagon, which often led to pressure from the secretary of defense to overestimate the strategic capabilities of the Soviet Union and to prevent the CIA from doing net assessments of the relative strength of the Soviet Union and the United States. Secretary of Defense Laird was strongly opposed to the negotiations of the SALT treaty and the ABM treaty in 1972 and strongly pressed for intelligence assessments that overestimated the quantitative and qualitative aspects of Moscow's strategic missile force, as well as its surface-to-air missile system. Secretary of Defense Weinberger inflated the capabilities of Moscow's SS-20 missile system in an effort to prevent the INF treaty in 1987 and wanted the intelligence community to do the same. Ironically, Weinberger resigned along with the author of the INF Treaty, Richard Perle, when the Reagan administration decided to sign the treaty. Secretary of Defense Rumsfeld pressured the CIA to bolster its assessments on Third-World nuclear programs in order to make the Bush administration's case for deployment of national missile defense.

Role of Expertise

The inevitability of surprise and the inability of experts to anticipate change are directly responsible for the huge number of tactical intelligence failures over the past sixty years. Intelligence failures should lead to internal post-mortems, congressional inquiries, and academic studies, but there have been few examples of such studies. As a result, there is no intelligence literature on lessons learned, which is an important device in the military. The Pearl Harbor and 9/11 failures are very similar, with sufficient premonitory evidence of an attack against the United States, but there was no evidence of any willingness to alter preconceived notions that argued against an attack. A very junior and inexperienced analyst at the CIA's Office of Current Intelligence, the late Gene Wicklund, predicted the Soviet invasion of Czechoslovakia in 1968, but he was silenced and even ridiculed by senior mentors and mangers at both the CIA and the Department of State's INR. A relatively junior CIA analyst in the field, Bob Layton, predicted the Tet offensive in 1968, but he was ignored by senior managers. More typical were the examples of the senior analysts on Iran (Ernie Oney), Poland (John Kachold and Terry Bender), and China (Douglas Paal and Bob Suettinger) who incorrectly predicted that the Shah would not fall, the Polish military would not resort to martial law, and the Chinese military would not use its weapons at Tiananmen Square, respectively. There seems to be a corollary between the presence of senior expertise and the incidence of intelligence failure, with greater expertise leading to greater incidence of failure. The overwhelming majority of CIA financial and human resources were devoted to the Soviet Union and the Soviet Bloc, but no one anticipated the collapse of the Berlin Wall and the Soviet empire in 1989, the Warsaw Pact in 1990, and even the Soviet Union itself in 1991.

Single-Outcome Forecasting

The failure to challenge assumptions and the reliance on straight-line forecasting has led to some of the worst intelligence failures, including the October War in 1973 and the fall of the Shah in Iran in 1979. The analysts in the Middle East division of the Office of Current Intelligence were highly experienced and had worked the problems of Arab–Israeli affairs and the Persian Gulf for significant periods of time. They had spent a great deal of time arguing against the likelihood of war between Arabs and Israelis throughout the early 1970s and were convinced that the Egyptians and the Syrians lacked the skill and temerity to attack a stronger nation such as Israel. There were only two analysts devoting full-time efforts to Iran but they had more than fifty years of experience between them and, for much of this time, were challenging frequent interventions from senior managers and policymakers who worried about the longevity of the Shah.

Lack of Collection . . . and Lack of Imagination

The recent war between Israel and Hezbollah produced noteworthy intelligence failure for Israel's Mossad, as well as the CIA. In addition to the large number of rockets and missiles that Hezbollah was able to launch against northern Israel, the power and sophistication of the missile and rocket arsenal caught Israel and the United States completely off guard, particularly the use of a sophisticated antiship cruise missile that damaged an Israeli naval vessel off the coast of Lebanon. The missile was the C-802, an Iranian-made variant of the Chinese Silkworm, which was totally unknown to the inventory of Hezbollah. Iran began buying dozens of these sophisticated antiship missiles in the 1990s, until the Clinton administration pressured Beijing to cease these sales. There was no information available to the United States or Israel that Iran had then supplied some of these missiles to Hezbollah, until its successful launching on July 14, 2006. Iran also had to train Hezbollah fighters on the proper use and maintenance of these weapons, since it is extremely unlikely (but cannot be ruled out) that members of Iran's Al Quds force (the faction of the Islamic Revolutionary Guards Corps that trains foreign forces) were present in Lebanon to fire and guide the missiles. Some of the rockets in Hezbollah's arsenal, particularly a 220-millimeter rocket used in a deadly attack on a railway site in Haifa, were built in Syria. Some of the Syrian-built rockets were filled with ball bearings, a method of destruction used in suicide bombings but not found before in warhead technology.

The CIA's greatest unstudied failure is the consistent exaggeration of Soviet intentions and capabilities toward the United States. U.S. politicians consistently painted the Soviet Bear as "ten-feet tall," and CIA analysts often supported these contentions with worst-case assessments. It is unlikely that a more measured and balanced assessment of the Soviet Union from the CIA would have guided various administrations toward a saner policy toward Moscow. The Nixon administration called a nuclear alert during the October War of 1973, even when the CIA and intelligence community had no corroborated evidence of heightened Soviet activity to justify such a risky step. Conversely, the mini-crisis over the so-called Soviet combat brigade in 1979 led to a major defeat for arms control and detente with the Kremlin simply due to a memory lapse in the CIA and NSA. The evidentiary record certainly did not support the aggressive military exercises of the Reagan administration in the 1980s that led to a "war scare" in Moscow. It would have required a combination of better intelligence and better policy to have reduced the length of the cold war and accelerated the pace of disarmament.

Following a period of underestimating the threat of terrorism toward the United States, the CIA is now exaggerating the problem. Despite the serious damage to al Qaeda in the U.S. use of force in Afghanistan in 2003, the CIA is still referring to that organization as the "greatest threat to the Homeland and U.S. interests abroad by a single terrorist organization." In doing so, the CIA is providing policy support to the Bush administration.[20] Congressional oversight committees need to demand open and closed sessions on our overall knowledge of al Qaeda and other nonstate terrorist organizations. Unfortunately, the chaos and uncertainly in Iraq, which was brought about by bad policy and bad intelligence, is being projected into a greater international threat against the United States. The CIA has argued that the "global jihadist movement . . . is spreading and adapting to counterterrorism efforts," but has offered no explanation of that assessment in terms of actual threats to the United States. Conversely, the CIA predicted that the loss of key terrorist figures, such as al-Zarqawi, would lead to "a less serious threat to U.S. interests," but the killing of al-Zarqawi led to increased mayhem in Iraq.[21]

The Iraq War has been a particular disaster for the reputation and credibility of the CIA. The official, bipartisan conclusion of the Senate Select Committee on Intelligence's review of prewar intelligence concluded that CIA's contribution to Secretary of State Powell's UN speech was "overstated, misleading, or incorrect." The assertions about chemical weapons were flat-wrong; the assertion about the nuclear program rested on a fabrication; the assertions about mobile biological laboratories rested on an alcoholic and liar who had never been debriefed by the CIA and was a brother of a top aide of Ahmed Chalabi, a known fabricator responsible for a series of phony assertions about Iraqi WMD. Senior managers at the CIA began to believe that the war with Iraq was inevitable and therefore decided to go along with it. The deputy chief of the CIA's Iraq task force told the Senate intelligence committee, "Let's keep in mind the fact that this war's going to happen, regardless of what Curveball said or didn't say, and that the powers that be probably aren't terribly interested in whether Curveball knows what he's talking about."[22] The chief of WINPAC, Alan Foley, told his senior managers, "if the president decides to go to war, it's our job to supply the intelligence to allow him to do so." Foley's comments took place only several days after Tenet assured President Bush that gathering intelligence support for a public case to go to war would be a "slam dunk."

Once the war started, CIA operatives in Iraq provided assessments to the U.S. military that were simply wrong. The CIA told the Pentagon the Iraqi military establishment would capitulate and entire Iraqi units might come over to the U.S. side, and Iraqi police could be counted on during the occupation process because of their professionalism.[23] CIA operatives dismissed the importance of the Fedayeen, and failed to locate the tons of arms cached in the cities and towns of southern Iraq. Agency operatives believed the Army and the Marines would get a strong welcome in the Shiite cities and towns in the south, where both U.S. and U.K. forces encountered extensive resistance. The military and the intelligence community believed that Baghdad was the "center of gravity" in Iraq and that the U.S. occupation there would enable a stabilization of the entire country. Of course, the entire Sunni triangle turned out to be the center of gravity and the Sunni-Shiite civil war led to an announced surge in U.S. forces in January 2007. Prior to the war, however, CIA warned of sectarian violence and even civil war, and provided an analysis of the British experience in Iraq in the 1920s that was a total failure due to chaos in Iraq.

The series of intelligence failures since the creation of the CIA points to the need for a professional effort to develop the means for more timely and accurate intelligence. There must be a system for challenging conventional wisdom, and there must be competitive forms of analysis. Devil's advocates and "red teams" that stress alternative means of interpretation offer opportunities to avoid the danger of group-think and to make sure that all sides of an issue have been given an hearing. Intelligence studies have determined that analysts are insufficiently rigorous in evaluating evidence that disproves their own analysis and much too accepting of evidence that corroborates their work. In recent years, the CIA has put a high premium on its accessibility to policymakers, and has downgraded the importance of the contrarians and the mavericks within the system that often offer important insights. Greater competition is needed within the system and greater access to outside expertise needs to be encouraged, particularly among demographers, socialists, and anthropologists who are not typically employed by the CIA in sufficient numbers. The high rate of failure on tactical intelligence issues points to the need for CIA self-criticism and greater outside review.

5

The Perils of Politicization

The CIA's mission to provide intelligence to policymakers renders the Agency vulnerable to political pressure, particularly when policies fail and policymakers are tempted to control the flow of intelligence. The CIA was created as an independent, nondepartmental agency precisely because its founders recognized the need for an intelligence service that was not part of a policy department and would, therefore, be less susceptible to manipulation in support of policy goals. Throughout the CIA's sixty-year history, there have been many efforts to slant analytical conclusions, skew estimates, and repress evidence that challenged a particular policy or point of view. As a result, the Agency must recognize the impact of politicization and introduce barriers to its practice. Unfortunately, it has largely ignored the problem.

CIA directors Helms, Schlesinger, Gates, and Tenet were guilty of politicizing intelligence, but no CIA director was as direct and vocal as Porter Goss in emphasizing that he would be tailoring intelligence on behalf of the White House. Two weeks after President George Bush's reelection in 2004, Goss sent an internal memorandum to all employees of the Agency telling them their job was to "support the administration and its policies in our work. As Agency employees, we do not identify with, support, or champion opposition to the administration or its policies."[1] Thirty years earlier, Schlesinger didn't put it in writing, but he assembled the Agency's Soviet experts and warned them, "this agency is going to stop screwing Richard Nixon." I was one of those Soviet analysts, and Schlesinger's language was actually stronger and more vulgar.

Schlesinger's objective was to rein in the CIA, which had produced analysis that challenged the Nixon administration on the war in Vietnam. It is not unusual for presidents to blame the inadequacies of intelligence when their policies and actions begin to fail. In 1995, former secretary of defense Mc-Namara wrote a memoir, *In Retrospect: The Tragedy and Lessons of Vietnam*, bemoaning the lack of reliable information on Vietnam for the crucial decisions that were made in the early 1960s. In fact, the CIA, the State Department's INR, and even the DIA produced outstanding intelligence on Vietnam that accurately anticipated the failure of military force in Vietnam. When Lt. Col. John Paul Vann came back to Washington in 1963 with his account of the corrupt South Vietnamese government, he was not permitted to brief the Joint Chiefs of Staff. Also in 1963, a State Department analyst on Vietnam, Louis G. Sarris, wrote a memorandum for Secretary of State Dean Rusk with a critical analysis of the military situation. Rusk forwarded the memorandum to McNamara.[2] The chairman of the Joint Chiefs, General Maxwell Taylor "hit the ceiling" over the INR report. McNamara warned Rusk not to issue "military appraisals without seeking the views of the Defense Department." Rusk agreed that the State Department would never again issue an "independent assessment of the overall military situation in Vietnam."

McNamara was responsible for politicizing intelligence in the early years of the Vietnam War, as well as for ordering a special staff to write a top secret *History of U.S. Decision Making in Vietnam, 1945–1968*, known as the *Pentagon Papers*. The annexes of the *Papers* reveal the highly accurate analysis of the CIA and INR on the course of the Vietnam War. This explains why national security advisor Kissinger called Daniel Ellsberg "the most dangerous man in America," who "must be stopped at all costs."[3] Ellsberg was responsible for the volume on the Kennedy administration and for releasing the overly classified *Pentagon Papers* to *The New York Times*. Nixon and Kissinger subsequently ordered a break-in at Ellsberg's psychiatrist's office to obtain information to smear and discredit those who exposed the lies on Vietnam.

The DoD ignored good intelligence analysis in order to defend a failed military strategy. The Pentagon echoed the Kennedy and Johnson administrations that the war against the Viet Cong was going quite well, although intelligence available to CIA strongly pointed to a far different and gloomier conclusion. McNamara arranged a corrupt quid pro quo; the Joint Chiefs of Staff endorsed the secretary's policies on the war in return for concessions on issues that had nothing to do with Vietnam. This pattern is being replicated in Iraq, with U.S. military commanders putting the best face possible on U.S. military actions, as Iraq falls into greater disarray. The most pessimistic analysis on Iraq is coming from CIA, particular from station chiefs in Baghdad who, like clandestine operative Tom Polgar in Saigon in the 1960s, are tracking the steady decline in U.S. fortunes and, in the process, putting their careers at risk. According to Tenet, the CIA's senior officer in Baghdad was dismissed as a "defeatist" for providing the first warnings in 2003 of the dangers of a growing Iraqi insurgency. Once again, the military is withholding its criticism of the war in return for larger defense budgets and increases in Army and Marine fighting forces.

As early as 1963, the intelligence community knew that the Vietnam War was slipping away. The Sarris memorandum was corroborated by intelligence assessments from the CIA that used statistical analysis supplied by the U.S. military mission in South Vietnam to demonstrate there was an "unfavorable shift in the military balance," a decline in Viet Cong casualties, weapons losses, and defections and an increase in Viet Cong military attacks. Nevertheless, in 1967, General William Westmoreland, the commander in Vietnam, told a joint session of Congress that there was great progress in the war; several months later, the Tet offensive, which was predicted by Sarris at the State Department and Bob Layton at CIA, took place. Sadly, it took the United States another seven years and tens of thousands of fatalities and casualties to withdraw.

The Tonkin Gulf Resolution, which gave the Johnson administration a military blank check to pursue victory in South Vietnam, was based on an intentional misreading of intelligence. Forty years after the Resolution legislated the use of force against North Vietnam, we learned senior officials at the National Security Agency (NSA) distorted critical intelligence the White House used to secure an overwhelmingly popular vote in the Congress to endorse the use of force. In 2001, the senior NSA historian, Robert J. Hanyok, found a pattern of translation mistakes that went uncorrected and altered intercept times, that indicated there had been deliberate skewing of key evidence.[4] Johnson had doubts there had actually been a second attack on U.S. ships and told Undersecretary of State George W. Ball, "Hell, those dumb, stupid sailors were just shooting at flying fish!" Thus, the escalation of a war that led to 58,226 American and more than 1 million Vietnamese deaths turned on intelligence that was doctored and then covered up. Ironically, NSA officials were moving in 2002 to declassify Hanyok's work, but the support for declassification lost momentum because of the controversy over the misuse of intelligence on Iraq.

In 1970, when the Nixon administration was planning the "incursion" into Cambodia, the CIA's Board of National Estimates concluded that an "American invasion of Cambodia would fail to deter North Vietnamese continuation of the war."[5] CIA director Helms refused to deliver this estimate to the White House, knowing the decision had already been made to invade Cambodia. He was one messenger who did not want to be shot. Helms also suppressed the accurate CIA analysis on the numbers of communist guerrillas and self-defense forces in South Vietnam, preferring to forward the politicized figures of the Pentagon that deliberately undercounted the enemy presence in Vietnam.

Helms was not willing to take on the Pentagon and national security advisor Walt Rostow at the White House.

The Politics of Team A Versus Team B

Following the withdrawl from Vietnam, President Gerald Ford removed the director of central intelligence, William Colby, and replaced him with a political appointee, George H. W. Bush. Ford, on the advice of his chief of staff, Dick Cheney, and Secretary of Defense Rumsfeld, then appointed a team of right-wing academics and former government officials, headed by Harvard Professor Richard Pipes, to draft their own intelligence estimates on Soviet military power. Whereas Colby refused to permit the Pipes' team to review CIA estimates, Bush was quick to permit the exercise to begin. Pipes and his team (Team B) had consistently labeled the Soviets an aggressive imperialistic power bent on world domination, and Team B estimates were drafted in order to reify Pipes' worldview. Team B predictably and falsely concluded that the Soviets rejected nuclear parity, were bent on fighting and winning a nuclear war, and were radically increasing their military spending. Other members of Team B, particularly Wolfowitz, deputy secretary of defense in the administration of George W. Bush, believed Moscow would use its nuclear advantage to wage conventional war in the Third World. Team B also applied worst-case reasoning to predict a series of Soviet weapons developments that never took place, including directed-energy weapons, mobile ABM systems, and anti-satellite capabilities. As a result, the CIA began to exaggerate its assessments of Soviet military spending and the capabilities of military technology, and it was a decade later before the CIA began to correct and lower these estimates. In the meantime, the Reagan administration used inflated estimates of Soviet military power to garner a trillion and a half dollars in defense spending in the 1980s against a Soviet Union that was in decline and a Soviet military threat that was greatly exaggerated.

The CIA's Tilt to the Right

The CIA learned no lessons from its Team A/Team B experience. Two decades later, it responded to another worst-case study that involved some of the same players from the early experience, particularly Rumsfeld. In 1998, Rumsfeld chaired the Commission to Assess the Ballistic Missile Threat to the United States, which warned that North Korea, Iran, and Iraq (soon to become the "axis of evil" in President Bush's State of the Union address in 2002) could deploy operational intercontinental ballistic missiles (ICBMs) with "little or no warning." A more balanced assessment of global ballistic missile arsenals over the past twenty years would reveal that the threat was confined, limited, and changing relatively slowly, but Rumsfeld wanted to justify a headlong rush to deploy a national missile defense. Just as NSC-68's exaggerated notions of the Soviet threat took on greater meaning because it was issued just before the start of the Korean War, the report of the Rumsfeld Commission received greater attention because it coincided with nuclear tests in India and Pakistan, Iran's test of its Shahab-3 medium-range ballistic missile, North Korea's test of its Taepodong-1 missile, the Cox Commission's exaggerated report of China's alleged thefts of U.S. nuclear secrets, and al Qaeda's attacks on two U.S. embassies on the Horn of Africa. The test of the Taepodong and the apparent willingness of North Korea and Pakistan to export their missile technology contributed to the notion that the United States could soon face the possibility of a rogue nation missile threat to the U.S. homeland.

As a result of considerable policy pressure, the intelligence community in 1998–1999 began to lower its standards for judging strategic threats, describing known missile programs as more immediate threats than did previous assessments. There had been no change in the intelligence on the subject of a missile threat and no actual threat in the capabilities of key foreign nations, but a very definite change in the evaluative criteria for examining the threat that accounted for nearly all of the differences between the 1999 NIE and previous estimates and assessments. The 1999 estimate concentrated almost exclusively on the possible threat from North Korea, Iran, and Iraq and emphasized who "could" test a long-range missile over the next five to ten years, instead of when a country "would" deploy a long-range missile. This change in syntax marked a shift to worst-case assumptions, independent of any significant political or military change.[6] Nearly ten years later, there are still no long-range missiles in the inventories of North Korea, Iran, and Iraq.

The 1999 estimate also shifted standards from when a country would *deploy* a long-range missile to when a country would *test* the missile, which took advantage of the five-year difference between first test and likely deployment. The CIA also raised the possibility of "shorter flight test programs—perhaps only one test" in order to raise the possibility of an earlier availability of the missile, without referring to the reduced reliability of such a limited testing program. The Indian experience with the Agni missile is telling, since the Agni program that began in the mid-1980s was flight-tested in 1994 and 1999 and has yet to enter production, despite Indian declarations to deploy and substantial financial and scientific resources devoted to the program, and CIA warnings of imminent deployment.

Finally, the 1999 estimate raised the threat to any part of the fifty states of the United States instead of the usual reference to the continental United States, which marks a shift in range of approximately several thousand kilometers, the distance between Seattle and the western-most tip of the Aleutian Island chain in Alaska. Therefore, the CIA could assert that an intermediate-range missile, such as the Taepodong-1, was threatening as an intercontinental-range missile, although it could not reach any part of the continental United States with a large payload. Conservatives on the Hill lambasted the CIA for appearing to be less concerned with citizens of Alaska and Hawaii, but in fact a North Korean threat to the sparsely inhabited areas of those two states would make little strategic sense.

These three syntactical changes account for virtually all the differences between the 1999 NIE and previous estimates on this subject. Therefore, the 1999 estimate (like the October 2002 estimate on Iraqi weapons of mass destruction in comparison with earlier estimates) did not represent some new, dramatic development in the strategic threat, but a lowering of the standards for judging the threat and the intelligence on the threat. In fact, there had been no significant technological leap forward in Third World missile systems or Iraqi WMD.

Both the 1999 estimate and the 2002 estimate contributed to an exaggerated sense of the strategic threat, giving a distorted view of the military balance, and failing to note that in both cases the threat had diminished. With respect to the missile threat, the number of intercontinental ballistic missiles with ranges over 5,500 kilometers had decreased dramatically since the height of the cold war, from 9,540 Soviet nuclear warheads on 2,318 long-range missiles in the 1980s to fewer than 5,200 Soviet warheads on 1,100 missiles in 2000, a decrease of more than 50 percent in the number of missiles capable of striking the United States. The number of intermediate-range ballistic missiles (with ranges of 3,000 to 5,500 kilometers) decreased dramatically with 1,846 Soviet weapons in this category in 1987, and virtually none after the signing of the Intermediate Nuclear Forces Treaty (INF) in that year. Finally, only six nations have medium-range missiles with a 1,000- to 3,000-kilometer range (Israel, Iran, India, Pakistan, North Korea, and Saudi Arabia), but these weapons do not threaten the United States. India, Iran, North Korea, and Pakistan are trying to extend the range of the missile force. Thus, there is a decreasing threat from long-range missiles, a limited capability to launch medium-range missiles, and only a widespread capability to launch short-range missiles, mostly highly inaccurate Scuds, that do not threaten the United States.

The only intelligence department to consistently challenge the politicized estimates of the CIA on strategic issues has been the State Department's Bureau of Intelligence and Research (INR). INR dissented from the conclusions of the 1999 estimate, arguing that the "prominence given to countries that 'could' develop strategic missiles gives more credence than is warranted to developments that may prove implausible." Over the years, INR's dissents from key NIEs on significant strategic issues involving Soviet political and military policy, Soviet strategic capabilities, Iraqi WMD, and ballistic missile threats have proved far more accurate than CIA assessments and military intelligence. The fact that INR is an intelligence bureau inside a policy department gives the lie to the conventional wisdom that the most objective and balanced intelligence emanates from outside the policy community. Over the years, INR has developed a stronger reputation for objective intelligence than any other intelligence agency, including the CIA. INR's small size and limited resources also points to a lesson for intelligence reorganization for its analysts, having a much larger piece of the intelligence pie than its counterparts at the CIA, develop a more sophisticated strategic view.

CASEY AND GATES "COOK THE BOOKS"

Bill Casey and Bob Gates guided the first institutionalized "cooking of the books" at the CIA in the 1980s, with a particular emphasis on tailoring intelligence dealing with the Soviet Union, Central America, and Southwest Asia. After he left the CIA in 1993, Gates admitted that he became accustomed to Casey fixing intelligence to policy on many regional issues. In fact, Casey's very first NIE as CIA director, dealing with the Soviet Union and international terrorism, became an exercise in politicization. Casey was convinced that a Soviet conspiracy was behind global terrorism. Casey and Gates pushed this line in order to justify more U.S. covert action in the Third World. In 1985, they ordered an intelligence assessment of a supposed Soviet plot against the Pope, hoping to produce a document that would undermine Secretary of State Shultz's efforts to improve relations with Moscow. The CIA also produced an NIE in 1985 that was designed to produce an intelligence rationale for arms sales to Iran, with NIO Graham Fuller collaborating with the NSC.

Casey and Gates were conducting an aggressive policy in Central America that included covert action in Nicaragua (Iran-Contra) and a covert role for the CIA in the civil war in El Salvador that found the United States supporting the brutality of the Salvadoran government. The U.S. ambassador in El Salvador, Robert E. White, was so unhappy with the role of the CIA that he wanted to replace the CIA chief in San Salvador. White accused him with filing politicized reports to justify continued military support for the government, arguing that Casey "put intelligence at the service of policy and provided justifications for ever-deeper involvement."[7] White also took issue with a State Department white paper, drafted by CIA analysts, falsely picturing a "flood of arms" from such Soviet allies as Vietnam, Ethiopia, and Bulgaria through Nicaragua to El Salvador. CIA analysts were pressured to make their assessments match the reports of the CIA station chief in El Salvador. Secretary of State Alexander Haig eventually fired White because of his contrarian views, and several analysts were forced out of the CIA's Central American branch because of their opposition to politicization.

Casey and national security advisor William Clark locked horns with Secretary of State Shultz, and his assistant secretaries of state for Latin America, Thomas O. Enders and Langhorne A. Motley, over policy toward Central America. Casey wanted covert action against Nicaragua, and Shultz campaigned for a diplomatic strategy to stabilize Central America. Nicaragua also provided an excellent example of Gates' efforts to truckle to the hard-line views of Casey on Central America. In a memorandum to the CIA director in December 1984, Gates referred to Nicaragua as a "second Cuba in Central America" and called for American air strikes on the "Nicaraguan military build-up."[8] Gates reminded Casey that U.S. "attempts to reach an accommodation with Castro" and "our Vietnam strategy of half-measures" ended in negotiations, which became a "cover for consolidation of communist control." Gates wrote a series of these memoranda to Casey to establish his hard-line bona fides and ingratiate himself with the CIA director.

In 1985, the Reagan administration charged the Soviets with trying to introduce MiG-29s into Nicaragua to provide alternative basing to Soviet facilities in Cuba. Secretary Shultz was particularly concerned with such a step, because of its consequences for renewing détente and reopening arms control talks; he warned his Soviet counterpart, Eduard Shevardnadze, against such a step. In the Office of Soviet Analysis, I commissioned an intelligence assessment to present the case for and against delivery of the MiGs. The paper explained the structure and nature of the debate (including the evidence and lines of argument on both sides), and offered the judgment that the Soviets would not deliver the MiGs—a conclusion that did not coincide with Casey's views. The paper was rejected by Gates because, he stated, we should not "go out on a limb" on this issue. The paper was never published, and it became one of many that failed to reach the policymakers. If the CIA cannot go out on a limb, there is no purpose for intelligence analysis as an instrument of support for policymakers. In any event, no MIGs were nitroduced to Nicaragua.

Gates also blocked papers in 1985–1986 that analyzed signs of a Soviet withdrawal from Afghanistan, and a general retreat from the Third World. Casey and Gates were totally committed to making the case for a Soviet presence in Afghanistan in order to justify increases in U.S. spending on defense and intelligence, as well as greater covert action in Southwest Asia. As a result, they blocked intelligence assessments that correctly predicted Gorbachev's desire to withdraw from Afghanistan and elsewhere. Covert action against such Soviet-supported regimes as Afghanistan, Nicaragua, Angola, Ethiopia, and Cambodia required Gates' censoring of intelligence products anticipating Moscow's reduced interest and activity in these places.

Casey's covert actions undercut U.S. policy in southern Africa, particularly Washington's efforts to negotiate a broad settlement in the region. Casey maneuvered against the assistant secretary of state for Africa, Chester Crocker, who favored the use of diplomacy to stabilize southern Africa. Crocker ended up in the middle of a feud between Shultz, who favored the role of diplomacy in bringing about Angolan national reconciliation, and Casey, who became an indirect party in the Angolan civil war in order to block any Soviet and Cuban efforts to establish a presence in southern Africa. Casey, NSC advisor John Poindexter, and White House communications director Pat Buchanan were close to the South African lobby, and determined to stop the diplomatic efforts of Shultz and Crocker. Crocker's memoirs documented the efforts of Casey to slant CIA intelligence on policy-sensitive subjects regarding Africa.[9] Crocker argued the State Department could never anticipate CIA's analytic objectivity because of Casey's preferred policies in Angola and Mozambique.

State Department policy called for weaning the government of Mozambique from its Marxist origins, but Casey exaggerated the strength of the Renamo insurgency in Mozambique in order to discourage those officials hoping to find a diplomatic solution. He undercut Crocker's diplomatic efforts in order to enhance the efforts of the neoconservatives in the Reagan administration to support the rebels. In his memoirs, Crocker recorded the efforts of the CIA to stymie the viability of a diplomatic approach to solving both the Angolan and Mozambiquan crises, and traced the impact of CIA covert action on the intelligence analysis of the Agency.[10] Casey and Gates then managed a Special NIE with a political purpose, undermining the argument for pressing the South African government to pursue negotiations with the African National Council. The Reagan White House permitted the CIA and the Defense Department to sabotage virtually every aspect of the State Department's efforts to negotiate a successful conclusion to the fighting in southern Africa. When Shultz tangled with Weinberger or Casey, the Reagan White House always sided with the conservative opposition to Shultz.

Politicization was a major reason for CIA's failure to track the decline and demise of the Soviet Union. In the 1970s and early 1980s, SOVA analysts "reported Soviet military spending growing at the enormous rate of 4 to 5 percent a year."[11] But, in 1983, these analysts realized they had significantly exaggerated the growth rate and that a growth rate of 1 percent was closer to the mark. Gates would not permit the paper with the revised growth rates to be published, but warned Weinberger, who "went nuts," according to two former CIA analysts. Two years later, in 1985, Gates finally permitted the paper to be circulated, but he refused to publish a paper arguing that the "Soviets had made a deliberate decision to curtail their spending on strategic forces in the mid-seventies, when they attained strategic parity with the United States."[12] Even in 1987, when analysts were arguing that Gorbachev's failure to modernize Soviet industry would ultimately lead to lower defense spending, Gates ordered his economists to forward an assessment to Weinberger on increased Soviet economic strength.[13]

Presumably, it would have been more difficult for President Reagan to get his unprecedented peacetime increases in the U.S. defense budget from 1981 to 1986 if the CIA had published accurate assessments of the troubled Soviet economy and the backward aspects of the Soviet military. The late Senator Daniel Patrick Moynihan (D-New York) asked in 1990, "Would we have spent as much on our military during the 1980s if we had believed that the Soviet defense burden simply was not sustainable? I think not, and if I am correct, then the issue has been a momentous one for the state of the American economy."[14]

After Gates left the CIA in 1989 to move to the NSC, the CIA immediately changed its analytical line on the Soviets and warned policymakers about the signs of Soviet weakness. The incoming Bush administration, led by such conservatives as NSC advisor Brent Scowcroft and Secretary of Defense Cheney, were opposed to the Reagan arms control policies and committed to an image of a powerful Soviet Union. They rebuffed CIA's new line of analysis at every opportunity. Cheney, who had been critical of the Agency's Soviet analysis since joining the Ford administration in 1975, complained that the CIA was making it difficult for the Pentagon to generate congressional support for the defense budget. He particularly objected to CIA director Webster's testimony to the House Armed Services Committee in 1990 that the "collapse of Soviet and Warsaw Pact military power was irreversible," which made the Pentagon furious.[15] Eventually, Webster was forced to resign, and Gates was named CIA director with a mandate to return to the tough anti-Soviet line. Ironically, the Soviet Union had virtually collapsed by the time Gates moved through a rough confirmation process into his executive suite in CIA headquarters.

Despite the signs of regional tensions that were being reported in the Soviet press in the 1980s, it was not until the spring of 1991 that the CIA's *National Intelligence Daily*, which was delivered to hundreds of national security officials at home and abroad, began to run a daily situation report on the internal situation in the USSR, with particular attention begin given to the non-Russian Republics. A few months later, Foreign Broadcast Information Service (FBIS) also began to issue a new series of translations of unclassified materials from the fifteen Soviet republics. Actually, the CIA was running far behind the Pentagon and the State Department on the nationalities issues. The

Pentagon began to hire regional specialists in 1989 to track the signs of tension in the Soviet Union, and the State Department had a strong specialist on Soviet nationalities, Paul Goble, who single-handedly tracked the ethnic and nationality tensions in the former Soviet Union and outperformed the CIA. The chairman of the Joint Chiefs of Staff, General Powell, among others, began to realize that using the Soviet rationale to justify the defense budget would probably soon be losing resonance on Capitol Hill. He was far ahead of both Secretary of Defense Cheney and Secretary of State Baker, who forced Goble to resign from the State Department.

The Reagan doctrine had no stronger supporters than Casey and Gates. Even after Gorbachev's initial speech announcing the withdrawal of all Soviet forces from Afghanistan, Gates and his NIO for the Soviet Union, Fritz Ermarth, produced an NIE declaring that Moscow would not withdraw. Gates and Ermarth ignored protests from the State Department's INR, as well as the CIA's political analysts. They put their money where their mouths were and lost bets to several high-level State Department officials on the issue of whether there would be withdrawal in the near term.[16] Casey had sponsored a covert investment of $2 billion in Afghanistan from 1981–1986, and he was not going to tolerate intelligence analysis that claimed the Soviets had become war weary. He wanted intelligence that supported a continued U.S. covert involvement in the Third World, and Gates and Ermarth obliged.

While Gates was suppressing a series of reports that pointed to Soviet withdrawal from the Third World, he was making his own series of speeches, as late as 1988, claiming incorrectly that the Soviet Union was becoming a stronger adversary. The CIA deputy director warned the United States would "face in the 1990s and beyond, a militarily powerful, domestically more vital, and politically more adroit Soviet Union whose aggressive objectives abroad and essential totalitarianism at home remains largely unchanged."[17] When Gates continued to make these charges as deputy national security advisor in 1989, Secretary of State Baker intervened with Gates' boss, General Scowcroft, to exercise firmer control over the substance of Gates' remarks. Gates, like his patron Casey, was trying to undermine secretaries of state Shultz and Baker, who were engaged in diplomatic negotiations with Soviet foreign minister Shevardnadze.

Suppressing Sensitive Intelligence on Nuclear Proliferation

One of the costliest suppressions of intelligence evidence in the 1980s involved sensitive details on Pakistan's nuclear program. The Reagan administration wanted to turn a blind eye to this program because the Pressler Amendment in the summer of 1985 had stipulated that continued U.S. military assistance to

Pakistan would stop if there were evidence of Pakistani possession of a nuclear explosive device. Since Pakistan was the conduit for record amounts of covert assistance to the Afghan rebels, the Reagan administration did not want anything to complicate bilateral relations with Islamabad. The Symington Amendment in 1961, moreover, demanded that Washington terminate military assistance to any nation developing a nuclear weapons capability. This legislation actually had forced the Carter administration to stop military assistance in early 1979, when the U.S. intelligence community discovered Pakistan was operating a clandestine uranium enrichment facility at Kahuta. During the campaign against Carter in 1980, Reagan asserted that "nuclear nonproliferation is none of our business," which foreshadowed the shift to a closer military relationship with Pakistan that abandoned nonproliferation. The strategic retreat from nuclear nonproliferation was completed in the Bush administration with the abrogation of the ABM Treaty, the building of a national missile defense, and the cooperative nuclear arrangement with India, a nonmember of the nonproliferation regime.

In 1984, there were reports that Pakistan was trying to circumvent U.S. export controls to purchase krytron switches to trigger a nuclear device, and a leading Pakistani nuclear scientist, A. Q. Khan, began bragging in public about the achievement of a nuclear weapons capability. In the previous year, U.S. intelligence discovered China was providing the Pakistanis with a design for solid-core nuclear weapons, and Pakistan was having success in uranium enrichment, which Khan confirmed in 1984 when he announced Pakistan crossed the nuclear threshold. In 1986, Deputy Director Gates issued an ultimatum there would be no reporting on Pakistani nuclear activities in the *National Intelligence Daily* that was sent to the Senate and House intelligence committees. Sensitive materials presumably made their way into the President's Daily Brief, which is not seen by the intelligence committees and is distributed to only a half dozen high-ranking principles.

Shultz should have complained about the politicization of intelligence on Pakistan's nuclear program, but he refused to do so because he favored the continued use of Pakistan as a conduit for military assistance to the Afghan rebels. He was a stronger supporter of the transfer of military weapons, including Stinger missiles, than Secretary of Defense Weinberger and CIA director Casey, who actually opposed the transfer of Stinger missiles. It was not known at the time, but the pressure for delivering Stingers to the rebels came from the State Department, particularly the chief of INR, Morton Abramowitz, and one of his senior deputies, Curtis W. Kammen. Shultz supported the Reagan administration's policy of providing military assistance to Pakistan even though the Pakistanis were not "clean" with regard to its nuclear activities throughout the 1980s. As a regular reader of the PDB, Shultz was witting of Pakistan's covert nuclear activities.

By 1984, several hundreds of millions of dollars in military aid, including surface-to-air Stinger missiles, were being covertly transferred to the Afghan rebels through the Pakistani conduit. When there were intelligence leaks in major American newspapers on the Pakistani nuclear program, Casey demanded all government officials, including those in the Cabinet, submit to a lie detector test to find the source of the leaks. When Shultz threatened to resign on December 19, 1985, if the White House proceeded with such an executive order, Reagan backed down.[18] Twenty years later, CIA director Goss orchestrated an extensive lie detector program at the CIA to learn the source of the leaks to Dana Priest of the *Washington Post* and James Risen of *The New York Times* on CIA "secret prisons" and NSA "warrantless eavesdropping" on American citizens, respectively.[19] Leak investigations are rarely successful, and these were no exception.

The CIA cooperated with the Reagan administration and made sure that no finished intelligence on Pakistani nuclear activities got beyond the six or seven readers of the PDB. The annual certification of Pakistan had become a farce. In 1993, the former deputy director of the CIA, Richard Kerr, told Seymour Hersh "there is no question that we had an intelligence basis from 1987 on" to deny military aid to Pakistan.[20] Since the Pakistani leaders were well aware of Washington's cover-up of their secret nuclear program, they presumably believed there would be no reprisals for providing nuclear assistance to other countries. As for Pakistan's nuclear program, even after the Soviet withdrawal from Afghanistan in February 1989, President George H. W. Bush gave another waiver to Pakistan to allow the sale of sixty additional F-16 fighter jets to Pakistan. In view of the U.S. dependence on Pakistani support against al Qaeda and the Taliban, it is possible that the CIA is once again suppressing intelligence on Pakistan nuclear activities.

Two CIA analysts, Richard Barlow and Peter Dixon, helped to uncover Pakistan's efforts to acquire nuclear weapons but, when they tried to expose the attempts to mislead the Congress on this issue, their security clearances were revoked and their careers were ruined. Both Barlow and Dixon tracked the work of A. Q. Khan to produce nuclear weapons in Pakistan and to provide nuclear technology to Third World states. Barlow received the CIA's Exceptional Analyst Award in 1988, and became the first intelligence officer in the office of the secretary of defense the following year. He was fired when he wrote a series of memoranda in 1989 that demonstrated the sale of F-16 fighter jets to Pakistan would violate the Pressler Amendment. A study of the Government Accountability Office in 1997 vindicated Barlow, who had his security clearances restored but received no job offers from the intelligence community and no federal pension.

In addition to Pakistan, there were other nuclear-related issues that led to politicization of intelligence. Whenever an assessment was produced that discussed Moscow's interest in preserving and strengthening the Nonproliferation Treaty, Deputy Director of Intelligence Gates or his directors for the Office of Global Intelligence, first James Lynch and then David Cohen, blocked the draft in order to maintain the fiction that the Soviet Union had no interest in the NPT and would do anything to expand strategic holdings in the Third World. Lynch was awarded with a high-ranking position as director of the Office of Security for which he was not qualified, probably contributing to the long delay in arresting Aldrich Ames, the long-time spy for the Soviet Union. Cohen was made the director of operations, although he had no background in operational matters, and his appointment led to bitterness and even resignations from the directorate. Cohen is now the deputy director for intelligence in the New York City Police Department, establishing counterintelligence units that monitor legitimate antiwar and antinuclear activities not only in New York City, but throughout the United States and even in England.

Commissioning Reports to Take the Preferred Line

Gates often created his own line of analysis on sensitive subjects when he disagreed with the consensus within his intelligence directorate. In order to boost support for President Reagan's Strategic Defense Initiative, Gates gave speeches that distorted the intelligence record on Soviet strategic policy in order to create the impression of a major Soviet strategic defense effort. In a speech in San Francisco in November 1986, Gates said that the CIA estimated the Soviet Union had spent $150 billion on its own SDI over the past decade, but he omitted the fact that most of this spending was on air defense and not antimissile or strategic defense. He falsely claimed Soviet activities in this field were "more significant and more ominous than any one previously considered," and suggested the Soviet Union "may be preparing" an ABM defense of its national territory with laser weapons. There was no intelligence to support the notion of a Soviet ABM with laser weapons, but Gates' statement was used by the Heritage Foundation to release a report calling for the speedy deployment of sophisticated ground-based interceptor missiles at Grand Forks, North Dakota.

Intelligence analysts knew the Soviets had limited their missile defense to the Moscow area and had no intention of breaking the ABM Treaty of 1972 that was so important to the Kremlin. But journalists, including some who should have known better, reported Gates' remarks at face value.[21] Gates' distorted the intelligence record in order to conduct a campaign of policy advocacy among influential American political organizations, which was disturbing to CIA analysts. CIA director Tenet used a similar technique in 2002, when he sent an unclassified letter to the chairman of the Senate intelligence committee, Bob Graham (D-Florida) claiming there was "reporting . . . that Iraq has provided training to al Qaeda members" in chemical and biological weapons and the manufacturing of conventional bombs.[22] Once again, DI analysts were vexed, but did nothing. Their ability to report objectively on this controversial issue had been compromised by the political actions of the CIA director, but there is no record of any attempt to inform the Inspector General of the CIA or the Congressional oversight committees.

The worst example of commissioning an intelligence estimate to support operational policy took place in 1985, when the NIO for the Middle East, former DO officer Graham Fuller, wrote a flawed estimate on Iran. Fuller's NIE became the intelligence product justifying the policy of Iran-Contra. There were many officers in the DDI who disagreed with the estimate's conclusions that Iran was reducing its support for international terrorism, that the Soviet Union was on the verge of gaining a foothold in Iran, and that there were moderates in Iran who wanted to open a dialogue with the United States. But Gates provided them no channel to express their opposition to the final product. Meanwhile, Fuller had been briefing both DDI Gates and relevant NSC officers, particularly Howard Teicher, with the progress of the draft estimate, and had lined up their substantive and bureaucratic support. Gates picked Fuller to draft an estimate that would provide intelligence support to the illegal sale of weapons to Iran, just as Gates picked the drafters of the Papal Plot assessment that was done *in camera*. This is a process that I referred to as "judge-shopping in the courthouse" in my testimony to the Senate intelligence committee in October 1991.

Casey and Gates wanted an estimate to demonstrate there was reason to sell military arms to Tehran, which was central to the Iran-Contra covert action. In fact, there was no evidence that Iran was modifying its position and sufficient evidence to demonstrate that Iran, which was involved in the attacks on the U.S. embassy and the Marine barracks in Lebanon in 1983, was still plotting terrorism. Iran's support for terrorism had been central to all U.S. policy decisions toward Iran. Casey also created the false impression with President Reagan that Iran was losing its war with Iraq, although intelligence demonstrated unambiguously that Iran had the upper hand.

The shift in the analytical line toward Iran took place in November 1985, when the DI suddenly began to report that Iran's support for terrorism had "dropped off substantially" in 1985.[23] Previously the DI had reported no change in Iranian activity and, just as the line changed in November 1985, it mysteriously returned to the conventional wisdom in May 1986 after HAWK surface-to-air missiles were delivered to Iran in November 1985. A senior CIA clandestine operative, Clair George, commented that the analytical de- parture "was an example of a desperate attempt to try to sort of prove some- thing was happening to make the policy look good, but it wasn't happen- ing."[24] In late November 1987, Gates claimed publicly that "no CIA publication" had asserted that Iranian support for terrorism was waning, which was of course false. He repeated this canard in his confirmation hear- ings for the position of CIA director in 1991.

In fact, the CIA falsely claimed an Iranian reduction of support for terror- ism in three different publications on three occasions: a *Near East and South Asia Review* article on November 22, 1985; a *Terrorism Review* article on Jan- uary 13, 1986; and an Intelligence Assessment on May 15, 1986, which stated that Iran had become more pragmatic on the issue of using terrorism as a tac- tic. In the *Washington Post* on November 29, 1987, Gates asserted, "No ana- lytical expert in the CIA believed in 1985 that Iran was losing the war, and only one or two believed Iranian support for terrorism was waning. And no CIA publication asserted these things."[25] The CIA's in-house journal, *Studies in Intelligence*, published Gates' false assertions, as did the journal *Foreign Affairs*. Gates repeated his false statements during the defense of his confir- mation before the SSCI in September 1991.

Shultz knew that Casey and Gates were spinning the intelligence analysis on Iran, particularly on the issue of whether Iran had reduced its support for terrorism. Shultz knew from his own intelligence analysts that CIA assess- ments of Iran had been politicized, and pointed to a "structural flaw in that the intelligence-gathering and assessment function had been joined together with the operational function." The secretary of state clearly understood the politicization process at CIA, where Casey fused the analysts and operations officers in order to shift and toughen the analysis. In forming the Counterter- rorism Center in 1986, Casey for the first time in the Agency's history fused two major DI and DO components that were designed to be separate. In ad- dition to manipulating intelligence and operations at the directorate level, Casey and Gates maneuvered the preparation of NIEs in order to tilt toward policy lines they favored.

The descriptions of the efforts of Casey and Gates were brought to the at- tention of the Congressional committees investigating Iran-Contra in 1987, as part of their efforts to study the politicization of intelligence on Iran and Cen- tral America. The report of the Tower Commission in February 1987 con- cluded there was undue pressure on the CIA from the White House, but did not accuse the White House or the CIA of politicizing intelligence, which is more difficult to prove. Shultz told the Iran-Contra committees in July 1987 that he was prepared to resign his post because of the politicization of intelligence, and told President Reagan in August 1987 that he had become "uneasy with intelligence."[26] The deputy director of INR, Frank McNeil, also charged that the Reagan administration had put pressure on intelligence analysts about their views. The debate over politicization became so intense within the Reagan administration that Casey's successor, William Webster, said that he was determined to end any doubts about the reliability of analysis and would make sure that divergent points of view were disclosed in all intelligence products.

The battle over Iran-Contra was also waged at the State Department, where McNeil challenged assistant secretary for Latin America, Elliott Abrams, over support for the Contras. McNeil resigned from the State Department; Abrams pleaded guilty to two misdemeanor counts of withholding information on the Contras to Congress. The most unsavory aspect of Abrams' role in the early 1980s found him testifying to Congress (along with Assistant Secretary of State Thomas Enders) that the descriptions of the El Mozote massacre in El Salvador were false or at least wildly exaggerated.[27] President Bush pardoned Abrams on Christmas Eve 1992, along with several CIA officers, who were part of Iran-Contra and the cover-up. (Abrams is back in the White House as the national security advisor for the Middle East, where he is one of the strongest supporters of the war in Iraq and a critic of the Bush administration's diplomatic negotiations with North Korea.)

CIA involvement in covert action led directly to pressure on analysts to tailor their conclusions to support operational policies. Casey and Gates pressed analysts to downplay the increased evidence of Iraqi use of lethal weapons against innocent civilians in the 1980s in order not to compromise CIA covert actions supporting U.S. military assistance to Saddam Hussein. This activity was largely unknown during the 1991 confirmation hearings for Gates, but, in 1995, former NSC adviser Teicher filed a sworn affidavit linking Gates to the illegal sale of weapons to Iraq during the 1980s war with Iran. According to Teicher, both Casey and Gates were behind the effort to sell cluster bombs and other munitions to Iraq. Teicher's affidavit corroborated earlier testimony in the 1980s linking Gates to the weapons sale, but, at that time, Gates was protected by George Tenet, then staff director of the Senate intelligence committee.

Repressing Reports that Do Not Support the Preferred Line

During the Vietnam War, CIA directors McCone and Helms suppressed intelligence reporting that did not agree with the policies of the Kennedy and Johnson administration. In 1963, McCone sided with the Kennedy administration on the issue of Vietnam policy and largely ignored his professional analysts.

Several years later, Helms had no stomach for a battle with the Pentagon over order of battle issues, particularly the numbers of Viet Cong, and censored the work of the Agency's senior analyst on the subject, Sam Adams. Thus, Helms sided with the Military Assistance Command, Vietnam (MACV) and DIA, who were wrong. Helms' senior analyst on Vietnam, George Carver, also ignored the warnings from the field in Saigon that would have provided premonitory intelligence on the Tet offensive in January 1968, because he did not want to be the bearer of bad news to an optimistic Johnson administration in an election year.

The Vietnam experience clearly demonstrated that CIA managers and senior analysts who were close to administration policymakers were more likely to tell the policymakers what they wanted to hear. Conversely, the further removed the analysts from the policy community, the more likely they were to tell it like it was. This experience was demonstrated again in the run-up to the Iraq War, with senior officials, such as Paul Pillar and Alan Foley, providing the Bush administration with a case for going to war, and failing to make sure their intelligence analysis reflected the integrity and objectivity of the intelligence process. Pillar and Foley forgot that their main mission was to "tell truth to power" and not to corroborate the opinions of the policy community's principals.

Altering or Streamlining the Intelligence Structure to Control the Finished Product

While serving as deputy director for intelligence from 1982 to 1986, Gates wrote the manual for manipulating and centralizing the intelligence process to get the desired intelligence product. Since its creation in 1947, the CIA had maintained a competitive analytic process, permitting independent offices to pursue competitive analysis and alternative methodologies. In this way, there would be constant debate over substantive issues, creating the best opportunity for challenging assumptions and creating a balanced product. But Gates changed this in 1982, when he became the DDI. He made himself the final reviewer of all intelligence products before they were delivered to the CIA director. As both DDI and chairman of the NIC, he accumulated unprecedented control over finished intelligence. He was the final reviewer of the PDB; he also controlled the agenda for NIEs and appointed NIOs. As DDI, he supervised most of the estimate drafters and had the power to prevent CIA dissents to an estimate, which he did on numerous occasions.

Serving in these capacities, Gates placed loyalists in management positions in both the DI and the NIC; he loosened standards to permit publication of desirable analysis and "tightened" standards to prevent publication of undesirable analysis. As there was no other outlet for the papers he rejected, they were effectively killed. Finally, Gates required that no drafts of intelligence products could be sent to other intelligence agencies for review or comment until he had seen them. As Robert Parry noted in his book *Secrecy and Privilege: Rise of the Bush Dynasty from Watergate to Iraq*, Casey and Gates changed the entire culture of the DI, introducing a successful corporate-style takeover of the CIA's finished intelligence. Their campaign was modeled after the novel *Wall Street*, with Casey serving as the corporate raider, Gordon Gecko, and Gates serving as his protégé, Bud Fox.[28]

A senior CIA clandestine officer, the late John Horton, resigned because of Casey's efforts to get Horton, the NIO for Latin America, to support the Reagan administration's policies. Horton had a distinguished career in the DO, had been station chief in Mexico, and retired with the CIA's Distinguished Intelligence Medal. He was called out of retirement to become the NIO for Central and Latin America. But Casey's efforts to get Horton to produce an NIE describing Mexico on the brink of revolution led to major battles between the two. After fighting the good fight, Horton decided to quit the Agency. Unfortunately, resignations are rare in these circumstances, and the congressional oversight committees rarely display any interest in those who resign on matters of principle. Just as it is easy for an administration to manipulate the media in order to marginalize the efforts of critics and whistle-blowers, it was easy for Casey and Gates to deputize another senior analyst, Brian Lytell, to draft the estimate they were seeking. Lytell was a typical example of "judge-shopping in the courthouse," as he was carefully selected as a "hired pen" for the task Horton refused.

When the CIA failed to produce all the intelligence Cheney and Rumsfeld demanded to justify the use of force against Iraq, they created the Office of Special Plans in the Pentagon to distribute analysis CIA opposed. As director of central intelligence, Tenet should have opposed the creation of OSP outside the intelligence community and taken the fight to the White House or the congressional oversight committees. Tenet lacked the energy or, more likely, the courage to do so. In fact, Tenet himself became part of the problem and not part of the solution when he overruled his own analysts and sent a letter to the chairman of the Senate intelligence committee, falsely claiming Iraq provided training to al Qaeda members in the use of chemical and biological weapons.[29] It is extremely difficult for CIA analysts to prepare objective and balanced intelligence on a subject when the CIA director himself has gone on record distorting the intelligence record and, in the case of the Tenet letter, creating his own intelligence.

Manipulating the Analytic Process by Changing Either Personnel or Procedures

It is particularly interesting to trace the careers of the individual analysts who were rewarded by Gates during the period of politicization of intelligence in the 1980s and then reappeared in prominent roles nearly twenty years later in the run-up to the Iraq War. During the Gates era, the careers of McLaughlin, Pillar, and Foley moved forward; all three were involved in the politicization of intelligence in the run-up to the Iraq War. Conversely, in the 1980s, the senior managers and analysts who were accurate in tracking the decline of the Soviet Union were driven from their posts. Douglas Garthoff, James Noren, and this author lost their positions as managers of intelligence on the Soviet Union; experienced analysts, such as Carolyn Ekedahl, Peter Clement, Paul Cheek, and Gene Wicklund, took more than sixty years of experience on the Soviet target to other areas in the DI.

Encouraging the Publication of Reports that Take the Preferred Line

The worst example of an assessment to support a policy position with no credible intelligence reporting took place in 1985, when the CIA director ordered a paper to make the case for Soviet complicity in the attempt on the life of Pope John Paul II in 1981. Between 1981 and 1985, there were numerous credible reports that made it clear the Soviets had nothing to do with the assassination attempt and had even warned their Eastern European colleagues to avoid contacts with nonstate terrorist organizations. Virtually all analysts who worked on the problem of the Papal Plot found no credible evidence to support such a hypothesis, and even DDI Gates told congressional intelligence committees in 1984 there was no evidence of Soviet involvement. But in 1985, a clandestine report from a Bulgarian source operating with third-hand information and no contact with the Soviet or Bulgarian KGB referred to Soviet complicity. For Casey and Gates, but only Casey and Gates, this was the "smoking gun." Given the nature and plethora of intelligence reporting, it is always possible to find some report that makes a needed argument at a particular time.

Casey's portrait at CIA headquarters is labeled facetiously "Great White Case Officer," and his management of the specious intelligence assessment on the Papal Plot displayed all the manipulative skills of a case officer in the field. He commissioned Gates to prepare a paper on Soviet complicity and to do the paper *in camera*, a highly unusual step at the CIA. Gates found three willing DDI analysts, two Soviet analysts from my own office and a third from the Office of Global Intelligence, which was known for its worst-case views on international issues. The three analysts were instructed to make sure that the Agency's experts on the issue of terrorism in the DI and DO did not see the paper. All three received cash awards and promotions for their efforts. If there is cynicism within the intelligence community, then this is the kind of episode that is a breeding ground for cynics. At the time, I was the senior analyst on Soviet affairs in the Office of Soviet Analysis, but I was not told about the project.

The final paper was sent only to the president, the vice president, the secretaries of state and defense, and the national security advisor at a critical point of decision making on U.S.–Soviet relations. The distribution of the paper served the interests of Casey, who opposed improved bilateral relations with Moscow and wanted to undermine Secretary Shultz's efforts in this direction. Gates' contribution was a cover note to the president, vice president, secretary of state, secretary of defense, and national security advisor alerting them to the "first comprehensive examination of who was behind the attempted assassination. . . ." He went on to say, "While questions remain and probably always will, we have worked the problem intensively and now feel able to present the findings with some confidence."[30] In testifying against the nomination of Gates as CIA director in 1991, I briefed the Senate intelligence committee on the contents of previous CIA publications that ruled out a Soviet hand in the plot, including an intelligence assessment in 1983, an Agency briefing to the intelligence committee in 1984, and an NIE in 1985, all of which concluded that there was no credible evidence of Bulgarian or Soviet involvement in the attempt to assassinate the Pope. The Russian and Bulgarian governments in the wake of the 1991 communist revolutions disclosed a good deal of information on the covert actions of the communist regimes, which contained no evidence of any Bulgarian–Soviet connection with the assassination attempt.

Two Agency postmortems were critical of the intelligence assessment, noting that alternate views were not included in the key judgments of the paper, conflicting evidence was played down, and alternate scenarios were not provided. The utmost secrecy was observed in drafting the paper, and every aspect of analytic tradecraft was breeched. The panel of senior managers who reviewed the paper found "no one at the working level in either the DI or the Directorate of Operations (DO)—other than the primary authors of the paper—who agreed with the thrust of the assessment." In pointing to the "irregularities" that accompanied the drafting of the paper, the managers nevertheless concluded they could not find examples of politicization. Indeed, the irregularities themselves were acts of politicization, introduced to manipulate the system and obtain the desired analytical result. The group of managers included the eventual deputy director of CIA, John McLaughlin, who had an even bigger role in the politicization of intelligence in the run-up to the Iraq War in 2003. According to the chief of one of the postmortem teams, Ross Cowey, McLaughlin was the only team member who wanted to hide the hand of Gates in manipulating the publication.[31]

Another CIA deputy director, Richard Kerr, also denied there was evidence of politicization. Kerr disingenuously explained that CIA assessments were exercises in "hypothesis testing," setting up a scenario and pursuing it to see if the evidence would support it."[32] Incredibly, a senior CIA analyst, James Worthen, defended the approach of "hypothesis testing," terming it essential for the CIA to analyze the only aspect of the Papal Plot that "interested U.S. policymakers."[33] In other words, one-sided hypotheses of issues important to policymakers are essential, and making the case for controversial hypotheses on sensitive issues is acceptable to the intelligence community. The CIA applied the same methodology in 2007, when it produced a NIE on Iraq that discussed the dangers of a U.S. troop withdrawal without addressing any other scenario confronting U.S. interests.

If the Papal Plot assessment was merely hypothetical, then DDI Gates should not have written a cover note referring to his "confidence" in this "comprehensive examination." The job of intelligence analysis is to provide objective analysis on complicated issues, and not to play devil's advocate for unlikely scenarios. Kerr thus offered the kind of rationale for politicization that dominated the finished intelligence of CIA in the run-up to the Iraq War. In other words, if policymakers were interested in examples of Iraqi WMD and links between Saddam Hussein and bin Laden, then it was the mission of the CIA to provide such ammunition. Or, as the director of WINPAC, Alan Foley, told his senior managers on WMD, if the Bush administration wants to go to war, then it is up to the CIA to find the intelligence that enables him to do so.

The assessment on the Papal Plot was the last straw for me. I discovered the paper in its final drafting stages, took it to the chief of the Soviet office, MacEachin, and to the DDI, Gates. I raised issues of integrity with both, which angered Gates and led to an immediate falling out between us. At the confirmation hearings for Gates in 1991, MacEachin testified that Gates wanted me removed from SOVA, but MacEachin only agreed to remove me from my job as chief of Soviet–Third World affairs. MacEachin conceded that I had "carried a lot of water for SOVA," and it would be unfair and unreasonable to end my service to the office. Nevertheless, MacEachin, who went on to become the DDI and a key staffer on the 9/11 Commission, feigned embarrassment over the paper that he approved, although he possibly deserved credit for making sure it was not passed to Casey's journalist friend in Europe, Claire Sterling. Sterling, a freelance journalist, was published regularly in the *Reader's Digest* and *The New York Times*, and consulted for NBC and the Voice of America. The Papal Plot assessment, which I provided to the Senate intelligence committee, was considered to be the closest thing to a "smoking gun" in considering the nomination of Gates for CIA director in 1991. The head of the Soviet office, George Kolt, who was brought into the CIA by Gates from the U.S. Air Force in the mid-1980s, approved of the paper and played his own role in the politicization of intelligence. He was mortified to learn the intelligence committee had received a copy, along with Gates' incriminating cover notes.

Gates' Hearings Document Politicization

The hearings before the SSCI regarding the nomination of Gates as CIA director documented the efforts of Casey and Gates to politicize intelligence.[34] The preparation of such documents as the 1981 NIE on international terrorism, the 1985 NIE on Iran, and the 1985 intelligence assessment on the Papal Plot offer a guidebook to the how and why of politicization, particularly the pressure from senior levels of the CIA to shift the line of analysis, prevent publication of undesirable analysis, or exclude from consideration "unacceptable" views in order to support Casey's policy agenda. In some cases, such as the 1981 NIE on terrorism and the 1985 Papal Plot assessment, Casey simply ordered a particular line of analysis to be advanced. This is the most efficient way to politicize intelligence, but it is also the most risky. It is risky because it flatly contradicts both the stated mission of intelligence and the professional ethics of the analytical cadre. The experience of the politicization on intelligence on the Soviet Union in the 1980s should have made intelligence analysts more resolute in protesting the misuse of intelligence in the run-up to the war in Iraq in 2002–2003, but the Agency had misplaced its moral compass once again.

Gates survived the nomination hearings in 1991 because the chairman of the Senate intelligence committee was David Boren (D-Oklahoma). Boren and Gates had developed a close working relationship between 1989 and 1991, and the staff director of the committee, George Tenet, was supportive of both Boren and Gates. The Boren-Tenet-Gates triangle consisted of Boren's support for Gates as CIA director, Gates' later support for Tenet as CIA director, and a mutual admiration society of all three men to support and stay on good terms with the Bush administration. This arrangement enabled Tenet to survive the 9/11 intelligence failure in order to remain as CIA director, although the failure on Iraqi WMD eventually forced Tenet's resignation.[35] Tenet's memoir, *At the Center of the Storm*, carefully avoided any direct criticism of the president.

Boren introduced Gates to the Senate Armed Forces Committee in 2006, when Gates was confirmed as secretary of defense.

The confirmation hearings in 1991 for Gates as DCI provided a guide to the problem of politicization and an opportunity for critics to describe the tools of politicization applied to intelligence in the 1980s. Politicization rarely involves a direct order to tailor the intelligence to policy; there are other approaches that are slower and more cumbersome, but are more difficult to detect and pose less risk. These are insidious steps that involve manipulating the analytic process by changing either personnel or procedures. This can be done by finding "right-thinking" analysts to do the reporting; removing or excluding "wrong-thinking" analysts from the process; hiring or moving those who will advance the desired line into key management positions; encouraging the publication of reports that take the preferred line; repressing reports that do not support the preferred line; and altering or streamlining the intelligence structure in order to control the finished product. All of these methods were used during the Casey-Gates era to affect intelligence production, and some of these methods were revived in 2002–2003 to support the Bush administration's case to go to war.

Gates was no stranger to controversy. He was first nominated to be the DCI in 1987, but had to withdraw his nomination because of his connection to Iran-Contra and the belief of many members of the Senate intelligence committee that he lied about his role. His confirmation hearings became controversial the second time around because of his role in helping former CIA director Casey politicize the product of finished intelligence on behalf of the Reagan administration. The committee heard from five senior officials and analysts on Gates' suitability as CIA director, with three opposed to the nomination and two favorable. The hearings began in secret session in May 1991, but the provocative testimony led Senator Sam Nunn (D-Georgia) to demand paradoxically, "this material was much too sensitive to be handled in closed session. We need to go into open session as soon as possible."

The open sessions took place in October 1991 and produced 2,000 pages of congressional testimony as well as a 200-page committee staff report that gave unprecedented treatment to the issue of politicization.[36] The documentary account involved the testimony and sworn affidavits of dozens of intelligence analysts who discussed the five major techniques used by Casey and Gates to politicize intelligence. The testimony of analysts on politicization was unique for the CIA and the intelligence community. In his memoir, Gates described my testimony as a "sucker-punch," although I had confronted Gates five years earlier about his lack of integrity in politicizing the intelligence on the Papal Plot.

The denials of politicization by such Agency careerists as Deputy Directors Kerr and McLaughlin helped Gates survive the confirmation process, although he immediately had to face the issue upon arrival at CIA headquarters in November 1991. At the CIA, Gates had done his best for the Reagan administration to portray the Russian Bear as ten feet tall, although the Soviet Union ironically collapsed during the period of his confirmation. The chairman of the Senate intelligence committee, Boren, tried to persuade Gates to establish safeguards at the Agency to prevent another period of politicization, threatening Gates that the intelligence committee would not permit any signs of retribution against the CIA employees who testified against him or submitted sworn affidavits to the committee. Boren's threat caused a great deal of chagrin among his committee colleagues because there was no way to enforce such a threat. Gates appeared to get the message and made personal calls to some of his detractors in an attempt to convince them there would be no hard feelings, no retribution.

Gates' first memorandum as CIA director established the CIA's first Task Force on Politicization under a former deputy director for intelligence, Ed Proctor, ironically one of those who routinely politicized intelligence on the Viet Cong during the Vietnam War.[37] Proctor's memorandum to Gates found a "sufficient level of concern about politicization . . . to warrant remedial action" by the CIA director. He recommended steps to "prevent the concern from worsening," comparing the DI to a "car driven hard, but not broken. It does need minor repairs, as well as regular attention to maintenance." This trite analogy essentially dismissed the problem of politicization.

Proctor's memorandum failed to recognize the problem of politicization is related to the deficiencies of individuals in the DI and not the process of analysis. Soon after Gates left the CIA as its acting director to become a member of General Brent Scowcroft's NSC, the CIA deputy director for intelligence sent a memorandum to the chairman of the NIC, charging him with doing a better job of protecting the "objectivity, quality, and usefulness" of the NIEs. Although the DDI denied Gates had any role in politicizing intelligence, he recognized the deficiencies of the most important corporate product of the intelligence community and realized that under Gates the product had lost much of its integrity and credibility. He didn't call for a change in the process for producing NIEs, realizing that "individuals, not process, are the critical element in the integrity and objectivity of NIEs. Without individual integrity and objectivity at all levels, particularly at the top, no process will work; with it, any process will be successful."[38] The DDI understood the NIEs produced by Graham Fuller, Larry Gershwin, and George Kolt on the Near East, Soviet strategic weapons, and the Soviet Union, respectively, had become corrupt. These individuals tended to draft the most policy-sensitive estimates themselves, instead of selecting drafters and making sure that the final product contained a full and clear expression of all views in the community.

Three years after the invasion of Iraq, a senior CIA analyst, Paul Pillar, documented the efforts of the Bush administration to politicize the intelligence of the CIA on Iraqi WMD and so-called links between Iraq and al Qaeda.[39] Pillar accused the Bush administration of using policy to drive intelligence production, which was the same argument offered by the chief of British intelligence in the Downing Street memorandum prior to the war, and aggressively using intelligence to win public support for the decision to go to war. Pillar could have added that the administration also used politicized intelligence to achieve an authorization to use force against Iraq in October 2002. Pillar does not explain why no senior CIA official protested, let alone resigned, in the wake of the president's misuse of intelligence on Iraq's so-called efforts to obtain uranium ore in Africa. Pillar falsely claimed "for the most part, the intelligence community's own substantive judgments do not appear to have been compromised," when it was clear that the CIA was wrong on every conclusion and had to politicize the intelligence to be so egregiously wrong.[40] In his memoir, Tenet's lame defense of himself and his Agency was, "The intelligence process was not disingenuous nor was it influenced by politics."[41] In other words, he continues to believe that the errors were honest ones.

Politicization of the National Security State

One of the most remarkable features of the Bush administration has been the politicization of virtually every agency in the national security arena, not just the CIA. In addition to the politicization of intelligence to make the case for war against Iraq, the CIA has been brought into a world of "secret prisons," extraordinary renditions, and torture and abuse to support the war against terrorism. The NSA developed an illegal and unnecessary intrusion into the privacy of all Americans with a program of warrantless eavesdropping that is far more comprehensive than we have been led to believe. The wiretapping program was conducted without congressional or judicial approval, although it was challenged by former attorney general John Ashcroft and Senator Jay Rockefeller (D-West Virginia), the ranking minority member of the Senate intelligence committee. The program was established by a secret executive order that ignored the criminal prohibitions against such surveillance in the FISA Act of 1978. NSA's spying has inundated the FBI with thousands of "leads" that turned out to go nowhere.[42]

Similarly, the FBI has used the Patriot Act to issue more than 30,000 "national security letters" every year to individuals and businesses across the country that require telecommunications companies and financial institutions to disclose information about their customers. These letters are issued without any judicial review and prohibit recipients from disclosing the FBI request. The American Civil Liberties Union obtained documents in 2005 that tracked FBI investigation of activist groups, including Greenpeace and People for the Ethical Treatment of Animals.

The FBI has also conducted an aggressive campaign of ethnic profiling against Arabs and Muslims that has led nowhere. After 9/11, more than 80,000 Arabs and Muslims were required to register, another 8,000 were called in for interviews, and more than 5,000 were locked up in preventive detention. Since none of these individuals has been convicted of a terrorist crime, the FBI's record is zero for 93,000.[43] The Bush administration boasts that it has obtained more than 400 criminal indictments and over 200 hundred convictions in "terrorism-related cases, but virtually all of these convictions were for minor, nonviolent crimes such as immigration fraud or false statements.[44] The only criminal convicted of a terrorist act since 9/11 was shoe bomber Richard Reid, who was corralled by an alert flight attendant who noticed a strange-looking man trying to set fire to his shoe.

The Pentagon played a major role in the campaign of politicization, falsifying intelligence to make the case for war, and creating the ad hoc OSP and the Counter Terrorist Evaluation Group to circulate intelligence the intelligence community considered worthless. The Pentagon created the Counter Intelligence Field Activity in 2003 to conduct surveillance against American citizens near U.S. military facilities or in attendance at antiwar meetings. In the summer of 2004, CIFA monitored a small protest in Houston, Texas, against Halliburton, the giant military contractor once headed by Vice President Cheney. The then undersecretary of defense Wolfowitz also created a fact-gathering operation called TALON (Threat and Local Observation Notice) to collect "raw information" about "suspicious incidents."[45] The unauthorized spying of CIFA and the computer collection of innocent people and organizations for TALON are illegal.

The Senate intelligence committee and the Silberman-Robb Commission contended that there were no examples where CIA analysts actually altered or shaped their judgments on Iraq because of political pressure, but this is a case of setting the bar too high to document politicization. These panels essentially asked analysts whether policymakers had pressed for specific judgments, but this of course is not the way politicization is achieved, and it would be a rare analyst who would admit to having been intimidated by such blatant interference. The administration was very effective, however, in creating an atmosphere of politicization, where analysts in the intelligence community were acutely aware of both the intelligence the administration was seeking to make the case for war and, more importantly, the intelligence that policymakers didn't want to confront because it compromised the case for war. Vice President Cheney and his then-chief of staff, Lewis Libby, made numerous trips to the CIA to make it clear what the White House was and wasn't seeking.

Pillar corroborates my own experiences with politicization of intelligence in the 1980s. He notes that senior managers are well aware of the intelligence that policymakers want to see and, as a result, review finished production with an editorial eye on the audience. In the run-up to the Iraq War, for example, it was far easier to publish intelligence for the PDB that made the case for WMD or Iraqi–al Qaeda links than to argue negatively on these matters. Any evidence of WMD, no matter how weak or lacking in credibility was highlighted; authoritative evidence against the presence of WMD, even reporting from credible Iraqi officials was typically ignored.

In the 1980s, there was no difficulty in publishing intelligence assessments that dealt with Soviet propaganda aimed at the United States or Soviet actions in the Third World that compromised interests of the United States. Conversely, it was extremely difficult to get approval for intelligence production that made the case for Soviet interest in arms control and disarmament or Soviet withdrawal from the Third World. There were many pieces of intelligence collection in the mid-1980s that described Soviet withdrawal from Afghanistan and Vietnam, but analysis that incorporated such evidence ran into the censorship of DDI Gates. The Silberman-Robb Commission pointed to such inconsistencies in the case of the Iraq War, but attributed it lamely to bad management. In the 1980s, senior reviewers would not acknowledge that politicization had taken place but disingenuously pointed to a "perception" of politicization. Until the Congressional oversight committees offer genuine protection to contrarians and dissenters within the intelligence community, it will remain difficult to learn the truth about the politicization of intelligence.

In the final analysis, the only protections against politicization are the integrity and honesty of the intelligence analysts themselves, as well as the protection of competitive analysis that serves as a safeguard against unchallenged acceptance of conventional wisdom. In the 1980s, Casey and Gates made sure that the conventional wisdom on the Soviet Union dealt with a ten-foot tall Russian Bear; as a result, a plethora of evidence of Soviet weakness and decline was suppressed and ignored. Prior to the Iraq War, the CIA asserted there were significant stocks of Iraqi WMD despite a lack of credible evidence and a near total reliance on single-source intelligence. Competitive analysis is a safeguard against biased and politicized intelligence, but the creation of a centralized director of national intelligence and placing key positions in the intelligence community in the hands of the military provide no assurance there will be genuine safeguards.

6

The CIA and the Soviet Union:
Success and Failure

The CIA was created in 1947 to provide objective intelligence to policymakers. From 1947 to 1991, when the Soviet Union collapsed, the Agency devoted more than 70 percent of its resources and more than half of its personnel to the Soviet target. Unfortunately, this commitment did not prevent one of the worst intelligence failures in the history of the CIA—the failure to monitor the decline and fall of the Soviet Union. Neither did the CIA's sophisticated intelligence collection platforms enable the Agency to avoid a series of tactical intelligence failures, including the failure to anticipate Moscow's atomic testing in the 1940s, the invasions of Hungary in 1956 and Czechoslovakia in 1968, and virtually every step of the national security revolution conducted by Mikhail Gorbachev and Eduard Shevardnadze in the 1980s, particularly Moscow's intense interest in arms control and disarmament. The Agency provided no warning of the coup d'etat against Nikita Khrushchev in 1964 and were slow to monitor the political opposition to Gorbachev and Shevardnadze that led to coup plotting in the summer of 1991. Most of these mistakes were honest ones, however, until the 1980s, when Bill Casey and Bob Gates politicized the intelligence on the Soviet Union that blinded the CIA to the Kremlin's efforts to build a new détente relationship with the United States and its virtual "capitulation" to U.S. policy. As a result of the campaign of politicization, the CIA completely missed the political revolution in Central Europe in 1989 and the fall of the Soviet Union in 1991, arguably the greatest victories of political liberalism in modern history.

Notwithstanding the problem of politicization, the CIA's overall intelligence record against the Soviet Union from 1947 to 1991 included some successes. The Soviet Union never introduced a strategic weapon to its military arsenal that caught the U.S. policy community and weapons planners by surprise. At some point in the design, testing, or procurement stage, U.S. technical collection obtained advance information of Soviet weapons plans, including the parameters of the weapon's lethality and capability. U.S. policymakers and politicians were prone to exaggerating the capabilities of Soviet weaponry, and it usually fell to CIA analysis to refute such politically inspired campaigns as the "bomber gap" in the 1950s or the "missile gap" in the 1960s. There were gaps in those years, but in both cases, it was the forces of the Soviet Union that suffered from the huge quantitative and qualitative gaps in the relative arsenals of the two superpowers.

Unlike most residents of the White House, President Dwight D. Eisenhower understood the important strategic issues that divided the United States and the Soviet Union. He used CIA assessments to refute proponents of the bomber gap, and he ignored Pentagon assessments exaggerating the muscle in Moscow's strategic weapons programs that were designed to increase defense spending. He applied the lessons of the so-called bomber gap and assumed the Pentagon was exaggerating Soviet strategic capabilities and intentions. The introduction of U-2 overhead photography in the 1950s and the successful launching of Corona in 1960, the first U.S. photo satellite, demonstrated that Eisenhower was right. National intelligence estimates (NIEs) had credited the Soviet Union with 140 to 200 intercontinental ballistic missiles; the first photographs from Corona made it clear the Kremlin had at least 10 intercontinental ballistic missiles (ICBMs), but no more than 25. Without satellite photography, there is no question that the United States would have been building strategic programs that were not necessary and, in the words of President Johnson, "harboring fears that we didn't need to have."

Prior to the successful launch of Corona, the CIA was using U-2 photography to determine there was no evidence of a buildup of intercontinental weapons and no evidence of operational intercontinental bases. The Air Force, however, was trying to protect its share of the military budget and, using worst-case analysis of the Soviet threat, exaggerated the extent of Soviet weapons procurement and deployment. The Air Force falsely charged in the 1950s that the Soviets were building intercontinental weapons at a brisk rate, which reflected the personal views of Air Force Chief of Staff General Curtis LeMay. LeMay had an important backer on the Hill in Senator Stuart Symington (D-Missouri), a former secretary of the Air Force and well connected to the aeronautics industry. LeMay's politicization of intelligence on these strategic issues revealed the extent of the harmful influence of a service chief over the intelligence production of his service.

Eisenhower, who was suspicious of the military-industrial complex from the beginning of his presidency, ignored the Air Force assessments, as well as the threats from Khrushchev regarding the production of SS-6 intercontinental ballistic rockets. He intuitively believed that the Soviets were a long way from producing intercontinental weapons in large numbers, and he was right.[1] But, incoming President John F. Kennedy, far less sophisticated than Eisenhower on strategic issues, ignored the cautious CIA assessments and began an unnecessary and provocative increase in missile competition that required years of intense diplomatic negotiation to reverse. Kennedy had no way of knowing that Khrushchev was bluffing, but he should have known that the Air Force was hyping the threat to make its own case for greater strategic weaponry. The interesting juxtaposition between a sophisticated military veteran like Eisenhower, who did not want to waste investment on the military budget at the expense of needed domestic spending, and an inexperienced commander-in-chief like Kennedy, who forsook his liberal domestic agenda in order to boost military spending unnecessarily, pointed to possible uses and misuses of strategic intelligence. Kennedy proceeded to the next generation of strategic intercontinental missiles, the multiple independently targeted reentry vehicles (MIRVs), despite the U.S. ICBM advantage, which sparked another phase in the missile race.

The critics of arms control in the Congress immediately accused the CIA of tailoring the numbers of Soviet missiles to conform to the policy interests of the Eisenhower administration. Senator Symington and others led the charge against the CIA, ignoring the fact that it was Air Force intelligence that was tailoring its product to suit the policy interests of General LeMay. This would not be the last time that conservatives would accuse the CIA of cooking the books, favoring hard-line intelligence to support more defense spending and more aggressive foreign policies. Senator Henry Jackson (D-Washington) accused the CIA of cooking the books in the 1970s to support the arms control policies of the Nixon administration, and there are conservative voices in the Congress currently who believe that the CIA is covering-up China's strategic defense programs in order to support the Bush administration's efforts to improve Sino–American relations.

Prior to the Casey-Gates era, the CIA usually could be counted on to resist pressures to slant intelligence to support policy toward the Soviet Union, particularly in the sensitive area of arms control and disarmament policy. This was particularly true during the Nixon administration, when the CIA demonstrated that Soviet surface-to-air missiles could not be upgraded to an antiballistic missile defense, which opened the policy doors to the negotiation of the Anti-Ballistic Missile Treaty in 1972. Similarly, the CIA maintained that the Soviet SS-9 ICBM was not sufficiently accurate and was not equipped with MIRVs, and therefore it could not threaten the U.S. ICBM force. This line of analysis allowed the Nixon administration to ignore the

Pentagon's opposition to arms control negotiations with the Soviet Union, which led to the 1972 Strategic Arms Limitation Treaty (SALT). CIA assessments on the Soviet military invariably provided early warning of new weapons systems, which allowed U.S. weapons planners to focus their attention on the reality of the Soviet threat and not the worst-case assumptions of right-wing critics, who favored greater defense spending. With the exception of the first Soviet nuclear testing in the late 1940s, which stunned the Truman administration, few Soviet strategic developments surprised U.S. policymakers, with warning often provided when Soviet weapons were still in the design phase. While the CIA often exaggerated the operational dates and rates of procurement of many weapons systems, its track record was better than that of any other institution, particularly the Pentagon's Defense Intelligence Agency (DIA), which faced intense pressure from the civilian and military leaders of the DoD to provide worst-case analysis. The "bomber" and "missile gaps" of the 1950s and 1960s were designed in part to justify increases in defense spending.

CIA scientists and technicians worked closely with their counterparts at various laboratories at Harvard University, the Massachusetts Institute of Technology, the Cornell Aeronautical Laboratory, and the Polaroid Corporation to make major breakthroughs in the collection of strategic intelligence. This collaboration contributed to the development of the U-2 and SR-71 reconnaissance aircraft and satellite reconnaissance vehicles, which played a major role in U.S. intelligence collection capabilities and gave the United States a decided advantage in flash points involving the former Soviet Union, including the Cuban missile crisis in 1962 and the nuclear dust-up during the October War in 1973.

The CIA's objectivity on the Soviet Union was initially threatened during the Nixon administration, when CIA director Schlesinger summoned all senior intelligence managers on the Soviet Union and told them that they would no longer be allowed to "screw" President Nixon. The Schlesinger stewardship at the Agency was short-lived, but his immediate successor, George H. W. Bush, permitted the White House to place a group of hard-liners inside the CIA's directorate of intelligence (DI) to drive the CIA's analysis on Soviet strategic issues far to the right at the very time the Kremlin was reducing its increases in defense spending and signaling a need for détente and disarmament with the United States. This exercise, known as Team A/B, was sponsored by White House Chief of Staff Cheney and Secretary of Defense Rumsfeld, who were dissatisfied with the influence of the CIA's independent analysis on White House decision making. Cheney and Rumsfeld remained critics of the CIA for the next thirty years, and eventually cut the Agency down to size with their support of the Intelligence Reform Act of December

2004, the creation of the office of the Director of National Intelligence, and the appointment of military officers to head both CIA and DNI in 2006.

IDEOLOGY AND INTELLIGENCE

From 1947 to 1991, there were two major efforts to politicize the intelligence toward the Soviet Union and to push the Agency's conclusions on Soviet issues far to the right. In addition to the Ford administration's Team A/B exercise to manipulate CIA intelligence on Soviet strategic issues, there was a campaign of politicization in the 1980s, when President Reagan's CIA director, Bill Casey, and his deputy, Bob Gates, manipulated virtually all intelligence judgments on the Soviet Union. Casey arrived at the CIA with an agenda for intelligence and policy, believing the Soviet Union was responsible for every international problem concerning the United States, particularly international terrorism. Reagan made Casey the first CIA director to serve in a presidential cabinet, bringing Casey into the president's inner sanctum. Casey in turn appointed Gates to the joint positions of deputy director of intelligence and chairman of the National Intelligence Council, marking the first time that one individual controlled all CIA intelligence production, both current intelligence and NIEs. Gates appointed Douglas MacEachin (who eventually became DDI) and then the late George Kolt (who became National Intelligence Officer for Russia) to head the Office of Soviet Analysis from 1984 to 1992. This triumvirate of intelligence hawks was in command of Soviet assessments during the period of politicization of intelligence on the Soviet Union; they thoroughly missed the decline and fall of the Soviet Union.

Casey and Gates used the CIA, both its operations and its intelligence, to support the confrontational style and policies of the Reagan administration. These policies led to a dangerous juncture in Soviet–American relations in the early 1980s, with the outbreak of a "war scare" in the Kremlin. British intelligence sources learned that Moscow was profoundly concerned about CIA covert action, particularly in Eastern Europe, and the Pentagon's more aggressive military maneuvers in Soviet waters and air space, which included "parking" strategic submarines in Soviet territorial waters to conduct espionage. The aggressive actions of the CIA and the Pentagon led to an unusual Soviet intelligence alert for indications of imminent American attack. The source for this information was Oleg Gordievsky, a senior KGB officer who was recruited by British intelligence and eventually spirited out of Moscow in mid-1984. Gordievsky reported to the British that the KBG stations in London, Washington, and West European capitals had been ordered to declare an intelligence alert in late 1981 that lasted until 1984. KGB headquarters in

Moscow ordered its residencies in NATO and Japan to observe and report any activities that might indicate preparations for mobilization. This program was called "RYAN," the Russian acronym for "nuclear missile attack." There was no comparable military alert during this period, and no reason given to the KGB for the extraordinary intelligence alert, although it was known that former KGB leader and Soviet party chief Andropov was concerned with the possibility of a U.S. nuclear strike against the Soviet Union. The CIA learned about this alert in 1984 after Gordievsky defected to England.

When Casey was briefed on this material, he found it serious enough to report to the president. Casey flew to London in 1984 to meet with Gordievsky, who eventually flew to Washington to be debriefed by small groups of policy and intelligence officials. My own meeting with Gordievsky convinced me that the extraordinary alert, which seemed implausible to many, was genuine and that the confrontational style of the Reagan administration was partly responsible. The British possibly withheld the information on the alert because they did not want to imply they accepted Moscow's reasons for any alert, particularly its concerns with President Reagan's aggressive policies toward the Soviet Union. The Soviet Defense Ministry's journal specializing in foreign developments noted that the "activity of all forms of U.S. intelligence operations increased with the arrival of the new administration in the White House in January 1981."[2] The memoirs of Soviet Ambassador to the United States Anatoly Dobrynin also termed the early 1980s as particularly dangerous years because of a lack of trust between the United States and the Soviet Union and the aggressive policies of the Reagan administration.

Casey met with President Reagan in December 1984 and convinced the president that there was a heightened Soviet perception of an increased threat of war, which shocked the White House. This was an important development because DDI Gates and many CIA military analysts were not willing to believe that the Soviet "war scare" was serious. Fortunately, Reagan took the matter seriously and there was a marked change in the pattern of U.S. military exercises near Soviet borders. The President's Foreign Intelligence Advisory Board reexamined the entire episode in 1990 and concluded that the CIA had underestimated the anxiety in the Kremlin and was too quick to conclude that the event was nothing more than Soviet posturing for political effect.[3]

THE PROCESS OF POLITICIZATION

The politicization of intelligence was responsible for the CIA's unwillingness to recognize the importance of the Soviet "war scare" in the early 1980s, as well as for the Agency's failure to chart the decline and dissolution of the Soviet Union and the Warsaw Pact. There was a plethora of political, economic, and military clues that accompanied the Soviet and Eastern European decline throughout the 1980s. Nevertheless, the collapse of the Warsaw Pact in 1990 and the Soviet Union in 1991 totally surprised U.S. policymakers, with the CIA providing no warning. Former president George H. W. Bush said he had no idea the Berlin Wall was going to come down and his national security advisor, Brent Scowcroft, could not recall any CIA warning about the Soviet demise. General Powell, President Reagan's last national security advisor, said CIA specialists could not "anticipate events much better than a layman watching television." Former CIA director Stansfield Turner concluded the Agency's "corporate view missed by a mile" and it "should not gloss over the enormity of this failure to forecast the magnitude of the Soviet crisis." The CIA did, in fact, gloss over its failure, and produced documentary studies that claimed it "interpreted and predicted the rapidly unfolding events that led to the collapse of communism and the end of the cold war."⁴

The memoir of former secretary of state George P. Shultz, *Turmoil and Triumph*, offers the best description of the CIA's failure to track the Soviet decline. Shultz believed that "CIA analysis was distorted by strong views about policy" and accused Casey of providing "bum dope" to the president. He warned the White House that the Agency was "unable to perceive that change was coming in the Soviet Union." He charged acting CIA director Gates with "manipulating" him, and reminded Gates the CIA was "usually wrong" about Moscow, having dismissed Gorbachev's policies as "just another Soviet attempt to deceive us." "When it became evident that the Soviet Union was, in fact, changing," Shultz wrote, "the CIA line was changes wouldn't really make a difference." Shultz, of course, was spot-on; Casey and Gates were using assessments to pander to the ideologues in the Reagan administration and to build support for a more aggressive U.S. foreign policy.

Gates defended Casey from charges of politicization during his confirmation process in 1991, but after his short tenure as CIA director ended, he admitted the intelligence process had been corrupted during the Casey era. After publishing his memoir, *From the Shadows,* he acknowledged watching Casey "on issue after issue, sit in meetings and present intelligence framed in terms of the policy he wanted pursued." Gates also conceded missing the dramatic change of course in Soviet policy, Gorbachev's strategic retreat abroad, and the destruction of the Soviet system at home. Indeed, Gates was wrong about the biggest intelligence issues of the cold war: the strength of the Soviet Union and the intentions of its leaders toward the United States and arms control and disarmament. And he made sure that the CIA was wrong, as well.

As a major part of their politicization campaign, Casey and Gates rejected intelligence papers that were incompatible with their beliefs and encouraged assessments that reinforced their views on arms control and the Third World. Senior managers who continued to produce papers that didn't meet the Casey-Gates agenda were replaced, including Douglas Garthoff, who authored special assessments on Moscow's interest in arms control and disarmament, James Noren, who documented the weakness of the Soviet economy, and the author of this book, who documented Moscow's withdrawal from the Third World.[5] Many CIA papers in the 1980s correctly analyzed Soviet national security, but, not suiting the Casey-Gates policy agenda, they were never published. These papers included the first comprehensive assessment of Soviet problems in Afghanistan, which appeared two years before Gorbachev signaled his interest in withdrawal from Afghanistan; an outstanding work on Soviet interest in destroying chemical weapons stocks, which preceded Moscow's interest in a chemical weapons ban with the United States; and a comprehensive review of Moscow's failures in the Third World.

Instead of attempting to determine what went wrong, however, the CIA worked hard to exonerate itself. Determined to gloss over the Agency's analytical failures, Gates proclaimed in 1992 that the CIA had looked into the matter of politicization with care and found little to fault in its performance. His successors, Woolsey and Deutch, never understood the issue and accepted his verdict. When I served as director of the CIA's Center for the Study of Intelligence in the summer of 1990, I inherited a dubious program that funneled hundreds of thousands of dollars in research grants to Harvard University's John F. Kennedy School to finance case studies on the CIA, particularly to demonstrate the CIA "got it right" on the issue of the Soviet Union. The program was called the Harvard Intelligence and Policy Project, and it began in 1987. The Kennedy School produced twenty documents in this series, and the most offensive one was published after I resigned from the CIA in the summer of 1990. The case study was Kirsten Lundberg's "CIA and the Fall of the Soviet Empire: The Politics of 'Getting it Right,'" based on documents given to Lundberg by the CIA. Lundberg did not consult with CIA analysts who opposed the nomination of Gates as CIA director and were in a position to comment authoritatively on the politicization on intelligence on the Soviet Union. Certainly, if the CIA had "gotten it right," then such policymakers as George Shultz and Colin Powell and such members of the SSCI as Senators Bill Bradley and Daniel Patrick Moynihan, would not have insisted that the Agency got it wrong.

The office director for the Soviet Union during much of the 1980s, when the work of politicization was undertaken, Douglas MacEachin, was sent to Harvard as intelligence officer in residence to help the director of the case studies, Philip Zelikow, prepare these studies. MacEachin testified on Gates' behalf at the confirmation hearings in 1991 and, while on sabbatical at the

Kennedy School, he completed a monograph praising the Agency's track record on the Soviet Union; not surprisingly, the Agency published the monograph. In 1993, MacEachin became the CIA's deputy director for intelligence, even though he had managed the Agency's intelligence on the Soviet Union in the 1980s when the CIA missed the decline and fall of the Kremlin. Zelikow and MacEachin were reunited in 2004, when Zelikow was named staff director of the 9/11 commission and appointed MacEachin a team leader on the staff. Zelikow and MacEachin made sure that the commission did not indict the CIA for its contributions to the 9/11 intelligence failure.

Instead of studying the reasons for the corporate intelligence failure, the CIA began a tax-supported public relations campaign to boast of its "successes" against the Soviet target. CIA director Tenet sponsored symposia at Texas A&M, where Gates was director of the George H. W. Bush School of Government and Public Service, and Princeton University, to permit selected outsiders to examine carefully selected CIA assessments to demonstrate the Agency's "success" analyzing the Soviet threat. According to Fred Hitz, former inspector general of the Agency, the CIA carefully controlled the documents that were released and prevented the attendance of CIA critics. The CIA documents did not deal with the exaggerations of the strength of the Soviet military and economy, the underestimates of the burden of Soviet defense spending, and the omissions of Gorbachev's efforts to engage the United States in a series of disarmament agreements.

The Agency was engaged in an exercise in self-deception. As one of the Agency's Soviet analysts during the 1980s, I had a front-row seat from which to view its dismal performance. The CIA was engaging in a sleight of hand in making public a set of documents produced from 1988 to 1991, hoping to be applauded for warning in 1989 that Gorbachev's prospects were "doubtful at best" or, as one of the declassified documents shows, because it said in November 1990 that the "Soviet Union, as we have known it, is finished." By that time, the endgame was upon us and discerning observers did not need classified intelligence to see that the Soviet regime was in trouble.

The CIA also provided carefully selected materials to such former consultants and employees as Abraham Becker of the Rand Corporation and freelance writers Jeffrey Richelson and Bruce Berkowitz to encourage support for its track record and to deny that the Agency had "cooked the books." The Agency's defenders focused much of their commentary on the narrow issue of whether the Agency predicted the coup attempt against Gorbachev in 1991, obfuscating more important questions. But the CIA must be judged on whether it provided U.S. leaders with accurate assessments of Moscow's weakness and vulnerability and whether it recognized Gorbachev's stated intentions were genuine. The CIA failed on both counts. It issued only limited warnings of Soviet weakness and no warning that the strategic relationship between the United States and the Soviet Union was about to change radically. It, therefore, could not predict, anticipate, or even imagine the convulsions that accompanied the Soviet decline. CIA estimates in the mid-1980s simply bolstered Gates' personal views, concluding that Gorbachev endorsed "well-established goals for expanded Soviet power and influence" and that Soviet leaders were "attempting to prepare their military forces for the possibility of having to fight a nuclear war." Ironically, the 9/11 Commission concluded that the CIA's intelligence failure on terrorism included a lack of imagination about the actions and motives of the terrorists; the same could be said about the intelligence failure regarding the Soviet Union in the 1980s, when a lack of imagination prevented a full discussion of Soviet weakness and decline. In the latter case, however, the politicization of intelligence was crucial to the failure. Many of the methodologies for politicization of intelligence on the Soviet Union were applied in the run-up to the Iraq War in 2003, when the CIA helped the Bush administration develop an intelligence rationale for going to war in Iraq.

MISSING THE DECLINE AND FALL OF THE SOVIET UNION

The politics of Casey and Gates made sure that the CIA was dead-wrong on the most important question of our time: Was Gorbachev serious about a strategic retreat at home and political and economic reform at home? As a consequence, the CIA missed every sign of change during the Gorbachev era, beginning with the significance of moving Andrei Gromyko out of the foreign ministry where he had exercised great influence over three decades and naming a relatively obscure party leader in the Georgian Republic, Eduard Shevardnadze, as Gromyko's successor. This singular move presaged a revolutionary change in Soviet national security policy, which the CIA failed to acknowledge. The revolution of Gorbachev and Shevardnadze, particularly in the areas of arms control and disarmament and the Soviet retreat from the Third World, created an entirely new setting for Soviet–American relations. In 1986, however, Casey, Gates, and the CIA still argued that Gorbachev gave "every indication of endorsing well-established Soviet goals for expanded power and influence."

Despite signs of anti-Sovietism throughout Eastern Europe, the CIA, as late as May 1988, saw no "unraveling of Moscow's Eastern European empire" and no "diminished military threat posed by the Warsaw Pact." The "Berlin Wall will stay," according to an estimate issued less than a year before the wall's collapse, despite "whatever tactical advantages Gorbachev might see in its removal." The Agency even predicted that, if necessary, Gorbachev would sponsor a "crackdown to preserve Soviet influence." After the collapse of every communist regime in Eastern Europe, the CIA still refused to change its assessments of Soviet influence in the region. An estimate issued in April 1990 maintained that the Soviet Union's "size, geographical proximity, security concerns, raw materials, and markets will continue to make it a major factor in Eastern Europe." None of the Agency's estimates suggested that the successful Eastern European revolutions of 1989 would weaken the Soviet Union and lead to increased demands for comprehensive Soviet change as well.

Casey and Gates did their greatest strategic damage at home by distorting CIA estimates on Soviet military and economic strength. Exaggerated estimates of the Red Army's military power were used to justify increased U.S. defense spending and led to the most significant U.S. intelligence failure since Pearl Harbor. According to Representative Les Aspin (D-Wisconsin), the Reagan and Bush administrations withheld information about declining military expenditures, which corrupted Congressional discussion of U.S. defense priorities.[6]

The full record shows that the CIA did not anticipate Moscow's retreat from abroad and its vulnerability at home. During the mid-1980s, the Agency issued only limited warnings of Soviet weakness and nothing to indicate that the strategic relationship between the United States and the Soviet Union was about to change radically. As a result, the CIA could not predict, anticipate, or even speculate about the consequences of the Soviet decline. Honest intelligence from the CIA on the Soviet military may not have led to less U.S. spending on defense during the Reagan administration, just as honest intelligence on Iraqi WMD would not have deterred the Bush administration from the war against Iraq. But, in both cases, the CIA failed to do its job of providing objective and balanced assessments, and serving as a check and balance on the ambitions of the White House and the exaggerations of the Pentagon's military intelligence.

Some historians of the cold war argued the U.S. military buildup helped put pressure on the Soviet Union, but that's not a defense for faulty intelligence work. Such a strategy is the province of policymakers; the CIA's job is to provide its best analysis of the facts, which it did not do. The CIA missed the facts that would have provided warning of the Soviet retreat from Third World, including the withdrawal from Afghanistan, Cam Ranh Bay in Vietnam, and the littoral states of Africa. The CIA even rejected Moscow's claims that it would withdraw from Afghanistan—the first major step in its strategic retreat—helping to set the stage for anticommunist revolutions in Eastern Europe and the reunification of Germany.

The CIA also missed the Kremlin's two major decisions on Afghanistan: failing to warn the Carter administration about the decision to invade that took place in December 1979, and failing to warn the Reagan administration about the decision to withdraw in 1989. There were months of indicators pointing to the Soviet use of force in 1979, and there were two years of indicators before the Soviets withdrew their forces in 1989. The Carter administration had no idea of the size and scope of the Soviet military intervention in Afghanistan in 1979, and the CIA's leading Soviet experts (Gates, MacEachin, and Ermarth) told the Reagan administration to ignore the signals that the Gorbachev regime was preparing to withdraw from Afghanistan. The CIA's Senior Review Panel, a special advisory group of seasoned policy and intelligence veterans, studied the reasons for the failure in 1979, but there was no attempt to understand the reasons for the failure in 1988–1989, which had greater strategic consequences for U.S. interests. Indeed, the consequences of the failure of the Reagan and Bush administrations to cooperate with the Soviet withdrawal and to stabilize the Afghan government include the formation of the Taliban government and the sanctuary for al Qaeda. Instead of cooperating with Moscow, U.S. policy contributed to the instability in Afghanistan and, thus, abetted the radical destabilization of Afghanistan. And now history is repeating itself. Not long after the successful overthrow of the Taliban government and the routing of al Qaeda forces in 2001, another Bush administration is confronting a steady increase in Taliban and al Qaeda violence against the Kabul government.

CIA estimates provided no warning that the Gorbachev agenda was designed to end the competition between the superpowers and, as late as December 1988, argued that Moscow was determined "not to let the West affect the fundamental nature of the Soviet system or its superpower status." Gorbachev's agenda had attracted strong opposition in 1987, but CIA estimates for the next several years ignored his radical goals, the strength of his opponents, and the constraints on his political actions. On December 7, 1988, the forty-seventh anniversary of the attack on Pearl Harbor, Gorbachev announced force reductions in Central Europe and along the Sino–Soviet border at the United Nations. His chief of the General Staff, Marshal Akhromeyev, resigned in protest, an obvious demonstration of the military's opposition to the force reductions. The CIA, however, attributed the resignation to poor health and ignored all political implications. Ironically, a year earlier, the two most vociferous hawks in the Reagan administration, Secretary of Defense Weinberger and Assistant Secretary of Defense Richard Perle resigned to protest President Reagan's willingness to pursue the Intermediate-Range Nuclear Forces (INF) Treaty.

This period marked the political turning point for Gorbachev, as the increased power of the conservatives led to "new men" in the party leadership:

Boris Pugo, Vladimir Kryuchkov, and Anatoly Lukyanov. The CIA estimated that these new leaders "made Gorbachev's position relatively secure over the next two years." Wrong again! These were the very men, along with Defense Minister Dmitri Yazov, who led the coup against Gorbachev in August 1991. Ironically, Yazov was the first commander of the Soviet brigade in Cuba, the so-called "combat brigade," that was central to the intelligence failure leading to the crisis in Soviet–American relations in 1979.

Until 1991, when even casual observers of the Russian scene could anticipate the disarray within the Soviet Union, the intelligence estimates of the CIA carried a message of business-as-usual, with no alarms for U.S. policymakers. When the die was cast and, in the words of General Colin Powell, the CIA "could no longer anticipate events much better than a layman watching television," the Agency frantically tried to catch up to events with worst-case analyses that were deeply wrong. In April 1991, a memorandum for the NSC warned that "Gorbachev, Yeltsin, and other lesser but nevertheless important leaders could die under the incredible strains in which they work or be assassinated with incalculable consequences." By the end of the year, an estimate predicted the "most significant civil disorder in the former USSR since the Bolsheviks consolidated power." The Agency predicted the overthrow of the Yeltsin government, serious unrest among Soviet forces in Eastern Europe and the Baltics, and "even acts of terrorism." Nothing of the sort took place as the Agency's analytic pendulum took world surveys at the Soviet target.

The CIA even tried to take credit for predicting the coup attempt against Gorbachev in August 1991. Actually, two months earlier, Ambassador Jack Matlock received sensitive information from the liberal mayor of Moscow, Gavril Popov, and quickly passed the information to President Bush. Popov accurately named the conspirators, all well-known reactionaries, including Kryuchkov, Prime Minister Valentin Pavlov, and Yazov, who were involved in the actual coup attempt six weeks later. When Bush called Gorbachev to inform him of the coup attempt, the president named Popov as the source of the report. Incredibly, for a former director of central intelligence, he did so on a telephone line that was monitored by the KGB.[7] When Gorbachev received the information from President Bush, the Soviet leader assured Ambassador Matlock he was grateful for the warning. But Gorbachev was actually dismissive of the warning and, when he saw Popov during the state dinner for President Bush in Moscow in July, he shook his finger at the Moscow mayor and accused him of "telling tales to the Americans."[8] If the coup had succeeded, then Bush, who committed a terrible breach of security, would have sealed Popov's fate.

Missing the Soviet Economic Collapse

The CIA's failure to understand the shaky political edifice in the Soviet Union was matched by the failure to understand the decrepitude of the Soviet economy. The latter omission was particularly stunning because of the ability of any seasoned traveler to walk the streets of the Soviet Union and observe the transparent backwardness of the infrastructure and the commercial environment. The economy had been stagnant for a period of two decades in the 1970s and 1980s, when the CIA attributed a steady growth of 2 to 4 percent for the Soviet economy. The CIA was convinced the Soviet Union was increasing its spending on weaponry in the mid-1970s, when new information began to arrive pointing to great strains on the Soviet economy and, as a result, the beginning of reduced increases in defense spending. The CIA put a great deal of assets and resources into defense costing for the Soviet Union and the Warsaw Pact, without ever understanding the weakness of Moscow's high-technology sectors and the overall economic burden related to defense spending. CIA counted the trees, but it missed the decrepitude of the forest.

As a result, the CIA stuck with its positive forecasts right up to the collapse of the Soviet Union in 1991, telling several Congressional committees that the Soviet Union claimed the second largest economy in the world, with a gross national product of $2.8 trillion, thus bigger than Japan and the two Germanys combined. Of course, this missed the fact that Japan and West Germany were major players in the international economy and the Soviet Union often approached the major economic powers with hat in hand. Former CIA director Admiral Stansfield Turner could not believe the "enormity of the failure to forecast the magnitude of the Soviet crisis."[9]

The Soviet economy had fallen into the early stages of collapse from 1976 to 1986, and economists, such as Sweden's Anders Åslund, the Soviet Union's Abel Aganbegyan, and Soviet émigré Igor Birman, pointed out fissures in the Soviet economy and flaws in CIA analysis. Unlike CIA analysts, these economists had no access to classified information, let alone sensitive clandestine sources. Nevertheless, in the early 1980s, Birman predicted a Soviet economic collapse by decade's end. Swedish and British analysts had long regarded the Soviet economy as functionally Third World—an Upper Volta with a nuclear arsenal—but CIA economists continued to exaggerate the size of the Soviet economy and to underestimate the economic burden of maintaining a large military. Gates was particularly dismissive of such émigrés as Birman. As a result, the CIA ignored Moscow's pleas for "breathing space" in the international arena, let alone the implications of such pleas.

CIA analysts estimated the size of the Soviet economy in 1986 to be nearly 60 percent that of the U.S. economy. Åslund's figures suggest that estimate was inflated by nearly twenty percentage points. The CIA finally began to report lower growth rates for the Soviet economy in the mid-1980s, but, by then, Aganbegyan concluded there had been "practically no economic growth" in the Soviet Union between 1981 and 1985, the very years during which the Reagan administration was using CIA data to challenge arguments against increased defense spending. The Agency failed to assess the burden of the military on the economy, placing the military's share of Soviet gross national product (GNP) between 15 to 17 percent, while critics argued it was closer to 35 percent.

These arguments were not academic. The CIA analysis describing a Soviet economy sustaining military expansion supported the policy of higher U.S. defense spending. In the late 1980s, for example, the CIA argued incorrectly that Soviet growth in industrial investment and GNP would allow for increased military procurement and influence abroad. The CIA predicted no significant shifts away from military production in the near future, but such shifts were already occuring. Several months before Gorbachev announced unilateral cuts in Soviet ground forces, the CIA predicted Soviet forces would be modernized, and Gorbachev would place a "new emphasis on organizing and planning sustained conventional theater offensive operations."

The CIA completely misread the qualitative and comparative economic picture and provided no warning to policymakers of the dramatic economic decline of the 1980s. Fortunately, in 1990, Shevardnadze's top aides briefed Secretary of State James Baker and others about the plight of the Soviet economy. This information allowed the chairman of the U.S. Council of Economic Advisors, Michael Boskin, to tell a Congressional committee in 1990 that "Soviet GNP is probably . . . only about one-third of the GNP of the United States." He ignored CIA assessments that—as late as the 1980s—estimated Soviet GNP to be three-quarters of the American level. At the same time, the CIA completely miscalculated the trends in Soviet defense spending, especially for the procurement of weaponry and for investment.

The CIA also failed to predict the economic collapse in Eastern Europe, which diminished the effectiveness of Warsaw Pact forces and hurt Soviet industrial production. The Soviet military-industrial complex was dependent on Eastern Europe, particularly for machine tools denied by the West. Production problems in Eastern Europe presaged the reduced procurement of key weapons systems in the Soviet Union, which began in 1976. As late as 1986, the CIA still believed that East Germany was ahead of West Germany in per capita production. Also, the CIA never understood the tremendous burden of defense spending on the overall Soviet economy.

The CIA falsely claimed the Soviets were continuing to increase their defense spending, which conservatives cited to charge Moscow with taking advantage of U.S. interest in détente and arms control. Whereas Soviet defense spending did increase in the early 1970s at a rate of four to five percent a year, it was widely known throughout the intelligence community that the rate of increase dropped to two percent a year in the mid-1970s, with investment and procurement leveling off and no increase in the rate of growth until the mid-1980s. In 1983, the CIA finally conceded that the Soviets "did not field weapons as rapidly after 1976 as before. Practically all major categories of Soviet weapons were affected—missiles, aircraft, and ships."[10] Thus, the earlier CIA estimates about the "relentless Soviet buildup" were flat-out wrong. The so-called spending gap was no more accurate than earlier "gaps" concerning bombers, missiles, antiballistic missile defense, civil defense, and—the favorite of the neoconservative Committee on the Present Danger—the so-called intentions gap.

The first acknowledgment of CIA's exaggerations of Soviet defense spending for the previous seven to eight years came in an unclassified briefing to the Congress and not in a classified paper or national estimate. As director of intelligence, Gates scrutinized the published record of intelligence on the Soviet Union far more carefully than the briefings on the Hill for low-level subcommittees. CIA analysts knew the opportunity for providing objective and balanced intelligence was far greater in briefings on the Hill than in the President's Daily Brief or the *National Intelligence Daily*. As a result, analysts looked forward to briefing Congressional committees because their remarks were not subject to Gates' filter.

The urgency of Gorbachev's efforts to reform the Soviet system and reach accommodation with the United States on arms control should have been a clue to CIA economists, but the Agency overstated the value of the ruble, the volume of Soviet investment relative to the United States, and the rate of growth of the Soviet economy. It made errors in estimating Soviet investment in fixed capital, particularly machinery and equipment, which contributed to alarming accounts of the size and capability of Moscow's military-industrial complex. CIA analysts totally missed the qualitative disparities between the two countries, arguing that the rate of growth of personal consumption in the Soviet Union from 1951 to 1988 exceeded growth rates in the United States. As a result, they concluded that the "USSR was much less constrained than the United States by domestic considerations." On balance, the inflated estimates of Soviet consumption and investment contributed to the CIA's misunderstanding of the defense burden on the economy, the critical need for reform, and the imminent economic crisis. These errors led to the CIA's unwillingness to accept, let alone comprehend, Gorbachev's commitment to change.

Soviet commentators had been engaged in a public debate on the backwardness of the Soviet system since the 1960s, but as late as 1985, an NIE

(*Domestic Stresses on the Soviet System*) described a "very stable country" that was a "powerful and acquisitive actor on the international scene." According to this NIE, the Soviet Union would use:

> Assertive diplomacy backed by a combination of military power, propaganda, and subversive tactics to advance its interests. Its ruling elite, now and for the *foreseeable future,* sees its mission in history, its security, and its legitimacy in maximizing its ability to control political life within and outside Soviet borders. The domestic problems of the USSR are unlikely to alter this quality of the Soviet system and the *international appetites* that spring from it. [emphasis added]

In fact, Moscow's severe domestic problems, which the CIA failed to acknowledge, already had produced the policies of strategic retreat, which were also missed.

Making the Russian Bear Ten Feet Tall

The CIA's most important series of national intelligence estimates in its first forty years was titled *Soviet Capabilities for Strategic Nuclear Conflict.* As late as 1983, six years after Leonid Brezhnev signaled reduced growth in Soviet defense spending, the annual NIE in the series concluded that the Soviets sought "superior capabilities to fight and win a nuclear war with the United States, and have been working to improve their chances of prevailing in such a conflict." Ignoring dissent from the State Department's INR, CIA analysts used language that catered to Casey's notions of threatening communist intentions: "[The Soviets] have seriously addressed many of the problems of conducting military operations in a nuclear war, thereby improving their ability to deal with the many contingencies of such a conflict, and raising the possibility of outcomes favorable to the USSR." The notion that the Red Army could conduct military operations on a nuclear battlefield was, of course, ludicrous.

Gates, as deputy and acting director of the CIA from 1986 to 1989, was directly involved in every aspect of the politicization of intelligence on the Soviet Union. He distorted NIEs on Soviet strategic defense programs to buttress the Reagan administration's case for the Strategic Defense Initiative or "Star Wars." In a 1986 speech, Gates claimed that the USSR had spent more than $150 billion on its Star Wars programs; he failed to mention that nearly all of this money was used for air defense, not antimissile defense—a fact he knew. He charged incorrectly that the Soviets were preparing an antiballistic missile defense of their national territory. Gates's role in the politicization of intelligence, particularly on the Soviet Union, led directly to the votes of thirty-one U.S. senators against his nomination for CIA director 1991.

The CIA depiction of a Soviet military Goliath with global reach and control of international terrorism bolstered the Reagan administration's portrayal of an "evil empire." CIA publications regularly discussed a "relentless Soviet buildup" and a "disquieting index of Soviet intentions," but these descriptions reflected bias at the CIA and not reality. It gave right-wing critics an opportunity to discuss a so-called spending gap, which was no more accurate than so-called gaps dealing with bombers, missiles, civil defense, and ABM systems. Missing the reduced investment and expenditures of the late 1970s and early 1980s led the CIA to miss the slowdown in the growth of military procurement. The CIA exaggerated the capabilities of important strategic weapons in the Soviet arsenal, such as the flight range of the TU-22 Backfire bomber (which justified counting the airplane as a strategic intercontinental bomber) and the accuracy of the SS-19 ICBM (which contributed to the myth of the "window of vulnerability"). Although these errors were eventually acknowledged by the CIA in Congressional testimony in 1989, after Gates left the Agency to join the NSC, they continued to appear in the unclassified DIA publication, *Soviet Military Power*, a propaganda vehicle for the Department of Defense. Then Secretary of Defense Cheney, who became the Bush administration's major force in politicizing intelligence on Iraqi WMD, was a major promoter of the DIA publication. The CIA, created as an independent agency, had failed in its role as "honest broker" between intelligence and policy, permitting the DIA to tailor intelligence on key strategic issues.

The CIA also distorted the military power of Warsaw Pact forces and never anticipated the pact would dissolve. As late as 1990, only months before the collapse, the CIA concluded the pact had matched or exceeded NATO's modernization programs. CIA assessments and NIEs ignored Moscow's concerns about U.S. modernization, particularly the presence of Pershing II and ground-launched cruise missiles in Europe, which threatened Moscow's early warning system and its retaliatory capabilities. Overall, the CIA presented the Warsaw Pact as an important Soviet military asset; in fact, the Warsaw Pact and its Eastern European membership was a military liability to the Soviet Union, witness the need for military intervention in East Germany, Hungary, and Czechoslovakia in the 1950s and 1960s. The Soviets did not intervene in Poland in the early 1980s when the Solidarnost labor organization became a threat to political and economic stability there, but Moscow's crisis management in 1980–1981 was a costly diversion.

One of the problems of CIA intelligence on military matters was taking the official pronouncements of Soviet leaders at face value and not taking into account the propaganda value of these statements. When Khrushchev boasted in the early 1960s that ICBMs would be "turned out like sausages," there was a tendency for the CIA to substantially overestimate the number of ballistic missiles to be deployed. After satellite imagery became available in the 1960s, very few ICBMs were located and the Agency's projections were scaled back accordingly. Actually, the Soviets were completing their deployment of medium-range missiles opposite Western Europe and solving technical problems with their first-generation ICBMs. As a result, the CIA did not anticipate the massive buildup of ICBMs later in the 1960s. One of the advantages of SALT in 1972 was to establish a ceiling on strategic nuclear delivery vehicles and, thus, remove a great deal of the uncertainty regarding Soviet deployments. In any event, the CIA never discussed a major Soviet vulnerability in terms of Soviet reliance on strategic forces in fixed ICBM silos (representing 75 percent of Soviet strategic power) as opposed to less than 25 percent of U.S. strategic warheads on more vulnerable land-based systems.

Nevertheless, the CIA successfully countered the so-called window of strategic vulnerability, which suddenly emerged in the late 1970s and early 1980s as a campaign issue exaggerating the power of the Soviet Union. The right-leaning Committee on the Present Danger cited intelligence sources to argue that the larger Soviet ICBM force would be a strategic threat to the U.S. introduction of the MX and Trident II missiles, but it did not account for the fact that the greater American strategic force would be in a position to destroy a larger percentage of the Soviet force. As Ambassador Raymond Garthoff argued in his authoritative two-volume study of Soviet–American relations, "even if 90 percent of U.S. ICBMs could be destroyed by the Soviet SS-18 force, that loss would represent the destruction of only 1,980 warheads, or 18 percent of the U.S. strategic force."[11] The U.S. could have used its ICBMs to target Soviet ICBMs (SS-17s, SS-18s, and SS-19s) and thus destroy nearly 40 percent of the Soviet strategic force. So the window of vulnerability, like the bomber and missiles gaps that preceded it, was largely a sham concoction of the enemies of détente and arms control. Actually, all of these equations deal in notions of fantasy because they assume extremely high accuracy ratios, as well as the fact that the targeted missiles had not already been fired on warning of an incoming attack.

The CIA stuck out its neck in the late 1960s and early 1970s when it concluded that the Soviet SS-9 was not compatible with a MIRV system and that it was, therefore, two generations behind the U.S. Minuteman program. This was a courageous position to take in Congressional and policy circles because National Security Advisor Kissinger and Secretary of Defense Laird were citing the SS-9 as a MIRV in order to justify the construction of an antiballistic missile system. The CIA termed the SS-9 only as MRV capable, which meant that the various warheads were not independently targetable. According to the CIA, the SS-9 was viewed as consistent with McNamara's concept of mutual assured destruction and not a first-strike weapon. Kissinger was furious when he learned that the CIA had delivered this testimony to Senator Fulbright's Senate Foreign Relations Committee and demanded a revised report from the CIA. The revised CIA study reached the same conclusions about the SS-9, and Congressional support for the U.S. ABM system declined somewhat, although the program squeezed through the Senate by one vote.

The intelligence community's exaggerations of the range of the Soviet Backfire bomber were typical. Soviet party chairman Leonid Brezhnev told Secretary of State Kissinger in January 1976 that the Backfire's range was 3,400–3,500 nautical miles, which classified the bomber as a medium-range bomber and not a heavy bomber.[12] The experts at McDonnell-Douglas did an exhaustive study for the CIA that was based on all available intelligence, which supported Brezhnev's contention. But Secretary of Defense Rumsfeld wanted the bomber classified as a heavy bomber, and the DIA went along with the secretary and argued that the range of the Backfire was six thousand nautical miles. The lower CIA estimates of the Backfire's range led to charges from Robert Novak, George Will, and the editors of *Aviation Week and Space Technology* that Kissinger had pressured the CIA into the lower estimates, leading the secretary of state to note that "no service is done to the nation by those who portray an exaggerated specter of Soviet power and of American weakness."[13]

CIA distortions on military issues delayed arms control negotiations with the Soviet Union as well. Estimates of Soviet military manpower in Europe, a key issue in negotiations for mutual and balanced force reductions, assumed 95 percent staffing levels when the actual average was much less. Soviet military manning and procurement was never as robust as the CIA estimated. The CIA overestimated Soviet chemical warfare stocks, and Gates delayed the release of an assessment demonstrating a change in Soviet thinking about chemical warfare that signaled the Kremlin's interest in destroying chemical weapons stocks. This assessment would have supported an earlier decision by U.S. policymakers to seek a chemical weapons ban.

Former secretary of state Shultz's memoir documents the CIA's failure to track the revolution in Moscow's disarmament policy, which included Gorbachev's willingness to accept intrusive on-site inspections, asymmetric agreements, and unilateral reductions. American negotiators, according to Shultz, were unprepared for Gorbachev's flexibility. Time after time, U.S. negotiators in Geneva, Reykjavik, and Vienna were caught off guard without negotiating positions because they had not anticipated Soviet initiatives and even conciliation. The CIA, for example, told U.S. policymakers that Soviet negotiators would not arrive in Reykjavik in 1986 prepared to negotiate, but the talks in Iceland actually marked an intellectual breakthrough on disarmament, particularly on strategic arms and the INF Treaty. Shultz believed Moscow was caving in to

U.S. positions because it wanted U.S. help in getting out of Afghanistan, but Gates harrumphed that Gorbachev was merely searching for a "breathing space" in order to "gather strength for another era of conflict with us."[14] Like Shultz, Secretary of State Baker used his memoirs to record his difficulties with Gates, particularly Gates's opposition to Baker's arms control and détente policies.

The NIEs on arms control became highly politicized documents that ignored changes in Soviet negotiating positions and missed Moscow's motives for conciliation. In January 1977, Brezhnev stated that nuclear war would be suicidal for both sides and that no victory was possible. His speech signaled a decisive shift toward Soviet cuts in the procurement of weapon systems and a decline in the growth of military spending. Brezhnev elaborated on this message at the 26th Communist Party Congress in 1981, and Gorbachev expanded it at the 27th Party Congress in 1986. But the CIA, as late as 1988, dismissed the Soviet statements as self-serving. Gates argued Moscow was merely exploiting disarmament issues to weaken the West. The State Department disputed this view, accepting Moscow's interest in disarmament, but the CIA redacted State's dissent when the Agency released a declassified NIE. (The CIA repeated this technique in October 2002, when it issued a declassified White Paper on the Iraqi WMD program without highlighting State Department and Energy Department dissents to CIA positions.)

It is noteworthy to track the career paths of those individuals who were responsible for the politicization of intelligence on the Soviet Union. Unsurprisingly, the corrupters of intelligence have prospered. Bob Gates, whose failure to be forthcoming about Iran-Contra forced him to withdraw his name for Senate confirmation as CIA director in 1987, was named secretary of defense nearly twenty years later. Ironically, the then CIA director Deutch named Gates to head a panel in the 1990s to determine whether an NIE on strategic threats to the United States had been politicized, as its critics had charged.

The promotions of the politicizers did not stop with Gates, however. Two senior officials, George Kolt and Douglas MacEachin, who were responsible for corrupting intelligence on the Soviet Union, became the NIO for Russia and the DDI, respectively. The project manager of the Papal Plot assessment, David Cohen, became one of the Agency's highest-ranking officers, the deputy director for operations, and is currently the deputy director for intelligence in New York City's police department. Kay Oliver, the coauthor of the papal assessment became the CIA's historian, and her mentor, Gary Hodnett, received numerous cash awards. John McLaughlin, the coauthor of the postmortem for the Papal Plot, which dismissed the issue of politicization, became the deputy director of central intelligence. McLaughlin was the highest-ranking CIA career officer directly responsible for the flawed and fallacious intelligence on Iraqi WMD; David Kay considered him the "villain" behind the politicized intelligence on Iraq. After all, McLaughlin failed to respond to analytical doubts about the credibility of clandestine sources on Iraq's so-called mobile biological warfare units, and encouraged Secretary of State Powell to deliver a speech to the United Nations that contained the specious intelligence. Powell blamed McLaughlin for failing to provide warning about the tenuous intelligence that was used in the secretary's speech to the UN in February 2003. He told an interviewer in September 2005 that his detailed description of Iraqi WMD that turned out not to exist "was painful" at the time and remains "painful now."[15] He added that it was "devastating" to learn that senior intelligence officials knew the information was unreliable but did not speak up.

The Agency still needs to examine the entire record of politicization from the 1980s, particularly after Gorbachev came to power in 1985. During the 1980s, the CIA exaggerated the strength of the Soviet military and economy, underestimated the burden of Soviet defense spending, and ignored Gorbachev's effort to engage the United States in a series of disarmament agreements. I am not alone in my view of the Agency's failings. Various Reagan administration officials—including Shultz, who was secretary of state, and Powell, Reagan's last national security advisor—have said that they were not well served by the CIA's estimates (as these forecasts are known in the intelligence community). The CIA was unable to convince those policymakers, including the former president Bush and his national security advisor, Brent Scowcroft, who have said that they were surprised by the disintegration of the Warsaw Pact and the Soviet Union. The most compelling voice was that of Shultz, who believed that the "CIA analysis was distorted by strong views about policy" that blocked any discussion of Soviet weakness. Shultz recorded that "when it became evident that the Soviet was, in fact, changing, the CIA line was that the changes wouldn't really make a difference." Baker also described the efforts of Gates to misuse intelligence in an effort to undermine détente policy. Gates conceded in his memoirs that the Agency had underestimated the dramatic change of course in Soviet policy and had neither anticipated Gorbachev's retreat abroad nor the destruction of the Soviet system at home. He made no reference to the senior analysts who made authoritative cases for these developments, let alone the fact he had them removed from their managerial roles to make sure these analytical streams were not pursued.

The politicized intelligence in the case of the decline and fall of the Soviet Union, as well as the run-up to the Iraq War, can be traced to the directors of central intelligence, Casey and Tenet, respectively. Casey, Reagan's handpicked director of central intelligence, only wanted information that would support the president's view of the Soviet threat and a strategy of confrontation with Moscow. Reagan's view of the Soviet threat and the need for arms control changed radically in his second term, but such cabinet members as Casey and Secretary of Defense Weinberger refused to shift gears and remained adamantly opposed to any sign of détente and any policymaker, such as Shultz and Powell, who adopted a conciliatory stance. Some have argued that the U.S. military buildup helped put pressure on the Soviet Union, but that's not a defense for faulty intelligence work. Such a strategy is the province of policymakers; the CIA's job is to provide its best analysis of the facts.

Tenet's posturing on behalf of the Bush administration resembled the role of his hero at the CIA, Richard Helms. Both started out trying to provide the best analysis of the facts, including evidence of the difficulty of the policy tasks against Vietnam and Iraq that relied on force. Both, however, began to provide the administration the intelligence that it needed in order to maintain their access to the president. Helms was found guilty of withholding intelligence that didn't support the views of President Johnson and national security advisor Rostow. Tenet's CIA went even further, allowing an intelligence fabrication to work its way into the president's State of the Union address in 2003, only weeks before the start of the war, and orchestrating a UN speech for Secretary of State Powell that was strewn with misinformation. Worst of all, Tenet told President Bush in December 2002 that the CIA's ability to make a public case for going to war against Iraq was a "slam dunk," thus making the CIA director an advocate for policy. As a result, Tenet dishonored his oath and obligations to the CIA.

If, in the future, the CIA wishes to avoid mistakes like the ones it made when the cold war was ending, playing games with the intelligence records is not a good way to start. In 1998, the Senate defeated ratification of the Comprehensive Test Ban Treaty in part because CIA director Tenet inexplicably decided the Agency would not be able to verify that other nations were complying with the ban. The sudden inability to monitor a treaty is chilling testimony to the continued politicization of the CIA, as was the Agency's decision, in an age of glasnost, to publish incomplete and deceitful defenses of its analysis on the former Soviet Union. Unfortunately, the Agency's estimate in 1999 on the ballistic missile threat to the United States, which has become a rationale for the national missile defense system, indicates that the Agency still prefers worst-case analysis to clear thinking and puts the nation's strategic intelligence at the service of a political agenda. The CIA's role in supplying misinformation and disinformation to the White House, the NSC, and the Congress on Iraqi WMD is more than enough reason to start over at the Agency.

The point here is not to compile a litany of the CIA's failures. After all, the Agency was not alone in getting it wrong on the collapse of the Soviet Union. Virtually every member of the media and the academy was wrong about the weakness and collapse of the Soviet Union. Only the CIA, however, has tried to convince itself and the public that its analysts were right all along. Major research centers and think tanks have conducted seminars to determine "what went wrong." But the CIA maintains that it "predicted the rapidly unfolding events that led to the collapse of communism and the end of the cold war." It is almost a cliché to repeat philosopher George Santayana's words: "Those who cannot remember the past are condemned to repeat it." But if the CIA is unwilling to learn from its mistakes, it will undoubtedly make similar fundamental errors in the future.

CIA director John Deutch told graduates of the National Defense University in 1995 that the primary mission of intelligence was to provide the president with the best possible information on sensitive policy matters: "We have to maintain an unassailable reputation for unvarnished treatment of the facts, never allowing ourselves to tailor our analysis to meet some policy conclusion that may be of convenience to one of our leaders at one time or another. If we do so, it will quickly destroy [our] credibility." The CIA's credibility was virtually destroyed, however, when Casey and Gates distorted intelligence on Soviet military and economic power and the political intentions of Soviet leaders. A decade later, the CIA distorted intelligence on Iraq's WMD and its so-called links to terrorist organizations to enable the Bush administration to make the case for war. Once again, the Agency lost its claim to integrity and credibility in the intelligence and policy communities in Washington.

The creation of the position of DNI has only worsened the malaise at the CIA without assuring any reform for the Agency and the intelligence community. The sudden departure of the first DNI in December 2006, John Negroponte, for a lesser position at the State Department will mean that the reform process will start over under a new, less experienced DNI, retired Admiral Mike McConnell. Currently, the major positions throughout the community, the DNI, the CIA director, and the undersecretary of defense for intelligence, are in the hands of retired or active-duty general officers, which marks the Pentagon's takeover of the intelligence community. The Pentagon already controls nearly 85 percent of the $50 billion intelligence personnel, and nearly 90 percent of the 100,000 intelligence personnel. Military officers have never been known for distinguishing themselves in long-term geopolitical thinking or in solving problems of strategic intelligence, which are the major problems confronting the analytical community of the CIA. And the absence of an independent civilian counter to the power of military intelligence threatens civilian control of the decision to use military power and makes it more likely that intelligence will be tailored to suit the purposes of the Pentagon. None of these issues were debated in the Congress when DNI McConnell, CIA director Hayden, and Undersecretary of Defense James Clapper—all general officers—were easily confirmed.

7

The CIA and the Threat of Terrorism

All we're doing is holding the ring until the cavalry gets here.
—CIA officer to the 9/11 Commission on the Agency's role
against al Qaeda and Osama bin Laden

For the past twenty-five years, the CIA largely failed in its task to provide urgent strategic warning to policymakers about the nature and threat of terrorist organizations to the United States. The formation of al Qaeda in the late 1980s did not escape the attention of the CIA, but it was more than a decade before the Agency understood the threat of international terrorism to the United States and not merely U.S. facilities overseas. The CIA lacked the imagination to anticipate the threat of kamikaze-like attacks from hijacked commercial aircraft against vital targets in major cities, as well as al Qaeda's ability to run a sophisticated operation with many moving parts out of several foreign countries.

The issue of terrorism had been politicized in the early 1980s when CIA director Bill Casey and deputy director Bob Gates exaggerated the Soviet role in international terrorism in order to support the Reagan administration's depiction of the "evil empire" and Secretary of State Haig's view of the Soviet Union as the organizer of terrorism the world over. Like Bush, Cheney, and Rumsfeld, who could not believe that al Qaeda was alone in its responsibility for 9/11, Reagan, Haig, and Casey could not accept that nonstate terrorist organizations, located in Europe and the Middle East, could conduct terrorist operations without the encouragement and support of the Soviet Bloc.

The analytical failure regarding terrorist organizations was similar to the CIA's difficulty in understanding the processes and pathologies of authoritarian societies, particularly the Soviet Union and China. On the one hand, CIA analysts assumed total or totalitarian control by leaders in Moscow and Beijing, and were slow to understand the complexity of decision making in both capitals. In the 1990s, the CIA underestimated the impact and influence of nonstate terrorist organizations without the backing of state actors. A series of CIA failures regarding terrorist attacks from 1993 to 2001 convinced policymakers the CIA could not be trusted for premonitory intelligence. Michael Eisenstadt warned, "If U.S. intelligence analysts and policymakers fail to understand the assumptions and choices of enemies in past wars, they will almost surely be surprised again by enemies in future wars."[1] The Bush administration made the mistake of adopting the Israeli tactic of wholesale use of force as the answer to instability in the Islamic world.

The CIA's directorate of intelligence (DI) was particularly slow to react to the threat of terrorism from bin Laden and al Qaeda. There was limited understanding in the CIA that the jihadist movement was beginning to coalesce around bin Laden and al Qaeda. The conventional wisdom within the intelligence community was articulated best by Philip C. Wilcox, the State Department's coordinator for counterterrorism, who believed "there are informal contacts among Islamists—especially abroad, where their leaders often find safe havens and fund-raising opportunities—but there is little hard evidence of a coordinated international network or command and control apparatus among these groups."[2] The CIA's perception of bin Laden was that he served as the "Ford Foundation of Sunni extremism," writing checks for worthwhile projects, which was particularly unsettling to NSC director Anthony Lake and his senior advisor on terrorism, Richard Clarke.[3]

Lake and Clarke were ahead of the CIA in anticipating the threat of terror to the United States, particularly the threat from bin Laden and al Qaeda, and they had to prod the CIA to be more aggressive both operationally and analytically. The chief of the Counterterrorism Center (CTC) in the 1990s, Cofer Black, and the chief of the Alec Station, Michael Scheuer, were zealots in believing the terrorist threat was indeed a serious one, but they failed to penetrate al Qaeda to obtain tactical warning of specific attacks. They also failed to gather the operational intelligence on bin Laden's whereabouts that would have been certain enough to permit the White House to sanction a military attack.

Nevertheless, the CIA was far out in front of other departments of government, particularly the Department of Defense, in anticipating the threat and devising operational plans against the Taliban government and al Qaeda in Afghanistan. As a result, in the wake of 9/11, the CIA planned and executed the assault to overthrow the Taliban government and to rout al Qaeda from its Afghan sanctuary. Only the CIA knew how to galvanize local units such as the Northern Alliance in Afghanistan and to give its paramilitary forces maximum flexibility on the ground. The Pentagon was unprepared.

CIA tactical failures regarding the threat of terrorism, particularly the inability to penetrate terrorist organizations, led many CIA critics to argue the so-called leash on the Agency was too tight and should have been loosened in order to have success against terrorist organizations. The typical explanations for the "tight leash" were the impact of the Church and Pike Congressional investigations of 1975–1976 that were created to address illegal CIA domestic spying in violation of U.S. law during the Vietnam War. The Church Committee was blamed for the prohibition on CIA assassinations that was put into place by President Jimmy Carter with an executive order in 1978. In the wake of clumsy CIA involvement in various assassination attempts against Fidel Castro in Cuba, Patrice Lumumba in the Congo, Ngo Dinh Diem in South Vietnam, and Guatemalan president Jacobo Arbenz, Carter believed it was time to act. Castro survived numerous assassination attempts, some rather bizarre, but others were killed when local groups got to their targets before CIA teams could reach them.

There was additional evidence the CIA was involved in assassination attempts against Colonel Abdul Kassem, Saddam Hussein's predecessor as prime minister, and General Rafael Trujillo, the dictator of the Dominican Republic. As often as the CIA tried to conduct assassinations, it always failed. As CIA director William Colby remarked, "It wasn't for want of trying."[4] Nevertheless, it was often the awareness of CIA attempts to conduct particular assassinations that emboldened indigenous groups to get into the hunt. The Belgian-sponsored assassination of Lumumba was put into play after Belgian intelligence learned of CIA plotting. U.S. fortunes in Vietnam and Guatemala grew worse in the wake of assassination attempts, and a series of Washington administrations became responsible for national security in Guatemala over the next five decades because of the instability created by the assassination of Arbenz. None of these assassination attempts helped U.S. national security interests, and all of them led to increased violence, even terrorism.

The CIA and International Terrorism

The CIA has never assessed the impact of its own terrorist acts, such as political assassination and the sponsorship of military coups d'etat, on the terrorist actions of anti-U.S. organizations in the Middle East. The CIA's first National Intelligence Estimate (NIE) on international terrorism did not take place until 1981, when the Agency was instructed to evaluate the role of the Soviet Union on the conduct of international terrorism. The NIE on terrorism was requested by the State Department's Ronald J. Spiers, who wanted to examine possible links between the Soviet Union and international terrorism. Spiers wanted to defuse the issue at the Department where new Secretary of

State Alexander Haig had arrived with an anti-Soviet agenda that was based in part on Haig's belief that the Soviet Union was the source for all acts of international terrorism, including the attempt to assassinate him in June 1979, only four days before he stepped down as Supreme Allied Commander Europe. Haig made his first claim of a close connection between the Soviet Union and international terrorism in his confirmation hearings on January 14, 1981, the same day that the Senate confirmed Bill Casey as DCI by a vote of 95 to 0.

Haig charged Moscow with "training, funding, and equipping" international terrorists and, in an aside that dismissed the foreign policy agenda of the Carter administration, added that "international counterterrorism will take the place of human rights." He promised to put a stop to Moscow's "conscious policies . . . that foster, support, and expand" rampant international terrorism. With the exception of Assistant Secretary of State Paul Wolfowitz, another anti-Soviet ideologue, there were very few State Department officials who agreed with Haig. Spiers told Haig privately the intelligence record would not support his hard-line views. Another State Department official, Phillip Stoddard, facetiously remarked, "Yes, the Soviet Union orchestrated terrorism like a giant Wurlitzer organ." They decided that an NIE on the subject would be a safe and nonconfrontational way to disabuse Haig of his views on the Kremlin's support for terrorism. Haig agreed, knowing he had a high-level supporter for his views, the incoming president. Ronald Reagan, whose campaign oratory against the Soviets regularly referred to "Soviet-trained terrorists who are bringing civil war to Central America," requiring "a stand against terrorism in the world."[5]

What Spiers had not counted on was the anti-Soviet paranoia of the new CIA director, Bill Casey, and Casey's interest in making a personal mark on his very first intelligence estimate. Casey was familiar with the work of Team A/Team B six years earlier and wanted to continue the effort to push the CIA's intelligence in a hard-line direction. He believed CIA political analysis was naïve and unsophisticated, and wanted an estimate on terrorism for key policymakers to demonstrate a new era had begun at the Agency. It was unfortunate that Casey cut his bureaucratic teeth on this particular estimate because it convinced him the CIA's Soviet analysts were not only naïve, but apologists for the Soviet Union. And the exercise convinced many Agency analysts that Casey was an ideologue and polemicist, and the new NIO for the Soviet Union, Bob Gates (soon to become Casey's special assistant, and then deputy director for intelligence, and then deputy for central intelligence) would be a weather vane for all of Casey's hard-line views.

There had not been this kind of tension in the CIA's analytic community since the disputes over Vietnam fifteen years earlier, particularly the politicized dispute over the numbers of Viet Cong. But Casey was a more mean-spirited, bullying type of individual than Richard Helms, and Gates was the perfect bureaucratic filter for Casey's views. As a result, there was terrible personnel turbulence during this period and, in many ways, the CIA has never recovered from the bruising battles over the Soviet Union and international terrorism. Casey was an incoherent mumbler in the best of circumstances, but he was direct and even brutal in dealing with CIA analysts and their managers, including the veteran director of intelligence, Bruce Clarke. At one meeting to discuss views on terrorism, Casey glowered at Clarke and said "half of what you say makes sense and the other half makes no sense, but the problem is I can't tell which is which." Clarke soon retired, and he and his wife moved to Vienna, Austria, far away from his beloved Agency and its erratic leader.

Just as the State Department bureaucracy was convinced Haig was wrong and had to be disabused of his polemical notions, the CIA bureaucracy knew Casey would be cutting his teeth on a very difficult issue, but he, too, was wrong. A senior intelligence official, the late Richard Lehman, who facetiously referred to policymakers as "our masters," told a group of us "Casey and Haig would have to be let down, but that it was your job to let them down easily." Thus, we were well aware of the difficult bureaucratic task we faced, but we were also aware there was no evidence of Soviet support for international terrorism in Western Europe and the Middle East. To the contrary, there was excellent evidence that documented Soviet efforts to get insurgent and radical groups to foreswear terrorism, particularly the Palestine Liberation Organization. In my twenty-four years at the CIA, I cannot recall another time where there was such unanimity between the collectors of intelligence in the DO and analysts of intelligence in the DI. There is typically parochial rivalry between these two groups and some difference of views could be expected on a controversial subject, but not on the subject of the Soviet Union and international terrorism.

As the Deputy Division Chief for Soviet relations in the Third World, I was heavily engaged in the first draft of the estimate on the Soviet Union. I appointed the senior analyst in the branch, Carolyn McGiffert Ekedahl, who had a well-earned reputation for tough-minded and balanced analysis, to write the draft, the first official Agency document on the subject. The draft was coordinated at a working level meeting of analysts from CIA, DIA, INR, and various military intelligence agencies, but it ran into a blistering attack from Casey who was convinced that terrorism was indeed a "gigantic Wurlitzer" played by the Kremlin. Unlike Stoddard, Casey was not being facetious. In a meeting with the authors of the draft, the senior leadership of the DI, operatives from the DO, and a representative from INR, he denounced the draft as an "exculpatory brief" and ridiculed everyone around the table. Casey cited the writings of Claire Sterling and noted that he stopped at a book store recently and picked up her latest work, *The Terror Network*, for $13.95 and "it told me more than you bastards whom I pay $50,000 a year." When members of the DO tried to tell Casey that much of Sterling's evidence was black propaganda placed in the European press by CIA operatives, he was totally dismissive. To paraphrase UN inspector Hans Blix, who was critical of CIA intelligence on Iraqi WMD twenty years later, it was another case of "100 percent certainty and 0 percent knowledge."

Haig, too, had read Sterling's book, several days before his comments linking Moscow to international terrorism. Sterling's collaborator, Michael Ledeen, convinced Haig the Soviets were responsible for all acts of terror, and Haig upon confirmation brought Ledeen into the State Department as a special assistant.[6] Ledeen had close ties to the chief of the Italian Military Intelligence and Security Service (SISMI), General Giuseppe Santovito, and SISMI operative Francesco Pazienza, who were convinced that the Soviets were behind the Papal Plot in 1981. The attempted assassin, Mehmet Ali Agca, even accused Pazienza of offering him freedom from prison in exchange for implicating Bulgaria in the plot—as he later did. The gullible victims of Ledeen's disinformation included Henry Kissinger, Zbigniew Brzezinski, and former ambassador Malcolm Toon, who accepted the notion of a Bulgarian–Soviet link to the Papal Plot. Brzezinski even said that it was "utterly scandalous" that State and CIA officials were "unwitting . . . or witting tools" in a campaign "pooh-poohing what turns out to be a very serious plot."

The fact that the assassination attempt against Pope John Paul II took place on May 14, 1981, in the middle of the CIA's debate over terrorism, gave Casey and Gates more reason to press for a hard-line document. Similar to the intelligence prior to the Iraq War, the policy decisions dealing with Moscow and international terrorism were about the personal predilections of high-level members of the Reagan administration and had nothing to do with intelligence information. Just as CIA director Tenet told President Bush that providing intelligence to support the war in Iraq would be a "slam dunk," Casey and Gates assured the Reagan administration there would be sufficient intelligence to support the branding of the Soviet Union as an "evil empire." Along with Secretary of Defense Weinberger, they planned to stop Secretary of State Shultz from pursuing détente with Moscow.

Casey's solution for the problem of an NIE on international terrorism was to take the draft away from the CIA and give the job to the Defense Intelligence Agency. The chief of DIA, General Eugene Tighe (known to CIA analysts as "General Tighraid"), had written Casey a letter outlining his differences with the Agency draft and arguing that the Soviets were involved in international terrorism, even if there were no evidence to say so. (A similar article of faith on Iraqi WMD became the ostensible rationale for using force against Iraq in 2003.) Therefore, Casey turned the project over to DIA where a director, such as Tighe, and analysts, such as Charlie Davis, virtually guaranteed the CIA director would be given a draft to his liking. Casey got more than even the senior managers of the CIA were willing to live with, a polemical and tendentious draft essay that was not supported by any credible intelligence information and totally unacceptable to the senior managers of the CIA and the State Department's INR. Casey, thus, had in his hands what he termed an "exculpatory brief" from the CIA on the subject of the Soviets and international terrorism and an extremist polemic from the DIA that was laughable to those analysts who knew the subject best.

The DIA draft was predictably compatible with Casey's own views of the Soviet threat, and he turned to it often in preparing briefings for the Senate intelligence committee where Senator Barry Goldwater (R-Arizona) shook his head in disgust and disbelief at the CIA director's outlandish views. It is particularly difficult for CIA analysts to properly brief members of the Congressional intelligence committees after CIA directors have gone on record with false information. The intelligence committee recognized Casey's briefings were unreliable and that its unanimous confirmation of the DCI earlier in the year was, in the words of Winston Churchill, "worse than a mistake, it was a blunder." (The CIA and the DI had a similar problem in October 2002, when CIA director Tenet falsely informed the SSCI there was evidence of ties between Iraq and al Qaeda, making it difficult for DI briefers to deny such evidence.)

The leaders of the CIA had to reach a compromise: turn over both draft estimates to the CIA's senior review board where Lincoln Gordon (former U.S. ambassador to Brazil and president of Johns Hopkins University) would find an acceptable solution. Gordon was extremely critical of the CIA draft, terming the definition of terrorism too narrow because it dealt only with such "pure" terrorists as the Baader-Meinhof Gang in West Germany, the Red Brigade in Italy, and the Red Army faction in Japan. Gordon correctly referred to these groups as nihilists who were interested in terror for the sake of terror, and ignored the fact that the draft estimate was designed to address the Soviet role vis-à-vis such groups. No one disputed the fact that the Soviets supported wars of liberation against entrenched autocratic regimes or others sympathetic to the West, and provided arms, training, and other assistance to encourage liberation. Gordon never examined the evidence, although he acknowledged the DIA went too far in terming any violent action against constituted authority as a form of terrorism.

As part of the compromise, the leadership of the NIC changed the terms of reference and allowed a new scholar-in-residence from Rutgers University, Professor Richard Mansbach, to produce what turned out to be the third and final draft. Instead of responding to the terms of reference dealing with Moscow and international terrorism, Gordon instructed Mansbach to broaden the subject to so-called "revolutionary violence," taking into account the actions of national liberation struggles, as well as terrorist organizations. This compromise was a response to those critics who believed that the CIA experts had defined the subject of international terrorism too narrowly. The new definition was so broad that it became meaningless, but Gordon was anxious to reach a compromise on this tendentious issue. Mansbach was new to the world of intelligence and international terrorism, and did not take full advantage of the extensive files on terrorism and Soviet activities in the Third World. Not even Mansbach could conclude that the Soviets had a direct hand in fomenting international terrorism, but he did conclude that Moscow was "deeply engaged in support of revolutionary violence worldwide," and that national insurgencies the Soviet Union supported "directly or indirectly" often "carry out terrorist activities as part of their larger programs of revolutionary violence." As I testified to the Senate Select Intelligence Committee in 1991, the final draft, which took eight months to complete, did not include the original assessment based on ample evidence that the "Soviets have opposed international terrorist activity in public and, in private, have urged their own clients to avoid its use . . . they do not encourage the use of terror by their Third World clients."

There was sufficient intelligence to support these judgments, but it did not agree with the views of Casey and Gates. The intelligence record demonstrated the Soviets were not playing a mighty Wurlitzer organ of terrorism and that the Soviets had in fact tried to discourage acts of terrorism. Moscow believed terrorism undermined the discipline and unity of the groups that conducted terrorist acts. Moreover, Moscow was willing to work with Washington to prevent terrorism. As Bob Woodward noted in *Veil: The Secret Wars of the CIA 1981-1987*, U.S. ambassadors had even been warned by the Soviets of kidnap plots involving Arabs, and the Bulgarians had supported the arrest of Baader-Meinhof gang members.[7] The Soviets cut off military assistance to the PLO after terrorist acts, particularly attacks on El Al aircraft in the 1970s.

The final product was released in 1981 to the policy community where it was quickly ignored and quietly shelved. Most of the policymakers who had any familiarity with it found it to be tendentious and polemical. When William Webster took over for the late Bill Casey in 1987, he quickly dissociated himself from the NIE and emphasized future NIEs would be improved under his command. His deputy, Richard Kerr, immediately directed the NIC to be more rigorous in pursuit of analytical judgments and not to fall victim to politicization. Twenty-five years after the estimate was released, and with access to the secret archives of the former Soviet Union and its Eastern European allies, there still was no evidence that the Soviets directly fomented international terrorism. Ironically, however, the failure in the Reagan administration to understand that nonstate actors could conduct terrorist actions on their own without governmental backing returned to bedevil the Bush administration in its belief that al Qaeda could not conduct the terrorist acts of 9/11 without state (read Iraqi) backing.

The CIA and the Papal Plot

Casey and Gates were never fully satisfied with the CIA estimate on terrorism, which partially exonerated the Soviets of directing terrorism. Four years later, they got the kind of intelligence product they sought when a poorly sourced and poorly documented piece of hearsay from the Bulgarian intelligence service attracted their attention. The document alleged Soviet and Bulgarian intelligence services had cooperated in conducting the assassination attempt against the Pope in 1981. The fact that the source got his information "third-hand" and was a GRU military intelligence official and not a KGB intelligence official meant nothing to Casey and Gates. The report was so weak and implausible that the DO had no plans to issue the document to the policy community. The GRU was responsible for the security of the armed services and collected military and political intelligence abroad; it would not have access to sensitive information on a political assassination. The KGB was responsible for both internal security and foreign counterintelligence responsibilities and also collected intelligence abroad; the Agency's KGB and Eastern European sources confirmed that the Soviets had no role in the Papal Plot. But Casey saw the raw report and it represented Christmas in July to the CIA director. The techniques of politicization that were used on the terrorism estimate thus were put into play in an intelligence assessment entitled, "Agca's Attempt to Kill the Pope: The Case for Soviet Involvement."

Mehmet Ali Agca fired a gun into the stomach of Pope John Paul II on May 13, 1981, in St. Peter's Square, and for four years, CIA officials at the highest levels told policy and congressional sources that the intelligence record exonerated the Soviets and Bulgarians from any involvement. Even Gates' briefings to the Congress as late as the winter 1983–1984 emphasized that the Soviets and Bulgarians were not involved in the assassination plot. For four years, however, Casey pushed the DI for evidence that the Soviets were directly involved, which was similar to Vice President Cheney's efforts to prove a link between Iraq and al Qaeda in 2002–2003. Casey was getting a great deal of pressure from Senator Alphonse D'Amato (R-New York) to produce a document on the Soviet role, and Clair Sterling was needling CIA officers in Rome about their unwillingness to point an accusing finger at the Kremlin. At a cocktail party in Rome, where Sterling was elaborating her theory on Soviet complicity, a CIA clandestine agent dismissed her conspiracy theory. According to one witness, "That pissed her off. She climbed all over the guy."[8] When D'Amato was in Rome, he pressed CIA officials for evidence, but was told there was no evidence to substantiate the allegations. The senator immediately wrote the CIA director to tell him his chief in Rome was a horse's ass. Casey also met with Sterling, who told the director that his analysts and operators were "leftist sympathizers," which Casey happened to agree with in the wake of the 1981 NIE on international terrorism.[9] Casey, who had a low boiling point to begin with, was furious; Gates' role as the good sycophant was to encourage Casey's hostility in order to ingratiate himself with the director.

Like the estimate on international terrorism in 1981, when Casey pointed to a book by Sterling, the CIA director pointed to another Sterling book, *The Time of the Assassins*, which traced the 1981 assassination attempt to the KGB. When the CIA produced a specious assessment in 1985, charging the Kremlin with the attempt against Pope John Paul II, its politicization of intelligence on the Soviet Union reached rock bottom. The DO informed Casey and Gates that Moscow had stopped political assassinations and that neither the Soviets nor the Bulgarians had been involved. Just as there was one young analyst in CIA who believed Iraq's aluminum tubes were for nuclear weapons, there was one operative, Ami Totzi, who believed Moscow was behind the Papal Plot. She did what all polemicists do—ignore authoritative intelligence if you don't happen to agree with the conclusions, but accept the flimsiest accounts possible if the conclusions are attractive.

Casey was playing for bigger stakes than just an analysis of international terrorism. He badly wanted an intelligence assessment to undermine Shultz's efforts to improve relations with Moscow, and Gates wanted to please his boss, making sure that carefully selected CIA analysts worked *in camera* to prevent proper vetting and coordination. Casey detested Shultz, in part because Shultz was occupying the position at State that Casey sought after helping to engineer Reagan's election victory in 1980. And Gates wanted to maintain his viability to succeed Casey as director of central intelligence, which he eventually did several years later in George H. W. Bush's administration. For both Casey and Gates, it was another case of "judge-shopping in the courthouse," finding the analysts who believed there was Soviet involvement and putting them on the case.

An internal CIA postmortem concluded the assessment had "stacked the deck" and "circumvented" the coordination process; the authors of the postmortem—a panel of CIA managers—described the assessment as "deliberately skewed" and stated they could find "no one at the working level in either the [directorates of intelligence] or [operations]—other than the two primary authors of the paper—who agreed with the thrust" of the assessment. The only manager on the panel who tried to water down the postmortem was John McLaughlin, who later became Tenet's deputy director and a major supporter of the effort to provide the Bush administration with the intelligence needed to go to war against Iraq.

The 1985 assessment, *Agca's Attempt to Kill the Pope: The Case for Soviet Involvement,* "read like a novelist's fantasy of Red conspiracy," according to *New York Times* columnist Anthony Lewis. The character of the still-classified report is revealed in its reasoning: "The Soviets were reluctant to invade Poland" in 1981 "so they decided to demoralize [the Polish] opposition" by killing the Polish Pope. The facts of the assassination were not complicated: there was no credible evidence of Soviet or Bulgarian involvement with the Papal Plot, and excellent evidence that the Soviet and Bulgarian intelligence services were not involved. There was also excellent evidence depicting Moscow's use of the Pope to mollify the crisis in Poland, where the Soviets used his influence to try to calm the Polish labor union Solidarnost.

Casey was not one to let the facts stand in his way, and Gates pandered to the Casey agenda, making sure that the draft document was reviewed in less than twenty-four hours and was not seen by officials familiar with the issue, according to testimony at Gates' confirmation hearings in 1991. Gates claimed at his confirmation hearings in 1991 that the CIA assessment only represented a hypothetical case, but his statement was compromised by his cover note to the president and vice president that referred to the assessment as a "comprehensive" examination he forwarded with "confidence."

The assessment became the classic example of the politicization of intelligence. Two Agency postmortems took the assessment and its three authors (Kay Oliver, Beth Seeger, and Mary Desjeans) to task for their flawed work. Their careers did not suffer as a result, however. All three moved higher in the CIA's bureaucracy, with Desjeans becoming chief for all intelligence on the former Soviet Union and an assistant to the deputy director for intelligence, and Oliver becoming the chief of the Agency's historical staff. All three also received generous cash awards for their efforts in support of Casey and Gates. Casey's efforts to worsen Soviet–American relations did fail, however.

NSC officials were aware that the CIA effort to blacken the image of the Soviets was masterminded by a CIA station chief in Europe, Paul Henze. Henze directed the effort to place black propaganda in the European press and give disinformation to writers, such as Sterling, to make the phony case against the Soviets.[10] When several analysts and operatives tried to explain the "blowback" of CIA propaganda to the United States, Casey contemptuously dismissed them.

The CIA and Iran-Contra

In addition to exaggerating Moscow's connection to international terrorism and the attempt to assassinate the Pope, Casey and Gates prepared the intelligence groundwork for Iran-Contra. In 1985, for example, they underplayed Iran's role in sponsoring terrorism, which included the financing for attacks against the U.S. embassy and the Marine barracks in Beirut, Lebanon in 1983. The sale of surface-to-air missiles to Iran required that Tehran had reduced its support for terrorist activities, contained a group of moderate politicians who favored reopening of relations with the United States, and faced a threat of Soviet influence. The extent of Iranian support for terrorism was a key part of the debate on U.S. policy toward the Iranian government because, if Iran's support for terrorism had not waned, it would not be possible to sponsor arms sales to Tehran. Casey and Gates and NIO Graham Fuller ignored the fact that all three of these suppositions were false; the analysts who tried to inform them of this were ignored.

By this time, Casey and a flamboyant DO officer, Dewey Clarridge, had developed a close working relationship in Iran-Contra. Clarridge, the former chief of operations in Europe, was an experienced and unctuous operations officer who helped Colonel Oliver North arrange the illegal flights of TOW missiles from Israel to Teheran. When the CIA's deputy director John McMahon learned about Clarridge's role, he was furious and his complaints to Casey led the CIA director to get Clarridge out of any operational role with Iran-Contra. McMahon may have thought Clarridge was sidetracked when he was given the job of finding new ways to combat international terrorism, but it turned out Clarridge could create havoc even in this ostensibly bureaucratic task. No one in the CIA bureaucracy or the NSC raised the red flag that the U.S. role in supplying surface-to-air missiles to Iran, a state that supported terrorist operations, would undermine U.S. credibility and effectiveness in the counterterrorism campaign. When Gates lied about his knowledge of Iran-Contra in his 1987 confirmation hearings for CIA director, the SSCI turned against him and he had to withdraw his nomination.

Clarridge wanted to shake up the Agency and he convinced Casey the best way to do that was to create a new organization outside of the traditional directorates. Clarridge wanted to merge the analytical experts of the DI with the operational agents of the DO in order to centralize the resources, expertise, and intelligence of the CIA. With the creation of the Counterterrorism Center under their direct control, Casey and Gates could ignore the DI and directly obtain the intelligence analysis they wanted. The dramatic increase in international terrorism in 1985, particularly the seventeen-day hijacking of TWA Flight 847 and Abu Nidal's terrorist attacks at the Rome and Vienna international airports in December 1985 that slaughtered twenty-five people, convinced Casey and Clarridge to use the Center to marshal the resources of the CIA.

There was resistance from both the DO, which did not want to share its sensitive information on sources and methods, and the DI, which did not want to see its intelligence analysis compromised by the worst-case approach of the operational personnel. But Casey was frustrated in his effort to control the DI and the DO, and believed that the creation of a joint center under a reliable zealot, such as Clarridge, would be the most direct bureaucratic means to achieve his policy ends. It worked for Casey and Gates and it produced politicized intelligence for the White House and the NSC.

The fusion centers were supposed to centralize the tasks of collection, dissemination, and analysis, but they had just the opposite effect. Moreover, the creation of a joint DO-DI center became the model for other intelligence missions, particularly counternarcotics and counterproliferation. These centers weakened the traditional roles of the deputy directors for intelligence and operations who had become powerful figures within the Agency bureaucracy and permitted Casey and Gates to have tighter hands-on control of the joint centers, thus bypassing the large and unwieldy directorates. The DO detested the independence of the CTC and its direct line to Directors Casey and Tenet in the 1980s and 1990s. Since the DO was responsible for supplying both resources and officers to the CTC, there was constant tension and bickering over the use of these resources and its personnel. Prior to 9/11, there was much bureaucratic resistance from the DO to provide additional funding to the CTC. The DI was the major loser in the creation of the fusion centers, where worst-case analysis was the dominate methodology and a backseat was given to the production of objective and balanced intelligence.

The CTC was designed to increase the Agency's ability to penetrate terrorist organizations, although the likelihood of penetrating Islamic groups such as Hezbollah, Hamas, or al Qaeda was slim. The fact of the matter (and a well-kept CIA secret) was the DO's lack of success recruiting assets abroad. The CIA relied on defectors, walk-ins or write-ins, who had financial and personal motives for turning to the other side. With small, nihilist terrorist organizations or even networks, the most important information was in the hands of very few people, honoring an extremely strict "need to know." Terrorist operatives did not work in the diplomatic circuit, and virtually all CIA officers abroad, like State Department foreign service officers, rely on diplomatic contacts for their information. Most DO operatives are assigned to Third-World countries, where clandestine sources are extremely unreliable. In fact, nearly all the arrests of al Qaeda targets have been made with liaison information and assistance, particularly the intelligence services of Pakistan, Saudi Arabia, and Egypt. Even Syria has been helpful on occasion.

In any event, senior policymakers and even some senior CIA officials could not accept the fact that small nonstate actors were responsible for the most heinous cases of terrorism around the world, and not large state actors. So, in the 1980s, the focus was on the Soviet Union as the major backer of international terrorism, and in the 1990s, particularly in the wake of the Iran-Iraq War, the focus was on Iran and Iraq as major backers. In November 1991, President Bush ordered government agencies and departments to identify their intelligence needs through the year 2005.[11] Terrorism was given a high priority, but the emphasis was on state-sponsored terrorism, and not the nonstate, nongovernmental, organizations such as al Qaeda. In 2001, President George W. Bush was convinced that Iraq was behind the terrorist attacks on Washington and New York.

Even when the CIA did provide evidence of the role of state actors in actions of terrorism, the White House typically did nothing. The Reagan administration, for example, ignored Iran as a backer of Hezbollah's terrorism, including Iran's financing of the truck bombs that devastated the U.S. embassy in Beirut and the Marine barracks in Lebanon in 1983. Syria and Iran were clearly implicated in these attacks, according to sensitive intelligence. Iran also supported the groups that tortured and killed the CIA station chief in Beirut, William Buckley, and a Marine colonel who was assigned to the UN peacekeeping team in Lebanon. Despite this activity, the DI was slow to sponsor NIEs or special assessments on the problem, even though CIA had no idea how these groups moved their resources globally. The CIA and the FBI were particularly uninformed on the system of "hawala"—an ancient system of moving money internationally without a paper trail and without the movement of funds across borders.

The CIA and al Qaeda

The CIA was slow to take al Qaeda seriously as an organization, bin Laden seriously as a terrorist organizer, and the jihadist movement as anything more than a "Veterans of Foreign Wars for Arabs who had fought in Afghanistan."[12] In the mid-1990s, when national security advisor Lake and counterterrorism expert Clarke were "foaming at the mouth about bin Laden," leading CIA specialists, such as Paul Pillar, merely conceded that bin Laden had an important role to play in raising money for Islamic insurgent organizations, but would go no further. The Agency was late in understanding the implications of the close relations between bin Laden and Khalid Sheikh Mohammed, and seemed to think that bin Laden was funding al Qaeda's terrorism out of his own pockets. An obscure office in the Treasury Department, the Office of Foreign Asset Controls, had a bigger role to play in tracing and understanding the international financial network of al Qaeda than the CIA.

The Clinton administration, particularly Lake and Clarke, became extremely impatient with the reluctance of the CIA and the Pentagon to pursue bin Laden more aggressively. On one occasion, Lake and Clarke drove to the CIA to meet with the head of the Counterterrorist Center, which is particularly unusual for high-ranking NSC officials. In my twenty-four years at the CIA, the only NSC official I can recall coming to the Agency for briefings was William Quandt, the senior official for the Middle East in several administrations, including the Carter administration. CTC officials found bin Laden's role as financier of terror to be intriguing, but it took pressure and persuasion from Lake and Clarke for CTC to agree in 1996 to create its first "virtual station"—the UBL station—not overseas, but in the Washington area, to collect intelligence against bin Laden and his organization. The first chief of the UBL station, however, was not an experienced operations officer but an eccentric intelligence analyst, Michael Scheuer, who named the station after his son Alec—thus, the Alec Station was born in a Virginia office park just a few miles from CIA headquarters in Langley, Virginia. Scheuer, the author of *Imperial Hubris*, was a controversial and divisive figure within the intelligence community, and the Agency eventually forced him to resign in 2004. But Scheuer was one of the few Agency analysts who understood the threat of bin Laden and he had direct access to CIA director Tenet, who came to share Scheuer's views. Scheuer was a zealot, who had few supporters within the Agency. Tenet was also a zealot, who raised alarms about the threat of terrorism, but failed to exercise programmatic control over the CIA and the intelligence community in a way that would improve collection and analysis against the terrorist target.

The sad fact of the matter was that, until 9/11, there was a bureaucratic hesitancy throughout the policy community about taking strong action against the terrorism threat. In late 1998 and 1999, the Pentagon launched air attacks against Iraq, but there was a general unwillingness to bomb targets in Afghanistan where bin Laden had a virtual safe haven. Deputy national security advisor James Steinberg noted that hitting targets in Afghanistan offered "little benefit, lots of blowback against a bomb-happy U.S." And when a Pentagon group under the leadership of Assistant Secretary of Defense for Special Operations and

Low Intensity Conflict Allen Holmes finally approved a recommendation for a "more aggressive counterterrorism posture," it was rejected by Undersecretary of Defense Walter Slocombe as "too aggressive."[13] (Slocombe's fingerprints are also on the failure of policy in postwar Iraq, where he ignored CIA operatives in Iraq and sponsored the de-Baathification and demilitarization policies that left Iraq without experienced individuals to run the government and combat the insurgency.)

When President Clinton and his senior advisors were prepared to use greater force against the terrorist threat, the military services and the intelligence community were dragging their heels. The chairman of the Joint Chiefs of Staff, General Hugh Shelton, believed previous embarrassments for the military in the hostage rescue attempt in Iran in 1980 and the downing of a Black Hawk helicopter in Somalia in 1993 had created a risk adverse culture in the Pentagon. Even General Anthony Zinni, the commander-in-chief of the U.S. Central Command, which would lead any military assault in Afghanistan, was opposed to missile strikes or the use of special operations forces. His proposal was particularly feckless, calling for a buildup of local counterterrorism capabilities in neighboring countries, such as Uzbekistan, and refusing to commit U.S. forces to the problem. In view of the intelligence support that the Taliban and al Qaeda were receiving from high-level Pakistani intelligence officials, including Interservices Intelligence Directorate chief Hamid Gul, it would have been impossible for the United States to lead any counterinsurgency strategy through the use of surrogates on Afghanistan's borders, who were not trustworthy.

The DI contributed to the cautious environment with its analysis. In the last NIE on terrorism before the 9/11 attacks, which was complete in late 1997, bin Laden was mentioned in only three sentences and, despite the importuning from Lake and Clarke, he was still described as a "terrorist financier."[14] There were no references to his organization, al Qaeda, which was about to celebrate its tenth anniversary. History repeated itself six years later, when an NIE on the sources of violence and instability in Iraq did not regard the insurgency as "sufficiently serious or likely to continue growing."[15] The State Department's intelligence analysts wanted a tougher document, but they were outvoted.

The CIA, in any event, was in no position to provide "actionable intelligence" that would allow the Pentagon to operate with any acceptable level of confidence. On one of the rare exceptions to that rule, the CIA identified bin Laden at a specific location in Kandahar in December 1998, but the principal advisors to President Clinton, including the military, ruled against a strike using cruise missiles that would risk an unacceptable level of collateral damage. High-precision strike aircraft would have ameliorated some of this problem, but General Zinni blocked the forward deployment of such aircraft. In February 1999, the CIA placed bin Laden near a large hunting camp in the Helmand province of Afghanistan, but he was accompanied by high-level officials from the United Arab Emirates who frequented this particular hunting preserve. The top CIA official in the region called the intelligence reliable, but policymakers were concerned that a strike might kill an Emirati prince or other senior officials who were with bin Laden. Even aggressive officials, such as Clarke, opposed the use of force because the UAE was our best counterterrorism ally in the region. Soon after, bin Laden moved on from Helmand and, in March, the entire camp complex was hurriedly disassembled, suggesting that the logistical details of the operation had been compromised. Scheuer recorded that "having a chance to get UBL three times in thirty-six hours and foregoing the chance each time has made me a bit angry.

Not even the suicide attack on the USS *Cole* on October 12, 2000, led to any increased urgency. The *Cole* attack should not have been a total surprise because bin Laden's modus operandi included a return to operations that had failed in the first go-round. Just as the WTC attack in 2001 followed the flawed attempt of 1993, the Cole bombing followed an attack in January 2000 when al Qaeda jihadists tried to bomb the USS *The Sullivans* with identical tactics. The earlier plot failed when the skiff carrying the explosives sank under their weight. General Zinni, in fact, had been warned about using the waters of Yemen for off-shore refueling, but he chose to ignore the State Department and CIA warnings. As Mike Sheehan, the State Department representative on the CSG, said: "Yemen is a viper's nest of terrorists. What the fuck was the *Cole* doing there in the first place? Who the shit do they think attacked the *Cole*, fuckin' Martians?"[16]

The attack on the USS *Cole* made it clear that al Qaeda was becoming more active and threatening in its planning and directing of terrorism attacks against the United States. The CIA and the FBI moved very slowly in reaching a final conclusion about responsibility for the deadly attack that left seventeen sailors dead and thirty-nine injured. Both agencies knew that there was a large al Qaeda cell in Yemen, where the terrorist organization conducted a good deal of its logistical activities, and that the Egyptian Islamic Jihad, also based in Yemen, had announced a merger into al Qaeda. NSA officials had made a credible case pointing to al Qaeda, but the CIA continued to waffle. Berger was leaning on Tenet but, as late as December 21, the Agency lacked a definitive answer on the "crucial question" of outside direction of the attack. The State Department and the Pentagon had reservations about retaliation in any event, citing the inability of the CIA and the FBI to point authoritatively at the responsible group. At one Principals Committee meeting, Berger upbraided Tenet so severely that the CIA director got up and walked out of the meeting.

In response to pressure from the White House, the Pentagon eventually prepared thirteen options for wider-ranging strikes, but none of these options included a contingency plan for an invasion of Afghanistan. The Pentagon simply did not want to get involved in Afghanistan and its response remained cautious and risk adverse, stressing that military options were limited. It gave this message to the Clinton administration on the way out and it gave the same message to the Bush administration on the way in. Like good accountants, the Pentagon believed that hitting inexpensive and rudimentary training camps with costly missiles would not be cost effective, ignoring the importance of simply disrupting their activities.

Although terrorism carried a high priority within the Clinton administration, particularly because of the interest and prodding of Lake and Clarke, the Bush administration clearly had other priorities. Clinton had created a small group at the highest level, including National Security Advisor Berger, CIA director Tenet, Secretary of State Madeleine Albright, and Secretary of Defense Bill Cohen to discuss such topics as the threat of bin Laden or a response to Khobar Towers, but the lack of any paper record meant that little information was disseminated to senior-level managers who needed to make decisions. Moreover, the absence of a clear chain of command and insufficient sharing of intelligence meant there was always some level of misunderstanding and tension when Clarke chaired the Counterterrorism and Security Group (CSG) for the members of the policy and intelligence communities. Clarke was controversial and unpopular within this structure, but Berger believed that Clarke occupied an important role in pushing the interagency process to fight bin Laden. As Berger put it, "I wanted a pile driver."[17] The turning point for the CSG was the bombings of two American embassies in East Africa in August 1998. Before those attacks, the U.S. focus was on such Iranian-sponsored groups as Hezbollah. Now the emphasis on bin Laden was accepted unanimously, with Clarke creating *Plan Delenda,* from the Latin word "to destroy," evoking the Roman vow to erase rival Carthage.

The embassy bombings and *Plan Delenda* led to the need for military strikes against al Qaeda, but, in the wake of attacks on U.S. embassies on the Horn of Africa, retaliation consisted of pin-prick strikes against ramshackle al Qaeda training facilities in Afghanistan and a pharmaceutical plant in Khartoum that had nothing to do with production of lethal chemicals. Berger and Clarke claimed the Sudan strike was based on the best intelligence ever collected for such operations, but that was a lie. The CIA operatives responsible for the soil sample at the pharmaceutical plant found the results inconclusive and called for another investigation. Tenet overruled them, bowing to White House pressure to get the military strike underway. Clarke told me that Tenet stood by the intelligence, although Tenet knew the first test was inconclusive.

Tenet refused to permit a second test, although later intelligence on the site in Khartoum made it clear that the plant had nothing to do with the production of lethal chemicals or terrorist organizations. The administration simply wanted to be seen as doing something.

During the Millenium period, there was greater pressure on the security services in Pakistan to turn over particular suspects to the United States, and there were more domestic surveillance warrants for investigations in the United States. About this time, an alert U.S. Customs agent, Diana Dean, apprehended Ahmed Ressam, an Algerian jihadist, in a routine screening on the U.S.–Canadian border. Ressam refused to make eye contact with Dean, and he was pulled out of line; he ran from the ferry boat, leaving his car on the boat. Dean gave chase, placed him in custody, found his car and learned that Ressam was trying to cross the border with explosives and a map of Los Angeles International Airport. For the first time, the FBI was convinced of the need to share information about its domestic investigations with the NSC.

The Clinton administration did a good job of getting greater Congressional appropriations for counterterrorism, but a poor job in getting the CIA to use the additional funds against bin Laden or on operational efforts overseas. Despite Tenet's so-called declaration of a war on terrorism, CIA spending and staffing on counterterrorism remained flat. When the NSC tried to get the CIA to fund Ahmed Shah Masood and the Northern Alliance, the Agency dragged its heels and argued that he was no match for the Taliban, even though the Northern Alliance controlled nearly one third of the country. Clarke's anger with the Agency persuaded him to review the CIA's spending on counterterrorism and, working with the Office of Management and Budget and the CIA's own auditors, he learned that all of its spending against al Qaeda was coming out of Emergency Supplementals. There were almost no baseline CIA funds being thrown at al Qaeda, and the DO refused to transfer funds from other projects to pursue al Qaeda.[18] White House pressure did lead the CIA and the Air Force to resolve its differences over the use of the Predator reconnaissance aircraft in Afghanistan, but the armed version of the Predator was not ready for use until after 9/11.

A case for holding CIA director Tenet responsible for the intelligence failure on 9/11 would be based on his failure to back up the so-called war on terror with resources or personnel. Tenet could talk-the-talk in front of a Congressional committee about the al Qaeda threat, but he didn't walk-the-walk to discipline the intelligence community, not even his own Agency. Similarly, the directorate of operations, led by James Pavitt, could claim that it was fixated with the al Qaeda threat, but it provided no additional support to the Counterterrorism Center led by Cofer Black, who shared Clarke's passion for a more aggressive approach.

The problem of terrorism also surfaced the traditional tensions that existed between the Pentagon and the CIA. The two institutions had disagreed over the nature of the Soviet threat, the role of arms control and disarmament in American national security policy, and all assessments of the relative power of the United States and its various enemies. On the subject of terrorism, the Pentagon simply wanted nothing to do with the problem. The uniformed military wanted no part of any campaign against terrorism or any tactics that involved operations in Afghanistan, and essentially ignored the warnings of the Clinton administration to prepare operational programs against such groups as al Qaeda. When President Bush decided to move against al Qaeda and the Taliban in the wake of the 9/11 attacks, the Pentagon had no plans on the shelf and Secretary of Defense Rumsfeld was particularly angry about being outmaneuvered by Tenet.

Unlike Rumsfeld's Pentagon, Tenet's CIA had a strategy for Afghanistan that turned on using cash, guns, and rice to buy its way into the tribal community, and then would use the tribal allies to conduct sabotage operations against the Taliban forces and to conduct reconnaissance operations to identify possible escape routes for bin Laden and other al Qaeda leaders.[19] The Agency relied on their contacts with the Northern Alliance, particularly the ethnic Tajiks and Uzbeks within the Alliance, to secure the northern half of Afghanistan and to create a safe passage for supplies from Pakistan. CIA teams located military targets for the Pentagon, and U.S. bombing operations made it possible for the Northern Alliance to reach Kabul. CIA paramilitary teams were fully operational in Afghanistan before the Pentagon could put boots on the ground.

The Pentagon, for its part, had borne a grudge against the CIA since Desert Storm in 1991, when it criticized the lack of intelligence support for the fighting. A DoD member of the CSG accused the CIA of "underfunding critical programs," which pointed to failure at the highest levels of the CIA.[20] Berger was becoming increasingly frustrated with both institutions, and commented that "unfortunately the light at the end of the tunnel is another tunnel." There were White House officials interested in using the Delta force against bin Laden, but the Pentagon said no. Others in the White House wanted to use the Air Force against al Qaeda, but, again, the answer was no. Sheehan eventually asked, "Does al Qaeda have to attack the Pentagon to get their attention?"[21]

The Bush administration did no planning for military operations and capabilities against the Taliban and al Qaeda before the 9/11 strikes. It lacked any sense of urgency regarding bin Laden and the need for operational planning and, as a result, valuable time was lost. Unlike Clinton and National Security Advisor Berger, Bush and National Security Advisor Rice placed no pressure on the CIA for greater intelligence collection against terrorism or greater operational involvement. Secretary Rumsfeld had other priorities, particularly national missile defense, and failed to appoint an assistant secretary of defense for counterterrorism until the day after the 9/11 attacks. He was briefed by outgoing secretary, William Cohen, on the threat of terrorism but didn't recall the briefing. The outgoing assistant secretary of defense for special operations and low intensity conflict (SOLIC) never briefed Rumsfeld. Lower level SOLIC officials knew that Rumsfeld was focused on other issues and not especially interested in their counterterrorism agenda. These officials, as well as members of the special forces, were frustrated with the lack of military planning, but the Pentagon in general believed that neither the Congress nor the American people would have supported large-scale operations against Afghanistan prior to 9/11.

Other high-level officials in the Bush administration had interests other than terrorism despite the urgent briefings from their Clinton counterparts in January 2001. The new undersecretary of defense, Douglas Feith, arrived at the Pentagon in July 2001 and was told to focus on dissolving the Anti-Ballistic Missile Treaty in order to prepare for the deployment of a national missile defense, Rumsfeld's number one priority. In June 2001, deputy national security advisor Hadley circulated a presidential directive on policy toward al Qaeda that called for a new set of contingency military plans regarding al Qaeda and the Taliban, but the NSC had not obtained a presidential signature for the directive. Hadley called Deputy Secretary of Defense Wolfowitz directly and advised him to start preparing new plans in response to the forthcoming directive. But Rumsfeld ordered no planning prior to 9/11, and Hadley and Wolfowitz conceded the Pentagon's plans presented to the Bush administration after 9/11 were unsatisfactory. Rumsfeld told the 9/11 Commission he could not remember any particular counterterrorism issue that engaged his attention before 9/11. He conceded the DoD before 9/11 was not organized or staffed to deal with terrorism.[22]

The Pentagon simply dragged its feet in response to the Clinton administration's effort to plan military options against al Qaeda and Afghanistan. Wolfowitz explained the Pentagon's inaction by describing the *Cole* attack as "stale" by the time the Bush administration came into office. Instead of looking at response scenarios, Rumsfeld and Wolfowitz instructed the Pentagon to work on force protection. Clarke was kept in the NSC to maintain some continuity on issues of counterterrorism, but his role and influence was severely downgraded; he was told to report to the Deputies Committee rather than directly to the principals. Unlike his relations with Clinton, Clarke never directly briefed Bush on terrorism prior to 9/11. The entire Bush White House and much of the CIA bureaucracy looked at Clarke as a "chicken-little alarmist."

The White House had its own excuses for lack of action. Berger argued he never received a definitive judgment from the CIA on al Qaeda's responsibility for the *Cole* attack, and therefore could not respond with military force. The Bush administration never had a strategic plan or understanding of the problem of terrorism in the Middle East, and believed the CIA never made an urgent case regarding the threat of terrorism. Tenet, Black, and Scheuer were emotional and graphic regarding the threat, but there was no programmatic effort to inform the administration in a dramatic way that the serious political and social issues of the Middle East were contributing to the problem of terrorism. In his memoir, Tenet conceded he and Black warned Rice, Clarke, and Hadley about a "significant terrorist attack in the coming weeks or months," but failed to take the message to President Bush because the president was not an "action officer."[23] The CIA never linked the absence of a peace plan in the Middle East to the problem of instability in the region, let alone the need for reducing Islamic support for such terrorist groups as al Qaeda. Strategic efforts were needed in the Middle East to counter the increased anti-Americanism in the region, particularly Islamic hostility toward the United States in the wake of any U.S. invasion of Iraq. Even in the wake of the Israeli invasion of Lebanon in the summer of 2006, the Bush administration saw no need for greater diplomatic involvement in the region, particularly the need to sponsor Arab–Israeli peace negotiations. The invasion of Iraq in 2003 and the Israeli invasion of Lebanon in 2006 worsened these problems, generating more terrorism and Arab–Israeli tensions.

Bush asked Vice President Cheney to chair an effort to examine preparations for managing a response to any WMD attack and other problems of national preparedness, but Cheney had barely started when 9/11 took place. Although Cheney gave little thought to the problem of terrorism before 9/11, he certainly exploited the attack as a transformative event to expand the powers of the presidency, an outcome he supported thirty years earlier as President Gerald Ford's chief of staff. National Security Advisor Rice was simply uninterested. Berger told her she would be spending more time on terrorism than any other issue, but Rice demonstrated no interest in the issue until after 9/11. She ignored a particularly dire and direct warning in a briefing from Tenet and Black in July 2001, only two months before 9/11.

Clarke tried to arrange Principals Committee meetings on these issues, but had no success until one week before the 9/11 attacks. He wanted the principals to agree that al Qaeda was a "first-order threat" and not a routine problem exaggerated by "chicken-little" alarmists, but there was no response. Clarke also wanted to revive covert assistance to the Northern Alliance and other groups in Afghanistan and for Predator reconnaissance missions. But Rice and Hadley agreed with the CIA's position that Predator reconnaissance should be delayed until the armed version was ready. And prior to 9/11, no funding had been found to get the program underway. The covert action budget was stalled in the Congress, and the stalemate was broken by the 9/11 attacks themselves.

Alarming reports were coming in from the field between April and July; in late June, Clarke informed Rice that the threat reporting had reached a crescendo, and in early July, the FBI issued a national threat advisory. On July 6, the CIA told CSG participants that al Qaeda members "believe the upcoming attack will be 'spectacular,' qualitatively different from anything they have done to date."[24] But the Pentagon was still unwilling to retaliate in response to the attack on the USS *Cole*, and Tenet was opposed to Predator reconnaissance flights until the arming of the Predator had been completed. Clarke believed that Tenet's position was typical of a risk-averse DO; Tenet found backing from the Pentagon and prevailed.[25]

In early August, the CIA prepared a PDB item on the possibility of a terrorist attack in the United States, although neither the White House nor the CSG had received specific, credible information about any threatened attacks in the United States. When the CIA finally hand-carried the PDB item to the president's ranch in Texas on August 6, 2001, which was titled "Bin Laden's Determination to Strike in United States," Bush dismissed it as the Agency's attempt to "cover its ass." In fact, the PDB lacked any sense of urgency. The lead sentence, for example, cited media reports in arguing that bin Laden had wanted to conduct terrorist attacks in the United States *since 1997* and the reference to recruitment efforts in New York was dated *1998*. There was nothing in the PDB item to cause any alarm or increased preparedness. Nor did the CIA inform Clarke or the CSG about the August 2001 investigations that produced the discovery of suspected al Qaeda operatives in the United States; similarly, the FBI did not inform them of the arrest or investigation of Zacarias Moussaoui in Minnesota.

Six years after 9/11, the intelligence and policy communities are more alert to the problem of terror, but there are still institutional reforms that have not been taken. The CIA has not fixed its problems in the field of strategic intelligence, and the operational side has been weakened by the use of secret prisons, torture and abuse, and extraordinary renditions. These tools have weakened liaison relations with foreign intelligence services that object to CIA violations of European law. Meanwhile, the CIA is still having difficulty dealing with the strategic picture regarding terrorism. The National Intelligence Council's NIE on trends in terrorism that appeared in April 2006 incorrectly predicted the loss of such key leaders as al-Zarqawi would "exacerbate strains and disagreements" in the movement and "pose a less serious threat to U.S. interests."[26] Actually, terrorism and recruitment in Iraq increased after the death of al-Zarqawi. The NIE also incorrectly predicted that any jihadist losses would hurt their recruitment efforts, when in fact Mujahideen losses in Afghanistan against the Soviets led to greater volunteers and the same trend has been seen in Iraq. A civil war was already taking place in Iraq even before the bombing of a Shiite mosque in Samarra in 2006, but CIA continued to refer to it as mere sectarian violence. The NIC did not refer to civil War in Iraq until February 2007, when it finally conceded there was a civil war.

The problem of strategic intelligence remains. The DI is giving too much attention to so-called target analysis for the CTC in its operational missions, and the CTC has been taken out of the analytical field. The analysis of terrorism and counterterrorism is done at the NCTC, which now reports to the DNI. The NCTC, moreover, is now led by Naval admirals, which does not suggest that strategic intelligence is being taken seriously. The appointment of general officers to manage not only the CIA, but the entire intelligence community as well, also points to a failure to address the strategic problems in the intelligence picture. Worst-case analysis rather than rigorous strategic intelligence is the name of the game. Finally, until the United States develops a robust and aggressive strategy for dealing with al Qaeda in Afghanistan and Pakistan, intelligence strategies will fall short. Donald Rumsfeld asked his military commanders several months after the invasion of Iraq whether we were "capturing and killing" more terrorists than the "radical clerics . . . were recruiting and deploying?" We knew even then that the U.S. occupation of Iraq compromised the strategic task against terrorism and created more terrorists.

8

The 9/11 Tragedy and the Failure of Strategic Intelligence

One week after the attack on the Pentagon and the World Trade Center, national security advisor Condoleezza Rice told the press corps, "This isn't Pearl Harbor." No, it was worse. Sixty years ago, the United States did not have a director of central intelligence, or fifteen intelligence agencies, or a combined intelligence budget of more than $50 billion to provide an early warning of enemy attack. Just as intelligence was unimaginative, divided, and diffuse on the eve of Pearl Harbor, there was little innovative thinking on terrorism within the intelligence community prior to September 11, 2001. The lack of intelligence sharing was central to the failure at Pearl Harbor, although the problems of sharing have probably been exaggerated in the case of 9/11. And like Pearl Harbor, nearly three thousand lives were lost in the 9/11 attacks because of systemic flaws within the intelligence community. But like Pearl Harbor, there was enough intelligence collected prior to 9/11 to prevent the attack.

There was one major difference between Pearl Harbor and 9/11. The surprise Japanese attacks led to a major investigation and reform of the national security community in the form of the 1947 National Security Act, which created the CIA, the NSC, the Department of Defense, and the Joint Chiefs of Staff. The 9/11 attacks led to a Presidential Commission in 2003 and an Intelligence Reform Act in 2004 that were totally inadequate to the task. In fact, the creation of an intelligence tsar and the centralization of intelligence analysis may have made future intelligence failures and the politicization of intelligence more likely, particularly in view of the decline in competitive analysis and the enhanced role for the White House and the Pentagon in the structure of intelligence. Placing the top three positions in the intelligence community in the hands of general officers will not help solve the problem of inadequate strategic intelligence.

Less than two weeks after the surprise attack on Pearl Harbor, President Franklin D. Roosevelt appointed a high-level military and civilian commission to determine the causes of the intelligence failure. Following the September 11 attacks, President Bush, CIA director Tenet, and the chairmen of the Senate and House intelligence committees adamantly opposed any investigation or postmortem. The president's failure to appoint a statutory inspector general at the CIA until April 2002 deprived the Agency of the one individual who could have started an investigation regardless of the CIA director's opposition. Overall, the unwillingness to begin a congressional inquiry for nearly eight months or internal investigations at the CIA and FBI for nearly two years increased the suspicion that indicators of an attack had gone unheeded. The unwillingness of the 9/11 Commission to examine the personal failures prior to the attacks and to assess blame for failures created the impression of a major cover-up. The CIA's reluctance to declassify its full accountability report for 9/11, the only agency not to do so, adds to the impression of a cover-up.

The eventual Senate and House intelligence committee investigation of the September 11 failure, which began in June 2002, was mishandled at the outset. The original staff director for the investigation, former CIA inspector general Britt Snider, had the stature and experience for the job, but he was soon pushed out by then Senate intelligence committee chairman Richard Shelby (R-Georgia), a staunch critic of CIA director Tenet, but never an advocate for reform of the intelligence community. Tenet and Snider had a close personal and professional relationship, which led Shelby to protest the appointment of Snider as staff director, although he was extremely well qualified for the position. Shelby's behavior was unprofessional and counterproductive; he had no quarrel with Snider, he simply wanted to punish Tenet.

The Congressional staff itself was too small and inexperienced to do the job seriously. The August 2002 decision of the chairmen of the Senate and House intelligence committees, Senator Bob Graham (D-Florida) and Representative Porter Goss (R-Florida), to order an aggressive FBI investigation of the joint intelligence committee, ostensibly to uncover leaks of unclassified information, marked a blatant violation of the separation of powers between the executive and legislative branches of government. Much time was lost as senators and representatives debated whether committee members should submit to unprecedented polygraph examinations, a move designed to placate President Bush and Vice President Cheney, who never wanted a Congressional or independent investigation in the first place.

The Bush administration, moreover, established roadblocks to the investigation from the start, preferring an inquiry that was quick and dirty to one that was thorough and authoritative. The president did not permit his secretaries of state and defense to testify to the joint congressional investigation in public session, and President Bush refused to accept questioning from the 9/11 Commission unless he was accompanied by Vice President Cheney. Sensitive intelligence items, particularly intelligence reporting from the PDB, were kept from the full membership of the Commission. According to Senator Shelby, the Republican chairman of the committee, the administration "delayed cooperating fully, knowing it [the committee] has a deadline to meet."[1]

To make matters worse, the Congressional oversight process was broken, and even in the wake of the 9/11 and Iraq War intelligence disasters, there was no sign that the Senate and House intelligence committees would scrutinize the intelligence community. Senator Charles Grassley (R-Iowa) observed, "Everyone's in awe of them [intelligence agencies]. Everyone just melts in their presence, and so they have always gotten a long leash." Representative David Obey (D-Wisconsin) agreed, adding that Congressional oversight has been "miserable." Representative Saxby Chambliss (R-Georgia) conceded that the congressional intelligence committees have a "share in the blame for not providing better oversight." The 9/11 Commission was particularly critical of the oversight committees; nevertheless, in the wake of its report, Senator Pat Roberts (R-Kansas) still stopped his committee from investigating the politicization of intelligence on the Iraq War, and Representative Peter Hoekstra (R-Michigan) prevented the House committee from investigating CIA war crimes in Guantanamo, Afghanistan, and Iraq.

Despite the opposition from the White House and the short deadlines for its work, the preliminary report of the joint intelligence committee did a decent job of ferreting out evidence documenting some of the failures at the CIA and the FBI.[2] The report described a director of central intelligence who declared a war on terrorism in 1998, but allocated no additional funding or personnel to the task force on terrorism; an intelligence community that never catalogued information on the use of airplanes as weapons; and a CIA that never acknowledged the possibility of weaponizing commercial aircraft for terrorism until two months after the attacks on the WTC and the Pentagon. The CIA never believed there would be a terrorist attack inside the United States and consistently warned the Clinton and Bush administrations that attacks would come against U.S. facilities overseas; meanwhile, the FBI told the White House that al Qaeda lacked the resources and the logistical network to conduct an attack at home. One could not cite a more profound failure of imagination and investigation than the wrong-headed assumptions of the two key intelligence agencies for counterterrorism.

Nevertheless, the joint inquiry of the Senate and House managed to identify the problems that kept CIA and the FBI from providing strategic warning to the White House, the Congress, and the American people of the 9/11 attacks. Their work pointed to the particular inadequacy of DCI Tenet, who never created a strategy for counterterrorism for the intelligence community. The resources and the expertise of the entire community were never marshaled, even though the first attack on U.S. soil took place in 1993, eight years before the horror of 9/11. The weakness of CIA strategic analysis was obvious on the issue of counterterrorism, and there is still no indication this weakness has been corrected. The National Intelligence Council did not produce an NIE on the crucial subject of terrorism and the threat to the United States in the four-year period before 9/11, and there was no strategic coordination of collection and analysis on the overall subject of international terrorism. There were individuals such as Tenet, Cofer Black and Michael Scheuer at the CIA, and John O'Neill and Daniel Coleman at the FBI, who shared the worries of such NSC members as Tony Lake, Sandy Berger, and Dick Clarke, but the CIA and the FBI refused to believe al Qaeda would attack in the United States or had the network or the individual cells to do so. There was insufficient information sharing, abysmal linguistic capabilities, and no coordination on funding to correct the problems regarding terrorism. The primary problem, however, was one of flawed assumptions with no mechanism for challenging conventional wisdom.

The Congressional joint inquiry, moreover, refused to examine the problem of accountability in terms of who was responsible for the failure. Instead, the Senate and House, in November 2002, asked the inspectors general of the CIA, the Justice Department, the Defense Department, and the State Department to determine whether individuals could be held accountable for failure in their performance. They also asked the IGs to recognize those individuals who should be recognized for outstanding performance in the field of counterterrorism. With the exception of the DoD, which dragged its heels on this assignment from the outset, the relevant IGs over the next two-and-a-half years completed their studies. The FBI, State Department, and Defense Department reports have been declassified, but CIA directors Goss and Hayden have stubbornly refused to declassify the full CIA report. Only the executive summary was declassified and released, following pressure from Senators Rockefeller, Ron Wyden (D-Oregon), and Kit Bond (R-Missouri). With the exception of Senator Wyden, the Senate has made no serious attempt to gain access to the full report, and the various 9/11 survivors groups and family members have not used their considerable influence to lobby for greater access. Unlike the Pearl Harbor investigations during World War II, the nation continues to operate in the dark about who was to blame and, just as important, who should be commended. Never has there been so much need for illumination in the field of national security and rarely has there been such indolence in trying to secure it.

We know from the preliminary report of the joint inquiry and the staff reports of the 9/11 Commission that the timely use and distribution of intelligence data could have prevented the terrible acts of terrorism in 2001. The co-chairmen of the 9/11 Commission have stated as much in public, but the partisan balance of their commission (five Democrats and five Republicans) prevented serious analytical conclusions in the final report. Several Democrats on the Commission were particularly zealous in blocking criticism of the Clinton administration; several Republicans served the same purpose for the Bush administration. Moreover, the refusal of the White House and the CIA to declassify information provided to the president before the attacks, some of which had already been reported in the international press, indicated important information did not make its way to the highest levels of government. Tenet and CTC chief Black gave a sensitive briefing to national security advisor Rice in July 2001 about the likelihood of a terrorism attack in the United States, but 9/11 Commission staff chief Philip Zelikow circulated this report to only one or two members of the Commission and it was never part of the Commission's final report. This is one of the best examples of the 9/11 Commission's cover-up of important information, with Zelikow protecting his close friend, Condi Rice.

The CIA learned about the first Soviet atomic testing in the late 1940s from the Associated Press and the first Indian nuclear tests in 1974 from United Press International; so it is not surprising that the CIA and even NSA learned about the terrorist airborne attack on New York and Washington from CNN. Prior to 9/11, there had not been an airline hijacking or bombing in the United States for nearly a decade, and the focus of the intelligence community on terrorism was marred by the lack of a strategic approach and the absence of analytical imagination. The best analysts were not interested in the issue of counterterrorism and the best operational officers considered nonstate terrorist organizations to be impenetrable. At the time of the attack, Tenet was having breakfast at the St. Regis Hotel in downtown Washington with his former boss at the Senate intelligence committee, David Boren. Boren had weighed in with the Bush administration in 2000 to make sure that the new president would keep Tenet, a nominal Democrat and Boren's good friend, as CIA chief.

The flawed assumptions of the analytical community meant the collection was ultimately misused or often ignored. For seven years prior to 9/11, for example, there was no cataloguing of information on weaponizing aircraft to be used against civilian targets. For three years prior to 9/11, there was sufficient information on al Qaeda's interest in attacking the United States, but, with the exception of a single PDB item in August 2001, there was no attempt to rigorously or systematically analyze this information. When President Bush dismissed the August briefing as a "cover your ass" exercise, he was right. NSA had several timely intercepts with direct relevance to 9/11 that were not translated until after 9/11. The CIA underestimated the importance of the two key al Qaeda leaders, bin Laden and Khalid Sheikh Mohammed, and prepared no special assessment on al Qaeda after the bombings of two U.S. embassies in 1998. The CIA knew that two al Qaeda members entered the United States in January 2000, but did not watchlist these individuals until several weeks prior to 9/11. The two hijackers befriended an FBI informant, but the FBI could not locate them. Virtually every failure was a personal or individual failure, but the suggested reforms of the 9/11 Commission and the congressional reform act dealt with process and not people. Since the CIA's full report on 9/11 accountability has never been declassified and only seen by several Congressional leaders, the American public has limited knowledge of how its intelligence agencies failed to deal with terrorism. The reference to rearranging the deck chairs on the *Titanic* was never more apt than in describing the government's response to the causes of the 9/11 failure.

THE PATTERN OF FAILURE

The failure of the CIA to anticipate the 9/11 attacks—and the reluctance to thoroughly investigate the failure until forced to do so by the Congress—was the latest in a long series of CIA blunders and cover-ups, consistently abetted by the unwillingness of the Congressional intelligence committees to conduct oversight. Over the past half-century, U.S. presidents have accepted the poor performance of the CIA, presumably because the Agency offers a clandestine and relatively inexpensive instrument for American foreign policy. President Eisenhower employed the CIA in a series of covert actions in Guatemala, Iran, and Cuba that contributed to instability in these countries and complicated U.S. bilateral relations in the Caribbean, the Middle East, and Southwest Asia. U.S. presidents sanctioned covert actions that had pernicious long-term consequences for U.S. security. Operations in Indonesia, Congo, Angola, and Chile harmed U.S. regional interests. In the field of intelligence analysis, the CIA provided no strategic warning for the Korean War in 1950, the Soviet invasions of Hungary and Czechoslovakia, the 1973 October War, the 1982 Israeli invasion of Lebanon, or the 1983 terrorist bombings that killed 250 U.S. Marines and destroyed the U.S. embassy in Beirut. Intelligence missed the signs of an Iraqi invasion of Iran in 1980, the Iraqi invasion of Kuwait in 1990, and Indian nuclear testing in 1998. In my twenty-four years at the CIA, the only time CIA analysts were held accountable for an intelligence failure followed their inability to anticipate the coup against Soviet leader Nikita Khrushchev in 1964. The following year there was a complete shake-up in the intelligence office that analyzed internal Soviet affairs, although—unlike the other cited failures—why should CIA anticipate an event hidden from a Soviet leader and his high command?

The performance of the intelligence community worsened in the 1990s. When the CIA and the National Geospatial Intelligence Agency missed Indian nuclear testing in 1998, Director Tenet stated, "We didn't have a clue."[3] A major share of the $50 billion intelligence budget is devoted to satellite and signals intelligence to prevent such strategic failures, which have important geopolitical consequences. In this case, the failure to monitor Indian testing and Tenet's inexplicable testimony that CIA could not guarantee verification of disarmament treaties led to the Senate' unwillingness to ratify the Comprehensive Test Ban Treaty. The CIA also failed to monitor the third-stage capability of the North Korean Taepodong missile, which was tested in August 1998, leading to Congressional calls in the United States for a national missile defense and Japanese suspension of talks to establish diplomatic relations with North Korea.[4] As a result of the North Korean failure, the CIA analysis of Third-World missile programs has taken on a worst-case flavor, exaggerating the national security threat to the United States and politicizing the intelligence data in the process. The CIA's worst-case analysis was used by the Bush administration to abrogate the Anti-Ballistic Missile Treaty of 1972 and proceed with the deployment of an untested national missile defense, which is now the most expensive weapons item in a record $620 billion defense budget. The CIA's exaggeration of the North Korean threat from 2001–2005 led to a worsening of U.S.–North Korean relations, the ouster of international inspectors, and a North Korean missile test.

The 9/11 failure was particularly stunning because, in 1995, the CIA had access to the infamous Bojinka plot, which outlined such U.S. targets as Wall Street, the Pentagon, and even the CIA headquarters building in Langley, Virginia. But the CIA didn't link the activities and relations between bin Laden, his deputy Ayman al-Zawahiri, and Ramzi Yousef, who masterminded the 1993 World Trade Center (WTC) bombing and drafted the Bojinka plot. The CTC never understood the connection between Yousef and the al Qaeda organization until it was too late. The same can be said about the connection between Khalid Sheik Mohammed (KSM) and al Qaeda, particularly the crucial relationship between KSM and bin Laden. The CIA did not believe bin Laden was anything more than a financier—rather than an organizer—of terrorist activities. Nor did the CIA recognize KSM as a "senior al Qaeda lieutenant" and a major factor in terrorist planning. CIA analysts ignored the reports that KSM was "sending terrorists to the United States to engage in atrocities on behalf on bin Laden."[5] As a result, the CIA expected an attack abroad, not at home. Even when the Philippines intelligence services provided the CIA with evidence in January 1995 linking Yousef, a nephew of Khalid Sheik Muhammad, to a terrorist plot to hijack and destroy nearly a dozen U.S. airliners in the Pacific with liquid explosives, the CTC changed no assumptions. Yousef was captured the very next month in Pakistan and immediately rendered to the United States.

Prior to 9/11, the CIA had information linking KSM to terrorist plans to use aircraft as weapons and to terrorist activity in the United States, but missed his role in the al Qaeda hierarchy. His role in the 9/11 attacks came as a surprise to the CIA. Indeed, KSM's confession to a military hearing at Guantanamo Bay on March 10, 2007, revealed his involvement in more than two dozen terrorist plots around the world, including the WTC in 1993, Richard Reid's shoe-bomb operation in 2001, and the nightclub bombing in Indonesia in 2002.[6] National security advisor Lake and counterterrorist expert Richard Clarke were ahead of the intelligence community in seeing the dangerous relationship between bin Laden and KSM, particularly their tenacity and dedication to strike the United States.

Yousef's plan included the use of a small nitroglycerine device that could not be detected by airport security, which was central to an abortive plot in London in August 2006. His uncle, KSM, brought the original plan to bin Laden in 1996, calling for two waves of hijacked planes, five from the East Coast and five from the West Coast. Bin Laden was noncommittal at that time. Fortunately, Yousef was captured in Pakistan in 1997 and, during his trial, the Bojinka plot surfaced. Two years later, bin Laden and KSM resumed the debate over Yousef's plan, with bin Laden dropping the West Coast option, but adding the training of al Qaeda terrorists to actually fly the aircraft. By then, in 1994, a terrorist organization based in Algeria, the Armed Islamic Group, had hijacked an Air France commercial airline and planned to have it flown into the Eiffel Tower in Paris, but this event led to no obvious alarm at CIA headquarters.

Yousef was more cautious the second time around, and limited his targets to the White House, the U.S. Capitol, and the Pentagon; KSM added the WTC, which Yousef tried to bring down in 1993.[7] Instead of blowing up the planes in midair, the new plan called for trained pilots and a knowledge of English that was required for a pilot's license. Two of the eventual pilots, Khaled al-Mihdhar and Nawaf al-Hazmi, were known to the CIA as early as January 2000, thanks to the Malaysian secret service. The CIA knew the two men traveled to Malaysia in January 2000 to "participate in a meeting of suspected terrorists."[8] Nevertheless, the Agency did not notify the State Department to place their names on a terror watchlist and did not notify the FBI to begin surveillance of these men until several weeks before the 9/11 attack. Even when the CIA learned that Hazmi and Mihdhar had flown to Los Angeles, the Agency did not notify the FBI or the State Department that al Qaeda operatives were in the United States.[9]

Similarly, the foiled plot to bomb Los Angeles International Airport in December 1999 did not heighten concerns over the ability of al Qaeda to strike inside the United States.[10] The FBI's John O'Neill, who played a leading role in the capture of Yousef, became convinced al-Qaeda had sleeper cells in the United States that could conduct terrorist operations, but FBI director Louis Freeh repeatedly told the White House that al Qaeda presented no domestic threat. National security advisor Berger told the joint intelligence inquiry in September 2002 that the FBI repeatedly assured the White House that al Qaeda lacked the ability to launch a domestic strike. The CIA provided similar assurance that overseas facilities were the likely targets. As a result of these flawed assumptions, the CIA tracked al Qaeda operatives but never placed them on the immigration service watchlist. Meanwhile, the FBI ignored Arabs attending flight schools who were behaving in suspicious fashion.

The failure regarding al Qaeda and its sponsorship of terrorism was a corporate community failure. During the period from January to March 2000, "50–60 community analysts and operatives read one or more cables" concerning travel information on al-Hamzi and al-Mihdhar, but shared none of the information. The officers from the CIA, NSA, and FBI ignored a pattern of activity that was modeled on Hezbollah's successful campaign (with the assistance of Syria and Iran) to force the United States to evacuate Lebanon in 1983. Al Qaeda, however, wanted to force the United States out of the entire Middle East, and the timid U.S. responses to a series of anti-American actions, particularly the 1998 bombing of two embassies and a naval warship in 2000, convinced al Qaeda's leaders they could be successful.

Although the al Qaeda organization was formed in 1988, it was not until 1999 that the CIA's directorate of intelligence (DI) began to take the group seriously in its writings and publications. The NIC prepared no national intelligence estimate on terrorism between 1997 and 2001, and the CIA's directorate of operations (DO) had no collection strategy for al Qaeda. CTC issued no strategic assessment on al Qaeda, and no CIA component did any comprehensive analysis on bin Laden from 1993 to 2001. There was limited analytic focus on the United States as a potential target. During this same period, the Congressional oversight committees held no hearings on the subject of terrorism and demonstrated no interest in critiquing the spotty work of the intelligence community. As a result, neither the intelligence agencies nor the Congressional intelligence committees issued any serious warnings regarding acts of terror inside the United States. At the same time, however, there were defectors from various terrorist organizations, as well as liaison reports from foreign intelligence services in Pakistan and Egypt that provided early warning, but all to no avail.

The 9/11 attacks exposed the inability of analysts and agents to perform strategic analysis, to challenge flawed assumptions, and to share sensitive secrets. The major failure was the absence of any challenge to flawed assumptions. No agency in the intelligence community could imagine a terrorist operation conducted inside the United States using commercial airplanes as weapons, although al Qaeda had planned such operations in the mid-1990s in Europe and Asia and the French security services had foiled such an operation targeting the Eiffel Tower in 1994. Just as there was ample warning of a Japanese military attack against a U.S. facility in 1941, there were sufficient indicators of a terrorism plot against the United States. The CIA received a "modest, but relatively steady stream" of reporting that pointed to the possibility of terrorist attacks *within* the United States, but there was no change in the assumptions.[11]

A major factor in the CIA's underestimation of the al Qaeda problem was the lack of focus on the anti-American animus of Islamic terrorist groups. One of the keys to understanding the anti-Western fanaticism of these groups is their opposition to the political and military policies of the United States toward the Arab world, the deployment of U.S. military forces on behalf of some of the most repressive regimes in the region, and the unbalanced U.S. support for Israel and Israeli reliance on military force. Since CIA analysts are not permitted to address the role and actions of the United States in their assessments, there will always be a missing element in their analysis. After all, the policies of the most important economic and military power in the world—the United States—must be analyzed in order to assess international developments. U.S. policies eliciting increased anti-Americanism and acts of terror must be explored and analyzed. There was a similar problem during the cold war when the CIA exaggerated Soviet military power because its analysis never explored the superior military power of the United States and the Soviet drive merely to catch up to U.S. nuclear and conventional power, let alone the superior U.S. geopolitical position. The U.S. domination in power projection was never explored by CIA military analysts and, as a result, Soviet power projection was overestimated in CIA military analysis.

Religious and Islamic fundamentalism grew out of a very specific context, particularly the view among many Islamic activists of a Western–Israeli scheme to maintain dominance over the Islamic community. The Gulf War in 1991 and its immediate aftermath found U.S. military forces occupying the lands of the Islamic holy places and cozying up to the most secular states in the region, particularly Saudi Arabia, Egypt, and Jordan. A double standard in U.S. foreign policy accepts and even encourages nuclear development in Israel and India, but labels Iraqi and Iranian WMD as unacceptable. When Arab members of the coalition that forced Iraq out of Kuwait in 1991 went to the Madrid Conference to accept Israel's right to exist, there was additional fodder for the Islamic fundamentalist campaign.

Bin Laden placed the United States at the center of all anti-Islamic events. He believed the United States would have to be challenged by an Islamic counterforce. He didn't hide these views, but brandished them in a series of fatwas that, as early as 1991–1992, emphasized "we cannot let the American army stay in the Gulf area and take our oil, take our money, and we have to do something to take them out. We have to fight them." Other fatwas focused on driving American forces out of Islamic lands. Several months before the bombing of the U.S. embassies on the Horn of Africa, bin Laden described the "Jihad against Jews and Crusaders." Many of these documents were recorded in Scheurer's useful compendium of the al Qaeda campaign against the United States, which was published anonymously in 2002. Ironically, the inability of the al Qaeda leaders to be successful in their own secular lands, such as Egypt and Saudi Arabia, convinced them to shoot at a much bigger and more distant target—the United States.

When the CIA and the FBI were slow to recognize the problem of al Qaeda and terrorism, National Security Advisor Lake, his deputy Berger, and Clarke confronted these agencies to pressure them to be more active in the pursuit of al Qaeda. As early as 1994, Lake and Berger met with Attorney General Janet Reno and her key deputies to create a better exchange of intelligence information on terrorism. The FBI position was that information developed in criminal investigations could not be shared with "civilians," but Reno and Lake agreed to sign a Memorandum of Understanding for exchanging information on terrorism involving foreign powers or groups with senior NSC officials. According to Clarke, they never did.[12]

Lake and his colleagues also spent time at CIA headquarters, where a handful of CIA officials, particularly Tenet, Scheuer, and Black, understood the power of the jihadists in the Middle East. Nevertheless, this trio also expected attacks overseas and not at home. Black had been the CIA chief in Khartoum, Sudan, where he was the target of an al Qaeda murder or kidnap plot, which contributed to his focus on al Qaeda. So for Black, it was personal. The same was true at the FBI, where O'Neill and Coleman were ahead of the curve in understanding the threat to the United States. With their superpower mentality, however, it was difficult for the senior officials of the CIA and FBI to believe that a group of troglodytes in Afghanistan could threaten the military and economic interests of the United States, let alone the United States itself. As a result, it took continued pressure from the White House and the NSC to make the CIA more aggressive. The Pentagon took the easy way out, virtually ignoring the problem.

CIA and FBI leaders, however, initially fought the creation of a separate organization, such as the Alec Station, to target bin Laden, believing the traditional clandestine organizations would lose power and influence on the problem of counterterrorism. As a result of their opposition, the best people did not gravitate to these units, and in the case of the CIA, very few operational officers were interested in serving there. Thus, the first chief for Alec Station was an analyst and not a clandestine agent and most of his initial staff of fewer than a dozen officers were analysts. He failed to create a good working relationship with CTC and the DO as well as with key CIA elements in the Middle East. His group was largely female, which created an additional problem. Predictably they had difficulty in gaining the cooperation of the DO and the key stations in the Middle East and Southwest Asia for collecting and tracking against terrorism suspects. There is an overwhelming machismo culture in the DO, and hard-bitten station chiefs were not going to take on the requests and demands from desk-bound intelligence analysts without an operational background, particularly female analysts, in Washington, D.C. Members of the OBL station told the 9/11 Commission their zeal toward bin Laden and al Qaeda was the subject of ridicule from both the DI and the DO.[13] Scheuer, in any event, had none of the management skills essential to such a delicate assignment. The organizational tension that accompanied the creation of the CIA and FBI units prevented any real progress in the campaign against terrorism.

The al Qaeda bombings of the U.S. embassies on the Horn of Africa in 1998 led to more aggressive planning against bin Laden and al Qaeda, including a plan for attacks against bin Laden as he traveled in his convoy along Afghan roads. The CIA authorized the recruitment of a network of agents to gather intelligence inside Afghanistan about bin Laden and al Qaeda, and a plan to capture him. By 1998, the plan called for the recruitment of Afghan tribal fighters to assault a terrorist compound where bin Laden might be found, but it was never recommended to the White House for approval because of the high risk associated with such a capture. Other operations were aborted because of the presence of women and children in the convoy, tight al Qaeda security, or a change in bin Laden's plans. There was too much reliance on Afghan proxies in the operational planning against al Qaeda and, during this period, no one from the CIA ever laid eyes on bin Laden. As a result, morale sagged in the OBL station.

The Emptiness of Tenet's "Declaration of War"

Months after al Qaeda's attacks on the American embassies in Kenya and Tanzania and President Clinton's signing of a Top Secret "Memorandum of Notification" authorizing the use of force to capture bin Laden and his top deputies,

CIA director Tenet issued a feckless "Declaration of War" in December 1998 on bin Laden and al Qaeda.[14] Tenet told the CIA and other intelligence agencies that "we are at war" and "I want no resources or people spared in this effort, either inside CIA or the community." But Tenet was unwilling or unable to marshal the resources of the intelligence community, even the CIA, and did not establish a comprehensive approach to the problem of al Qaeda. He did nothing to transfer funds or personnel to the programs designed to counter al Queda or bin Laden, and most intelligence agencies were entirely unaware of the director's directive. The "declaration" was not hand-carried to the various principals in the intelligence community, but faxed to their watch offices where it got lost in the myriad pieces of paper that arrive there hourly. Several directors of the various intelligence agencies testified they never saw the memorandum. Tenet considered his declaration an example of his strategic approach to the problem of terrorism, but the handling and distribution of his document pointed to his inability to develop a comprehensive approach and to ensure that there would be monitoring of the various contributions within the community. Tenet sounded the tocsin about the threat, but failed to follow through on his warnings; he demonstrated that he was all hat and no cowboy.

The prodding from the NSC enabled the CTC and the Pentagon to come up with a plan to fly an unmanned drone—the Predator—over Afghanistan to relay footage of al Qaeda activity. CIA's senior management and the DO were extremely reluctant to go ahead with the Predator program. In addition to concerns about cost and who would pay for the Predator, some Agency officials believed that if the Taliban spotted the reconnaissance version of the Predator, there would be no element of surprise for the armed version of the Predator that would soon come on line. But the NSC persisted and there were at least two occasions in 2000 when photo interpreters believed that a security detail around a tall man in a white robe pointed to the presence of bin Laden. It was exactly one week before the 9/11 attacks, when the Principals Committee of the NSC finally agreed CIA should fly reconnaissance missions with the Predator.

The CIA and the military were still risk adverse, counting on proxies such as the Northern Alliance to move against bin Laden. The CTC wanted an aggressive program involving Northern Alliance forces against both the Taliban army and al Qaeda fighters, but its director, Cofer Black, didn't receive enthusiastic support from within his own agency. The Clinton administration in its last months was not responsive. Not even the bombing of the USS *Cole* in October 2000 led to more aggressive operations against al Qaeda. And when the CTC resumed its push for more aggressive measures against al Qaeda in 2001, it received no response from the Bush administration. Black strongly felt that the only recourse against al Qaeda was a paramilitary campaign to end bin Laden's use of Afghanistan as a sanctuary, but the Clinton administration turned a deaf ear and the Bush administration paid little attention until after 9/11. According to the 9/11 Commission's staff studies, two unnamed members of CTC were so concerned about the likelihood of a terrorist attack and the inattention of the Bush administration that they were prepared to resign and go public.[15] Tenet told the commission that the administration understood the urgency, but his deputy McLaughlin and CTC chief Black were frustrated with new policymakers who failed to understand, and even began to question, the validity of the intelligence that was being collected. McLaughlin testified that the Bush administration failed to understand the gravity of the reporting or the urgency of the task.

In the 1990s, the intelligence community did not have a robust professional cadre of intelligence analysts on the problem of terrorism. Regional priorities, such as dealing with the politics and social conditions of the Middle East and the Southwest Asia, always took precedence over the problem of Islamic fundamentalism or Muslim terrorism. There was an unwillingness on the part of the most senior CIA experts to concentrate on the politics and policies of terrorism, and the Pentagon never gave the requisite priority to counterinsurgency and counterterrorism problems. More than four years after the invasion of Iraq, the Pentagon still hasn't gotten a handle on the insurgency or committed sufficient forces to the problem in Afghanistan.

Counterinsurgency deals with "winning hearts and minds," which is not suited to the training and experience of U.S. military forces that deals with the application of maximum force. While I was a member of the National War College faculty in the early 1990s, the commandant of the college dropped a segment of the international relations program that dealt with insurgency, arguing that the problem was not a military one for the United States. He may have been right in one way because the United States's use of force against Iraq has certainly created more terrorists than it has eliminated, and the heavy-handed tactics of the U.S. Army and Marine Corps has created more sympathy and support for insurgents and jihadists. As U.S. forces get up close and personal with the insurgent enemy in Iraq and Afghanistan, they are more likely to experience the intense fear that doesn't stem from fighting at a distance with heavy artillery and armored personnel carriers. The element of fear, with soldiers and marines frustrated and fearful in an alien environment, has led to some of the worst abuses against innocent Iraqi civilians. In any event, the U.S. superiority in firepower and maneuverability does not translate into immediate success against armed guerrillas; the Israeli experience against the Hezbollah fighters in Lebanon in 2006 resembled the American failures in Iraq.

In August 2001, the FBI's Minneapolis field office detained Moussaoui, a French national enrolled in flight training in Minnesota, where FBI agents suspected he was involved in a hijacking plot. An aggressive FBI program against Moussaoui would have led to additional clues regarding the 9/11 attacks, but attorneys at FBI headquarters, failing to understand the legal standards for obtaining a court order under the Foreign Intelligence Surveillance Act (FISA), missed an opportunity to link Moussaoui to the entry of al-Mihdhar and al-Hazmi into the United States. The acting director of the FBI, Thomas Pickard, testified that he didn't learn about either the memorandum or the detention of Moussaoui until after 9/11. In view of the cautious behavior of bin Laden in similar circumstances, the compromising of at least three al-Qaeda operatives could have led to a major postponement of the 9/11 attacks, thus giving more time to the CIA and the FBI to connect the dots.

Without the benefit of classified information and foreign liaison, Rex A. Hudson of the Federal Research Division of the Library of Congress and University of Pennsylvania Professor of Political Science Stephen Gale did anticipate hijacking of commercial aircraft and warned both the CIA's National Intelligence Council and the Department of Transportation.[16] Hudson's report, "The Sociology and Psychology of Terrorism: Who Becomes a Terrorist and Why?" was prepared for the intelligence community; it was far more sophisticated than any CIA assessment before 9/11. Hudson's report warned that "suicide bombers belonging to al Qaeda's Martyrdom Battalion could crash-land an aircraft packed with high explosives into the Pentagon, the CIA, or the White House."[17] Thus, Hudson had defined a paradigm shift in terrorist tactics in his September 1999 study, which had escaped CIA analysts. Conversely, as late as the CIA's PDB of August 6, 2001, there were no references to the weaponizing of aircraft or the possibility of targets in the United States; it merely rehashed intelligence data from the mid-1990s. The CIA was also aware of the presence of radical Islamic activists in Germany, some with connections to bin Laden, but did not aggressively pursue these contacts.

Nowhere in the thirteen agencies of the intelligence community did any analyst explore the possibility that bin Laden would return to the World Trade Center as a target for a terrorist attack. Perhaps bin Laden wasn't personally responsible for the 1993 attack, but his modus operandi clearly indicated that he often returned to failed operations until there was success. The destruction of the USS *Cole* in 2000 followed the failed attempt against the American destroyer, USS *The Sullivans,* earlier in the year. The fiberglass skiff that was supposed to target *The Sullivans* in Aden harbor sank because it was overloaded with explosives. The skiff was retrieved with a marine crane and ten months later, attacked the *Cole.* There was no response from the Clinton administration; key officials lamely insisted the lack of a positive identification of the affiliation of the terrorists prevented a military response.

STRUCTURAL FLAWS

The errors of the CIA and FBI in the period before the 9/11 attacks point to large organizational failures within these agencies. The CIA has an operational mission to collect clandestine intelligence and conduct covert action; it also analyzes and publishes NIEs. The Agency cannot perform both missions well, and operational demands have often politicized intelligence analysis. This has happened in such regions as Central and South America, where the CIA (and the Justice Department) collected intelligence supportive of policy objectives and ignored the demands of intelligence analysts. The DO helped to cover-up human rights abuses in Central America, and the CIA censored reporting on strategic weapons programs in Pakistan. Many of these acts took place during the stewardship of DCI Casey and his deputy Gates, who became secretary of defense in November 2006.

The FBI also suffers from a bipolar mission, with Walter Lippmann reminding us seventy years ago that it is essential to "separate as absolutely as it is possible to do so the staff which executes from the staff which investigates."[18] Just as the operations directorate of the CIA often contaminated the intelligence collection of the Agency, the FBI similarly put the operations cart in front of the analysis horse and weakened the intelligence mission there as well. Its traditional law enforcement mission involves reacting to crimes that have already occurred. Its counterintelligence mission, by contrast, requires a proactive role—ferreting out threats to national security before they occur. Under former FBI director Freeh, the FBI remained hostile to the inexact world of analysis and intelligence that is the basis of any investigation of international terrorism.

Turf issues abound between the intelligence agencies. The protection of "sources and methods" has been an obstacle to information sharing, with the CIA and the FBI having a long history of poor communication. The NSA had sensitive intercept information, but was unwilling to share raw data with intelligence analysts in other intelligence agencies. The NSA, for example, monitored satellite phone calls, but would not share this data with the FBI or the CIA, or even with Clarke at the NSC.[19]

The FBI was furious with the CIA failure to inform them of the two al Qaeda members, but the FBI, in turn, failed to aggressively pursue the CIA information when it was finally received. Hazmi and Mihdhar actually consorted with a Saudi informant for the FBI in San Diego, which suggests the CIA believed the two men were under surveillance or under contract to the Saudis. Mihdhar was listed in the San Diego phone directory, and Hazmi used a credit card in his own name. Both were active at the San Diego Islamic Center. Either one of these hijackers could have led the FBI to at least eleven of the nineteen hijackers and the plan to hijack and weaponize commercial airliners. Both of them also purchased the airline tickets that ten or eleven of the nineteen hijackers used on September 9, 2001. The CIA may have believed it could recruit one or the other and, for that reason, delayed sharing their names with the FBI. The CIA's failure to inform the State Department that Mihdhar held a multiple-entry visa to get into the United States and should be placed on the watchlist to prevent future reentry represented the Agency's greatest operational failure in the run-up to the 9/11 attacks. When an FBI analyst assigned to the Alec Station learned that Mihdhar and Hazmi were in the United States, he made sure they were placed on the watch lists of the FBI, INS, the State Department, and the Customs Department.[20]

As director of Central Intelligence, Tenet was personally responsible for failing to resolve the differences between the CIA and the FBI. The CIA's IG report recommended the establishment of an Accountability Board to review Tenet's inability to act "in an effective and timely manner," but Goss and Hayden refused to do so.[21]

The traditional tensions that existed between the CIA and the FBI, as well as between the CIA and the NSA, remain a major obstacle. The CIA has always been slow to pass along sensitive information to other intelligence agencies because of the risk of releasing information that could be embarrassing to the CIA or the tendency to place the needs of counterintelligence (protecting sources and methods) over the needs of counterterrorism. Occasionally, politicization of intelligence leads to an unwillingness to share sensitive information that does not support the intended position. For example, an informant told the CIA in the spring of 2001, a full two years before the invasion of Iraq, that Iraq had abandoned its uranium enrichment program, a major element of its nuclear weapons program, and that centrifuge components from the scuttled program were available for examination and even purchase.[22] This is particularly noteworthy because, several months earlier, the CIA had issued a classified assessment stating the Iraq had not taken significant steps toward the reconstitution of its nuclear program. In October 2002, without any additional new evidence, however, the CIA reversed direction and charged the Iraqis with taking energetic steps to reconstitute its nuclear weapons program.

Intelligence agencies and the Pentagon often locked horns, particularly on issues of threat perception, as well as arms control and disarmament. The CIA director, and now the director for national intelligence, is responsible for foreign intelligence, but lacks control and authority over 85 percent of the intelligence community, including the National Security Agency (NSA), the National Geospatial Intelligence Agency (NGA), and the National Reconnaissance Office (NRO), which are staffed and funded by the Department of Defense. During the important period of arms control agreements from 1972 to 1990, the

CIA and State Department's INR were at odds with the Pentagon and DIA on various aspects of disarmament. Over a forty-year period, the Pentagon opposed all major arms control agreements between the United States and the Soviet Union, beginning with the Partial Test Ban Treaty in the Kennedy administration. Throughout this period, there was a great deal of pressure on DIA and the intelligence branches of the various services to toughen the intelligence analysis on issues related to arms control. The Pentagon and Secretary of Defense Weinberger even opposed the Intermediate Nuclear Forces Agreement in the 1980s, which was designed by deputy defense secretary Richard Perle. Weinberger and Perle resigned from the administration when President Reagan sought confirmation of the INF Treaty.

The simple fact was that the so-called intelligence community was not a "community"; it made no serious attempt to share sensitive intelligence. The NSA had transcripts of al Qaeda phone conversations that it refused to share with the CIA or the FBI or even the National Security Council. The FBI was accumulating intelligence on al Qaeda that it hoped to use in a criminal case against bin Laden; therefore, most of this intelligence never left the compartmented areas of FBI headquarters. The CIA held back information on terrorist suspects when it had hopes of recruiting these suspects as sources. We have been led to believe the situation improved in the wake of 9/11 but, in view of the traditional cultural and professional animosity between these organizations, it would be unwise to assume that the problem of intelligence sharing has been resolved.

THE FAILURE OF THE 9/11 COMMISSION

Despite the opposition of President Bush and the Republican chairmen of the Senate and House intelligence oversight committees, the 9/11 Commission ended up with a broad mandate for investigation of the terrorist attacks. Nevertheless, the Commission ultimately failed to use the powers it had been given to explore the reasons for the 9/11 intelligence failure. It deferred unnecessarily to the White House's use of "executive privilege," and it even failed to stand up to CIA director Tenet who refused to permit the commissioners to debrief defectors and prisoners held by the CIA. The Commission had subpoena powers, but that power itself required a majority of the commission and the composition of the members (five Republicans and five Democrats) prevented a majority on controversial issues. Lacking sufficient experience in the world of the intelligence community, the Commission's report failed to provide a context for the debate over reform and provided little insight into the systemic problems of the CIA. The 9/11 failure was about personal failures, accountability, and bureaucratic cowardice; the Commission was focusing on budgets and funding, organizational problems, and structural issues within the intelligence community.

The Commission was not bipartisan per se, but was a balanced group of Democrats and Republicans who could block each other's judgments that were unacceptable for one reason or another. The composition of the group gave a veto power to the members who wanted to support either the Clinton administration or the Bush administration. The members were primarily lawyers with little intelligence experience or insight; the group suffered from insufficient stature in taking on the CIA, let alone the White House, or in gaining access to the media. On the Republican side, former senator Slade Gorton, former secretary of the navy John Lehman, and former governor James R. Thompson were particularly zealous in protecting the reputation of President George Bush. On the Democratic side, Jamie Gorelick, Richard Ben-Veniste, and Timothy Roemer were particularly active in protecting former president Bill Clinton. The intelligence experience of the membership was particularly thin, which begged questions about the failure to use such intelligence luminaries as General Brent Scowcroft, Admiral Stansfield Turner, former senator Sam Nunn, or former senator Nancy Kassenbaum. The commission also suffered from the absence of such distinguished political operatives as David Gergen, Lloyd Cutler, and Howard Baker whose work has been nonpartisan in the past. The Commission was bipartisan or contained a balanced partisanship; it needed to be nonpartisan and independent, but it was neither.

The Commission was insufficiently rigorous and tenacious in pursuit of the failures of the intelligence community. As a result, their only "reform" of the intelligence process has been the creation of a new management structure under the Director of National Intelligence. The Commission wanted a lean office of national intelligence, with a small but powerful staff based on three deputies for foreign, domestic, and military intelligence. Instead, the DNI sits atop a huge, lumbering, and bloated bureaucracy that includes a principal deputy director, four deputy directors, three associate directors, and no fewer than nineteen assistance deputy directors. The Office of the DNI has a huge budget (over $1 billion) to match this bureaucratic giant and has taken its management staff, for the most part, from such key intelligence agencies as CIA and INR, thus weakening the overall intelligence apparatus. Since the creation of the DNI, the intelligence community devotes more of its budget to independent contractors than to government employees. It took Hurricane Katrina in 2005 to teach us what a mess had been created in the creation of the Department of Homeland Security. Hopefully, we will not need an intelligence disaster to learn how much harm the Office of the DNI has done to the intelligence community and American national security.

The Commission emphasized the importance of public policy and, as a result, the Intelligence Reform Act of December 2004 was about process. But the 9/11 intelligence failure was about the culture and the personnel of the intelligence community. The failure exposed the need for new approaches to intelligence analysis, intelligence sharing, methodologies for collection, and making sure that an independent intelligence community tells truth to power. We needed to know something about accountability and responsibility in order to learn where and when the errors were made in the intelligence community and who made them. This is not about a search for scapegoats, but part of a larger effort to reform a dysfunctional intelligence system that provided no warning of a surprise attack nearly forty years after the surprise attack on Pearl Harbor led to the creation of an intelligence community that receives $50 billion a year.

The staff director, Philip Zelikow, had extremely close ties to the Bush White House, and he directed virtually all of the investigative work of the Commission. He was politically, personally, and ideologically involved with many of the key individuals to be investigated. Zelikow also was personally responsible for allowing a senior CIA official, Douglas MacEachin, who was responsible for the politicization of intelligence in the 1980s, to lead the investigation of the work of the CIA, establishing an obvious conflict of interest from the start. Zelikow, on MacEachin's recommendation, also appointed a career CIA case officer, Lloyd Salvetti, who was as an advocate for the CIA.

Zelikow was responsible for politicizing the case studies of Harvard University's John F. Kennedy School on the CIA, which were funded by the CIA. As staff director, Zelikow led a process that turned out good studies on the problems within the intelligence and law enforcement communities; as the editor and drafter of the Commission's final report, however, Zelikow turned out a bland document that largely ignored these studies. The fact that Zelikow (and even cochairman Thomas Kean) had to recuse themselves from some discussion begs serious questions about their suitability for the important tasks they inherited. Zelikow had a long and close relationship with Rice, and he was particularly protective of her reputation during the 9/11 investigation. He did not fully circulate the testimony of CIA director Tenet and CTC director Black, who briefed Rice in July 2001 on the numerous indicators of an imminent terrorist attack; she initially denied receiving such a briefing, and no more than two members of the Commission saw the evidence of her disinterest in the possibility of domestic terrorism.

The Commission had insufficient access to other reports being prepared on the 9/11 disaster, particularly the accountability reports of the CIA and the Justice Department, and the Robb-Silberman Report. The latter report could have disabused cochairman Kean of his fixation on possible Iraqi links to

9/11. The Scowcroft study could have alerted the Commission to the need to demilitarize the intelligence community. The staff studies of the Senate intelligence committee also provided intelligence that refuted the charge of links between Iraq and al Qaeda. There was no reason for the members of the 9/11 Commission to accept major impediments to their review of the President's Daily Brief, which carried the most sensitive information available to the intelligence community and the most authoritative and thorough record of the intelligence available to the president and his key advisers. But various members of the Commission had to travel to the New Executive Office Building to read the PDB; they couldn't take notes outside of the building and all were not cleared to read all the documents. Each member of the Commission, in fact, had a different level of access, which made no sense for an investigation of this type. It was impossible for the commission to make any assessment about the kind of intelligence provided to the president, as well as the actions taken by the president in response to the intelligence, without full access to all the PDB items related to terrorism and al Qaeda.

The Commission avoided any direct criticism of President Bush, although there were many former officials of the Bush administration who have written persuasively about the disinterest of the administration in the problem of international terrorism. Some of this disinterest could be attributed to the inexperience of a new administration, but a great deal could be attributed to senior officials who had greater interest in national missile defense, the abrogation of the ABM Treaty, and a policy of unilateralism in international affairs than in the issue of terrorism. On balance, the Commission kow-towed to the White House, allowing the president to be interviewed only along side the vice president, making sure that only several members of the commission reviewed the numerous items from the PDB on the relevant issues of terrorism, and then reading these items only in the friendly confines of the Executive Office Buildings.

Ironically the centralized organization, the office of the DNI, created by the Commission for the intelligence community, is the most likely way to ensure continued politicization of intelligence. The intelligence failure in the run-up to the Iraq War was marked by centralized intelligence free of dissent and debate. A retired naval admiral, Mike McConnell, has replaced John Negroponte as DNI, and a four-star general has taken command of CIA, which has led to less interest in strategic intelligence and more interest in centralization. Unfortunately, the important estimative process of the intelligence community is in the hands of general officers at the DNI and CIA. Flag officers also hold the top leadership at the National Counterterrorism Center.

The 9/11 Commission concluded that by putting a single person in charge of the community, a DNI, there would be greater likelihood of connecting the dots and making the intelligence case to the president. But a centralized framework almost ensures that diversity and competition in the collection and analysis of intelligence will be given short shrift. Truth is elusive within the intelligence process, and there is rarely a single answer to a controversial question or problem. Thus, a president and his senior policymakers deserve a range of alternative analysis so their own exclusive information, which is rarely shared with the intelligence community, can be tested by additional sources and assumptions, particularly contrarian ones.

The Bush administration has never displayed an interest in tough-minded intelligence analysis to inform its foreign policy decision making. Instead, it viewed the intelligence process as a support mechanism for decisions that were already taken. It claimed, for example, 100 percent certainty about its charges of Iraqi WMD and Iraqi links to al Qaeda, but could point to 0 percent knowledge in support of the charges that it made. The same pattern is developing in the case of Iran, particularly its nuclear industry and its reported support for insurgencies in Iraq and Afghanistan. Just as the intelligence community, particularly the CIA and the Pentagon's DIA, provides the intelligence information that the administration was seeking to justify war in Iraq, we are now reading about so-called intelligence collection that justifies the use of force against Iran. In both cases, we are seeing less interest in careful scrutiny of the collection and fewer doubts and dissents within the community.

The 9/11 Commission failed to address the major intelligence flaw prior to 9/11, the failure of imagination. National security advisor Rice argued before the Commission, "No one could have anticipated anyone using airplanes as bombs," but there was clandestine intelligence on such plans and operations in 1994 and 1995. The CIA's DI and the CTC never analyzed how a hijacked aircraft or any aircraft loaded with explosives might be used as a weapon against a target such as the WTC or the Pentagon. Using unclassified sources, however, there were three studies in the 1990s that anticipated such weaponizing of commercial aircraft. The first was prepared in 1993 for the Pentagon to investigate the possibility of airplanes being used as bombs. (A year after the report, a disgruntled Federal Express employee invaded the cockpit of a DC10 with the intention of crashing it into a company building.)

In addition to a lack of imagination on the possibility of weaponizing commercial aircraft, the CIA was lax in ignoring a series of warnings from foreign liaison intelligence services, including the French, German, Israeli, and Russian. The German service, BND, warned both CIA and Mossad in the summer of 2001 that terrorists were planning to hijack commercial aircraft and use them as weapons to attack U.S. targets. The Israeli security service, Mossad, issued its own warning to the FBI and the CIA in August 2001 that al Qaeda was planning to attack vulnerable U.S. targets. Excellent information has become available on the intelligence of the French intelligence service (General Directorate for Foreign Services or the DGSE) that was passed to the CIA and Western intelligence services, including reports on bin Laden's discussion with the Taliban on the subject of hijacking American commercial airliners.[23] At the very least, the CIA should have passed on the information that bin Laden had decided on targeting American Airlines and United Airlines. Liaison reporting and even the European press referred to a "blizzard" of warnings about potential attacks against the United States, which of course went unheeded.

From a professional standpoint, it is particularly shocking that the CIA, which was created to correct the lack of warnings intelligence prior to Pearl Harbor and had devoted a great deal of attention to warnings issues involving the Soviet threat, made no attempt to identify the appropriate indicators of a surprise terrorist attack and lacked a system for collecting intelligence against such indicators. More collection and analysis should have been devoted to evidence of individuals taking flight training on large commercial airliners. With such a set of indicators, the CTC may have reacted to the information forwarded by FBI agents in Phoenix and Minneapolis regarding such flight training. In the summer of 2001, the Phoenix station reported a significant number of Arabs interested in various kinds of flight training in Arizona and requested that other FBI stations examine the situation in California and Florida, where there were flight schools. The Minneapolis station reported the suspicious behavior of Moussaoui, and the FBI briefed the CIA director and other top Agency officials on the issue of "Islamic Extremists Learn to Fly," without eliciting any response from CIA director Tenet or the NIO for Warning, Charlie Allen, who currently heads the intelligence operations at the Department of Homeland Security. Neither the intelligence community nor the NSC looked into the issues of defending commercial aircraft or preventing suicidal bombings. Clarke told the 9/11 Commission he was interested in these scenarios because of the need to protect the Atlanta Olympics of 1996, the White House, and the G-8 summit in Genoa in 2001. He traced his interest to various novels he had read and not to any CIA warnings.[24]

Finally, there is no indication that the major lessons of the 9/11 failure have been learned. One of the keys to the intelligence failure was the lack of a central repository for all intelligence information on international and domestic terrorism, and there is no indication that a comprehensive repository has been created. Also, there is still no apparent central role for any of the various intelligence agencies in dealing with the problem of terrorism and particularly al Qaeda. Even in the wake of 9/11, the problem of central command continues. Who is actually running the military and operational presence in Afghanistan? Who is running the hunt for bin Laden and other key members of al Qaeda?

Who is coordinating the Pentagon and CIA operatives? Indeed, if there is a so-called war against terrorism, who is the commanding general of that war, and what is the strategic template for waging the war? And if Iraq is the center of the war against terrorism as the president proclaimed in September 2003, what is the counterterrorism strategy for waging the war in Iraq? There has been a major increase in terrorist violence in Iraq since February 2006, with no indication of any genuine change in strategy except for a "surge" of an additional twenty thousand troops, primarily for Baghdad, that was announced in January 2007. Iraq has now become the training base for terrorist attacks in Afghanistan, which now features suicide bombers for the first time. The appointment of a war "czar" in 2007 for wars in Afghanistan and Iraq that began in 2001 and 2003, respectively, points to the absence of a genuine central command for the so-called "war against terror." Little is know about the work of the czar, and his briefings to Congress have been uninformative. In an era of arms control in the 1970s, Secretary of State Henry Kissinger asked, "What is strategic superiority?" and "What we would do with it if we possessed it?" Today, we should demand intelligence indicators to measure U.S. successes in the war, but also ask, "What is the war against terror?" and how will we ever know when U.S. forces are winning such a "war."

The inability to share information between the three most important agencies for collecting intelligence (the CIA, the FBI, and the NSA) points to a larger problem within the policy and intelligence communities—the lack of central direction in the overall struggle of counterterrorism. There were several authoritative studies prior to 9/11 that pointed to the problem of terrorism as a genuine threat to U.S. security, but the Clinton administration was more concerned with biological warfare and the Bush administration saw terrorism simply in the context of justifying a national missile defense. Between 1991 and 2001, such government and congressional luminaries as Ambassador Paul Bremer, Senators Gary Hart and Warren Rudman, and Governor James Gilmore called for a higher priority for the problem of terrorism, but their warnings were observed in the breach. Even with the creation of the DHS and the National Counterterrorism Center, there is no indication of a centralized coordinating body to counter terrorism. If Hurricane Katrina exposed the problems of the Federal Emergency Management Agency in the new DHS, one can only hope that such important agencies as the Customs Service, the Border Patrol, and the Coast Guard have not been similarly weakened in the overall struggle against terrorism.

In many ways, the false U.S. accusations regarding the links between Saddam Hussein and bin Laden, which were used to justify the use of force against Iraq, provided the al Qaeda leadership with its biggest victory of all—the American occupation of Iraq and a concomitant worsening of U.S. standing in the Middle East and the war against terrorism. President Bush's branding of Iraq as the center of the war against terrorism has become a self-fulfilling prophecy and has placed more Americans at risk. U.S. policymakers and many intelligence analysts failed to understand that Saddam Hussein and bin Laden were natural enemies, the latter always referred to the former as the "socialist infidel." One was a secular leader; the other was a fundamental Islamacist who wanted to head a new caliphate. Hussein knew he never could control the jihadist fanatics and, therefore, he avoided any cooperation with them.

Now that it is known there were no ties between Iraq and al Qaeda, the Bush administration has shifted the argument to the possibility that Iraqi WMD (also nonexistent) could end up in the hands of al Qaeda and other terrorist groups to be used against U.S. interests. What we do know is that, in abandoning the campaign in Afghanistan against al Qaeda in order to invade Iraq in 2003, the United States began the occupation of a key Moslem country that attracted jihadists from throughout the region, just as the Soviet occupation of Afghanistan in the 1980s elicited Islamic support for the Mujahideen against the Soviet Union. As a result, the U.S policy and intelligence communities are facing tougher challenges in both Afghanistan and Iraq and throughout the entire region. The emergence of two failing states will complicate the regional situation as weak governments in Pakistan, Saudi Arabia, Iran, and Syria try to cope with new and far more unpredictable challenges. The preoccupation of the United States with its military situation in both Iraq and Afghanistan has translated into far less leverage and influence in the Middle East and Southwest Asia and has given such nations as China, India, Iran, North Korea, Russia, and Venezuela opportunities to counter U.S. influence. As a result, today's intelligence challenge is far greater than the cold war situation in the Third World, when the assessment of Soviet power and influence was the only major mission. Finally, there is also the fear that the "case" for war against Iraq, including WMD, links with terrorists, and democratization, could become the case for war against Iran.

Despite the intelligence failure, which analysts inside the CIA building referred to as "Pearl Harbor II," there has been neither a comprehensive nor authoritative exploration of the methodological and analytical reasons for the failure and to gain lessons learned from a postmortem of the crisis. In the 1990s, the CIA failed to give strategic warning of the decline and fall of the Soviet Union, but maintained that the Agency actually provided warning of the Soviet crisis. There was no call for a postmortem and no attempt to gain lessons learned. The Congressional oversight committees put no demands on the CIA, and the Office of the Inspector General conducted no inspections of the faulty collection and analysis of the Soviet Union over a ten-year period. In the wake of the 9/11 failure, there was an accountability report by the Office of the IG, but the two most recent CIA directors, Goss and Hayden, refused to establish an accountability board, and to issue an unclassified version of the full report. Both directors have ignored the demands of Senators as Wyden (D-Oregon), Rockefeller (D-West Virginia), and Bond (R-Missouri) for the circulation of the classified report to all members of the intelligence oversight committees.

There is still much to learn about the CIA's collection and analysis of intelligence on terrorism, particularly in the run-up to the 9/11 tragedy. CIA director Tenet declared a war on terrorism in December 1998, but failed to create a strategic plan against al Qaeda. He failed to stop bureaucratic turf battles between the CIA, the FBI, and the NSA, and poorly managed the resources of the Counter-Terrorism Center. The CIA underestimated the importance of key al Qaeda leaders, and more than fifty community analysts and operatives did not respond to sensitive cables on al Qaeda operatives who took part in 9/11.

THE NEXUS OF INTELLIGENCE AND TERRORISM

There is no more important tool against terrorism than intelligence, both intelligence collection and intelligence analysis. Intelligence was the key to dealing with terrorist groups in Western Europe, where the West Germans, the Italians, the British, and the Spaniards had to deal with their own nihilistic terrorist organizations. The Israelis also contend that intelligence is the key to dealing with terrorist activities and have had more success than most in penetrating small terrorist cells. Conversely, the United States, particularly the Bush administration, believes that the military instrument is the key to defeating terrorism and, in the wake of 9/11, even declared a "war on terrorism." But terrorism is a tactic and not an enemy, and just as President Franklin D. Roosevelt did not declare a war on the blitzkrieg in the 1940s, there should have been no declaration of war against terrorists that offer no front lines, no clear order of battle, and few military targets.

President Bush did a great favor for bin Laden when he followed the war on terrorism with the invasion of Iraq, which created a failed state in the middle of the Islamic world and provided a breeding and training ground for more terrorists. Since 9/11 and the invasion of Iraq, terrorist attacks have been carried out in Algeria, Egypt, England, Indonesia, Kenya, Morocco, Saudi Arabia, Spain, and Tunisia. There was a 25 percent increase in global terrorism in 2006, according to the State Department, and half of all the victims have been Moslems. Half of these "significant terrorist attacks" took place in Iraq, which President Bush declared the "center of the war of terrorism" in

September 2003, several months after declaring "mission accomplished" on the USS *Abraham Lincoln*. There has probably been no more profound self-fulfilling prophecy than the President's declaration of Iraq as the center of the war; prior to the invasion and the U.S. occupation, there was virtually no terrorism in Iraq and certainly no safe haven there for terrorists. The accusations of the Bush administration and CIA director Tenet regarding the so-called links between Iraq and al Qaeda were created out of whole cloth, just one of the many false assumptions and fabrications that supported the idea of U.S force. And despite the Pentagon's descriptions of the degraded operational capabilities of al Qaeda, the "sheer number and breadth of terrorist attacks suggest strongly that al Qaeda has morphed into al Qaedism."[25]

The fact that a small terrorist organization in the mountains of Afghanistan has now become a global political movement has worsened the security situation for the international community and the collection situation for the intelligence community. Former secretary of defense Rumsfeld asked in a confidential memorandum following the Iraqi War: "Are we capturing, killing, or deterring and dissuading more terrorists every day than the madrassas and the radical clerics are recruiting, training, and deploying against us?" CIA director Goss seemingly answered this question in the negative in February 2005, when he told the Senate intelligence committee: "Islamic extremists are exploiting the Iraqi conflict to recruit new anti-U.S. jihadists. These jihadists who survive will leave Iraq experienced in, and focused on, acts of urban terrorism. They represent a potential pool of contacts to build transnational terrorist cells, groups and networks in Saudi Arabia, Jordan, and other countries."[26] At a congressional briefing in May 2007, a senior CIA analyst testified that the U.S. presence in Iraq is "creating more members of al Qaeda than we are killing."[27]

Just as the cold war led to a CIA that was preoccupied with the Soviet threat, the 9/11 attacks created a CIA preoccupied with the problem of terrorism. The Soviet threat, however, was a strategic one that involved long-term analytical studies and multidisciplinary rigor in assessing the political, economic, and military requirements of the Soviet Union and the Soviet Empire. The terrorist challenge is more tactical in nature, turning on worst-case assessments and not lending itself to strategic evaluations and in-depth research. A former intelligence officer noted that the NCS "now directs its energy 'like a laser' on counterterrorism and Iraq, and a significant fraction of CIA's analytic cadre has been redirected toward counterterrorism both within the CIA and on assignment to Homeland Security, the FBI . . . and elsewhere."[28] Analysts and the managers of analysis are not going to spend their time on in-depth strategic assessments when the policy community is clamoring for constant reporting on the terrorist threat.

9

The Iraq War and the White House

From a marketing point of view, you don't introduce new products in August.

> —Andrew H. Card, Jr., September 2002
> (Card's explanation of a meticulously planned strategy to
> persuade the public, the Congress, and the allies of
> the need to use force against Saddam Hussein)

The President of the United States and the Secretary of Defense would not assert as plainly and bluntly as they have that Iraq has weapons of mass destruction if it was not true, and if they did not have a solid basis for saying it.

> —Ari Fleischer, White House Press Spokesman, December 4, 2002

But for those who say that we haven't found the banned manufacturing devices or banned weapons, they're wrong, we found them.

> —President George W. Bush, May 30, 2003

Many people have debated the issue of whether the White House distorted the intelligence it received on Iraq or whether the CIA provided bad intelligence to the White House. In fact, both the White House and the CIA had a hand in the distortion of intelligence; both contributed to making the phony case for war to the Congress and the American people. The Bush administration bears major responsibility for the war because the president, the vice president, the secretary of defense, and the national security advisor worked assiduously to create and employ a strategic disinformation campaign to convince Congress and the American people of the need for war. Their efforts to manipulate the American people is still not fully understood, and much of their disinformation became conventional wisdom, successfully linking Saddam Hussein to the 9/11 attacks and Iraqis to members of al Qaeda. These lies and distortions were central to the Bush administration's case for war.

President Bush, Vice President Cheney, Secretary of Defense Rumsfeld, and National Security Advisor Rice wanted the intelligence community to provide the justification for the use of force against Iraq. They consistently misused intelligence, used fabricated and fallacious intelligence, and even created intelligence out of whole cloth. Cheney and Undersecretary of Defense Wolfowitz, in the wake of the 9/11 terrorist attacks, argued that Saddam Hussein was responsible for the attacks; they wanted him removed. Rumseld was the first official to go on record for the use of force against Iraq, and he relished the opportunity to demonstrate the use of small, mobile forces. Bush's team believed that the American fear of Iraqi WMD was the only justification for the use of force against Iraq that the U.S. public would accept. Wolfowitz conceded privately the Bush administration had difficulty deciding on the case for war, but at least the nuclear rhetoric and WMD was the "one reason everyone could agree on."[1] Having settled on the preferred justification, they worked to develop an intelligence record to support the use of force.

In going to war, President Bush ignored the prescient advice of his father, President George H. W. Bush, and his father's national security advisor, General Brent Scowcroft.[2] In 1998, the elder Bush argued that the use of U.S. military power could lead to the breakup of the Iraqi state and compromise the long-term balance of power in the Persian Gulf. He cited the incalculable human and political costs of a U.S. invasion. General Scowcroft concluded that an invasion would lead to civil war in Iraq and any action would require a U.S. military presence for a protracted period "to stay to protect the people that sign on for [the new] government." Finally, Scowcroft said there would be no assurances about that government after the United States left. In October 2002, General Scowcroft, with the approval of the president's father, wrote an article urging the president not to go to war and reminding the Bush administration of the reasons for stopping Desert Storm in 1991 at the Iraqi border. After the war, Scowcroft warned the president that his vice president was undermining his presidency. He "consider[ed] Cheney a good friend— I've known him for 30 years. But this is a Dick Cheney I don't know anymore."[3]

The month of September 2002 brought a request from several members of the Senate intelligence committee for a National Intelligence Estimate on Iraqi WMD. The administration did not want an estimate. It preferred not to explore the differences of opinion within the intelligence community on the issue of WMD. The NSC knew the Department of State's Bureau of Intelligence and Research, the Department of Energy, and even the intelligence bureau of the U.S. Air Force disagreed with key aspects of the president's case for going to war. The NIE revealed these differences, but the CIA crafted a Key Judgments section on Iraqi WMD making the president's case for war without mentioning the significant dissents within the intelligence community. The CIA also prepared an unclassified White Paper on WMD to take to the American public. The estimate arrived on the Hill only days before the Congress voted on a resolution to go to war, but only five or six Senators bothered to read it.

This was not the first time that intelligence had been manipulated to make a case for war. It happened before the Mexican–American War to support the policies of President James Polk; the Spanish–American War to support the policies of President William McKinley; and the Vietnamese War to support President Lyndon Johnson. The Bush administration was probably unique in its zeal, however; the president's chief of staff, Andrew Card, admitted that the White House had a programmatic "marketing plan" to justify the war, which was put into play in September 2002.[4] The flawed analysis of the CIA, particularly the NIE and the White Paper, became vital parts of this public campaign.

As early as July 2002, the chief of the British MI6 intelligence service, Sir Richard Dearlove, knew the Bush administration was preparing for war and that it was manipulating the intelligence to make its case. In one of the so-called Downing Street memoranda, which was published in *The Sunday Times* of London on May 1, 2005, he warned Prime Minister Tony Blair of Washington's intentions. The July 2002 memorandum described Dearlove's talks with Tenet and other intelligence officials that referred to the misuse of intelligence and a U.S. public relations campaign to justify war.[5] Dearlove noted there had been a "perceptible shift in attitude" in Washington. He wrote that "military action was now seen as inevitable" and "intelligence and facts were being *fixed* [emphasis added] around the policy." Dearlove expected the war to begin in January, although the U.S. Air Force actually started operations in October, with 21,000 sorties attacking 350 targets in Iraq before the official start of the war in March 2003.

Although the Downing Street memorandum was ignored by the American press and dismissed by some pundits as the stuff of the "usual freelance chatterboxes," it provided the best evidence of the decision of the White House to go full speed ahead and the doubts of the CIA about going to war. The head of British intelligence, Dearlove, after all was reporting to Prime Minister Blair on his meetings with top CIA officials, including Tenet. The MI6-CIA meeting had been urgently requested by the British so that Blair could get an update on the thinking of the Bush administration. Blair wanted to get a gut-check prior to his exchanges with President Bush regarding Iraq and considered a meeting between the U.S. and British intelligence chiefs as the best way to do so. The day-long meeting at CIA headquarters included a private one-on-one meeting between Tenet and Dearlove.

Dearlove's discussion of a public campaign was a reference to the White House Iraq Group (WHIG) that was formed in the summer of 2002 to convince public opinion of the need for war against Iraq. The group met regularly in the White House Situation Room; the regular attendants included Karl Rove, Karen Hughes, Mary Matalin, Condi Rice and her deputy Stephen Hadley, and Lewis "Scooter" Libby, who represented Vice President Cheney. About this time Cheney and Libby also began meeting directly with CIA analysts at CIA headquarters in Langley, Virginia, an unprecedented procedure. Their purpose was to garner the intelligence justification for a preemptive war to remove Saddam Hussein in order to make a case to the Congress, the American public, and the international community.

The WHIG produced much of the language used to make the case for war, including such rhetoric as "the smoking gun should not be a mushroom cloud." The "smoking gun" and the "mushroom cloud" became favorite phrases for Cheney, Rice, Rumsfeld, and the president.[6] Rice repeatedly stated "we don't want the smoking gun to be a mushroom cloud." She used this phrase on CNN on September 8, 2002, the same day that Cheney told "Meet the Press" that "we know with absolute certainty" that Saddam Hussein was "using his procurement system to acquire the equipment he needs to enrich uranium to build a nuclear weapon." President Bush and Cheney were the most persistent supporters of the notion that Iraq was "reconstituting" its nuclear weapons program in order to gain congressional and public support for going to war. The president's State of the Union address in January 2003 and Secretary of State Powell's UN speech in February emphasized a nuclear threat. CIA analysts signed off on the president's address and crafted Powell's speech, relying on tainted and discredited intelligence to do so.

After the invasion, it became clear that the Administration had manipulated and even created the intelligence case for war. In 2006, the Pentagon released its Inspector General's report on the Office of Special Plans (OSP). The report confirmed British assertions that intelligence had been "fixed" to justify the war. For several years, Senator Carl Levin (D-Michigan) had been arguing that Undersecretary of Defense for Policy Douglas Feith had supplied bogus intelligence to the White House on Iraqi WMD and links to terrorist organizations in order to rally support for the use of force. The former chairman of the Senate intelligence committee, Senator Pat Roberts (R-Kansas), admitted that Vice President Cheney had pressured the committee to delay any investigation of the administration's misuse of intelligence. The Pentagon's acting IG, Thomas J. Gimble, charged in his report that Feith ignored the consensus within the intelligence community and issued "alternative intelligence assessments" and that he had done so with the authorization of Secretary of Defense Rumsfeld and his deputy, Paul Wolfowitz.[7] The Senate intelligence committee had not known before the war that OSP was engaged in intelligence-gathering operations, relying particularly on Iraqi defector Ahmad Chalabi. The CIA had warned the policy and intelligence communities in the 1990s that Chalabi, the head of the Iraqi National Congress, was a fabricator and not to be trusted. Nevertheless, key members of the Bush administration regularly used information provided by Chalabi and Feith in their statements to the Congress and to the public.

The modus operandi of Card's "marketing plan" was to leak unsubstantiated and flawed "intelligence" (supplied by Chalabi and his minions) to the press and then offer authoritative White House confirmation of the leaked information. The White House selected Judith Miller of *The New York Times* as the key recipient of these leaks. Miller had a front-page story in the *Times* on September 8, citing administration officials claiming that Saddam repeatedly had tried to acquire aluminum tubes "specially designed" to enrich uranium. Her article pointed to the aluminum tubes as the "smoking gun."[8] Four days later, President Bush took the aluminum tubes claim to the UN General Assembly. The aluminum tube issue was also central to Secretary Powell's UN speech.

The similarity in language used by both U.S. and British officials on Iraqi WMD and links between Saddam Hussein and al Qaeda as reasons for war pointed to significant coordination between the White House and 10 Downing Street.[9] Wolfowitz met regularly with British Ambassador to the United States Christopher Meyer to discuss ways and means to influence opinion in the parliament and legislature, as well as with the public. A major victim in all of this manipulation, besides the American and British people, was the intelligence community and the pursuit of objective and balanced intelligence. The Biblical inscription, "the truth will set you free," may be inscribed in the lobby of CIA headquarters, but, in this case, it was observed in the breach. However, British Foreign Secretary Jack Straw and Secretary of State Powell were nervous about the public relations campaign, doubting that regime change was justification for going to war.

A second Dearlove memorandum in January 2003 described a meeting between Prime Minister Blair and President Bush, and noted the United States intended to invade Iraq even if UN inspectors found no evidence of WMD.[10] If he found it necessary, Bush said, the United States would "fly U2 reconnaissance planes . . . over Iraq, painted in UN colors" to tempt Iraqi forces to fire on them, which would constitute a breach of UN resolutions. The justification for the war would be the "conjunction of terrorism and WMD," although there was never credible evidence of Iraqi links to terrorist groups, such as al Qaeda, and no confirmed evidence of Iraqi holdings of WMD. Dearlove concluded, "There was little discussion in Washington of the aftermath of military action"; he argued the Bush administration was ignoring the disastrous situation in Iraq that the British anticipated in the wake of the overthrow of Saddam Hussein. In a separate memorandum, Foreign Secretary Straw conceded Saddam was not threatening his neighbors and, in any event, his WMD capability was less than that of Libya, North Korea, or Iran.

Whenever the United States has pursued a war not based on self-defense, the decision has been a political one, having nothing to do with intelligence. The Iraq War was wanted by the Bush administration regardless of the intelligence input. Intelligence played no role in the decision making of the president's inner council, the Pentagon's strategy for the war, or the postwar situation. If the Bay of Pigs in 1961 was an example of a "perfect failure" in CIA's covert action, then the Iraq War of 2003 was an example of a "perfect failure" in the strategic decision to go to war. In the words of Pulitzer Prize winner Thomas E. Ricks, President Bush's decision to invade Iraq in 2003 ultimately may come to be seen as "one of the most profligate actions in the history of American foreign policy."[11]

Even if the CIA had gotten the intelligence right, had not drafted the October 2002 NIE and its unclassified version (the White Paper), and had not prepared the phony speech for Powell, the Bush administration would have gone to war against Iraq. The NIO for the Near East and South Asia from 2000 to 2005, Paul Pillar, told a Senate committee hearing in June 2006 that he received no requests from any administration policymaker on any aspect of Iraq until more than a year after the war began.[12] This is in stark contrast to the Vietnam experience when there was a healthy intelligence debate within the community on Southeast Asia, and the White House and the NSC were well aware of the debate. Nevertheless, the reports of the Senate Select Committee on Intelligence, the Iraq Survey Group, and the Presidential WMD Commission confirmed that the CIA failed to provide truthful intelligence on Iraq's WMD.

In the early going, prior to October 2002, the CIA resisted the White House on certain issues. As a result, Cheney and Secretary of Defense Rumsfeld cooperated in creating a "supersecret intelligence analysis operation at the Pentagon, totally separate and unknown to the members of the Intelligence Community."[13] The office initially was called Team B, and it opened with two neoconservative analysts, David Wurmser and Michael Maloof, who reported to Undersecretary of Defense for Policy Feith. The choice of "Team B" was an interesting one. Cheney and Rumsfeld had been critics of CIA analysis for more than three decades, even sponsoring the so-called Team A/Team B exercise in 1976 to force the CIA to adopt more threatening estimates of the Soviet strategic threat. "Team B" essentially reported to Cheney and Rumsfeld in 1976 and 2002.

By late summer 2002, with the Bush administration moving toward a decision to go to war, Team B was renamed the Office of Special Plans (OSP), absorbing the staff of the Iraq desk, and growing to eighteen staffers. Its major purpose was to provide intelligence to the White House that made the case for war, using intelligence information the CIA did not consider credible. OSP also coordinated activities with Chalabi's Iraqi exile opposition, and organized military training in Hungary for the so-called Free Iraqi Forces. The office communicated directly and frequently with Cheney's office in the White House. A former Pentagon intelligence analyst charged that the OSP "cooked the books" on intelligence for the war, reminiscent of the role of the NSC during the Iran-Contra crisis. The OSP also had close links with the Defense Policy Board, whose members—particularly Richard Perle, former CIA director Woolsey, and former Republican speaker of the House Newt Gingrich—peddled the OSP's disinformation to audiences at home and abroad.

The OSP under the leadership of Feith and Abram Shulsky was one of the major villains in making the specious case for war, creating intelligence out of whole cloth and ignoring the need for transition arrangements in Iraq in the wake of Saddam Hussein's downfall. It relied on information from the Iraq National Council's Chalabi, who was Judith Miller's favorite source on Iraq and WMD. Wolfowitz and Feith also accepted Chalabi's recommendation to dismantle the Iraqi army and security agencies as soon as the war ended, which contributed to the inability of U.S. forces to stabilize the Iraqi security situation. Although Chalabi was a known fabricator, the OSP took his reports directly to the offices of the president and the vice president, without any vetting from the intelligence community. The OSP was responsible for conducting meetings with such unreliable sources as Manucher Ghorbanifar, who was part of the Iranian arms-for-hostages negotiations in the 1980s. When the pressure from Congress and the news media became intense in the summer of 2003, Rumsfeld folded OSP quickly and quietly into the Northern Gulf Affairs office under the Pentagon's Near East and South Asia policy office. Under this arrangement, the Gulf Affairs office had more adult supervision than the OSP, but it still danced to the tune of Cheney's office in the White House, particularly to Scooter Libby.

The OSP was staffed with neoconservatives and ideologues loyal to the goal of regime change in Iraq and bent on using the reporting from Chalabi's Iraqi National Congress to make the case for war. The OSP was also designated to plan for postwar Iraq, but it gave no attention to the problem. According to the

Pentagon's Inspector General, OSP's major mission was to provide the White House with so-called intelligence to make the case for war.[14] This intelligence included "reporting of dubious quality or reliability" that supported the views of the White House and lacked the imprimatur of the intelligence community. The IG referred to Feith's activities as an "alternative intelligence assessment process." It represented a systematic politicization of intelligence to make a phony case for war. The IG failed to describe how Feith passed his classified work to Stephen Hayes of the *Weekly Standard*, which regularly published OSP's disinformation, and did not discuss Feith's briefings to Rumsfeld, Libby, and Hadley in August and September 2002, the crucial period for making the case to go to war.

Feith claimed his office "didn't do intelligence assessments," but one of his briefings to the White House and the NSC was titled, "Assessing the Relationship Between Iraq and al Qaeda," which was designed primarily to malign the work of the CIA and DIA, and prove the Iraq–al Qaeda link.[15] One of the key OSP documents was titled "Iraq and al-Qaida: Making the Case." It argued that a "mature, symbiotic relationship existed" between the two; it was released on July 25, 2002, soon after the British intelligence chief charged in a private memorandum that intelligence in Washington was being "fixed" to support the administration's policy. Feith personally delivered a briefing at the White House that contained a slide presentation termed, "Fundamental Problems with How Intelligence Community is Assessing Information." He did not include this in his briefings to the directors of the CIA and DIA.

Using the work of OSP, President Bush asserted in October 2002 that "Iraq has trained al Qaeda members in bomb-making and poisons and deadly gases," although several months earlier a CIA report discounted those assertions. Several days before the president's remarks, the NIE on Iraqi WMD programs termed the reporting on training and support for al Qaeda "second-hand or from sources of varying reliability," qualifiers that were dropped from Pillar's White Paper.[16] The NIE also noted the intelligence community "cannot determine . . . how many of the reported plans for CBW (chemical and biological warfare) were actually realized." And as late as January 2003, the CIA noted the lack of "evidence of completed training" and the lack of certainty whether "training was actually implemented."[17] The Agency termed much of the reporting "hearsay" and some of it "simple declarative accusations of Iraqi-al Qa'ida complicity with no substantiating detail or other information that might help us corroborate them." Cheney, for his part, regularly referred to the *Weekly Standard* as the "best source of information" on the relationship between Saddam Hussein and al Qaeda, and used the Feith-Hayes pipeline to publish the canard that 9/11 hijacker Mohammed Atta met with Iraqi intelligence officers in Prague.

At the State Department, Undersecretary of State for Arms Control and Disarmament John Bolton ran his own intelligence program, providing "white papers" on WMD that lacked support within the intelligence community. He used these papers to testify to congressional committees, exaggerating the WMD programs in Iraq, Syria, and Cuba. In 2002, he presented misinformation to the Congress on a Cuban biological weapons program; when the CIA challenged the accuracy of Bolton's information in 2003, he was forced to cancel a briefing on Syrian WMD for a House International Relations subcommittee. As the director of central intelligence, Tenet should have been more aggressive in countering the intelligence efforts of both Feith and Bolton and their band of neoconservatives.

THE WHITE HOUSE AND POLITICIZATION

The White House made a strong case for war on the basis of Iraqi WMD, despite the lack of credible evidence. The strategy of the Bush administration was simple and direct: tie Iraq and Saddam Hussein to al Qaeda and the 9/11 attacks; highlight the reconstitution of Iraq's nuclear weapons program with purported purchases of uranium from Niger and aluminum tubes from Europe; claim huge stocks of chemical and biological weapons, including mobile biological laboratories; and describe WMD cluster bombs and SCUD missiles. The CIA lacked credible evidence on these charges, and some of the claims were based on fabricated or specious reports. The administration officials who made the case were largely located in the NSC and the Pentagon; most of them (including Robert Joseph, Feith, Wurmser, Libby, and Shulsky) are no longer in the Bush administration.

In July 2002, high-level CIA officials told their British counterparts the Bush administration had made its decision to go to war. The British learned from CIA that the option to petition the United Nations was merely a face-saving measure to appease the international community and Secretary of State Powell, and that the intelligence was being tailored to support the war. Meanwhile, Foreign Minister Straw had already forwarded a memorandum to Prime Minister Blair that tried to explain the difficulty of making a case for war: "The truth is that . . . even the best survey of Iraqi's WMD programs will not show much advance in recent years on the nuclear, missile, or CW/BW fronts; the programs are extremely worrying but have not, as far as we know, been stepped up."[18] Blair's trip to Crawford, Texas in April 2002, and Richard Dearlove's trip to Washington in July were designed to slow down the U.S. plan to go to war.

Bush and Cheney, however, had no intention to slow down. In fact, they were moving full speed ahead to manipulate intelligence on Iraq in four key areas in order to make the case for war. The issues involved Iraqi purchases of enriched uranium from Niger, Iraqi purchases of aluminum tubes for nuclear testing, Iraqi mobile biological laboratories, and so-called links between Iraq and al Qaeda. All of these charges were false, but all were bolstered in one way or another by faulty or politicized CIA analysis. The White House had no basis whatsoever for telling international and domestic audiences the Iraqis were close to a deliverable nuclear weapon. Prior to the war, the CIA told the administration on every possible occasion that the Iraqis were several years away from developing a nuclear weapon, which was also an exaggeration; there was no reason to believe Iraq was about to develop such a weapon.

Enriched Uranium from Niger

Vice President Cheney was obsessed with the notion that Iraq was trying to reconstitute its nuclear weapons capability; it was his major justification for using force against Iraq. A week before the war began, Cheney charged on "Meet the Press" that Saddam Hussein "has, in fact, reconstituted nuclear weapons." He had unveiled his doomsday scenario on August 26, 2002, in a speech to the 103rd national convention of the Veterans of Foreign Wars, declaring with no equivocation that Saddam Hussein had "resumed his efforts to acquire nuclear weapons."[19] About this time, the vice president and "Scooter" Libby made their first of at least ten trips to the CIA to meet with senior officials and even junior analysts to press the case for intelligence supporting their charge that Hussein was stockpiling WMD. In my twenty-four years at the CIA, the only time a president or vice president came to visit CIA headquarters in Virginia was to take part in a ceremonial function or to bolster the troops. Cheney was also guilty of shooting the messenger, actually demanding the replacement of two senior PDB briefers whose intelligence assessments did not corroborate his views. As late as November 2005, Vice President Cheney lashed out at administration critics who accused the Bush administration of manipulating key intelligence information to make the case for war.

Cheney consistently dismissed warnings from the CIA and the State Department that the intelligence on Iraq and Niger had been discredited or fabricated. The discredited information was a British White Paper based on old information linking Niger to the reconstitution of Iraq's nuclear capability.[20] The president was going to link Iraq to a Niger deal involving uranium, but after a phone conversation between Tenet and NSC deputy adviser Hadley, this language was removed from the speech, angering Cheney and Libby. Tenet wrote Hadley on at least two occasions to convince the White House the Niger documents were flawed. Two months after the start of the Iraq War,

Hadley conceded he had received Tenet's warnings, but that he had forgotten them in the busy run-up to the war. State Department analysts had determined the Niger documents were bogus, and Secretary of State Powell personally had told Cheney they were phony. Less than two weeks after the president's State of the Union address, Powell omitted the Niger allegations from his UN speech, despite considerable pressure from Libby and Hadley to leave the Niger material in the speech.

In late December 2002, there was a second round of negotiations between the White House and the CIA on the Niger issue, with a far different outcome. The president was preparing to use the accusation in his most important speech of the year, the State of the Union message in January 2003. The CIA and the NSC entered into protracted negotiations over the draft language of the address, with the chief of CIA's Office of Weapons Intelligence, Proliferation, and Arms Control (WINPAC), Alan Foley, convincing the NSC's Robert Joseph that the Niger story could not be linked to CIA intelligence. Joseph wanted a strong statement regarding Iraqi efforts in Niger, but Foley maintained the CIA could not corroborate the story. They agreed on compromise language allowing the White House to cite British intelligence for the connection. Thus, Joseph and Foley enabled the president to make a false charge in the State of the Union: "The British Government has learned that Saddam Hussein recently sought significant quantities of uranium from Africa."

The statement was well calculated, negotiated in several tense secure-line telephone conversations, and was designed to mislead. Foley quickly retired when the heat generated by the controversy grew intense in the summer of 2004; Joseph replaced John Bolton at the Department of State as the undersecretary of state for arms control and disarmament, but left the administration in 2007 due to his opposition to a nuclear deal with North Korea.

The forged documents on Niger served an extremely important purpose for the White House. Never mind that virtually everyone in Washington knew the documents were a fabrication and that Mohamed El-Baradei of the IAEA had declared the documents "not authentic." As long as the rationalization for the war was to make sure that the "smoking gun was not a mushroom cloud," the Bush administration had to prove that Saddam Hussein was trying to reconstitute Iraq's nuclear capabilities. There was no credible evidence whatsoever that he was doing so, but the possibility of uranium purchases in Africa or the use of aluminum tubes for a nuclear centrifuge was the only evidence available to the White House. The Niger documents, although phony, became the "silver bullet," supposedly demonstrating Saddam's efforts to become a nuclear power. The White House would not let go of the Niger documents, although every key official in Washington knew they were forgeries. In addition to Tenet telling Hadley, the deputy director for intelligence at the CIA, Jamie Miscik, told National Security Advisor Rice; Carl Ford, the chief of the State Department's INR and a thirty-year CIA veteran, told Powell the documents were "crap," and, as a result, the information was not used in the secretary's address to the UN. As early as December 2001, State and CIA analysts believed the issue "was done, shot down," but the White House would not relent.[21]

The president's use of a fabricated document was no mistake, and it was not inadvertent. The use of the fabrication begs a series of questions about the role of specific individuals in preparing the case for war. Who in the White House was involved in removing language from the president's speech in October 2002 about efforts to obtain uranium from Niger, and who was involved in refusing CIA entreaties on the same subject for the State of the Union in January 2003? Who in the White House pressed the CIA for language on the uranium issue for the State of the Union? Why did White House pressure continue when it was obvious that the CIA did not believe in the reporting? What was the role of the Pentagon's OSP, which was created by Secretary of Defense Rumsfeld in October 2002, when the CIA refused to document the Niger link to Iraq and al Qaeda's links to Iraq? Why has there never been a counterintelligence investigation of fabrications that reached the White House and ended up in the State of the Union speech? These questions remain unanswered, but there is strong evidence that points to Cheney and Libby as the masters of the game.

The White House knew from the beginning that the reporting on Iraqi efforts to purchase nuclear materials from Niger was bogus. Nevertheless, this allegation became central to the administration's case for war, and the White House refused to abandon the charge. Cheney particularly hammered the CIA about Iraq's so-called search for uranium to assist its nuclear weapons program. In response to importuning from Cheney and Libby, the director of the CIA's Counter Proliferation Division (CPD) asked Ambassador Joseph Wilson to visit Niger. Wilson was a likely candidate for such a trip, as a retired career diplomat who had been an ambassador in West Africa, fluent in French, and extremely knowledgeable about the uranium industry. And this was not Wilson's first secret mission on behalf of CPD; several years earlier, he had traveled to Niger to learn about a visit to that country from the father of Pakistan's nuclear program, Abdul Qadeer Khan, who subsequently confessed to having run an illicit global nuclear-proliferation network.[22]

When Wilson's trip to Niger refuted Cheney's notions that Iraq was trying to obtain uranium from Niger and the ambassador described the visit in an op-ed in *The New York Times*, the White House's angry response included the outing of Wilson's wife, Valerie, a clandestine operative in the CPD. Libby and Karl Rove both revealed that Wilson's wife was a CIA operative. This was done to embarrass the ambassador and keep other officials from testifying against the White House's case for war. President Bush and Cheney also decided to leak intelligence information from the phony October 2002 NIE in order to strengthen the public case for Iraqi WMD and to demonstrate that the Niger story was true. They approved the declassification of the October 2002 NIE, which falsely charged that Iraq "had undertaken a vigorous effort to acquire uranium in Africa." Cheney authorized Libby to provide classified information to Judith Miller of *The New York Times*, with Libby and Miller meeting on two occasions in early July. In briefing Miller and *Time's* Matthew Cooper, Libby never mentioned the dissents of INR and the Department of Energy on the uranium charge.

In the process of retaliating against Wilson, the decision to "out" his wife Valerie was made to create the impression that she actually sent her husband on a "boondoggle" to Niger. Plame's Agency affiliation was given to syndicated correspondent Robert Novak and five other journalists, but only Novak published the information. Supporters of the war and the Bush administration have tried to insinuate that Plame was not an undercover operative, but her testimony to the Congress in March 2007 included a memorandum from the CIA director to the White House confirming her status as a clandestine CIA operative working under cover.

Both Bush and Cheney were involved in the campaign against Wilson and Plame, although the president has maintained that he was unaware of any attacks against Ambassador Wilson. Scooter Libby's lawyer, Theodore Wells, argued that Libby was a scapegoat to protect Karl Rove, the president's principal advisor. Cheney also charged that the White House was failing to "protect one staffer and sacrifice the guy this Pres asked to stick his neck in the meat grinder because of the incompetence of others."[23] Cheney ultimately scratched out "this Pres," and substituted "that was."

The campaign against Wilson and Plame led to a grand jury investigation of a possible violation of the 1982 Intelligence Identities Protection Act by two top officials in the White House, Rove and Libby. Libby was indicted and found guilty for lying to the grand jury and obstructing justice, and in July 2007 the president commuted Libby's 30-month prison sentence. No charges were filed against Rove, who also spoke to reporters about Plame's affiliation with CIA.[24] The White House determination to use the fabrication and to "out" Plame in order to punish her husband is one of the best examples of the administration's recklessness in conducting its campaign to support the decision to go to war. Plame was not only working under "non-official cover," which is a difficult and expensive process, but she was one of the few Agency operatives who understood the substance and technology of WMD proliferation.

The Saga of the Aluminum Tubes

The White House handling of the aluminum tubes issue is similar to the Niger-uranium story. Secretary of State Powell and National Security Advisor Rice used CIA intelligence to assert that the tubes, which Iraq possessed, were "only really suited for nuclear weapons programs." Serious experts inside and outside the government made a strong case that the tubes had nothing to do with nuclear weapons, and could not be used to for nuclear weapons. The fact that Saddam Hussein made no attempt to hide the purchases of these tubes argued against their secret use in nuclear weapons. It is incredible that Powell, a four-star general, who was trained as an infantry officer, could not see the difference in specifications between an artillery tube and a nuclear centrifuge, which required heavier and thicker tubing. At the very least, he could have called his artillery counterparts who could have disabused him of his foolish notions. After a year of exhaustive investigation, the Iraq Survey Group confirmed the Department of Energy's conclusion that the tubes were intended for use as battlefield rockets, as the Iraqi government had claimed all along.

"Curveball" or Screwball

The only source for the accusation that Iraq had mobile biological laboratories was code-named "Curveball," an asset handled by German intelligence. The intelligence from "Curveball" was wrong, and the Germans warned the CIA and DIA that Curveball exaggerated his claims during the run-up to war and that there was no validation for the claims. As a result, they were shocked when Bush and Powell used this intelligence in their speeches prior to the war.[25] Senior members of the German Federal Intelligence Service (BND) warned the United States that Curveball never claimed to produce germ weapons and never saw anyone else do so. "We were shocked," the official said. "Mein Gott!! We had always told them it was not proven . . . it was not hard intelligence."[26] The Germans knew that Curveball would say anything to ensure his family German visas. To make matters worse, the Germans believed that Curveball, the only source for CIA intelligence on mobile biological laboratories, was emotionally unstable.

Even DIA analysts referred to Curveball's intelligence as "garbage," but this didn't stop the information from reaching the White House. President Bush subsequently mischaracterized Curveball's information when he warned that Iraq had at least seven mobile laboratories brewing biological weapons. Powell did the same before the UN in February 2003. Powell's behavior is the most curious of all because he opposed the use of force in the summer of 2002 and convinced the president to go to the UN to obtain international support for any military action. He warned the White House, moreover, that Iraq was "like a crystal glass . . . it's going to shatter. There will be no government. There will be civil disorder."[27] Thus, Powell went from his Senate confirmation in 2001, when he called Iraq "fundamentally a broken, weak country," to the United Nations in 2003, when he termed Iraq's possession of the world's most deadly weapons a menace. After resigning as secretary of state in 2005, he came to grips with the errors in his UN address. He remarked, "The world is beginning to doubt the moral basis of our fight against terrorism."

In fact, Powell had doubts about the Curveball charges when he was at the CIA in late January to prepare his UN speech and he carried these doubts right up to the eve of the speech. From the very beginning, Powell insisted that there had to be multiple sources for every charge in the speech, and both Tenet and McLaughlin assured the secretary there would be no single-source intelligence. According to Larry Wilkerson, Powell's senior aide at the State Department, Powell now believes the CIA leaders lied to him about the sources of the speech, particularly on the mobile biological labs and the Iraqi–al Qaeda connections. Whenever Powell expressed strong doubts about one aspect of the speech or another, Tenet or McLaughlin would suddenly produce another source to corroborate one of the controversial allegations.

In his hotel room in the Waldorf Astoria on the eve of Powell's speech, the CIA director got an urgent phone call from Powell, who once again wanted personal assurance the intelligence in the speech was solid and reliable. Tenet personally endorsed the intelligence, although he had just talked to a senior CIA operative who strongly urged Tenet to drop the material on Curveball. Powell wanted assurances there were multiple sources for CIA's allegations because he was getting heavy criticism from intelligence experts at INR. The INR analysts wanted numerous items deleted from the speech, including the claims about mobile biological laboratories, Iraqi–al Qaeda contacts, the presence of bioweapons hidden in palm groves, descriptions of water trucks at Iraqi military installations as "decontamination vehicles" for chemical weapons, the use of Iraqi drones for bioweapons attacks, and the housing of WMD experts in one of Saddam's guest houses. Powell's dramatic moment at the United Nations, where he was backed by CIA director Tenet and UN Ambassador Negroponte, was nothing more than worst-case propaganda that marked a low point in U.S. diplomacy. Powell's descriptions of Iraqi WMD will always be compared to Soviet foreign minister Andrei Gromyko's phony denials of Soviet missiles in Cuba in 1962.

So-Called Links between Iraq and al Qaeda

The primary source for intelligence linking Iraq to training in chemical and biological weapons to al Qaeda turned out to be a fabricator, according to declassified portions of a study prepared by the DIA in February 2002, months before senior members of the Bush administration made their accusations.[28] The DIA concluded the al Qaeda source was "intentionally misleading the debriefers" in making claims about Iraqi support for al Qaeda's work with illicit weapons. The information declared "credible" by the Bush administration and cited in the president's speech in Cincinnati in October 2002 was considered disinformation by the DIA. The prisoner, who had been rendered by the United States and tortured by the Egyptians, did not officially recant his claims until nearly two years later, in January 2004, which finally prompted the CIA to recall its intelligence reports based on the source's reporting.

The CIA initially tried to convince policymakers there were no significant ties between Iraq and al Qaeda, but the president and vice president claimed to be convinced Iraq was behind the terrorism of al Qaeda. President Bush said on September 25, 2002, that "You can't distinguish between al Qaeda and Saddam when you talk abut the War on Terror." At a press conference in December 2005, he made the same claims.[29] Secretary of Defense Rumsfeld claimed on September 27, 2002, he had "bulletproof" evidence of ties between Saddam and al Qaeda, and Secretary of State Powell described a "potentially . . . sinister nexus between Iraq and al Qaeda, a nexus that combines classic terrorist organizations and modern methods of murder."[30] CIA officials provided Powell with the specious intelligence that was used in his UN speech describing the "sinister nexus," although most CIA analysts knew there was no corroboration for these claims.

Cheney's descriptions of a Prague meeting between 9/11 hijacker Mohammed Atta and Iraqi intelligence officers in April 2001 were also based on specious intelligence. He argued in December 2001 that this meeting had been "pretty well confirmed" and, in September 2002, he asserted Atta traveled to Prague "on a number of occasions. And on at least one occasion, we have reporting that places him in Prague with a senior Iraqi intelligence official a few months before the attack on the World Trade Center." As late as January 2004, Cheney raised Atta's travels to Prague and his meetings with Iraqi intelligence officers. In fact, both the CIA and the FBI had definitive evidence placing Atta in the United States at the time of the so-called meeting with Iraqi intelligence officials.

As late as April 2004, when the 9/11 Commission was approaching its conclusion that there was no Iraq–al Qaeda link, nearly half the American population believed that the link existed and that Saddam Hussein was involved in the 9/11 terrorist attacks against the World Trade Center and the Pentagon. Following the release of the 9/11 Commission's report, which debunked the notion of a relationship between Iraq and al Qaeda, President Bush proclaimed, "The reason I keep insisting that there was a relationship between Iraq and Saddam and al Qaeda [was] because there was a relationship between Iraq and al Qaeda."[31] Vice President Cheney referred to "overwhelming evidence" of these links, and Secretary of State Powell referred to links that existed "over the years" in a nexus that "combines classic terrorist organizations and modern methods of murder."[32] On the eve of Powell's UN speech, Secretary of Defense Rumsfeld said the link existed "over a span of some eight to ten years" and when Iraq denied any linkage, Rumsfeld flippantly replied, "And Abraham Lincoln was short."[33] After the invasion of Iraq, National Security Advisor Rice still repeated the myths of Iraqi training in chemical and biological weapons for members of al Qaeda, emphasizing that the United States needed to prevent the day that Saddam Hussein would hand "just a little vial of something" to terrorists.[34]

Postwar Iraq

The Bush administration did no planning for postwar Iraq and ignored intelligence reports predicting great difficulty in the wake of regime change. The White House ignored the good advice it received on constraints of power in Iraq and instead created a bogus case for the use of power in the prewar period and then cynical rationalizations for the lack of success after the invasion. The CIA's Middle East analysts anticipated correctly that the war and occupation would further politicize the Islamic community against the United States, would increase support for terrorists within the Islamic community, and would bring Arab extremists into Iraq to fight the infidels from the West. In January 2003, the National Intelligence Council warned the president that war in Iraq could lead to an anti-U.S. insurgency and "increased popular sympathy for terrorist objectives."

Cheney told numerous audiences that U.S. forces would be greeted as liberators, a message he was not getting from the intelligence community. The CIA, as well as the State Department's INR, tried to tell the administration that Paul Wolfowitz's dream of a democratic Iraq was a pipedream and that it would take a Marshall Plan-type effort to restore the Iraqi economy. Army Chief of Staff Eric Shinseki warned that it would take more troops in the postwar situation than for the battle against Saddam Hussein. Rumsfeld and Wolfowitz combined to marginalize Shinseki.[35] Wolfowitz argued that Iraqi oil revenues, and not the United States, would pay for the restoration of the Iraqi economy, and the chief of the Agency for International Development told the National War College faculty that the war would cost less than $2 billion.

However, the economic advisor in the White House, Larry Lynn, predicted in September 2002—just as the White House was beginning its marketing campaign—that the actual cost of rehabilitation would be over $200 billion; he was forced to resign. The projected cost of the war through 2008 exceeds $750 billion, making the Iraq War the second-costliest war in U.S. history.[36] Only World War II, which cost more than $3.2 trillion, was more costly. The Bush administration has budgeted only $50 billion for the Iraq and Afghan Wars in its 2009 projections and nothing for the eight years after that, so the World War II record is not safe.

Cheney's challengers were simply adhering to lines of analysis consistent with the past. Anyone familiar with the British experience in Iraq in the 1920s knew that a colonial occupation of an Arab country was far more likely to produce anarchy than democracy. Lawrence of Arabia warned in 1920 that the British had been led "into a trap from which it will be hard to escape with dignity and honor. . . . Things have been far worse than we have been told, our administration more bloody and inefficient than the public knows. . . . We are today not far from a disaster."

Cheney has remained aggressive in defending the Iraq War he wanted in the wake of the 9/11 attacks, although others in the administration have sounded more defensive. Rumsfeld's well-known response to the criticism of his military plan for Iraq was "sometimes you go to war with the army you have, not the army you would like to have." His opposition to the surge of American forces in 2007 led to pressure on him from the White House to resign. President Bush admitted, in his State of the Union address in January 2007, that "we are not in the fight we entered, but it is the fight we're in." Secretary of State Powell always had doubts about the reasons and rationality for war, despite his UN speech in February. Powell has become increasingly angry about the text for his UN speech that the CIA created for him based on flawed and unverified intelligence. All members of the administration will have to deal with UN inspector Hans Blix's question: "How could there be 100 percent certainty about the existence of weapons of mass destruction but zero percent knowledge about their location?"[37]

THE PRESIDENT'S CASE FOR WAR

Cheney and Rumsfeld, who had been critics of CIA intelligence analysis since the mid-1970s when they were chief of staff and secretary of defense, respectively, for President Gerald Ford, believed the CIA was a major obstacle to President Bush's case for war against Iraq. As a result, there was constant pressure on the Agency for intelligence to support the war, which eventually wore down the CIA leaders, particularly Tenet and McLaughlin, and the CIA caved in. President Bush found the CIA's intelligence support for the case to go to war inadequate; he wanted "something that Joe Public would understand or gain a lot of confidence from."[38] Bush turned to Tenet and remarked, "I've been told all this intelligence about having WMD and this is the best we've got?" The CIA director replied, "Don't worry, it's a slam dunk!" This was not, as Tenet writes, the seminal moment for the decision to go to war, but it was the seminal moment for the CIA signaling the White House would get the intelligence it wanted. Several days later, the chief of WINPAC, Alan Foley, told his senior staff, "If the president wants intelligence to support a decision to go to war, then it is up to the agency to provide it."

The Bush administration used misinformation for two more "slam dunks": the president's State of the Union in January and the secretary of state's UN address in February. The president's speech contained three pieces of misinformation or disinformation. The connection between Niger and enriched uranium was based on a fabricated document; the charges concerning high-strength aluminum tubes for a nuclear weapons program was disavowed by scientists at the Department of Energy and Department of State; and the evidence of mobile biological laboratories was from a discredited Iraqi defector known as "Curveball." Bush cited the British as his source for the allegation regarding Niger; the stories on Niger's "yellowcake" and Iraq originated in the phony reporting of Rocco Martino, a former member of the Italian military intelligence service (SISMI), who tried to peddle this story to Italian journalists. The former chief of INR, Carl Ford, asserted all the reporting on Iraq and Niger stemmed from the same source.[39]

The news of Powell's decision to spend several days at CIA headquarters, side by side with Tenet and McLaughlin, was received with outrage at the Department of State, particularly at INR. State's INR had serious problems with the CIA's handling of the intelligence on Iraqi WMD and knew Powell would need an independent audit on any speech provided by the analysts of WINPAC and the Counterterrorism Center. Powell's willingness to closet himself at the CIA to write a major speech was unprecedented; his own intelligence bureau had a far better record on intelligence issues involving Iraq. INR could have saved the secretary from the excesses of the UN speech that is the major blemish on an otherwise distinguished career in the military, the NSC, and the Department of State. The original draft for Powell's speech was actually written in the office of the vice president by Scooter Libby, a 48-page draft on Iraqi WMD. The secretary of state threw the draft into the air and pronounced, "I'm not reading this. This is bullshit." On January 29, 2003, Powell told his chief of staff at the department, Larry Wilkerson, that on the following day two more drafts would arrive: one on Iraq's involvement in terrorist activities and another on Iraqi human rights violations.[40] Powell immediately ordered Wilkerson to establish a task force to draft the speech with the assistance of CIA analysts at their headquarters in Virginia.

Powell's frustration over the Libby draft led Tenet to suggest using the October 2002 NIE as the basis for the UN speech. Compared to the Libby draft, the estimate was better sourced and better written, but no less polemical and no more accurate or convincing. The paper on terrorism was eventually reduced to seven pages; Powell and Wilkerson concluded it introduced no substantive evidence of Iraqi terrorist contacts other than Saddam Hussein's payments to the families of deceased Palestinian terrorists. Powell should have dropped the entire memorandum instead of including portions on Abu Musab al-Zarqawi's presence in Iraq, which Saddam Hussein opposed and tried to prevent, and alleged contacts between Iraq and al Qaeda regarding chemical and biological weapons training that had been obtained primarily from captured terrorist Ibn al-Sheikh al-Libi. Al-Libi's information on such contacts had been extracted following hours of torture at the hands of Egyptian intelligence officials; al-Libi eventually recanted this information in 2004. The DIA had given up on al-Libi's information on Iraqi-al Qaeda connections long before his recantation, more than a year before the CIA introduced this material into Powell's speech.

Powell was drafted to give the speech by the most hawkish elements within the Bush administration, led by Vice President Cheney. On the evening of April 12, 2003, Cheney had a small dinner party for Libby, Wolfowitz, and their major public spokesman for the war, Ken Adelman. They were dining to celebrate the victory over Iraq; it was Adelman who had written in February 2002 that the war would be a cakewalk. On April 10, Adelman wrote "Cakewalk Revisited" for the *Washington Post*, gloating over the expected quick victory.[41] They were euphoric about their victory in Iraq and particular derisive toward such skeptics as Brent Scowcroft, Jim Baker, Larry Eagleburger, and Powell, whose name drew chuckles around the table.[42] Cheney and Wolfowitz remarked that Powell loved to brag about his popularity and knew that selecting Powell to go to the UN would exploit the secretary of state's desire for the limelight. Probably the best critique of the speech came from Tenet, several years later, "It was a great presentation, but unfortunately the substance didn't hold up."[43]

If the Senate and House intelligence committees had fulfilled their task of intelligence oversight, the U.S. public would have known months before the invasion that the case for war was spurious. The chairman and vice chairman of the Senate intelligence committee, Senator Roberts and Senator Rockefeller, respectively, conceded the Senate would not have authorized the president to go to war in October 2002 if there had been accurate information regarding Iraq's programs of WMD.[44] The committee eventually concluded that Powell's UN speech was "overstated, misleading, or incorrect."[45] Of course, this should have been known at the time of the speech and, in any event, was confirmed by the report of the International Atomic Energy Agency in March 2003, nearly two weeks before the invasion. But, as late as 2004, when the Senate intelligence committee was finally trying to determine whether the CIA had provided false intelligence data to the White House, the Bush administration was withholding key documentation. At the same time, Roberts continued to block an investigation into the White House misrepresentation of the intelligence it received.

A former CIA analyst, Paul Pillar, has written an authoritative account of the Bush administration's misuse of the intelligence it received in order to "justify decisions already made," although he falsely argued the Agency did not compromise any of its own assessments or estimates in the process.[46] He conceded the White House requested his unclassified White Paper on Iraqi WMD for "public advocacy purposes . . . to strengthen the case of going to war with the American public," which was the reason Pillar had no business managing such an exercise.[47] The Bush administration paid no attention to intelligence assessments on Iraq and requested no specific intelligence on Iraq other than summaries of nonexistent WMD and nonexistent ties between Iraq and al Qaeda. Unlike the Johnson administration and the war in Vietnam, the Bush administration did not request CIA memoranda as a check on the intelligence provided by the Pentagon or the Joint Chiefs of Staff. Bush and the senior members of the administration created much of the intelligence they wanted, whether it was bogus intelligence on Niger's uranium stocks or unsubstantiated intelligence on Saddam Hussein's links to bin Laden. Bush and Cheney had their assumptions about Iraq and the need for war, and sensitive intelligence information was not about to change any of their thinking.

THE PRESIDENT'S DEFENSE AND
THE PRESIDENT'S DEFENDERS

Fifty days after the fall of Baghdad, on May 29, 2003, President Bush emphatically proclaimed that the United States "has found the weapons of mass destruction," which turned out to be the mobile biological laboratories.[48] This claim, the purported vindication for the invasion of Iraq, was repeated by every prominent member of the Bush administration for the next nine months. Nevertheless, at the highest levels of the Pentagon, the CIA, and the DIA, it was authoritatively known there were no mobile biological laboratories long *before* the president, the vice president, the secretary of state, and the secretary of defense heralded the so-called find as justification for the invasion of Iraq.

In the summer of 2003, the Pentagon announced withdrawal of the U.S. task force that had been sent to Baghdad to search for WMD, acknowledging that no chemical, biological, or nuclear materials had been found. In December 2003, U.S. military forces released nearly all of the captured Iraqi scientists, which indicated that the Pentagon no longer believed there was anything to be gained from additional interrogations. Before the war, the International Atomic Energy Agency issued its own report concluding that there was "no indication of resumed nuclear activities . . . nor any indication of nuclear-related prohibited activities at any inspected sites."[49] The IAEA reported there had been "no indication that Iraq has attempted to import uranium since 1990" and termed President Bush's assertion that Saddam was trying to purchase uranium in Africa bogus. The obvious question in all this was why a UN inspection team was able to monitor and verify the decrepit state of Iraq's political, economic, and military situation when the CIA could not.

In fact, the U.S. Army, according to its intelligence chief at the time, General James "Spider" Marks, went into Iraq with no intelligence regarding the location of WMD, whether chemical, biological, nuclear, or radiological munitions. "Nobody," according to Marks, "was thinking about intelligence about WMD, in warehouses or buried someplace, that would have any relevance" to the troops on the ground.[50] Marks received intelligence from the CIA and DIA that he termed old, sketchily sourced, or not sourced at all. When asked if the war planners genuinely cared about WMD, Marks replied, "They ostensibly cared, but their give-a-shit level was really low."

The president selected the Veterans' Day address on November 11, 2005 to deny his administration had skewed intelligence to make the case for war and to charge he received the same intelligence on Iraq the Congress and his immediate predecessor, President Bill Clinton, received. President Bush charged Democrats with accusing the White House of falsifying intelligence and thus providing aid and comfort to the insurgents and hurting the morale of American servicemen. This was a major reversal of his previous defense, which was to blame the CIA for providing faulty intelligence on Iraqi WMD. In actual fact, the policies of the Clinton administration had worked, with the destruction of all WMD programs achieved by 1998, the same year the UN inspectors left Iraq. The verification measures of the international inspectors also had worked; they were accurate, while the $50 billion intelligence industry failed.

President Bush also argued there was no political pressure on the intelligence community to provide analysis that would make the case for war, citing the first phase of the Senate intelligence committee's investigation on Iraq, as well as the 9/11 Commission. This aspect of Bush's defense is particularly disingenuous because former Senate intelligence chairman Roberts blocked the committee from investigating how the administration used the intelligence it received from the community. The ranking minority member of the committee, Senator Rockefeller called for such an investigation before the war began in March 2003, but Roberts blocked these efforts for the next two-and-a-half years. Roberts finally yielded in October 2005, after the Senate Democrats demanded an unusual secret session of the Senate to work out a compromise on investigating White House handling of sensitive intelligence matters, the so-called Phase Two aspect of the investigation. President Bush was also disingenuous in stating that the Congress had the same intelligence that was available to the president. Actually, the White House blocked sensitive intelligence from going to the committee, and Vice President Dick Cheney and Scooter Libby played a particularly aggressive role in this campaign. The committee had no access whatsoever to the daily copies of the PDB, which contains the most sensitive intelligence available to the community.

The new Democratic chairman of the intelligence committee, Rockefeller, promised in 2007 to reopen the issue of the Bush administration's misuse of intelligence on Iraqi WMD, which remains the key unexamined issue in the second phase of the committee's review of prewar Iraq intelligence. Rockefeller wants to learn if intelligence was misused in the public speeches of key members of the Bush administration to build support for the Iraq War, terming this assessment one of "our core responsibilities."[51]

Despite the denial of political interference with the intelligence process, there is no question that the White House placed tremendous pressure on the CIA to provide intelligence to support the case for war, particularly on WMD and Iraqi links to al Qaeda.

CIA officials acknowledged the White House pressure, and CIA ombudsman Barry Lee Stevenson told the Senate intelligence committee the administration's "hammering" on Iraq intelligence was harder than he had seen in his thirty-two years at the CIA. A former deputy director of central intelligence, Richard Kerr, remarked in 2003 that there was "significant pressure on the intelligence community to find evidence that supported a connection" between Iraq and al Qaeda.[52] Stevenson and Kerr ignored politicization of intelligence during their careers, so their reversal on this issue following their retirements is noteworthy. Kerr also headed a group of former senior intelligence officers that prepared three reports on the intelligence community's performance in the run-up to the Iraq War. These reports cited "intense policymaker demands in the run-up to the war, which some in the community believed constituted inappropriate pressure on intelligence analysts."[53] Kerr remarked that the White House was unrelenting in its demands on "WMD and Saddam's links to al Qaeda . . . in the months leading up to the war."[54]

As late as June 2006, there were still politicians claiming that WMD were discovered in Iraq and that the Bush administration had been exonerated. The former chairman of the House intelligence committee, Representative Peter Hoekstra (R-Michigan), and former senator Rick Santorum (R-Pennsylvania) held a press conference on June 28, citing an unclassified report by the National Ground Intelligence Center regarding five hundred chemical munitions shells that had been buried near the Iranian border. Even the White House and the Office of the Director of National Intelligence disavowed the report and explained these particular shells had been buried along the Iraqi–Iranian border during their war in the 1980s. In fact, the finding of the shells had been announced in 2004, and the CIA explained at the time that findings of degraded mustard gas and sarin nerve agents were not unusual and had nothing to do with the missing WMD. Hoekstra, Santorum, and various true believers cannot accept they were lied to by the Bush administration. Their efforts to conduct a futile search for WMD cost American lives, because it took time and attention from controlling stocks of conventional weapons that were used against U.S. forces when the insurgency began.

Clearly 100 percent of Iraq's nuclear program, including facilities and infrastructure, had been destroyed prior to the war. The weapons design facility and all production equipment had been destroyed, and the introduction of detection equipment on land and airborne would have detected any gamma rays that would have been emitted if Iraq sought to enrich uranium or plutonium. There could not be as much certainty about the chemical and biological weapons programs because of the more difficult verification and monitoring environment. Nevertheless, in this area as well, the destruction of the Muthanna State establishment meant there was no capability to fabricate new agents.

Five years after the start of the war against Iraq, the Senate intelligence committee has still not published a report to detail the Bush administration's use and misuse of the intelligence it received. The exaggeration of intelligence by the president, the vice president, the secretary of defense, and the national security advisor, particularly with reference to Iraqi nuclear programs ("the smoking gun cannot be a mushroom cloud") and Iraqi links with al Qaeda, was obvious, but there needs to be an official record of White House distortions. The British also played games with intelligence materials, releasing a report in September 2002 saying Iraq could launch biological and chemical weapons within forty-five minutes. British officials have conceded the report was "sexed-up" for release to the public.

THE MISUSE OF INTELLIGENCE

The Bush administration's misuse of intelligence has created serious consequences for the United States. The international community knows the so-called clear and present danger of Iraqi WMD used to justify the invasion did not exist, and that the claims of the president, vice president, secretary of defense, and CIA director were vastly exaggerated or simply false. The intelligence of the CIA, moreover, is not intended to be the personal weapon for the political use of the White House. The CIA director has no business taking part in a White House effort to make the public case for war, let alone guaranteeing that his Agency could do so.

- Misuse of intelligence by the White House, such as the forged documents on Niger, or politicization of intelligence by the CIA, such as the NIE and White Paper of October 2002, weakens the instrument of credible intelligence to prevent further terrorist acts and undermines U.S. national security. The misuse of intelligence during the Vietnam War prolonged a brutal and costly war. The manipulation of intelligence during Iran-Contra in the 1980s led to political embarrassment for the Reagan administration. The misuse of intelligence on the Soviet Union led to unprecedented peacetime increases in defense spending despite the decline and decay of the Soviet Union. Any administration's use of intelligence for political ends is unacceptable, particularly to make a specious case to go to war.
- Distortion of evidence of Iraqi WMD makes it harder to gain international cooperation in the war against terrorism and the campaign to prevent the spread of nuclear weapons. These efforts require international support. Information from foreign intelligence services has been essential in the capture of all al Qaeda terrorists thus far; any success in stopping the strategic weapons programs of Iran and North Korea, both more advanced than those of prewar Iraq, also requires foreign intelligence. The credibility of U.S. intelligence and national security policy is essential in such a campaign.
- The use of more than one thousand military and civilian analysts and technicians to search for nonexistent WMD took time away from the search for the conventional stockpile of weapons held by the Iraqi military and various sectarian and insurgent groups. The current civil war is being waged with weapons that could have been seized early in the war, when the U.S. military had relatively open access to most of the country and there was no sign of an institutionalized insurgency.

In addition to the specious NIE on Iraqi WMD in October 2002, the CIA produced an estimate on North Korean strategic capabilities that exaggerated the scope of Pyongyang's nuclear program. As a result, U.S.–North Korean relations worsened, North Korea made a decision to break the nuclear freeze and conduct a weapons test, and the political balance in Northeast Asia became more unstable. There are now efforts to find a diplomatic solution to the strategic problems on the North Korean peninsula, but faulty CIA intelligence contributed unnecessarily to tensions in the region.

- Finally, one of the worst possible scenarios for U.S. security interests, and those of the international community, would be learning that WMD materials had been looted or smuggled from Iraqi weapons sites. As former White House spokesman Ari Fleischer noted during the Iraq war: "[WMD] is what this war was about and is about. And we have high confidence that it will be found." We lost an opportunity to verify any remnants of WMD in Iraq in the spring of 2003 when the U.S. military occupation made no attempt to investigate possible WMD sites, not even Tuwaitha, where Iraqis previously stored supplied of enriched materials. The only way to ensure that such sites were not looted of old materials was to deploy international inspectors who had examined these sites in the 1990s.

Ari Fleischer was responsible for one of the more Orwellian remarks in the postwar period when he remarked on July 9, 2003, "I think the burden is on those people who think he didn't have weapons of mass destruction to tell the world where they are."[55] The burden of proof, however, is on the Bush administration, which insisted on going to war even while UN inspectors were doing their job—and obviously doing it well. It was the international agencies that effectively monitored the destruction of Iraqi WMD. The Nobel Peace Prize in 2005 was given jointly to the IAEA and its director, Mohammed El-Baradei, who argued that there was no evidence of a reconstituted nuclear capability or large stocks of chemical and biological weapons, and declared the evidence linking Saddam Hussein to purchases of uranium from Niger was fabricated. The Nobel Prize appeared to be a calculated response to the arguments of the Bush administration for going to war against Iraq. In addition to the award to El-Baradei, the Nobel Prize for Literature in 2005 went to British writer Harold Pinter ostensibly for his trenchant novels and plays in the 1960s and 1970s, but whose recent work condemned the foreign policy and national security policies of the United States in the wake of the Iraq War.

Increased anti-Americanism and a decline in American influence in the global community are just some of the consequences of the Iraq War, which has become a strategic nightmare for the United States. Many more Americans died in Vietnam than have been lost in Iraq thus far, but the strategic consequences of the Iraqi failure are far greater. The United States has far greater strategic and geopolitical interests in the Middle East and the Persian Gulf than in Southeast Asia, and those interests have become far more problematic in the wake of the U.S. occupation of Iraq. The potential for conflict beyond Iraq itself is far greater than the possibility of a wider conflict beyond Vietnam in the 1970s. The deceit in the run-up to the war, particularly the corruption of the intelligence process, and the absence of postwar planning will continue to create problems for the United States.

10

The Iraq War and the CIA

Don't worry, it's a slam dunk.

—CIA Director George Tenet, December, 21, 2002
(Tenet's response to President Bush's demand for
stronger intelligence on Iraq's weapons of mass destruction
to provide to the American people)

Let me begin by saying we were almost all wrong, and I certainly include
myself here.

—David Kay, January 28, 2004
(To the Senate Armed Forces Committee on Iraqi WMD)

The Truth Will Set You Free.

—Biblical inscription in the lobby of the CIA building

The U.S. rush to war against Iraq marked the worst intelligence scandal in the
history of the United States. The CIA cherry-picked the evidence to support the
case for war and thoroughly corrupted the intelligence process to convince the
Congress and the American people of the need for war. The Bush administration would have gone to war even if the CIA had gotten the intelligence right,
had not drafted a specious NIE and white paper, and had not prepared a phony
speech for Secretary of State Powell. This does not absolve the CIA of its own
abuse of power. It is conceivable, moreover, that honest leadership from George
Tenet and John McLaughlin and a strong CIA stand could have created more
opposition to the war from the Congress, the media, and the public.

Clearly the White House had no interest in intelligence that argued against
the case for war. The NIO for the Near East and South Asia, Paul Pillar, told

a Senate committee hearing in June 2006 that he received no requests from any administration policymaker on any aspect of Iraq until more than a year after the war began.[1] This is in stark contrast to the Vietnam experience when there was a strong debate within the intelligence community on Southeast Asia; the White House and the NSC were well aware of every aspect of the debate, including the controversy over the numbers of Viet Cong. In contrast, the Bush administration demanded only intelligence materials that demonstrated the presence of WMD in Iraq or linkages between Iraq and al Qaeda.

In several areas, the CIA initially tried to put forth the best available information and analysis in order to educate the White House. Early on, it debunked many of the notions being advanced by the pro-war crowd: Iraq's alleged efforts to obtain uranium from Niger, the canard about Saddam Hussein's links to al Qaeda, and the possibility of a reconstituted Iraq nuclear capability. The closer the run-up to war, however, the more willing the CIA was to cave to administration pressure. In certain areas, such as mobile biological laboratories and chemical and biological weapons, CIA tradecraft—both operational and analytic—was deeply flawed and corrupted.

Sadly, it was the CIA's most senior leaders who failed in their responsibilities. CIA director Tenet told the president of the United States that it would be a "slam dunk" to provide a stronger intelligence justification for the war to the American people. His deputy, McLaughlin, perverted the intelligence process, ignored briefings on the weakness of the intelligence on WMD, and tried to silence the chief of the Iraq Survey Group, David Kay, who found no evidence of any strategic weapons. McLaughlin was a key advocate for the notorious "Curveball," whose phony intelligence on mobile biological laboratories ended up in Secretary of State Powell's UN address six weeks before the start of the Iraq War. The NIOs for Strategic Weapons and the Middle East, Robert Walpole and Paul Pillar, respectively, were responsible for an NIE and an unclassified white paper that made a false and politicized case for the war. Senior analysts in the Counterterrorism Center (CTC) provided false intelligence on the so-called nexus between Iraq and al Qaeda that was used in Powell's UN speech. The rare operations officer or intelligence analyst who tried to get it right was marginalized by CIA's senior leaders and, in some cases, removed from his or her job. In their reports, the Senate Select Committee on Intelligence (SSCI), the Iraq Survey Group, and the Presidential WMD Commission agreed that the intelligence community, particularly the CIA, totally failed on the issue of Iraq's WMD.

Although intelligence played a minor role in the planning for war, the failures of intelligence were nonetheless stunning, pointing to major problems within the intelligence community. The CIA had no understanding of the intentions and motivations of Saddam Hussein; the decrepit state of Iraq's political, economic, and military situation; and the fact that there were no WMD and no programs for reconstituting the capabilities that existed before Desert Storm in 1991. Furthermore, the CIA displayed no subsequent interest in understanding the failures that took place. No postmortem and no lessons learned have been produced, raising the strong possibility that the CIA's errors with respect to Saddam Hussein's Iraq could be repeated in its approach to Iran and North Korea, where the collection of intelligence is limited due to the absence of an official American diplomatic presence.

The CIA's performance on Iraq raises serious questions about collection and analysis of intelligence at the nation's premier intelligence agency. The close interaction between the policy community and the intelligence community led to serious politicization of intelligence. President Harry Truman warned about the dangers of such interaction when he created the CIA, and intelligence professionals over the years have echoed his warnings. Former CIA director Helms told new recruits that the Agency existed to keep the policy process honest, but under Tenet, that lesson was honored in the breach. The failure to tell truth to power in the case of Iraq is the most serious intelligence failure in U.S. history, helping the Bush administration to initiate a preemptive war that will have long-term negative repercussions for the United States.

The CIA was wrong on every aspect of Iraqi WMD—nuclear, biological, and chemical, and there were no honest errors in the process. The CIA's conclusions about the so-called nuclear program were based on flimsy and, in one prominent case, fabricated information. The CIA and the intelligence community spend record amounts of money for technical collection, but these sophisticated collection systems were of little value in the run-up to the war. This raises serious questions about the role of technical collection in an era of non-state actor terrorism (al Qaeda) and internal sectarian warfare (Iraq). The only failure that rivals the intelligence failure is the failure of oversight, particularly the breakdown in Congressional oversight. The fact that independent bodies, such as the Robb-Silberman Commission and the inspection teams headed by David Kay and Charles Duelfer, had to examine the WMD problem points to the inability of the CIA to investigate itself. The silence of the CIA's Inspector General was deafening. These are systemic problems that must be addressed.

The CIA's comprehensive intelligence failure points to the absence of a historical office, such as the Special Research Staff (SRS), which was abolished in 1973. The SRS maintained the historical archives of the CIA, and the failure on Iraqi WMD points to the Agency's inability to maintain and pulse its own archives in preparing intelligence assessments. The DI never reexamined previous estimates on Iraq, and it accepted at face value unsubstantiated assertions that the Desert Fox raids in 1998 had failed to destroy Iraq's suspected chemical warfare facilities.[2] Lacking new evidence, CIA analysts assumed that

Iraq still had huge stockpiles of poison gas, as well as the capability to resume the production of chemical weapons. In December 2000, on the basis of disinformation supplied through European intelligence services, the CIA and the intelligence community produced an estimate, "Iraq: Steadily Pursuing WMD Capabilities," that concluded Iraq had stockpiled up to one hundred tons of mustard gas and sarin nerve agents, and had the potential to produce as much as several hundred tons of biological agents per year. Using the reports of the discredited German asset code-named "Curveball," the estimate raised the issue of mobile biological laboratories that became a major embarrassment to Secretary of State Powell who emphasized this canard in his UN speech. In producing these estimates, the CIA ignored numerous Iraqi sources with access to Saddam Hussein's weapons programs who reported there were no WMD to be found.[3]

The CIA was vulnerable to worst-case analysis on Iraq because it had underestimated Iraqi intentions and capabilities in the 1980s and early 1990s, and did not want to do so again. The CIA did not anticipate the Iraqi attack against Iran in 1980 and underestimated the damage to the Iraqi military and economy as a result of their eight-year war. The CIA misread Iraq's intentions in the aftermath of that costly war and, prior to the Iraqi invasion of Kuwait in August 1990, CIA intelligence had informed President Bush that Iraq would leave its neighbors alone for at least the next three years while it licked its wounds. An NIE in 1990 gave no hint of an imminent Iraqi attack against Kuwait, and previous CIA assessments missed Iraqi's strategic and nuclear programs prior to 1991.

Unlike the CIA, the Pentagon anticipated problems with Iraq and rewrote its war games in the late 1990s to include military scenarios involving Iraq, while the CIA focused on Iran as the regional threat. The CIA provided little useful intelligence to the Pentagon during Desert Storm, according to high-level American generals, and in the wake of Desert Storm the CIA overestimated Iraqi nuclear programs. In the 1980s the CIA suppressed intelligence on Baghdad's procurement network for nuclear weapons, supporting the policies of the Reagan administration that favored working with Saddam Hussein against Iran. The CIA also suppressed intelligence on Pakistan's nuclear network in order to protect the U.S.–Pakistani link for supplying arms and financial support to the Afghan Mujihideen.

THE CIA'S TRADECRAFT FAILURE

CIA managers and senior analysts violated every norm of the analytical process in helping the Bush administration make its case for war against Iraq, using fabricated intelligence, sole source information, unvetted information, and information that had been obtained through torture and abuse. The directorates of intelligence (DI) and operations (DO) have filters designed to prevent the introduction of fabrications into finished intelligence products; in this case, CIA managers and analysts ran through a series of red lights. Analysts, like investigative reporters, should be particularly leery of sole-source information, but single-source intelligence on Iraq's so-called mobile biological laboratories was central to Secretary of State Powell's UN speech prior to the war. Both Tenet and McLaughlin lied to Powell in claiming there were multiple sources for information on mobile biological labs. In another instance, information provided by a source who had been tortured was given unwarranted credibility. This source had been rendered to Egypt and tortured in order to garner the information. Tenet used this corrupt information in a letter to the Senate intelligence committee just several days prior to the vote authorizing the use of force. Sole source information was then used in the NIE of October 2002, when one of the major reasons for producing an estimate should be to exploit the multiplicity of sources central to good intelligence. The Commission on the Intelligence Capabilities of the United States Regarding Weapons of Mass Destruction concluded in March 2005 that the CIA's senior management was "remiss in not raising concerns" with senior policymakers before the war, but the Commission underestimated the corruption of the entire intelligence process.[4]

The CIA and DIA were also remiss in not being more skeptical of the intelligence information received from members of the Iraqi National Congress, who were trying to draw the United States into a war against Saddam Hussein by making the case for Iraqi WMD and Iraqi links to terrorists. The two agencies funded the collection and then used it in intelligence distributed to the White House and the NSC. Prior to the start of Operation Iraqi Freedom on March 19, 2003, false information from INC sources was used to support key intelligence assessments that were widely distributed throughout the intelligence community.[5] The source for intelligence linking Iraq to training of non-Iraqi Arabs on aircraft hijackings was affiliated with the INC.[6] The sole source for intelligence on the mobile biological labs had a brother with the INC. CIA operatives wrote memoranda calling attention to the inaccuracy of the INC information at the same time that CIA analysts were inserting this information into their assessments. Despite their skepticism about INC intelligence, both CIA and DIA often distributed information without noting the origin of these dubious sources, an egregious violation of analytical tradecraft. The CIA never communicated to the White House and the NSC its doubts about the accuracy and credibility of its dubious sources.

The CIA and the Niger Forgery

The allegation that Iraq was trying to purchase nuclear materials from Niger was one of the keys to the administration's case for war. The first report of such a purchase appeared in a DIA intelligence highlight on February 13, 2002. Vice President Cheney then used this report to hammer the CIA about its views on Iraq's search for enriched uranium. The CIA had doubts about the authenticity of the reporting and asked Ambassador Joseph Wilson to visit Niger to get additional details on a possible purchase. The CIA picked Wilson for the Niger trip because of his knowledge of the uranium industry and African politics; the Agency hoped that Wilson's bona fides would serve to disabuse Cheney of his zealous campaign to use the Niger documents to assert that Saddam Hussein was trying to reconstitute Iraq's nuclear capabilities. The request originated in the DO's Counter Proliferation Division, where Wilson's wife, Valerie Plame, worked as a clandestine officer under cover. According to several reporters, the proposal to send Wilson to Niger came from Plame's colleagues and not Plame, although Plame relayed the Division's request to her husband.[7] During this period, Marine Corps General Carleton Fulford and Ambassador Barbro Owens-Kirkpatrick conducted their own investigations and reported to their sponsors, the Joint Chiefs of Staff and the State Department, respectively. Wilson, Fulford, and Owens-Kirkpatrick each reported emphatically that there was no substance to the intelligence reporting that Iraq was trying to buy uranium yellowcake.

In addition to these missions, European intelligence liaison repeatedly told the CIA that the Niger reporting was based on a crude forgery. French intelligence dismissed the reporting as early as mid-2001 and as late as January 2003. The French view was authoritative because the French run the international consortium that produces uranium ore in Niger. The Italians were also dismissive, and even the popular Italian magazine *Panorama* refused to print the documents because the fabrication was so obvious. International organizations, including the International Atomic Energy Agency, also considered the documents to be fraudulent. There is no question that the CIA tried to have it both ways, initially making an effort to stop the White House from citing the intelligence in any public arena, but repeating the allegations in their own intelligence products. The fact that we still do not know who created the phony intelligence and why it was created points to the ineptitude of the counterintelligence capabilities of both the FBI and the CIA or, even worse, suggests a cover-up of an operation that would implicate former or current American intelligence officers. This would not be the first time that CIA "black propaganda" or misinformation designed for an European audience ended up in the United States, even in the White House, as unintended blowback.

The two-year investigation of the outing of Plame, which led to the unusual jailing of *The New York Times* reporter Judith Miller, revealed the extent of the risks that the White House would take to protect its phony case for war. In sanctioning the outing of Plame, an expert on the proliferation of WMD, the White House was weakening CIA collection against an extremely important target. The Wilson trip was not controversial until it led to the outing of his wife, Valerie, whose cover status was protected by federal legislation passed in 1982. Very little was done with Wilson's briefings upon return from Niger, and there is no record that Vice President Cheney was given a formal briefing.

When the White House persisted with the fiction of linking Iraq to uranium purchases in Niger, Wilson published an article in the *New York Times* in July 2003 denouncing the fiction. The article enraged Cheney, who orchestrated a program to intimidate Wilson and to prevent other officials from revealing the misuse of intelligence in the run-up to the Iraq War. President Bush authorized Libby to leak the language of the 2002 NIE that falsely tied Iraq to Niger, and Vice President Cheney authorized Libby to discuss Plame's CIA affiliation with journalists in Washington and New York. Only Robert Novak published the information. Cheney's central role in ridiculing Wilson and "outing" his wife serve as prima facie evidence of the vice president's passionate commitment to going to war with Iraq and the lengths he would go to protect his case.

The CIA played an unusual game. In the first instance, it tried to quell the use of the fabricated Niger report in the public statements of the White House in October 2002; in the second instance, it placed language in the October 2002 NIE that gave credibility to the idea of Iraq's acquisition of uranium from Niger. Although there was a consensus within the intelligence community that the clandestine reporting on a Niger deal was a fabrication produced by members of the Italian military intelligence service, the NIC used the Niger documents to conclude that Iraq was "shifting from domestic mining and milling of uranium to foreign acquisition."

In the same month of October, Tenet intervened personally to prevent President Bush from discussing the reputed Niger deal in a campaign speech in Cincinnati. Tenet called national security deputy advisor Hadley, who reluctantly removed the offensive language from the speech. At the same time, senior CIA officials repeatedly informed Congressional and White House officials that they doubted the reports of Iraqi purchases of uranium from Niger. On October 2, 2002, deputy CIA director McLaughlin, in response to a question from Senator Jon Kyl (R-Arizona), disagreed with the British white paper that charged Iraq with "seeking uranium from various African locations." The NIO for Strategic and Nuclear Programs testified two days later that "there's a question about those attempts [to buy uranium in Africa] because of the control of the material in those countries," an obvious reference to the international consortia that control the uranium industry in Niger. And on October 5, 2002, the CIA's associate deputy director for intelligence reported "concerns about the sourcing of the report and noted that international control of the mines in Niger would make it very difficult to get yellowcake to Iraq."[8] The CIA provided this information in a memo to Hadley, suggesting that the reference to an Iraqi purchase from Niger be removed from the president's speech. On October 6, the CIA sent a second memorandum to the White House with additional reasons for dropping the reference to Niger, including the fact that the clandestine reporting referred to a uranium oxide mine that was actually flooded and a second mine that was controlled by the French.[9] Senior CIA officials knew that the British reporting on Niger was from 1999, and that it had never been substantiated or corroborated.

Thus, in October 2002, the CIA had succeeded in getting the White House to drop its charge from the president's speech regarding uranium, but also used the information in the most authoritative corporate product of the intelligence community, an NIE on Iraqi WMD. In January 2003, however, the CIA failed to stop President Bush from using the discredited link between Iraq and Niger in his State of the Union speech. In October, Michael Morrell, a CIA officer who subsequently became a deputy director of the Agency under Director Hayden, directed the effort to keep the offensive Niger language out of the Cincinnati speech. He received full support from Tenet, who wrote a supporting memorandum to Hadley. In December 2002–January 2003, however, Tenet played no role in vetting the State of the Union speech and turned the matter over to his deputy director for intelligence, Jamie Miscik, who in turn delegated the matter to the chief of WINPAC, Alan Foley. Foley made sure that the speech did not link the Niger accusation to CIA intelligence, but accepted language asserting that "British intelligence" had learned of nonexistent Iraqi efforts to obtain uranium from a West African country. The CTC tried to introduce similar language into Powell's UN speech, but Powell's own intelligence cadre at INR made sure it was excised.

Vice President Cheney insisted that the president use the Niger report in his January address to the nation, although the CIA had been telling the NSC that the Niger story could not be linked to CIA intelligence. This time, Foley and a senior NSC officer, Robert Joseph, arranged a compromise that turned out to be the infamous sixteen words in the actual State of the Union: "The British Government has learned that Saddam Hussein recently sought significant quantities of uranium from Africa." The statement was a lie, presumably based on discredited information from the 1990s. But Foley could breathe a sigh of relief; the CIA was not directly implicated. Whereas State and CIA analysts believed that the issue "was done, shot down" as far back as December

2001, the White House finally got its Niger story in the president's State of the Union in January 2003.[10] Thus, the CIA used a full-court press to stop any mention of the Niger story in a presidential speech in October, but in December it refused to block an implicit reference to the purchase of uranium in West Africa.

In early December 2002, the CIA was involved in additional efforts to squelch the fabricated report on Niger. The State Department inserted the claim into a fact sheet, but the CIA's intervention caused State to remove it. The Pentagon asked for an authoritative judgment from the NIC and was told unequivocally, "The Niger story was baseless and should be laid to rest." DDI Miscik told National Security Advisor Rice to disregard the reporting. Miscik again objected to Cheney's accusations incorrectly charging that Iraq was "busy enhancing its capabilities in the field of chemical and biological agents," and continuing to "pursue the nuclear programs they began so many years ago."[11] Bush often cleared his speeches with the CIA; Cheney rarely did.

The Niger story began to circulate in Italy in early 2002, when Rocco Martino, a former member of the Italian military intelligence service (SISMI) tried to sell an Italian journalist assorted documents that alleged Saddam Hussein had acquired five hundred tons of "yellowcake," or processed uranium ore from Niger. Martino had worked with both the Italian intelligence service and the French intelligence service (the Direction Generale de la Security Exterieure or DGSE), and both services were known for being vulnerable to forged documents and disinformation.[12] The Italian journalist recognized the documents as fabrications or forgeries, and turned them down. But Martino peddled the documents to several European intelligence services, including the British, and the documents eventually landed in the hands of CIA officials in Rome, which delivered them to the CIA and INR. Both the CIA and the INR were leery of the authenticity of the documents, but they became the basis of President Bush's assertion in the 2003 State of the Union speech that Iraq was trying to procure uranium from Africa.

The CIA and the Aluminum Tubes

The CIA handling of the aluminum tubes issue also points to an effort to help the administration make its case for war. Both Secretary of State Powell and National Security Advisor Rice used CIA intelligence to assert that the tubes were "only really suited for nuclear weapons programs," although experts inside and outside the government had argued that the tubes were not compatible with a nuclear weapons program. The fact that Saddam Hussein made no attempt to hide Iraq's purchases of the tubes argued against their use for nuclear weapons.

The only "compelling testimony" of Iraqi efforts to reconstitute its nuclear program was provided by a relatively junior CIA analyst (referred to as "Joe") who cited Iraq's "aggressive pursuit of high-strength aluminum tubes" as the evidence. In fact, the Department of Energy and the State Department's INR believed the tubes were for Iraqi artillery. The Energy Department dissented from the estimate on the issue of the aluminum tubes and, even prior to the estimate, sent a memorandum to the CIA that eviscerated "Joe's" theory that the aluminum tubes were for nuclear centrifuges. This memorandum was given to National Security Advisor Rice, but she continued to maintain that the tubes provided clear evidence of an Iraqi nuclear program. Meanwhile, the managers of the October 2002 NIE made sure that the dissents on the aluminum tubes were printed far away from the judgment that "all intelligence experts agree . . . that these tubes could be used in a centrifuge enrichment program." In any event, the tubes were hardly evidence of a "grave and gathering danger," in the words of President Bush, particularly since the estimate stressed that Iraq would only achieve nuclear weapons if left "unmolested" to develop such a capability.

The CIA and the Curveball Concoction

Another egregious example of CIA use of disinformation was its handling of intelligence on the mobile biological laboratories. The sole source of the mobile labs was an agent code-named "Curveball," who was handled by German intelligence and was never vetted by CIA, as is customary in sensitive clandestine matters. Curveball was the brother of a senior aide to Ahmad Chalabi who led the Iraqi dissident effort to feed disinformation to the U.S. government and the media, particularly Judith Miller of *The New York Times*. There was little reason to give credibility to Curveball's information, because the two key factories producing anthrax and botulinin toxin had been destroyed long before the Iraq war, and Iraq could not have reconstituted a biological manufacturing base that was not monitored by Western intelligence agencies. Nevertheless, the CIA officers who protested the use of Curveball's information were ignored, and one of the officers was chastised and transferred.[13] And when David Kay, the chief of the Iraq Survey Group, told Tenet that Curveball was a liar and that Iraq had no mobile labs or other illicit weapons, he was assigned to a windowless office without a working telephone. When President Bush used the State of the Union message on January 20, 2004, to praise Kay and his Iraq Survey Group, Kay resigned and went public with his concerns.[14]

The Germans had warned the CIA early in the process that they could not vouch for "Curveball's" bona fides; some Germans warned that he was an alcoholic, others that he was a liar. The fact that he was trading information, in this case disinformation, for possible German citizenship was clear to many members of the German intelligence service and even to several clandestine officers from the CIA, including the chief of the directorate of operation's European Division, Tyler Drumheller. Drumheller knew "Curveball" was an Iraqi defector; was mentally unstable and a liar; and was trying to trade his bogus information to the Germans for immigration status for himself and his family. The Germans told Drumheller they were dealing with a crackpot. British intelligence also informed the CIA prior to the 9/11 attacks that "elements of Curveball's behavior strike us as typical of . . . fabricators." The CIA's chief in Berlin warned the Agency that "Curveball's" accusations could not be verified and that it would be wrong to "use information that cannot be verified on such an important, key topic." Curveball, who was granted political asylum in Germany in September 2001, continues to live in southern Germany under an assumed name, receiving a generous stipend that means he will never have to work.

Even Iraqi colleagues of Curveball dismissed his accounts as "water cooler gossip" and "corridor conversation." They knew him as a convicted sex offender, who was connected to Iraqi exile and Pentagon-agent Ahmed Chalabi.[15] Chalabi was the source of much disinformation, including a report that an Iraqi general witnessed the Iraqi military training of Arab fighters to hijack airplanes.[16] Chalabi regularly passed such inflammatory information to the Pentagon's OSP, which delivered the information to the White House and to Stephen Hayes at *The Weekly Standard*, where it often appeared.

Drumheller's warnings to CIA leaders started in October 2002, after he spotted the false information in the tainted NIE. But Foley, the chief of WIN-PAC, was doing his best to provide a case for war for the Bush administration and refused to yield on the mobile labs story. Foley told his senior staff in December 2002 that, "if the president wants to go to war, then it is the Agency's job to find the intelligence to allow him to do so."[17] In January 2003, CIA headquarters asked Drumheller if a U.S. official could refer to "Curveball's" mobile lab accounts in an upcoming speech, presumably Powell's speech to the UN scheduled for February, and if the Germans could verify Curveball's claims and if Curveball would stand by his account.[18] The Germans told Drumheller unequivocally they could not verify Curveball's account, and he forwarded this response to Tenet. Drumheller was dumbfounded when President Bush used the information in his State of the Union address on January 28, 2003. So were senior members of the German Federal Intelligence Service (BND).[19]

Drumheller then received the draft of Powell's UN speech, and once again there was the Curveball information including detailed drawings of mobile labs inspired by Curveball's accounts. This time, Drumheller sat down with

Deputy Director McLaughlin who promised to look into the matter. McLaughlin now says that he has no recollection of the meeting and "if someone had made these doubts clear to me, I would not have permitted the reporting to be used in Secretary Powell's speech."[20] Several Agency analysts had their own doubts about Curveball, but their protests were ignored.[21] Meanwhile, Powell's chief of staff, Larry Wilkerson, contends that he and the secretary were suspicious of the material because there was no photos of the alleged labs, but that the confidence of Tenet and McLaughlin and their assertions that there were multiple sources convinced Powell to highlight the materials over the objections of INR analysts.

Despite the authoritative disclaimers of Curveball's information, the CIA and DIA took part in an intelligence cover-up to protect a totally unreliable source that was the sole basis for Secretary Powell's claims to the UN about mobile biological laboratories. In late May 2003, the CIA and DIA jointly published a white paper describing the labs as the "strongest evidence to date that Iraq was hiding a biological warfare program." It emphatically refuted an explanation by Iraqi officials that appeared in *The New York Times* that referred to the trailers as mobile units for producing hydrogen, which turned out to be true.[22] The Pentagon also had a three-page field report from a team of U.S. and British experts in Iraq referring to the mobile equipment as "the biggest sand toilets in the world," but the CIA and DIA ignored this report.[23] Thus, within the corridors of the CIA and DIA, it was known there were no mobile biological laboratories *before* the president, the vice president, the secretary of state, and the secretary of defense heralded the so-called find as justification for the invasion of Iraq. Kay's Iraq Survey Group, which had been dispatched by the CIA, informed Tenet in October 2003 that the trailers were not only "impractical" for biological weapons production, but were in fact "almost certainly intended" for manufacturing hydrogen for weather balloons, just as the Iraqi officials had claimed six months earlier.

Tenet and McLaughlin were responsible for allowing disinformation to be used in Powell's speech. The night before the speech, the CIA director had two important conversations. The first exchange was with Drumheller, who personally appealed to Tenet to delete "Curveball's" information from Powell's speech. The second conversation was with Powell himself, who wanted Tenet to personally assure that the intelligence written for the speech was good. Tenet brushed off Drumheller and provided assurances to the secretary of state. Powell meanwhile, brushed off the intelligence analysts of INR, who also wanted "Curveball's" material removed from the speech. Several months after the speech, Tenet worked up the courage to inform Powell the "Curveball" story was a sham. Powell was furious with the fact that, one by one, his entire speech was crumbling, leaving behind shards of disinformation and misinformation. He was particularly angry with Tenet and McLaughlin, who never shared any concerns about the veracity of the material or the reliance on sole-source information. Several CIA operatives were aggressive in countering Curveball, but could not attract any interest from McLaughlin or Deputy Director for Operations Jack Pavitt. Unlike Tenet, who continues to believe there were honest mistakes, Powell remains embarrassed with his role in making the Bush administration's case to the UN.

Prior to his resignation from the CIA in May 2004, Tenet told an audience at Georgetown University that "when the facts are all in, we will neither be completely right nor completely wrong." The speech was part of his public defense of the intelligence analysis of the CIA. He ordered an unprecedented public campaign to proclaim that the "integrity of our process was maintained throughout and any suggestion to the contrary is simply wrong."[24] Tenet's remarks coincided with President Bush's assertions that two trailers found in Iraq were evidence of the mobile biological weapons labs. The DIA eventually disavowed the information, and several British and Australian intelligence officers resigned over their own governments' use of this material. But the CIA persisted in supporting the legitimacy of the reports, and no one resigned.

It took nearly another year before the CIA formally discredited Curveball and concluded he fabricated the information. In September 2004, the Iraq Survey Group, then under Kay's successor, Charles Dalgeish, reaffirmed that the so-called labs were mobile hydrogen units for weather balloons, which is exactly what Saddam Hussein claimed in his account of Iraqi weaponry in December 2002 that was roundly dismissed by the Bush administration and the CIA.

The CIA and the Nonexistent Links

The CIA initially tried to convince policymakers that there were no significant ties between Iraq and al Qaeda. Senior members of the Bush administration, particularly the president and the vice president, were either convinced that Iraq was behind the terrorism of al Qaeda or, more likely, wanted to manipulate Congressional and public opinion in that direction. When the CIA downplayed the reports on links between Iraq and al Qaeda, no one at the White House listened. A CIA report in June 2002 reported that knowledge of such links contained "many critical gaps," and even the infamous NIE of October 2002 gave a "low confidence" rating to the view that Saddam Hussein would share chemical or biological weapons with al Qaeda.[25] The CIA learned authoritatively in September 2002 from a high-level member of Saddam Hussein's inner circle, presumably Foreign Minister Naji Sabri, that Iraq had no past or current contacts with bin Laden and that Saddam Hussein himself considered the al Qaeda leader an enemy of the Baghdad regime.[26] As late as January 2003, the CIA informed the policy community that it had "no credible information that Baghdad had foreknowledge of the 11 September attacks or any other al Qaeda strike," and that the intelligence on links between Iraq and al Qaeda was based on contradictory sources "with varying degrees of reliability."[27]

The CIA would have had a decent record of trying to keep the White House honest on the so-called links between Iraq and al Qaeda, if it had not been for the role of Tenet in drafting a letter to the SSCI in October 2002 and helping to draft Powell's UN speech. Tenet's letter to the chairman of the SSCI claimed "solid reporting of senior-level contacts between Iraq and al Qaeda," training to al Qaeda members in the "areas of poisons and gases and making conventional bombs," and predicted that "Baghdad's links to terrorists will increase."[28] Tenet did not mention the letter in his memoir, although it was a communication that angered many Agency analysts who knew evidence of such ties was weak and unsubstantiated. Several months later, the Counterterrorism Center's text for Powell's UN speech discussed the "sinister nexus" between Iraq and al Qaeda, which is the formulation that Powell used in his speech to the Security Council. The CIA never suggested that there was any connection between Iraq and the 9/11 attacks. When Richard Clarke reported to the White House that there was no such connection, he was told, "Wrong answer. . . . Do it again."[29]

In responding to reports of chemical and biological assistance to al Qaeda, the CIA concluded "the level and extent of this assistance is not clear."[30] But it should have said there was strong evidence of no CBW assistance whatsoever. Instead, the Agency identified "many critical gaps" in the intelligence on Iraqi links to al Qaeda because of "limited reporting" and the "questionable reliability of many of our sources." The NIE on Iraqi WMD reported that the sources on training and support for al Qaeda are "third-hand, unvetted, or from sources of varying reliability."[31] It also noted that the intelligence community "cannot determine . . . how many of the reported plans for CBW (chemical and biological warfare) were actually realized." As late as January 2003, the CIA did note the lack of "evidence of completed training" and says most of the reports of training "do not make clear whether training" was "actually implemented."[32] The Agency report noted that much of the reporting was based on "hearsay" and that some of the evidence was "simple declarative accusations of Iraqi-al Qa'ida complicity with no substantiating detail or other information that might help us corroborate them." The Agency should have noted the primary source of Iraqi–al Qaeda links had been tortured by the Egyptian security service.

The DIA was more direct and honest than the CIA in dealing with the intelligence linking Iraq to al Qaeda. When the Pentagon's OSP supplied information on Iraqi–al Qaeda links to Cheney's office, DIA tried to destroy the credibility of the INC reports and the reliability of all sources on these issues. The CIA eventually recalled all intelligence reports based on his statements, but that was two years after the DIA informed policymakers that it believed a top al Qaeda operative, Ibn al-Shaykh al-Libi, had lied.[33] DIA noted in February 2002 that al-Libi's "confession" lacked details and suggested that he is most likely telling interrogators what he thinks will "retain their interest." Al-Libi added, "Saddam's regime is intensely secular and is wary of Islamic revolutionary movements. Moreover, Baghdad is unlikely to provide assistance to a group it cannot control."

The CIA had authoritative information that put the lie to Cheney's descriptions of a Prague meeting between 9/11 hijacker Mohammed Atta and Iraqi intelligence officers in April 2001, but in June 2002 referred to "contradictory" reporting on trips to Prague and meetings with Iraqis. It concluded falsely that Atta's travels could not be verified.[34] In January 2003, the Agency reported that the "most reliable reporting casts doubt" on the possibility of any such meeting.[35] In fact, there were sensitive telephone intercepts that placed Atta in the United States at the time of the so-called meeting with Iraqi intelligence officials. Initially, it was a Czech intelligence source that pointed to the Atta meeting with Iraqi intelligence officers, but the Czech intelligence service ultimately denied there had been such a meeting. The head of the DI, Jamie Miscik, was summoned to the NSC in January 2003 to defend one report concluding no such meeting ever occurred. She threatened to resign before returning to the NSC one more time, and CIA director Tenet gave her strong support. "She is not coming down," Tenet shouted into the phone to NSC deputy director Hadley. "We are not rewriting this fucking report one more time. It is fucking over. Do you hear me! And don't you ever fucking treat my people this way again. Ever!"[36] Even McLaughlin, who caved to the administration on so many issues, refused to redo some of the assessments, despite the importuning from Libby. McLaughlin sent a letter to Congress declaring the likelihood of Saddam using WMD "very low" unless attacked. McLaughlin stood up to Libby in January 2003 when the vice president's aide found the CIA intelligence too weak and wanted it reexamined; McLaughlin reportedly said, "I'm not going back to the well on this. We've done our work."

Ultimately the CIA and the intelligence community went too far in trying to accommodate the demands of the Bush administration to find evidence of links between Iraq and al Qaeda. The analytical community took a "purposely aggressive approach" in conducting exhaustive and repetitive searches to find such links. Pressure from the administration, particularly from Cheney and Rice, was also responsible in part for the failure to scrutinize the reporting on WMD in general. The Bush administration, particularly Cheney, Rice, and

Rumsfeld, made it clear what it wanted in the way of intelligence and kept sending reports back to be redone until it got the answers that it wanted. As a result, the CIA began to practice self-censorship and stopped distributing credible intelligence that argued against Iraqi WMD and links to al Qaeda.

Nuclear Reconstitution

The intelligence community repeatedly told the administration that the Iraqis were several years away from developing a nuclear weapon. There was no reason to believe, as the administration contended, that Saddam Hussein was on the verge of developing such a weapon. Even the NIE of October 2002 argued that Saddam Hussein would not use such a weapon against the United States and would not share the technology with terrorist organizations, unless the United States invaded Iraq and was on the verge of overthrowing his regime. The CIA should have indicated the entire Iraqi nuclear program, including facilities and infrastructure, had been destroyed, but it never did so. The weapons design facility and all production equipment were gone, and the introduction of gamma detection equipment on land and airborne could monitor any gamma rays that would be emitted if Iraq sought to enrich uranium or plutonium in order to reconstitute a nuclear program.

THE CIA'S FAILURE OF INTELLIGENCE

The CIA's failure in the run-up to the Iraq War was a total corporate breakdown, with the senior leadership of the Agency and the senior managers of the intelligence and operational directorates, playing key roles.

Intelligence Analysis

President Harry Truman created a CIA to pull together and make sense out of the vast amount of information available to the intelligence community and to ensure that the most trenchant analysis found its way to key policymakers. The failure at Pearl Harbor had resulted in part from the failure to analyze and distribute intelligence; the failure of 9/11 had resulted from a similar failure to connect the dots and to share information. The intelligence failure in the run-up to the invasion of Iraq was far worse, because it involved the corruption of the intelligence process and the politicization of intelligence data. A former director of the State Department's INR, Thomas Hughes, concluded that policymakers use intelligence the way a drunk uses a lamppost—for support, not for illumination.[37] In the case of the Iraq War, intelligence offered far too much support, far too little illumination.

The process of intelligence analysis begins with open-source analysis, DO clandestine reports, NSA intercepts, and State Department and DoD cables from the field. All of this intelligence feeds into the CIA's DI, which is responsible for providing premonitory intelligence for policymakers, and the intelligence community's National Intelligence Council, which is responsible for producing National Intelligence Estimates (NIEs). The estimates are the major corporate product of the intelligence community, signed by the director of national intelligence and representing the views of all sixteen agencies of the community. The CIA describes NIEs as the "most authoritative written judgment concerning a national security issue prepared by the Director of Central Intelligence." Unlike current intelligence, which describes the present, NIEs forecast future developments and address implications for U.S. security. The NIC has fewer than one hundred people, including a dozen national intelligence officers (NIOs) who are considered serious experts in their respective fields.

Intelligence analysis is never an easy or clear-cut process, but when intelligence analysts believe—as they did in the fall of 2002—that the United States was going to war, there is a tendency to resort to worst-case analysis.[38] In the case of the Iraq War, virtually all intelligence analysis on WMD was based on information that was collected prior to December 1998, when a UN inspection team left Iraq. An internal CIA study concluded that all Agency analysis was based on "untested, long-held assumptions" and "technical analysis that equates programs with capabilities."[39] This methodology leads to worst-case analysis, which exaggerated the power of the Soviet Union and the Warsaw Pact in the 1980s and did the same with Iraqi military capability in the 1990s. The fact that the CIA significantly underestimated Iraqi strategic holdings prior to Desert Storm in 1991 probably led to the latter exaggeration of Iraqi military capabilities. CIA errors regarding the Soviet invasions of Hungary in 1956 and Czechoslovakia in 1968 led to exaggerations of Soviet intentions in the 1970s and 1980s regarding Poland.

Although CIA political and regional analysts did provide some warning to the White House regarding the likely chaos following an American invasion, CIA analysts ultimately caved in to White House pressure and gave the Bush administration the intelligence it needed to make the case for war. The NIE in October 2002, which was requested by the chairman of the Senate intelligence committee, not the White House, was a perfect example of worst-case analysis to allow analysts to protect their reputations if American forces encountered Iraqi WMD. It was the most egregiously politicized estimate in the history of the CIA. The CIA's Counterterrorism Center (CTC) aggressively pursued evidence of possible links between Iraq and al Qaeda in order to satisfy White House consumers, often ignoring the absence of validation for the worst-case reporting.

Actually, there was a war in the CIA over intelligence on Iraq before the U.S. invasion. The CTC, which was administered by the DO, was engaged in worst-case analysis on Iraq and Saddam. The Near Eastern analysts of the DI developed more moderate and accurate assessments, and challenged the dubious assertions of Iraq–al Qaeda contacts. CTC analysts, however, received high-level support from DDCI McLaughlin and DDI Miscik, but DI analysts had to go out on a limb to press their conclusions. DCI Tenet and WINPAC director Foley simply decided to endorse the worst of the accounts regarding Iraq, and as Foley told his analysts in December 2002, "if the president wants to go to war against Iraq, then it is our job to provide him the intelligence to do so." The deputy director of the CIA's Iraqi Task Force noted, "Let's keep in mind the fact that this war's going to happen regardless of what Curveball said or didn't say . . . the powers that be probably aren't terribly interested in whether Curveball knows what he's talking about."

The CIA also pressed for evidence of Iraqi WMD long after it was realized that there would be no WMD to be found. Tenet and McLaughlin commissioned veteran inspectors Kay and Duelfer to head a huge task force to find WMD, and then tried to politicize their findings when they reported no evidence of such weapons. Meanwhile, the Pentagon announced soon after President Bush declared "mission accomplished" in May 2003 that it was withdrawing its task force that had been sent to Baghdad to search for WMD. It conceded no chemical, biological, or nuclear materials would be found. In December 2003, U.S. military forces released nearly all of the captured Iraqi scientists, which indicated that the Pentagon no longer believed there was anything to be gained from additional interrogations. Before the war, the IAEA concluded there was "no indication of resumed nuclear activities . . . nor any indication of nuclear-related prohibited activities at any inspected sites."[40] The IAEA's work demonstrated the value of independent, international inspections to remedy the danger of national inspections, which are subject to politicization.

Human Intelligence

There was no reason for the CIA to claim "high confidence" regarding its WMD finds, because there were no reliable sources in Iraq vouching for the existence of WMD. More importantly, the CIA ignored all Iraqi sources, including high-level ones with access to the leadership, who reported no sign of WMD in Iraq. An informant told the CIA in 2003 that Iraq had abandoned a major element of its nuclear weapons program, but the CIA did not share this information with other agencies or with senior policymakers.[41] When a senior CIA office remonstrated over the Agency's failure to share important intelli-

gence information, he was fired for questioning the CIA's assumptions on a series of weapons-related matters and the agency's intelligence conclusions."[42]

This is very familiar. In the mid-1989s, the three senior office managers
who actually anticipated the decline of the Soviet Union and Moscow's interest in closer relations with the United States were demoted. These three officers managed analysis for the Soviet economy, Soviet foreign policy, and
Soviet–American relations; all understood the weakness of the Soviet Union,
but were removed from their managerial responsibilities by the director of the
Soviet office, Douglas MacEachin, under the orders of the deputy director of
intelligence, Bob Gates.

I was one of those officers, and when I resigned from the CIA in 1990 because of the politicization of intelligence on the Soviet Union throughout the
1980s, I made an effort to see CIA director Webster to brief him on the issue
of politicization and my reasons for resignation. Webster was totally adverse
to confrontation and, for whatever reason, refused to see me, even though my
views did not address his stewardship at the Agency, but that of Director
Casey and Deputy Director Gates. Nevertheless, he arranged a meeting with
a long-time colleague, Richard Kerr, the deputy director for central intelligence, who marginalized my remarks and tried to maintain a jocular and col-
legial setting. But I wasn't joking and, perhaps as a result, I was not given the
usual resignation interview for senior officials of the Agency.

Clandestine Collection Calamity

The value of clandestine collection has been overemphasized, honoring the
myth that only technical collection can track the capabilities of foreign nations,
but human intelligence (HUMINT) is the final word on intentions of foreign
leaders. This theory is flawed; it is virtually impossible to divine the intentions
of a foreign leader unless the leader himself is the source. In view of our general inability to divine the intentions of our own leaders, it seems particularly
arrogant to assume that we can do better overseas. CIA sources failed to deci-
pher Khrushchev's intentions toward Hungary in 1956; Brezhnev's toward
Czechoslovakia in 1968; Sadat's toward Israel in 1973; Begin's and Sharon's
toward Lebanon in 1982; and Saddam Hussein's toward Iran in 1980 and
Kuwait in 1990. The CIA has a mediocre record of collecting intelligence on
the start of wars and possibility of coups. On balance, the intelligence community is good at finding things, counting things, and describing things, but
intentions remain an elusive quarry.

The CIA has had little success collecting intelligence in closed societies and
much of its clandestine reporting on the former Soviet Union, Eastern Europe,
and Cuba came from double agents who were controlled by their communist

masters. Currently, when the most important threats to U.S. interests emanate from Iran, Iraq, North Korea, and nonstate terrorist organizations, such as al Qaeda, there is very little useful clandestine information that is collected by CIA operatives. The only exception to this pattern was the clandestine gathering of intelligence on Soviet weapons systems during the cold war, which enabled all U.S. administrations to have a great deal of warning time on the procurement and deployment of new weaponry in the Soviet Union.

Far more intelligence, particularly in political and economic areas, can be gleaned from the reporting of U.S. embassy officers, who build close personal relations with influential government officials. Clandestine collection of intelligence has been marginal in closed societies and typically inferior to information from Foreign Service officers, military attaches, and journalists in open societies. It would be more cost-effective to shift resources devoted to clandestine collection to the State Department and other agencies, which have had to reduce their personnel in the field because of budget limitations. The State Department budget has been steadily reduced in recent years, while that of the intelligence community has been increased to match the increases in the defense budget. The State Department's current budget is smaller than the CIA's.

In the case of Iraq, the intelligence community recognized that it had a serious collection deficiency, but did nothing about it. Saddam Hussein was a particularly difficult target for collection, and he was the source of a series of strategic surprises for the United States in the 1980s and 1990s with his invasions of Iran and Kuwait. According to the Robb-Silberman report, one senior policymaker described the intelligence community as "running on fumes," depending on "inference and assumptions, rather than hard data."[43] Iraq in the 1980s and 1990s was an extremely difficult collection environment, which was typical of closed societies; the task of collecting useful intelligence on Iraqi weapons programs was particularly challenging. The absence of an American embassy meant that there was little possibility for assigning and stationing CIA clandestine operatives in Baghdad, and the absence of the United Nations inspection team from 1998 to 2002 removed the most successful CIA collection effort, which had infiltrated the team several years earlier to collect intelligence against Saddam Hussein specifically and Iraq in general.[44]

The clandestine collection offered no insight into the backward Iraqi political, economic, and military situation. An accurate picture of Iraqi society, which was well-known to Arab intellectuals throughout the Middle East, would have demonstrated the danger of any military action against a failing regime. There was no premonitory intelligence regarding the likelihood of total chaos in the wake of a U.S. invasion. There is no question that U.S. military planners were totally unprepared for the chaos in Iraq after a war perceived as "won." This failure to monitor the Iraqi society and economy throughout the 1990s was reminiscent of the CIA's failure to record the collapse of the Soviet economy throughout the 1980s. In both cases, access to man-on-the-street opinion would have confirmed the backwardness of life in the major cities, let alone the poverty of the hinterlands.

Technical Collection

Technical collection against WMD programs in Iraq presented a difficult challenge in view of the small size of chemical and biological weapons systems and the ease with which these weapons could be stored. The Iraq challenge was too much for technical collection systems; it required a better understanding of the political and cultural context in which these programs existed. Technical collection, particularly from satellites and ground-based intercept sites, is an excellent source against large-scale, widespread targets, such as those offered by the former Soviet Union during the cold war.

The Pentagon's domination of technical collection worsens these problems. With military domination of collection, there is insufficient collection against social, cultural, and economic problems that could have provided insight into the impact of conflict, sanctions, and isolation on Iraq for more than two decades. The CIA failed to assess the results of Desert Storm on Iraq's economic, social, and cultural fabric, and to monitor Iraq's steady decline. The sad intelligence truth, which was largely ignored, was that Iraq was collapsing like a house of cards from eight years of war against Iran and the impact of U.S. military containment since Desert Storm. The introduction of U.S. forces in 2003 pushed Iraq into a world of chaos and discontinuity that required a greater number of forces for occupation than were required for liberation, as well as billions of dollars for reconstruction. In many ways, this may have been the greatest intelligence failure, although trenchant strategic intelligence would not have deterred members of the Bush administration committed to war.

Estimative Process

The only corporate product of the intelligence community is the NIE, which is signed by the director of central intelligence (now the DNI) and represents the thinking of the community. NIEs were central to the policy community's understanding of the Soviet threat during the worst days of the cold war, and special NIEs were often prepared on an urgent basis to understand crisis situations and provide premonitory intelligence of fast-breaking situations. Several estimates in the 1960s warned the Johnson administration that its Vietnam policies would not succeed. There was no attempt in the run-up to the

Iraq War to warn the Bush administration about the constraints of force in a multiethnic and unstable environment such as Iraq.

The controversial NIE on Iraqi WMD in 2002 was chaired by a former Defense Department analyst, Robert Walpole, who surrounded himself with true believers from the CIA and DIA who shared the administration's views on Iraqi nuclear reconstitution. This was a perfect example of "judge-shopping in the courthouse," making sure that the manager and drafters of the estimate were worst-case analysts on Iraq. Walpole, the NIO for Proliferation, made sure that dissident voices did not find their way to the table. Two other managers of the estimate, Larry Gershwin and John Landry, were reportedly reprimanded for their work on the NIE. Gershwin was well-known for his efforts to politicize NIEs on Soviet strategic capabilities throughout the 1980s and 1990s.

The NIE entitled "Iraq's Continuing Programs for Weapons of Mass Destruction" (October 2002) was arguably the most politicized estimate ever produced by the CIA and the community. It took false reports regarding WMD and spun a fictitious tale of clear, present, and mortal danger. Its assumptions and conclusions were wrong; nearly every one of its claims was in error. The assessments concerning alleged stockpiles of chemical and biological weapons; nuclear weapons; unmanned aerial vehicles; and ties between Iraq and al Qaeda were false. The intelligence was tailored just as the British chief of intelligence concluded in the summer of 2002. The Senate intelligence committee concluded that analysts had "overstated" their key judgments and were guilty of "systematic weaknesses, primarily in analytical trade craft, compounded by a lack of information sharing, poor management, and inadequate intelligence collection." The Senate report was a political copout, blaming a "group-think" mentality for errors, and making no mention of pressure from the Bush administration or the politicization of intelligence.

Iraq simply did not have the weapons the CIA claimed it had and had no production programs for making such weapons. Even though administration officials alleged that Iraq had the "intentions" to restart these programs, the Iraq Survey Group could find no plans to do so. The neoconservatives in the administration contended that the weapons were moved to Syria or destroyed on the eve of the U.S. invasion, but most of these programs were destroyed during Desert Storm in 1991. The declassified estimate, the so-called white paper, was even more egregious, omitting the only key judgment of the estimate that may have been relevant (i.e., Saddam Hussein was highly unlikely to transfer WMD to terrorist groups). In omitting this assessment, the manager of the white paper, a high-ranking NIO and the CIA's leading Arabist, Paul Pillar, engaged in policy advocacy to support a decision to go to war, violating the CIA's charter that prohibits propagandizing political matters for the U.S. public. It is implausible that every one of these false assessments could be attributed to faulty judgment or just plain incompetence. Nevertheless, just as the former director of FEMA, Michael Brown, was told in the wake of Hurricane Katrina that he was doing a "heck of a job," CIA director Tenet was praised for having done a "superb job." He even received the nation's highest civilian award, the Presidential Freedom Medal. Presumably the "superb job" was a reference to the endorsement of an NIE that made the president's case for war.

The key judgments of the October NIE did not mention that several intelligence agencies dissented from major conclusions of the estimate. The State Department's INR dissented on the issue of reconstitution of a nuclear weapons program, demonstrating that an intelligence bureau in a policy department could maintain an independent and objective point of view, while the CIA catered to the whims of policymakers. INR dismissed the idea that Iraq was pursuing enriched uranium in Niger and that Saddam Hussein would share chemical and biological weapons with al Qaeda under any conditions. The director of intelligence and reconnaissance of the U.S. Air Force dissented from the description of UAVs, arguing correctly that the small size of Iraq's new UAV and its limited range "strongly suggests a primary role of reconnaissance."[45] Since the president had already accused Iraq of using these aircraft to target the United States, it took a certain amount of courage for the USAF to dissent. The Department of Energy did not believe that the aluminum tubes had anything to do with an Iraqi nuclear program. Secretary Powell ignored these dissents in delivering his UN speech.

The NIE and the white paper linked Iraqi military construction to chemical and biological sites, but neither the UN or the IAEA inspectors, who had visited many of the construction sites, agreed. The CIA's analysis on Iraq's SCUD missiles was wrong, ignoring the UNSCOM inspectors who correctly maintained there were only one or two SCUDs. Several months before the estimate appeared, the CIA told Congressional committees it did not know how many missile launchers or warheads were in Iraq. And, in January 2003, Mohamed El Baradei, the head of the IAEA, echoed the Energy Department's view that the aluminum tubes were for artillery rockets, not nuclear centrifuges. He told an interviewer in January 2003 that, "It may be technically possible that the tubes could be used to enrich uranium, but you would have to believe that Iraq deliberately ordered the wrong stock and intended to spend a great deal of time and money reworking each piece." It is mind-boggling that any career Army general officer, let alone former chairman of the Joint Chiefs of Staff Powell, could be so wrong on this issue.

The estimate's gratuitous judgments, often introduced without evidence, served as policy advocacy for a decision to go to war. This is a violation of all intelligence principles and ethics. Without any evidence whatsoever, the estimate concluded that Iraq reconstituted its nuclear weapons program about the time that UNSCOM inspectors departed in December 1998. With no specific information, the document concluded that Iraq had "stocked at least 100 metric tons and as much as 500 metric tons of CW agents"—*much of it added in the last year*, and even speculated on clandestine attacks against the United States with chemical or biological weapons. The estimate considered all key aspects of Iraq's biological weapons program to be active and that "most elements are larger and more advanced than they were before the Gulf War." As the former director of IAEA, Hans Blix, concluded, "Never before has a nation had 100 percent confidence about its intelligence with 0 percent information." Blix did not know that the CIA actually had numerous authoritative sources that denied the presence of WMD in Iraqi inventories, but this intelligence never made it to the Agency's estimates.

One of the most dishonest aspects of the estimate concerned the emphasis placed on Iraq's biological weapons program, which was described as "active . . . larger and more advanced than they were before the Gulf War."[46] The estimate's reference to "large-scale, redundant and concealed BW agent production capabilities" was largely based on the fantasies of "Curveball." UNSCOM and IAEA inspectors regularly investigated many of these facilities and recorded correctly that there were no active biological weapons programs at sites such as the Fallujah III plant. The estimate also contained worst-case language about a nonexistent anthrax program, and the white paper gratuitously added language about a potential threat to the U.S. homeland. Despite the estimate and the white paper, which were widely distributed to the Pentagon, U.S. military forces never investigated the so-called CBW sites that were discussed.

The insertion of the fabricated report describing Saddam Hussein's efforts to obtain uranium, or "yellowcake," from Niger was particularly egregious, allowing the CIA to claim falsely that Iraq was trying to reconstitute its nuclear weapons program. The NIE concluded, if "Baghdad acquires sufficient fissile material from abroad, it could make a nuclear weapon within several months to a year." None of the European intelligence services shared this provocative assessment, and even Powell refused to cite the Niger connection in his speech. Walpole omitted this charge from the key judgments, but allowed it to stand in the text.

"White Paper" or Black Propaganda?

Pillar's unclassified white paper was even more egregious than the NIE, dropping some of the balanced and nuanced language in the classified version, and substituting a certainty that didn't exist in the intelligence community. It was developed to circulate to the Congress and the American public, which placed the CIA in the center of a propaganda campaign for the case to go to war, a serious violation of the CIA's mission. Pillar's white paper conveyed the impression the divided intelligence community was of one mind and united on the Iraqi threat to the U.S. homeland. His efforts were unconscionable, involving the deletion of all uncertainty and the addition of worst-case views to support President Bush's view of a "gathering threat." Pillar has joined Tenet and former Defense Department undersecretary Feith on the faculty of Georgetown University's Foreign Service Institute, placing three of the major politicizers of prewar intelligence under one academic roof.

Pillar, who managed the coordination and production of the White Paper, took every opportunity to make it tougher than the NIE. Walpole's classified NIE estimated that Iraq would not obtain nuclear weapons until the period between 2007 and 2009, but Pillar's paper dropped the dates and suggested that the possibility was more imminent. The NIE contended, "Saddam does not yet have nuclear weapons or sufficient material to make them," but the white paper dropped the sentence.[47] Both the classified and unclassified versions developed scenarios for Iraq acquiring nuclear weapons within twelve months, although UN and IAEA inspectors found no facilities that were even capable of building a nuclear weapon or enriching uranium to weapons grade. These exaggerations beg questions on current CIA intelligence assessments on Iran and North Korea, which may also reflect worst-case analysis.

The white paper ignored the dissents in the classified estimate, but Pillar blamed Tenet for omitting the dissents. Pillar downplayed the expertise of the dissenters and exaggerated the confidence of his own judgments. The white paper created the impression that the intelligence community was of one mind on the threat of Iraqi WMD, and supported the Bush administration's view that WMD represented a threat to the U.S. homeland.[48] The CIA linked Iraq's attempts to obtain aluminum tubes to a centrifuge enrichment program, and Pillar noted there were "some intelligence specialists" who linked the tubes to conventional weapons. He never explained that the "some" referred to the opposition of the Department of Energy, which employs the intelligence community's most serious expertise on centrifuge technology. The several analysts at the CIA with their modest engineering credentials were certainly no match for the PhD scientists at the Department of Energy. As early as September 2002, British intelligence informed its CIA counterparts there was "no definitive intelligence that the aluminum tubes are destined for a nuclear program." The most authoritative think tanks in the United States and Britain, including the Institute for Science and International Security, called attention to the ambiguity in the intelligence on the artillery tubes. The white paper ignored all these caveats.

The white paper also exaggerated the possibility of Iraq renewing production of chemical agents and biological weapons. All of the evidence for these allegations was tainted or flawed or sole-source intelligence, and even the CIA eventually had to issue a classified report two years after the war that corrected the prewar assessments on chemical weapons and acknowledged that Baghdad abandoned its chemical weapons programs in 1991.[49] This report appeared a year after Tenet told an audience at Georgetown University, "when the facts of Iraq are all in, we will neither be completely right nor completely wrong." In fact, the CIA estimate from October 2002 was indeed completely wrong and at odds with a DIA report from September 2002, concluding there was "no reliable information on whether Iraq is producing and stockpiling chemical weapons." The CIA announced that additional corrections would be forthcoming in order to address errors on biological weapons and the nuclear weapons program. But CIA director Goss, who was paranoid about leaks and corrections, put a stop to additional postmortems on prewar intelligence, and Director Hayden has continued Goss's censorship.

Pillar finally conceded on a documentary by "Frontline," PBS's award-winning public affairs series, that he was directly responsible for politicizing intelligence for the Bush administration. The documentary, which was broadcast in June 2006, quotes Pillar saying that the white paper was "clearly requested and published for policy advocacy purposes . . . to strengthen the case of going to war with the American public."[50] It is particularly unconscionable for an intelligence analyst to distort intelligence information in order to help a president make a case for going to war. Pillar merely concedes that it wasn't "proper for the intelligence community to publish papers for that purpose."

Postmortem of an NIE

The NIE and white paper were prima facie evidence of a tipping point in the decision to go to war, perhaps the drop-dead decision. The administration did not want such an estimate because it was aware of the differences of opinion within the intelligence community and did not want a corporate product of the entire community that surfaced the doubts of the Department of State's INR (regarding nuclear reconstitution), the Department of Energy (regarding the aluminum tubes), and even the intelligence bureau of the United States Air Force (regarding the use of UAVs to target the United States with biological and chemical weapons). The final product did surface such differences, but that did not stop the CIA from distorting the intelligence on WMD before the Congress voted on a resolution to go to war. The postwar inspections of the Iraq Survey Group, which was operated by the CIA, found no evidence of any chemical or biological weapons programs and no stockpiles of the weapons themselves.

THE CIA DEFENDS ITSELF: THE KERR GROUP

Instead of instigating a rigorous investigation into what went wrong in the analytical process, the CIA maintained a stout defense of its finished intelligence on Iraq, merely acknowledging some analytic shortcomings in the intelligence process. In response to authoritative criticism from Congressional intelligence committees, the CIA had to cobble together a group of former Agency officers to review the finished intelligence from the prewar period. This group was known as the Kerr Group, named for its director Richard J. Kerr, who was deputy director of intelligence to Gates and deputy director of the CIA to Judge Webster. Kerr was a curious choice to head a panel on politicization, because he never accepted the documented evidence of politicization in the Casey-Gates era and, in 1990, refused to address my concerns about the politicization of intelligence on the Soviet Union, which was similar to the Iraqi process. His group consisted of former analysts who never distinguished themselves as tough-minded analysts willing to tell truth to power. The group produced two classified memoranda that documented the intelligence community's judgments before the war, without commenting on the accuracy of those judgments. The third report, which was unclassified, was presented in July 2004 to assess the performance of the intelligence community from a broad perspective, focusing on systemic issues that may have compromised analysts' evaluations and analyses.

Kerr's group tried to take the NIE off the hook by arguing that it "was done under an unusually tight time constraint—three weeks—to meet a deadline for congressional debate."[51] In actual fact, it was typical for the NIC (and previously the Board of National Estimates) to have short-fuse assignments in crisis situations, such as the run-up to war against Iraq. I participated in many of these exercises in which several weeks were given to prepare estimates on Soviet–Egyptian relations, the Horn of Africa, the Chinese invasion of Vietnam, Afghanistan, and Sino–Soviet tensions. This was not unusual. Tenet was being disingenuous in pointing to the short timeframe as an excuse for weakness of the NIE, because he led the effort to use the NIE to prepare Powell's UN speech, which took place four months after the publication of the estimate.

What is more pertinent with regard to the Iraqi estimate is that the NIC did not initiate the estimate, although its members believed that the United States was about to go to war. It is particularly unusual for members of Congress to request estimates, which begs the question of why the executive branch or the intelligence community didn't want an authoritative intelligence assessment of possible Iraqi resistance, WMD, the postwar situation, and the impact of use of force. In this case, the administration made it known that it had no interest in an estimate on any of these issues because it was well aware of the differences within the intelligence and policy communities, including the Pentagon, on the wisdom of invading an Arab country that had nothing to do with 9/11 or terrorism.

The Kerr Group also tried to exonerate the producers of the October 2002 estimate, noting that it was the "product of three separate drafters, each responsible for independent sections, drawing a mixed bag of analytic product," making "consistent application of analytic or evidentiary standards . . . next to impossible."[52] Again, this methodology was not unusual given the need to examine the three separate problems of nuclear, chemical, and biological weaponry, which demanded a stern managerial hand at the senior NIC level. If the estimate was inconsistent and lacking clarity, then that was the fault of NIC management, whose leader, Stu Cohen, was tasked by Tenet to lead a public relations effort to praise the estimate as the most authoritative document available to policymakers. Cohen made two appearances: a public one on ABC's "Nightline with Ted Koppel" and a closed door one at the National War College, where he argued that the NIE was an excellent document and would be given high marks after the work of the Iraq Survey Group had finished its inspections in Iraq. Cohen also guided the production of the declassified version of the estimate that thoroughly misrepresented the NIE only a week before the Congressional vote on the use of force against Iraq. Unlike Tenet and Cohen, the Iraqi Survey Groups of both Kay and Duelfer, and the Robb-Silberman Commission had few positive things to say about the CIA analysis on WMD.

The Kerr Group made no recommendations for fixing the systemic and methodological problems associated with the NIC and its estimate. Instead, the Group made a series of gratuitous judgments about the value of NIEs and the process used to produce them. Kerr, a former Soviet naval analyst, and Becky Donegan, a former inspector in the office of the IG, had never worked on NIEs, but that did not get in the way of their conclusion that NIEs "have not carried great weight in policy deliberations, although customers have often used them to promote their own agendas."[53] In fact, NIEs are the only genuine corporate product of the entire intelligence community, and these documents are invaluable in making strategic assessments about military challenges and threats, arms control and disarmament, and geopolitical concerns for American national security interests. Estimates have become valuable tools, for example, in the current debate over political and military developments in Iraq.

The Group did identify one major institutional failing of the CIA, noting that the Agency had shifted from "long-term, in-depth analysis in favor of more short-term products intended to provide direct support to policy."[54] The Group believes that this shift was "done with the best of intentions," but as a participant in these analytical debates over the years, I would stress that the shift was more a part of the dumbing-down of the DI that began after the collapse of the Soviet Union and the end of the cold war. There has been a definite weakening of the analytic skills of the CIA and the intelligence community since 1991. The CIA now spends millions of dollars on the training and education of its analytic cadre, with huge amounts of money going to independent consultants and contractors with very little accountability. Many of the former analysts who teach the tradecraft of analysis to new employees are the very people who politicized the intelligence on the Soviet Union in the 1980s, terrorism in the 1990s, and Iraq during the run-up to war.

The Group ignored many major failures in the intelligence system. First of all, the CIA repressed numerous reports noting the absence of WMD in Iraq, including the authoritative reports of Saddam Hussein's son-in-law, General Hussein Kamal, who defected to Jordan, briefed the United Nations inspectors, Jordanian intelligence, and the CIA, returned to Iraq, and was summarily executed. Kamal, the former Iraqi weapons program manager, told the debriefers in 1995 that Iraq's strategic program was larger than the CIA estimated before the 1991 Desert Storm War, but that it no longer existed. Kamal had first-hand knowledge that "chemical weapons were destroyed"; in fact, it was Kamal who ordered the destruction of the chemical stocks. The same was true for biological weapons, and "in the nuclear area, there were no weapons."[55] He also told United Nations officials in 1995 that Iraq had two SCUD launchers and one of them was disassembled.[56] Excellent intelligence on the absence of Iraqi WMD from Foreign Minister Sabri never got to the White House, and the Bush White House stopped the CIA from recruiting Sabri as a clandestine source.

The CIA even sponsored its own intelligence collection that collaborated all of Kamal's information on strategic weaponry and nuclear programs, but once again this essential information never found its way to policymakers. The Agency's assistant director for intelligence collection, Charles Allen, a specialist on warnings intelligence, commissioned an unusual program that involved Iraqi–Americans who lived in the United States. Allen's ingenious scheme sent about thirty of these individuals to Iraq to gather information from their close relatives who happened to be scientists with access to information on nuclear programs. As late as September 2002, Sawsan Alhaddad, a doctor living in Cleveland, reported to the CIA on her conversations with her Iraqi brother, an electrical engineer who worked in the Iraqi nuclear program.

The engineer contended that the nuclear program had been shut down for years, which corroborated information from other Iraqi scientists and engineers that had been gathered right up to the start of the war in March 2003. Many of the Iraqi–Americans returned to the United States in mid-September and reported that Saddam had abandoned all his WMD programs, but this intelligence never appeared in the NIE or the PDB.[57]

A History of Politicization on Iraq

The CIA has a history of slanting intelligence on Iraq, so it is not surprising that intelligence on Iraqi WMD was politicized for the Bush administration. The Reagan and Bush administrations, from 1881 to 1990, wanted to improve relations with Iraq (and Pakistan) to maintain pressure on Iran (and Afghanistan), so the intelligence community was pressed to conceal evidence of Iraqi (and Pakistani) nuclear activity as early as 1985. Gates was involved in the suppression of intelligence detailing Iraq's efforts to pursue a nuclear weapons program. Moreover, in the Iran–Iraq War, the United States provided intelligence to Baghdad in order to assure the defeat of Tehran. Assistant Defense Secretary Perle informed Secretary of Defense Weinberger in 1985 of CIA evidence on the Iraqi program.[58]

In the late 1980s, the State Department and the CIA were aware that Saddam Hussein had been diverting U.S. farm credits through an Atlanta bank to pay for nuclear technology and other sophisticated arms.[59] Secretary of State Baker received a memorandum in October 1989 that described the Iraqi program to launder U.S. farm export credits through the Atlanta branch of the Italian-owned Banca Nazionale del Lavoro (BNL) to procure nuclear-related equipment. President George H. W. Bush and Baker denied any knowledge of these reports in the wake of Desert Storm, but there was a paper trail from the CIA and the Departments of Justice, Energy, Treasury, and Agriculture detailing the transactions. Bush, moreover, had signed a secret National Security Directive in October 1989 that endorsed trade with Saddam Husssein. Between 1985 and 1990, Iraq received 771 export licenses from the United States, and 162 of these licenses were granted for technology with nuclear applications. Only several weeks before Iraq's invasion of Kuwait, the Iraqis were trying to obtain a shipment of high-temperature furnaces that were designed for Iraq's ballistic missile program, in view of this technology's ability to produce titanium and other super alloys for the construction of ballistic missiles. Bush and Baker were in favor of allowing the transaction, although Saddam Hussein had already gassed Iraqi Kurds, destabilized Lebanon with extensive weapons shipments, and resumed programs to develop WMD.

Ironically, the only obstruction to this support for Iraq was coming from then Secretary of Defense Cheney. When the Iran–Iraq war ended in August 1988, the departments of Treasury and Agriculture, as well as the Office of Management and Budget also opposed the extension of agricultural credits, but the State Department, led by Baker, Undersecretary for Political Affairs Robert Kimmitt, and Deputy Secretary Lawrence Eagleburger, successfully pressed for continuing $1 billion in loan guarantees annually. An FBI raid on the Atlanta banks in August 1989 uncovered the huge fraud that had transpired, but Bush and Baker continued to provide the loan guarantees, as well as military intelligence to Iraq. A CIA assessment provided to the Congress could have exposed the program, but the Agency refused to do so for policy reasons.

A congressional investigation around this time also learned that the CIA refused to cooperate in a Federal investigation of a multi-billion-dollar operation that benefited Iraq and an Italian-owned Banca Nazionale del Lavoro. When Representative Henry Gonzalez (D-Texas) tried to get to the bottom of this financial fraud, CIA director Gates supported the Bush administration in trying to squelch Gonzalez's efforts. The fact is that the Bush administration was engaged in an effort to subsidize and arm Saddam Hussein right up to the Iraqi invasion of Kuwait, and the CIA was totally aware of these efforts. Gates, in his confirmation battle in 1991, had promised to be "faithful to the imperatives of honest consultation with Congress," but instead he became busily engaged in a political campaign against a member of Congress trying to uncover illegal activity in the Bush administration.

What Needs to be Done?

If the intelligence community is ever again to be in a position to tell truth to power, then the intelligence ethics of collection and analysis must be restored. Curveball was the sole source for false intelligence that linked mobile biological weapons laboratories to Iraq, but the CIA pretended to have additional sources. The German intelligence service lost confidence in his reporting and was stunned by high-level American assertions that cited the "Curveball" allegations. The source for much of the intelligence linking Iraq to training in chemical and biological weapons to al Qaeda was a fabricator, according to declassified portions of a study prepared by the DIA in February 2002, months before senior members of the Bush administration made their accusations.[60] DIA concluded that the al Qaeda source was "intentionally misleading the debriefers" in making claims about Iraqi support for al Qaeda's work with illicit weapons. Yet, the disinformation was declared "credible" by the Bush administration and was cited in the president's speech in Cincinnati in October 2002.

The prisoner did not officially recant his claims until nearly two years later, in January 2004, which prompted the CIA to recall all of its intelligence reports based on the source's reporting. Finally, the sole source for Saddam Hussein's efforts to purchase "yellowcake" uranium from Niger was known to be a fabrication by former members of the Italian military intelligence service; only the British and American intelligence services were ostensibly fooled. This pattern of illicit tradecraft points to a larger ethical problem within the intelligence community that will not be fixed by creation of an office for the DNI, greater centralization of the intelligence process, and placing the management of the intelligence community in the hands of general officers.

11

The Failure of Congressional Oversight

There's a marked lack of curiosity around here.

— Staff member of House Intelligence Committee, 2005[1]

Oversight is an essential aspect of democratic government, an integral part of any system of checks and balances, and central to any effort to "watch and control the government."[2] Oversight is designed to improve the efficiency and effectiveness of the government, to detect arbitrary and capricious behavior, let alone illegal and unconstitutional conduct, to ensure compliance with legislative intent, and to prevent executive encroachment on legislative authority. Currently the Senate and House intelligence committees, which were created in the mid-1970s to ensure oversight of secret agencies, are observing all of these duties in the breach. Until the Democratic congressional victory in 2006, Senate and House intelligence chairmen, Pat Roberts (R-Kansas) and Peter Hoekstra (R-Michigan), respectively, were the cat's paw of the Bush administration and made sure that there was no accountability and no criticism of any actions of the intelligence community that could rebound unfavorably on the White House.

Over the years, the best-known examples of legislative oversight are the investigations by select committees into major scandals or failures. Recent examples of select committee inquiries have included "Watergate" in 1972–1974, intelligence agency abuses in 1975–1976, the Iran-Contra affair in 1987, and homeland security in the wake of the 9/11 terrorist attacks. Standing committees have examined the sharing of intelligence information prior to the 9/11 attacks and U.S. intelligence on Iraqi WMD. But Congress' current unwillingness to investigate the torture and abuse scandals, CIA secret prisons and extraordinary renditions, and NSA's conduct of warrantless eavesdropping indicates that the oversight process has atrophied.

With the creation of the oversight committees, there was no question that the Congress had the power to monitor the performance of the intelligence community. The committees had the power to legislate on all matters related to the intelligence community. The intelligence committees authorized the budget of the intelligence community for action by the full Senate and had the power to investigate allegations of criminality, intelligence failure, and fraud and abuse. The committees could monitor the operations of the community, including covert actions, and audited all expenditures. Finally, the Senate intelligence committee confirmed the most senior officials of the intelligence community, and received prior notification of covert actions after the president had signed the "finding." The committees could task intelligence community officials to supply sensitive information needed for oversight through printed reports, letters, testimony, and briefings.

There was no intelligence oversight from the Agency's creation to 1947 until the creation of the Senate and House intelligence committees in 1976. In the very beginning, the intelligence community was under the jurisdiction of the Senate and House Armed Services Committees, but oversight was nonexistent. When CIA director Allen Dulles wanted $50 million for a new headquarters building in Virginia, he visited the chairmen of the Armed Forces and Appropriations committees and discussed what was needed. Dulles and Senator Richard Russell (D-Georgia) drank bourbon and discussed how many millions were needed, and Russell made sure that Dulles left with more than was requested. The CIA was involved in assassination plots, coups d'etat, and various covert actions, but, according to Senator Leverett Saltonstall (R-Massachusetts), "There are things that my government does that I would rather not know about."[3]

It was not until 1976–1977 that the Senate Select Intelligence Committee (SSCI) and the House Permanent Select Committee on Intelligence (HIPSI) were created. The decisive event for the shift took place in 1973, when CIA director Richard Helms deceived the Senate Foreign Relations Committee, refusing to acknowledge the role of the CIA in overthrowing the elected government in Chile. Helms falsely testified that the CIA had not passed money to the opposition movement in Chile, and a grand jury was called to see if Helms should be indicted for perjury. In 1977, the Justice Department brought a lesser charge against Helms, who pleaded nolo contendere; he was fined $2,000 and given a two-year suspended prison sentence. Helms went from the courthouse to the CIA where he was given a hero's welcome and a gift of $2,000 to cover the fine. It was one of my saddest experiences in twenty-four years at CIA.

In the wake of the Senate (Church Committee) and House (Pike Committee) investigations of CIA abuses, the center of gravity shifted on Capitol Hill and large majorities in both houses favored the creation of select committees. Senator Harold E. Hughes (D-Iowa) and Representative Leo J. Ryan (D-California) used the foreign authorization bill to add a requirement that covert actions, such as the operation in Chile, be reported to the Congress. According to the Hughes-Ryan Amendment, covert actions could not be initiated until a presidential "finding" was reported to the Senate Foreign Relations and House Foreign Affairs Committees, as well as the Armed Services and Appropriations Committees of each house, which marked the first time that Congress specifically ordered the CIA to report anything at all.

The Church and Pike Committees called for the creation of Congressional intelligence oversight committees and, as result, the Senate created the SSCI in 1976 and the House created the HPSCI in 1977. The era of intelligence oversight began when these committees claimed jurisdiction over the Hughes-Ryan amendment to the Foreign Assistance Act in 1974. Initially, the Senate Armed Forces Committee, the Senate Appropriations Committee, the Senate Foreign Relations Committee, and their House counterparts claimed equal oversight jurisdiction. But, in 1980, the Carter Administration created the Intelligence Oversight Act that gave exclusive jurisdiction for oversight to the SSCI and the HPSCI.

The end of the Senate intelligence committee's reputation for bipartisanship occurred during the confirmation hearings for Bob Gates in 1991. Since 1976, the oversight committees effectively monitored CIA activities, but the confirmation process for Gates as director of central intelligence was politicized and partisan. President Reagan initially nominated Gates to the post of director of CIA in 1987 following Casey's losing battle with a brain tumor. Many members of the Senate intelligence committee believed Gates lied about his knowledge of the Iran-Contra affair, and Senate committee chairman Boren (D-OK) privately warned Gates that he could not get an approval from the committee. Gates wisely decided to withdraw his nomination and set about to launder his credentials and particularly to insinuate himself with Boren. In 1991, the White House checked with Boren to see if Gates could receive confirmation this time around, and Boren angered many Democrats on the intelligence committee when he guaranteed confirmation to White House aide Boyden Gray. When opposition to Gates mounted in the fall of 1991, President Bush, a former CIA director and the president for whom the CIA headquarters building is named, was shocked by the intensity of the CIA rank-and-file against the Gates nomination. Nevertheless, he immediately informed the Republican members of the intelligence committee that he was "going to the mat" for Gates and wanted his nomination confirmed at all costs.[4] The White House informed the minority director of the Senate intelligence committee staff, John Moseman, that "You've got to deliver a favorable outcome for the White House." Moseman carried out his assignment, with no Republican voting against Gates.

In the summer of 1991, I provided several classified briefings to the Senate intelligence committee on Gates' role as DDI in politicizing intelligence on sensitive matters dealing with the Soviet Union, Central America, arms control, and Southwest Asia. In his memoir, Gates said he took some satisfaction from the fact that all the complaints of politicization dealt with Soviet-Third World issues, but that was far from the truth. I described Gates' role as the intelligence filter for a myriad of policies and polemics of CIA director Casey, and numerous written affidavits were submitted to the Committee dealing with politicization on a variety of issues. In September, Gates accompanied President Bush to a resort on St. Simons Island, Georgia, where he wrote his defense, but failed to mention in his memoir that the president's concern about confirmation led the White House to call in Kenneth Dubberstein to lead the defense.[5] The Senate staff at that time was led by majority staff chief Tenet, who became director of central intelligence in 1997, and minority staff chief Moseman, who became Tenet's chief of congressional liaison and then executive director at CIA.

In the words of former CIA analyst and SSCI staffer Marvin Ott, "for the first time in a decade the proceedings of the SSCI were being heavily influenced by partisan politics."[6] Ott believed Gates secured his confirmation by guaranteeing Boren that he would take the views of the Senate intelligence committee "heavily into account" during his tenure as DCI. This "guarantee" was endorsed by *The New York Times*, which naively ignored Gates' predilection for saying what was necessary to garner confirmation.[7] Boren, in turn, claimed he extracted a pledge from Gates that, as DCI, he would not take adverse action against those analysts who testified against him, but several analysts were immediately called into the Office of Security for polygraph investigations and then barred from returning to their former offices in the DI. The discredited confirmation process for Gates marked the turning point in the history of the Congressional oversight process, setting the Senate intelligence committee on the road to partisanship that it has not reversed. The Republican party-line vote for Gates marked the first time the White House demanded strict party discipline within the intelligence committee. Meanwhile, the close relationship between Boren, Tenet, Moseman, and Gates continues to this day.

The confirmation of Gates appeared to be a "slam dunk" in the spring of 1991, when there was no new testimony linking him to the Iran-Contra scandal or CIA's illegal support for the Contras. It was not until a senior Agency official, Harold Ford, and two former analysts, Jennifer Glaudemans and this author, presented testimony in the fall of 1991 regarding the politicization of intelligence that the White House became alarmed. Their testimony was backed up by the sworn affidavits of several intelligence analysts, including Carolyn McGiffert Ekedahl and John Hibbits, who did considerable risk to their careers by stepping forward. As a result, the Gates nomination changed from a political confirmation game that was Gates' to lose into a confrontation that was his to win. The personal and political stakes were high. For the first time in the history of CIA, the integrity and credibility of intelligence analysis—and not the wisdom and legality of covert action—was being debated at the highest legislative levels. Never before had the congressional intelligence committees discussed and debated the tradecraft of intelligence analysis, let alone the politicization of intelligence.

The debate over Gates' confirmation turned on the politicization of intelligence on the Soviet Union in the 1980s that was used to justify unprecedented peacetime increases in the defense budget, calling a halt to the arms control and disarmament process in the first term of President Ronald Reagan, and avoiding summit leaders with the Soviet leadership for the first five years of the Reagan administration. Any compromise of the integrity and credibility of the intelligence process, let alone compromises that deal with issues of grand strategy, gravely weakens a central component of decision making in national security, the role of intelligence analysis.

Gates was sufficiently concerned that he resorted to pressure and blandishment with one of the key CIA witnesses, Douglas MacEachin, who led the Office of Soviet Analysis (SOVA) during the period of politicization. If Gates was Casey's filter in the DI for making sure intelligence would be slanted in the direction of policy, then MacEachin was Gates' filter in SOVA to make sure intelligence on the Soviet Union conformed to the Casey-Gates agenda. MacEachin was prepared to offer testimony in support of Gates as CIA director, but at the last moment he was beginning to have doubts about his role, not wanting to embarrass himself in front of a key member of the committee, Senator Bradley, who knew about MacEachin's earlier problems with Gates' lack of integrity. A staffer on the intelligence committee, Dick Combs, who represented Senator Sam Nunn (D-GE) on the committee, decided to meet with MacEachin, who conceded he could not support Gates in the final analysis and wanted to meet with Senator Nunn to discuss his change of heart. When Nunn told committee chairman Boren about MacEachin's *volte-face*, this led to a private meeting between Boren, Nunn, and MacEachin.[8] At this point, MacEachin became nervous and eventually called Gates. Both Gates and Boren put a great deal of pressure on MacEachin to support the nominee, and he did so.

Since Senator Nunn forced the deliberations of the committee to be held publicly, the United States witnessed an unprecedented debate on the role of intelligence and policy. These televised sessions did not have the drama and *dramatis personae* of the Army-McCarthy hearings in the 1950s, but there was intense partisan activity, particularly the intimidating tactics of Senator Warren Rudman (R-NH). Rudman raised the issue of McCarthyism against Gates' critics in order to staunch the flow of criticism of the Gates nomination from the rank and file of the CIA. Rudman's role was similar to Vice President Cheney's efforts during the Iraq War, when he tried to intimidate Ambassador Wilson who charged the Bush administration with using false intelligence to go to war against Iraq.

There would have been even more Democratic votes against Gates, if Nunn had not been pressured to vote for Gates, whom he held in extremely low regard. In addition to getting MacEachin to maintain his support for Gates, Boren told Nunn that the vote for Gates was becoming a test of the personal friendship that existed between the two senior senators. Nunn believed the politicization issue was genuine and that Gates was personally responsible; therefore, he was opposed to the nomination. But Nunn had told Combs many times that, while he was never bothered by the pressure from outside the Senate, he always had a problem with pressure from inside the Senate. Ironically, both Boren and Nunn took the issue of politicization seriously, but genuinely believed that the Senate intelligence committee would have influence over a CIA director and that would be a "feather in the cap" of the SSCI. Boren added, somewhat naively, that he would "own" Gates. He eventually persuaded Nunn to support Gates, which made his confirmation inevitable.

The "Dysfunctional" Oversight Process

The final report of the National Commission on Terrorist Attacks Upon the United States (hereafter referred to as the 9/11 Commission) was particularly critical of the congressional oversight process, choosing to call the process "dysfunctional," which is the same term the intelligence committees have used to describe the CIA and the intelligence community.[9] Over the past two decades, we have witnessed a series of intelligence failures (e.g., the Soviet intelligence failure, the Indian nuclear testing failure, 9/11 itself, and the run-up to the Iraq War), but there has been no attempt by either the House or Senate to consider serious reform. One of the best examples of the dysfunctional nature of the congressional oversight process has been the inability of the Senate and House committees to monitor the CIA's intelligence analysis. Although there have been significant strategic failures of intelligence over the past two decades, there have been no examples of committee members or staffers tracking the Agency's poor performance. In the 1980s, for example, CIA analysts warned committee members about the politicization of intelligence on the Soviet Union, but there was no attempt to example the Agency's finished intelligence until it became a political issue in the confirmation hearings for Bob Gates. Despite the pattern of international terrorism against U.S. interests that started in Yemen in 1992, the intelligence committees did not pursue the CIA's intelligence production on al Qaeda and other terrorist organizations. Not even the attacks on the World Trade Center in 1993, U.S. embassies in Kenya and Tanzania in 1998, and the USS *Cole* in 2000 led to an investigation by committee staffers of the Agency's National Intelligence Council and the directorate of intelligence. Finally, the congressional oversight committee ignored the corruption of the intelligence process in the run-up to the Iraq War in 2003. As a result, the congressional intelligence committees must share some of the responsibility for the failures over the past twenty years.

Even with the creation of the tougher oversight process in 1976, the CIA often chooses those events that it does not share with the congressional committees. In the early 1980s, CIA director William Casey did not inform the committees that the CIA was mining the harbor of Corinto in Nicaragua. Ten years later, CIA directors Webster and Gates did not inform the congress that CIA spy Aldrich Ames had comprised virtually every Soviet asset and every Soviet operation. The Agency has never acknowledged its intelligence failures with regard to the Soviet Union from 1985–1991. It also failed to inform the committees that nearly all the major intelligence information on Iraq in the run-up to the war in 2003 was single-source intelligence and that some of the single-source items were from known fabricators. For example, the Agency failed to inform the Congress before its vote in October 2002 on the use of force that the intelligence suggesting reconstitution of the nuclear industry was a forgery and that the intelligence on mobile biological warfare plants came from a single source who was not trustworthy. (In February 2002, the Pentagon's Defense Intelligence Agency had disavowed its intelligence on the so-called links between Iraqi officials and al Qaeda because the single-source in that case, a Libyan named al-Libi, was an established liar. Nevertheless, CIA director Tenet disingenuously assured the intelligence committees in October 2002 that there was evidence of links between Iraq and al Qaeda.)

The congressional intelligence committees neglected to push for investigations of the abuse and torture of detainees in CIA prisons and other overseas facilities. Senator Carl Levin (D-Michigan) has won no Republican support for his proposal to create an independent commission to investigate treatment of detainees since 2001. The administration's rejection of accountability for numerous cases of "cruel, inhuman, and degrading" treatment of foreign detainees, and the congressional failure to conduct oversight hearings, is a shocking and shameful scandal in its own right. There has been no investigation of Secretary of Defense Rumsfeld, his senior staff, and White House and Justice Department lawyers who drafted or approved policies for detainee interrogations. There has been no investigation of CIA personnel, ranging from former director Tenet to operational personnel in Afghanistan and Iraq, who have been involved in the illegal hiding of "ghost detainees" from the International Red Cross and the "rendition" of suspects to countries that practice torture. As a result, little or nothing is known about such CIA practices as where prisoners are held, how many there are, what access they have to medical treatment, and how many may have suffered injury or death while in the Agency's custody.

The dereliction of oversight reached its apogee in late 2002 when the Senate and House intelligence committees made no serious attempt to vet the intelligence analysis of the October 2002 NIE on Iraqi weapons of mass destruction. Members of the Senate intelligence committee had commissioned the estimate, which is unusual in itself, but few members took the time and effort to read the finished product or to react to the CIA's unclassified "white paper" of the NIE, which omitted the caveats, subtleties, and dissents from the classified version. The white paper was aimed at a domestic audience and represented policy advocacy. The NIE said that Iraq probably could not acquire a nuclear weapon for at least seven years, but the white paper left out the dates and suggested that the weapon could be acquired imminently. The NIE contained a dissent from the State Department on this issue, but the white paper omitted the dissent. The NIE incorrectly stated that Iraq was aggressively trying to obtain high-strength aluminum tubes for its nuclear weapons program, and the white paper downplayed the dissent from the Department of Energy, the most authoritative government agency to report on such developments.

An excellent example of the lack of interest and curiosity of the oversight committees is the most recent oversight failure. In December 2005, *The New York Times* reported that the Bush administration ordered the National Security Agency in 2001 to begin warrantless eavesdropping of American citizens, a violation of law and possibly the Fourth Amendment of the Constitution against "undue searches and seizures." Bush cited his inherent constitutional authority as commander-in-chief and the congressional resolution in the wake of the 9/11 attacks that authorized use of force. The president and former attorney general Alberto Gonzales also argued that they briefed Congress a dozen times on warrantless wiretapping, but the briefings actually involved only 8 of the 535 members of Congress. It took riveting testimony to the SSCI in 1986 to break open the illegality of the Iran-Contra operation; it will take similar testimony to get to the bottom of the executive order to sanction NSA's use of warrantless eavesdropping against American citizens.

Aptly Named "Oversight" Committee

George Orwell certainly would have appreciated the irony of referring to the SSCI as the Oversight Committee. For the past fifteen years, there has been no end to the examples of oversight on the part of the committee. The Senate intelligence committee has failed to investigate the major intelligence failures from the 1980s to the Iraq War, including the failure to track the decline, let alone collapse, of the Soviet Union; the Indian nuclear test failures of 1998; and the failure to monitor the terrorist campaign against the United States that began with the bombing of the U.S. embassy in Lebanon in 1983, when even high-ranking CIA officials were killed. Certainly in a world without Orwellian doublespeak, according to the *Los Angeles Times*, the intelligence committee would be referred to as the Senate Coverup Committee, although the Senate Oversight Committee could serve as the proper double entendre.[10]

Roberts single-handedly kept the committee from investigating the Bush administration's use of the CIA's intelligence information in the run-up to the Iraq War in March 2003 and the administration's warrantless eavesdropping program. Although the Bush administration resorted to a flimsy legal defense to conduct warrantless surveillance, citing the authorization to use force in Afghanistan in September 2001, Roberts did nothing to examine NSA's activity as an obvious violation of the 1978 Foreign Intelligence Surveillance Act, if not the Fourth Amendment of the Constitution against "unreasonable searches and seizures." President Bush and Senator Roberts essentially collaborated to get the Congress to pass a bill ex post facto to consider the surveillance legal under the previous FISA authority.

Roberts also dragged his heels in investigating the bogus intelligence of the CIA on Iraqi weapons of mass destruction and finally relented only after an outside commission headed by former senator Charles Robb (D-Virginia) and Judge Larry Silberman was appointed to investigate the matter. Roberts and CIA director Porter Goss also collaborated on the cover-up of the CIA Inspector General's accountability report on the 9/11 intelligence failure, preventing proper distribution of the report within the intelligence committees of the Senate and House, as well as a sanitized unclassified report, which is customary in such events.

The best example of the Senate intelligence committee's failure to pursue oversight of the executive branch and the misuse of the intelligence community turned on the issue of warrantless surveillance that surfaced in December 2005. A secret intelligence court exists to review classified applications for wiretapping inside the United States, but President Bush signed a secret executive agreement in September 2001, permitting NSA to monitor the conversations of American citizens in the United States. Most Republican congressmen favor an explicit authorization of such wiretapping and an exemption of it from the 1978 law. The FBI has already acknowledged that NSA's spying has inundated the FBI with thousands of leads that were worthless.[11]

A stifling partisanship within the Congressional oversight process meant that, for the first time since the intelligence committees were formed in the mid-1970s, the Senate failed to pass an intelligence authorization bill. Former intelligence committee chairmen such as Bob Graham (D-Florida) and David Boren (D-Oklahoma), remarked that they had never witnessed such a high level of animosity and partisanship. Ironically, former committee member Senator Warren Rudman (R-New Hampshire) urged that "politics should stop at the door of that committee," although it was Rudman who ushered in the era of partisanship in 1991, when he accused CIA critics of the nomination of Robert M. Gates for CIA director with "McCarthyism."

Representative Hoekstra maintained the same partisan lock on the House intelligence committee that Roberts placed on the doors of the Senate intelligence committee. Just as Roberts blocked inquiries and investigations of such illegal activities as warrantless eavesdropping and torture and abuse at secret prisons, Hoekstra made sure that the House committee doesn't open any of these Pandora's boxes. Ironically, the House of Representatives has a procedure that permits any Congressional committee to obtain factual information—not opinions—from the executive branch.[12] The procedure was used during the Vietnam War to obtain access to the *Pentagon Papers*, the Defense Department study of U.S.–Vietnamese relations, and information on CIA covert operations in Laos.[13] When the United States fought a secret war in Cambodia during the Vietnam War, it took a Congressional inquiry to learn the number of U.S. sorties and the tonnage of bombs and shells fired and dropped during certain periods. A month before the Iraq War, Representative Dennis Kucinich (D-Ohio) used a resolution of inquiry to obtain a 12,000-page Iraqi declaration on its weapons of mass destruction, which turned out to be far more accurate that CIA declarations on Iraqi WMD. A resolution of inquiry would be an effective device for gaining more information on such controversial issues as CIA extraordinary renditions and secret prisons, which Hoekstra refuses to investigate.

Meanwhile, the intelligence committees have not challenged the efforts of the Bush administration to restrict the need to know of the American people. In 1999, four years after the Clinton administration signed a declassification order, the CIA, the Defense Intelligence Agency, and several other agencies began removing thousands of historical documents from public access, including documents that had been published by the State Department and photocopied by private historians.[14] Some of the documents were decades-old reports from the Korean War and the early days of the cold war. The Bush administration accelerated the process when it came into office, and the impact of the 9/11 attacks put the program into high gear. The program has revoked access to approximately 9,500 documents since its inception, and more than 8,000 of these documents have been removed since the Bush administration came into power. There clearly has been a marked trend toward greater secrecy in the Bush administration that has increased the pace of classifying documents, slowed declassification, and discouraged release of some material under the Freedom of Information Act. The CIA under Porter Goss went even further, denying publication of materials that have no security classification and preventing CIA officials from addressing open meetings of academic associations. He also threatened the possibility of grand jury investigations in which reporters would have to reveal their sources of classified information or risk prosecution for espionage.

The intelligence committees have done nothing to challenge the efforts of the White House to shut off the flow of national security information to the American public. The White House and the Department of Justice are even using an espionage law from the days of World War I to prosecute two pro-Israeli lobbyists for receiving classified information from a Pentagon official who was sentenced to twelve years in prison in January 2006. The two lobbyists, Steven Rosen and Keith Weissman of the American Israel Public Affairs Committee, are facing jail sentences that would have a chilling effect on debate over national security issues. This would represent the first time that any administration has tried to stifle debate on national security issues by criminalizing the receipt of oral information as part of a lobbying or reporting process.

In addition to blocking any serious investigations of the misuse of intelligence, the Senate and House intelligence committees have also blocked the Government Accountability Office, the investigative arm of Congress, from monitoring the effectiveness of the nation's intelligence agencies. The GAO is uniquely qualified to investigate the world of intelligence; it has more than 150 officials who are able to audit intelligence information, but it has not audited the CIA and the NSA since the 1960s. In the mid-1970s, the Pike Committee, which investigated the intelligence community, recommended that the GAO should have the same authority to investigate and audit intelligence as other agencies. But the GAO needs authorization from Congress to begin an investigation, and the oversight committees have been particularly quiet since the intelligence failures that accompanied the 9/11 terrorist attacks. Both Roberts and Hoekstra stated that they have their own audit staffs within the intelligence oversight committees and have no need for GAO involvement.

The Congressional intelligence committees failed in other ways, allowing the CIA to hide behind a secret budget embedded in the huge defense appropriation, which violates Article I, Section 9 of the Constitution. Article I demands that a "regular Statement and Account of the Receipts and Expenditures of all public Money should be published from time to time." The overall intelligence community budget (now exceeding $50 billion) has been declassified only in 1997 and 1998, but the CIA budget (typically one-tenth of the overall intelligence budget, or about $5 billion) has never been declassified. The CIA maintains that, because of the openness in those two years, the release of old budget figures would "help identify trends in intelligence spending" that may permit correlations "between specific spending figures and specific intelligence programs."[15] In view of the fact that the United States outspends the entire world on intelligence matters, it is almost unimaginable that any harm could come to national security by the release of budget information. In fact, a deputy director for national intelligence, Mary Margaret Graham, divulged the overall intelligence budget in an on-the-record speech in San Diego in November 2005. Even when President Bush signed into law a requirement that the overall intelligence budget be made public, which the 9/11 Commission recommended, the House intelligence committee immediately blocked disclosure. Thus, an oversight committee is responsible for denying the American people access to spending on intelligence, which is needed in order to make informed decisions about national policy.

Finally, the intelligence committees have not been vigorous in monitoring the new office of the DNI and the new director of the office, Admiral Mike McConnell. The office has grown into a bureaucratic behemoth with a budget exceeding $1 billion. It has not sponsored any reform of the intelligence community and, with the exception of the CIA, has not brought any changes to the specific intelligence agencies. McConnell has not established control over the community and, in his briefings to the Congress, has displayed incredible ignorance of the Foreign Intelligence Surveillance Act (FISA). Under FISA, a secret court had to issue warrants for surveillance of communications involving anyone within U.S. borders. The 1978 Act has been useful in foiling terrorist activities, but McConnell incorrectly testified to various congressional committees that the process has been too cumbersome.

WHAT NEEDS TO BE DONE?

Reform of the oversight process would consist, for the most part, of enforcing the system that already exists. The congressional intelligence committees have great powers that have been increasingly observed in the breach. The committees legislate on all matters relating to the intelligence community, including the most sensitive aspects of covert action; authorize the budget of the intelligence community; investigate allegations of failure and fraud, let alone criminality; confirm key members of the community; and have access to sensitive intelligence, including reports of the Inspector General. The oversight committees may not be able to veto a covert action, but it is possible for them to deny the funding for specific covert actions. It would be foolhardy for the White House and the CIA to proceed with a covert action that the Congress opposed.

The 9/11 Commission suggested important reforms for the oversight process, but all of them were ignored by the committees. The powerful rule of the former Senate intelligence chairman, Senator Roberts, moreover, kept the committee from investigating key areas that pointed to an abuse of power by the White House over the use of intelligence or by the intelligence community itself. He promised to hold "closed meetings to move forward" on the administration's manipulation of intelligence, but never indicated when factual findings would be published. With the exception of Senator Carl Levin (D-Michigan), the Democratic minority has been extremely dilatory in pursuing its legitimate interests on intelligence matters. In the House, Representative Jane Harman (D-California) was no more aggressive than her Senate counterpart, and deferred unnecessarily to the Republican chairman, Representative Hoekstra. In a short period of time, Hoekstra became the same "advocate" for the intelligence community that his predecessor, Representative Porter Goss (R-Florida), had been. The new chairmen of the intelligence committee, Senator Rockefeller and Representative Silvester Reyes (D-Texas), seem to lack the tenacity and vigor needed to conduct genuine oversight.

Unless the Congressional oversight process returns to its bipartisan or nonpartisan roots, recruits an expert professional staff with the instincts of junkyard dogs, accepts the fact that objective, balanced intelligence analysis is just as important as clandestine operations, and appoints chairmen who do not see themselves as "advocates" for the intelligence community, the CIA and other intelligence agencies will not receive the guidance and monitoring they sorely require. With the dangerous increase in unchecked presidential power and the incompetence of the intelligence community prior to the 9/11 attacks and the Iraq War, the restoration of Congressional intelligence oversight is essential to American national security.

12

DCIs and the Decline and Fall of the CIA

The CIA's current difficulties can be traced to the failure of the past eight directors over the last twenty-five years, and not simply to flaws in organization or process. There is no silver bullet of reform that will halt the steady deterioration of the CIA unless the Agency receives stellar leadership. Beginning with William Casey in 1981, in the Reagan administration, and continuing to the present with General Michael Hayden in the second Bush administration, the decline has been incremental but perceptible. It is too early to judge General Hayden, who was named CIA director in June 2006, but the appointment of a four-star general does not augur well for an independent intelligence agency that must be free from military or policy bias. The fact that Hayden was the director of the National Security Agency during the inception of warrantless eavesdropping indicates that the general follows presidential orders, even those that break the law and the Fourth Amendment of the Constitution. A key charge in the impeachment process for President Richard Nixon in 1974 was the use of warrantless eavesdropping.

In June 2007, General Hayden declassified a huge 1973 CIA file known as the "family jewels," which detailed domestic spying, assassination plots, and numerous CIA crimes from the 1950s to the early 1970s. Hayden boldly proclaimed, "The documents provide a glimpse of a very different time and a very different Agency. I firmly believe that the improved system of intelligence oversight that came out of the 1970s gives the CIA a far stronger place in our democratic system. What we do now to protect Americans, we do within a powerful framework of law and review." Nothing could be further from the truth. In the 1970s, a series of presidential and congressional investigations (the Rockefeller Commission, the Church Committee, and the Pike Committee) addressed the abuses and intelligence scandals associated with

CIA covert action and assassination plots, recognizing the need for reform. These investigations led to the creation of the Congressional intelligence oversight process. Unfortunately, the examination of such failures as 9/11 and the Iraq War have produced no remedy other than the creation of an office of the director of national intelligence (DNI), which has contributed to the bureaucratic bloat in the intelligence community. No effort has been made to remedy the problems introduced by Bill Casey and George Tenet, who enthusiastically politicized intelligence for the White House. And there has been no attempt to reverse the militarization of the intelligence community begun by Bob Gates and John Deutch in the 1990s. Today's crimes include torture and abuse, secret prisons, and extraordinary renditions, which have not been addressed by the CIA's leader. In the final analysis, no large organization could survive the twenty-five years of stewardship that the CIA's leaders have provided. This corrupt leadership is the major reason for the CIA's loss of influence and credibility.

WILLIAM CASEY (1981–1987)

Reagan's appointment of Casey, a dyed-in-the-wool political operative as his intelligence chief, sent shock waves through the intelligence and policy communities in Washington, and marked the beginning of the end of the CIA's credibility. Casey was the first genuine political appointee at the CIA. He had made a huge fortune investing in Capital Cities Broadcasting Corporation and had gained influence with Reagan by campaigning for his successful race for California governor. He garnered large campaign contributions for Reagan's presidential race in 1980, and stuck by Reagan when his candidacy ran into rough spots on the campaign trail. Truman had designed the CIA to be above politics and policy, and never before had such a brusque and blatant partisan been appointed director of central intelligence (DCI).

Casey was the first ideologue to direct the CIA and the first director to become a member of the president's cabinet. The appointment to the cabinet violated the principle of keeping the CIA and its director outside the policy process. Casey strongly believed that the Soviet Union was the cause of all that was wrong in the international system, and favored an aggressive role by the United States and the CIA to counter the Soviet Union. Like William ("Wild Bill") Donovan, the chief of the Office of Strategic Services (OSS), during World War II, Casey was a veteran of the OSS, a New York lawyer, and a great believer in the role of covert action. He wanted the CIA to be aggressive in promoting covert action to bring down the Soviet empire, and he was not interested in congressional oversight and the rule of law. Casey ran the CIA the way Donovan ran the OSS, and Casey looked at the Soviet Union the way that Donovan perceived Nazi Germany. Ironically, Casey's aggressive tactics coincided with the emergence of Mikhail Gorbachev, who wanted to create a stable and peaceful Soviet–American relationship. Casey's belief that Gorbachev's international agenda was a sham led to the intelligence failure concerning the importance of the new Soviet leader to Soviet–American relations. Casey adamantly opposed Secretary of State Shultz's policy of détente, which worsened relations between the CIA and the State Department in the mid-1980s.

Casey's single-minded aggressiveness as CIA director led to the Iran-Contra scandal that compromised the Reagan administration. The fact that the Congress had passed the Boland Amendment to outlaw funding for the overthrow of the Sandinista government in Nicaragua meant nothing to Casey. He believed that the restrictions of the Boland Amendment applied to the CIA, but not to the NSC. Serious risks were no impediment for Casey; in 1984, he sanctioned an act of war against Nicaragua without informing Congress. The mining of the harbors at Corinto was managed by a CIA operative, Rudy Enders, who relished the opportunity to use the skills he learned at a demolitions course given by the U.S. Navy. During the Iran-Contra hearings in 1986, Enders told me the mining operation was his greatest moment in serving the CIA.

The Congress wasn't so enamored with Enders' efforts. Indeed, the Congressional intelligence committees were furious over this unsanctioned act and would have fired Casey if it had the power to do so. But President Reagan laughed off the issue, remarking that if anyone in his administration was pursuing such an initiative "no matter what time it is, wake me, even if it's in the middle of a Cabinet meeting."[1] Presumably, it never occurred to either Reagan or Casey that shopping around for funds for the Contras from third countries was a violation of law and, thus, an impeachable offense. And selling weapons to Iran, a supporter of terrorism against the United States, in order to obtain the release of American hostages in Lebanon, was a violation of every American principle on dealing with terrorists. The special investigation of Lawrence E. Walsh and the Tower Commission revealed Casey's fingerprints all over the Iran-Contra operation, but Casey's death from a brain tumor in 1987 helped his reputation and the unwillingness of the Congress to examine Iran-Contra for impeachment issues protected the image of President Reagan.

Casey communicated his desire to be secretary of state to Reagan on election night in 1980, but was told such an appointment was not in the cards.[2] Richard Allen, who would become Reagan's first national security advisor, told Casey "You don't look like a secretary of state. You don't talk like a secretary of state. You only think like one." What Allen could not have known was that Casey's bitterness at being passed over for Foggy Bottom led the CIA director to lock horns with Reagan's most important cabinet member, Secretary of State Shultz, in an effort to end Shultz's sponsorship of détente with the Soviet Union. Casey even sent several memoranda to President Reagan calling for Shultz's resignation. Casey failed in his confrontation with Shultz, who directed a successful policy of détente and, thereby, saved Reagan's reputation in his second term. Shultz's memoirs are filled with understandable anger at the CIA director, and his deputy Bob Gates, for undercutting the diplomacy of the secretary of state.

Casey never had the access to Reagan that Shultz cultivated, and the fact that Nancy Reagan took an immediate and intense dislike to Casey ensured that he would be no match for Shultz. Casey would write and call the president on a variety of substantive matters, but according to Gates, ". . . there was nobody listening at the other end."[3] Reagan and Casey wrongly believed that Moscow was going to use its negligible presence in Central America to challenge the United States, which was the background to the illegal U.S. support for the Contras and Iran-Contra. When Reagan and Casey plotted in 1984 to mine the harbors of Nicaragua, the Congress was not even informed, which led an Agency supporter like Senator Barry Goldwater (R-Arizona) to declare, "I've been trying to figure out how I can tell you my feelings about the discovery of the President having approved mining some of the harbors of Central America. It gets down to one, little, simple phrase: I am pissed off!"[4] Actually, Casey had pissed off his own operational leadership, which considered his covert action plans for Central America as "crazy" and "harebrained." While Reagan and Casey were playing with covert actions that proved feckless, Gates was truckling to his boss, writing memoranda that called for "air strikes to destroy a considerable portion of Nicaragua's military buildup" as the only way to bring down the Sandinista government.[5]

Casey could not have been a worse fit for the position of DCI. He had his own views about key national security interests and relied on an intuitive approach to international security. When a finished product of the directorate of intelligence (DI) ran up against his naturally hard line views, he immediately moved to kill the product and punish its authors. He was, first and foremost, a bully. I encountered this trait in 1981, when the CIA was charged with writing a special assessment on Soviet involvement in international terrorism. There were several meetings with Casey, and all of them were tense and tendentious. He strongly believed that the Soviet Union was responsible for every major act of terrorism around the world and insulted the intelligence of all those who disagreed with him. Casey shared Secretary of State Haig's view that the Soviet Union was behind the assassination attempt against Haig in Brussels, Belgium, in 1979. When there was an assassination attempt against Pope John Paul II, Casey was convinced that the KGB was behind it and that, as a result, he had justification for preventing détente and disarmament with the Soviet Union.

Both Casey and Haig strongly believed that the Soviet Union was an evil empire and therefore, it had to be involved in every act of international terrorism in the 1960s and 1970s. Casey had read Claire Sterling's *The Terror Network*, which argued the case of a Soviet terrorist conspiracy. Several of us met with Casey to try to tell the director that much of Sterling's so-called evidence was in fact CIA "black propaganda," anticommunist allegations planted in the European press and, thus, a prime example of CIA blowback to the United States. The directorate of operations (DO) was extremely angry over the issue of blowback and with the misuse of its clandestine reports. We called Casey's attention to this phenomenon of blowback, but he dismissed our case and contemptuously noted that he purchased the Sterling book with his own money and "learned more from Sterling than from all of you." Casey, of course, had high-level support from the neoconservatives of their day, including Secretary of State Haig, State Department officials Robert McFarlane and Paul Wolfowitz, and Department of State consultant Michael Ledeen.

The high-level interest in an estimate on international terrorism, the first ever done on the subject by the CIA, meant that a great deal of care and attention had to be given to the research and composition of the first draft. Every piece of evidence dealing with any sign of Soviet involvement, direct or indirect, with terrorist activity or terrorist organization was scrutinized. An annex was attached to the draft that included all the evidence, both good and bad, and the first draft of the assessment was a balanced view of Moscow's views and actions toward terrorism. The evidence overwhelmingly demonstrated that the Soviet leadership played no direct role in the conduct of international terrorism, believing it to be counterproductive. Moscow consistently stated publicly and privately that international terrorism was ill-advised and told groups they supported, such as the Palestine Liberation Organization, to stop such tactics.

Casey dismissed the draft as an "exculpatory brief," gave the assignment to more malleable analysts at the Defense Intelligence Agency, who produced just the accusatory document that Casey wanted. The DIA draft was so off the mark that even Casey agreed to give the assignment to a third drafter, a newly-named scholar in residence from Rutgers University who shifted the focus of the paper sufficiently to satisfy Casey's view on Moscow's support for revolutionary violence. The policy community understood that the intelligence assessment had been politicized and essentially dismissed the CIA's findings. Senior analysts at the CIA realized that the Casey stewardship would become a constant battle to find a way to tell truth to power; Casey concluded that liberals and leftists dominated the analytical community at his own Agency.

The excellent investigative work of Lawrence E. Walsh, the independent counsel in the Iran-Contra investigation, assigned Casey the major share of the blame for Iran-Contra, along with a few overzealous underlings, who were eventually pardoned by President George H. W. Bush. The operation involved trading U.S. arms for U.S. hostages held by Iranian terrorists, and placing the proceeds from these undercover sales in Swiss bank accounts. Some of this money funded the guerrilla activities of the Nicaraguan Contras, a counterrevolutionary group. The U.S. Congress had specifically forbidden the administration to support the Contras, however. Casey was only one of many key conspirators; he had a great deal of help from NSC adviser Admiral John Poindexter, as well as Colonel Oliver North. But Casey was the key operative in terms of managing or mismanaging the merger of two distinct covert actions into one called Iran-Contra. Casey's motivation was basic; he genuinely believed that, "If America challenges the Soviets at every turn and ultimately defeats them in one place, that will shatter its mythology, and it will all start to unravel. Nicaragua is that place."[6] It was the Reagan administration that nearly unraveled because of Iran-Contra, and it was Casey who took to his grave all the details of the illegal sale of arms to Iran and the funneling of the profits of these sales to the Contras.

Casey's deceit and duplicity at the CIA led the Senate Select Committee on Intelligence and its chairman, Senator Daniel Inouye (D-Hawaii) to create an independent and statutory Inspector General for the CIA. No CIA director had worse relations with the Congressional oversight committees, although Jim Woolsey and Porter Goss were forced to resign after less than two years as CIA directors for wearing out their welcome in front of the Congressional intelligence committees. Schlesinger and Gates were pushed aside by Presidents Nixon and Clinton, respectively. But Casey had protection from the White House that the others lacked. At the White House correspondents' dinner in 1984, Reagan facetiously told Goldwater that, from now on, he would receive advance notice of Casey's exploits, ordering the CIA director "no matter what time it is, wake me, even if it's in the middle of a Cabinet meeting."[7]

WILLIAM WEBSTER (1987–1991)

Judge William Webster has a reputation for integrity in Washington but, sadly, he too was drawn into the Iran-Contra cover-up. The key to the case against two important Iran-Contra players, Colonel North and Admiral Poindexter, was the testimony of Joseph Fernandez, the CIA station chief in Costa Rica, who led the southern front in the effort to guide the Contras in Nicaragua. When arms had to be dropped to the Contras in this area, Fernandez was responsible for coordinating the air drop with Costa Rican officials. But Fernandez gave false and misleading testimony to both the CIA Inspector General and the Tower Commission, and was ultimately indicted by a grand jury for making false statements and obstructing both investigations, and for conspiring to carry out an unauthorized covert action. Webster led the CIA effort to withhold documents from the Walsh investigation in order to force dismissal of the case against Fernandez. The Bush administration obstructed the investigation, and the case against Fernandez was dropped. Webster and National Security Advisor Scowcroft had conspired to prevent the trial of an individual who had admitted to making false statements.

Webster's background as FBI director should have given him excellent experience on counterintelligence and internal security matters, but he failed to focus on the problem and fell asleep during his first security briefing that named Aldrich Ames as the spy who had been providing sensitive operational intelligence to the Soviet Union since 1984. Ames eventually received more than $2.5 million from the Soviets, which he lavished on cars, real estate, and the finer things in life. The information supplied to Moscow led to the death or disappearance of at least twelve members of the Soviet security service, but it took six years after the initial briefing for Webster before the Agency understood the need for Ames' arrest in February 1994.

Inadequate CIA intelligence during Desert Storm and Webster's questioning of the degree of damage caused to Iraqi forces by the U.S. Air Force led to a backlash of dissatisfaction within the military toward the CIA director.[8] Key congressional members, including Senator Daniel Moynihan (D-New York), were exceedingly critical of Webster's nonrole during Desert Storm and the weakness of CIA analysis, and there was no rush from the policy or intelligence communities to defend Webster. As a result, the military could see that there was blood in the water on these issues and began to campaign for turning over satellite imagery analysis to the Pentagon and to block CIA analysts from conducting order of battle intelligence, as well as military damage assessments during times of war. Within five years, the Pentagon achieved most of its objectives, with Gates surrendering O/B analysis to the Pentagon and Deutch promoting the creation of the National Imagery and Mapping Agency in order to give the analysis of satellite photography to the military.

Both Casey and Webster believed the creation of intelligence centers would strengthen the operational and analytical effort on key national security issues. Casey was responsible for the first of these centers, the Counterterrorism

Center in 1986, and Webster added joint centers for collection and analysis on international narcotics, counterintelligence, and arms control. Webster also agreed in 1989 to move the CIA's Arms Control Intelligence Staff (ACIS) from the DI to the office of the DCI, where the director could influence the analytical products of the staff. CIA's arms control experts had developed a reputation for integrity and expertise under the awning of the DI, but this reputation was seriously eroded when the DCI and his NIO, Larry Gershwin, began to focus on worst-case estimates of Soviet strategic power.

The centers, moreover, never achieved the community unity that was sought and never improved the analytical skills of the CIA. In fact, just the opposite took place, and some of the best analysts in these particular areas were recruited from the directorate of intelligence (DI), which weakened the overall analytical capabilities of the CIA. By moving the centers closer to the office of the CIA director, it became easier to politicize the work of the centers, particularly in the important areas of arms control and counterterrorism. The counterintelligence center was particularly feckless; not even Director Webster, a former director of the FBI, could arrange for FBI participation and cooperation. Webster tried to get the CIA more involved in creating better security conditions for U.S. embassies, but Secretary of State Shultz resented the CIA's intrusion into what he considered a State Department management issue. Shultz's unreasonableness on this issue was actually the legacy of his bitterness toward the efforts of Casey and Gates to block Shultz's diplomatic initiatives toward the Soviet Union.

Despite his lack of attention to the intelligence community, Webster tried to reverse the impact of politicization that took place under Casey and Gates. Webster dissociated himself immediately from the CIA's work linking the Soviet Union to international terrorism and the attempted assassination of the Pope in 1981. He did the same with the CIA's intelligence on Central America and the Soviet Bloc. He tried to improve counterintelligence at the CIA and ultimately had the unfortunate task of informing President Reagan that all the Cuban agents recruited by CIA operations officers were "double agents" and thus controlled by the Cuban government. But Webster had a poor understanding of the strategic role of intelligence, and it was not until 1990 that he commissioned a study of the impact of the end of the cold war on the CIA's foreign intelligence relationships and foreign intelligence collection. The Pentagon's criticism of the CIA's role during the war against Iraq in 1991 and the Congressional commitment to enforce serious change at the CIA forced Webster to resign in May 1991. He told the president that he did not want to preside over an agency losing its centrality and some of its missions, particularly in military intelligence.

Actually, Webster never really developed a relationship with the president and had no idea that his access to the president was being blocked by Gates, the deputy national security advisor, who wanted to replace his former boss at the CIA. President Bush had made up his mind to nominate Gates at the first opportunity, which Webster's resignation provided in May 1991. While Webster was DCI, Bush's chief intelligence advisor was actually Gates. It was Gates who blocked CIA intelligence on Gorbachev's reform efforts from reaching the president, simply because Gates considered Gorbachev just one more Leninist and no different from his predecessors. Webster was smart enough to realize that the cold war was ending and that the Soviet Union was in decline, but he was not savvy enough to stop the politicization of intelligence by his senior managers on the Soviet desk, Fritz Ermarth, Douglas MacEachin, and George Kolt, who blocked intelligence assessments that suggested the old order in the Soviet Union was ending and the Kremlin was on its last legs.

ROBERT GATES (1991–1993)

Gates survived the most difficult and contentious nomination battle of any DCI, attracting thirty-one votes against his confirmation in 1991. Four years earlier, he had been nominated as DCI to replace his patron, Bill Casey, who lost his battle with a brain tumor in 1987. Gates had to withdraw his name at that time because the chairman of the Senate Select Committee on Intelligence (SSCI), David Boren (D-Oklahoma), told him that a majority of the committee simply did not believe his denials regarding any prior knowledge of the Iran-Contra scandal and that some senators believed he was involved in the Agency's machinations. Several high-level Agency officials, including his own deputy, Richard Kerr, had briefed Gates on the sale of surface-to-air missiles to Iran and the diversion of profits to the Contras. The case officer for Iran-Contra, Marine Colonel Oliver North, had told Gates about the Swiss bank accounts where the money for the Contras had been kept. And in view of Gates' close relationship with Casey, there was very little chance that the director had not kept his deputy director for intelligence up-to-date. Gates' withdrawal took place early in the process, but not early enough to prevent him from referring to Casey as the model CIA director, which did not serve him well before the Senate intelligence committee in view of Casey's lies to the intelligence committees on issues such as Nicaragua.

Members of the intelligence committee, both Democrats and Republicans, did not believe Gates' argument that he had forgotten about the retroactive signing of the presidential finding in December 1985 that authorized the CIA's role in the transfer of Hawk shipments to Iran to recover the American hostages. In preparing Casey's testimony before the Senate and House intelligence committees in November 1986, Gates testified that he had forgotten about the finding a year earlier. However, CIA general counsel David Doherty told the Senate intelligence committee that he had given Gates a draft of the finding only a day or so before Casey's testimony. Charles Allen, the NIO for Warning, also testified that he had warned Gates about the diversion of arms sales proceeds to the Contras, and that Gates "appeared irritated" when he received the warning.[9] CIA deputy director Kerr corroborated Allen's testimony and the warning about the diversion. The independent counsel in the Iran-Contra investigation concluded that Gates brushed off the warnings because he already knew about the diversion and obviously became irritated when new witnesses brought him information he preferred not to see.

The simple fact was that Gates was the bureaucratic creation of Bill Casey, and it was virtually impossible to believe that CIA director Casey was involved in sensitive shenanigans that were not briefed to Gates. Thomas Polgar, a high-ranking CIA operations officer and then a Senate intelligence committee staff member, testified about the close relationship between Casey and Gates, and concluded that Gates could not be "compartmented" out of sensitive information.[10] After all, Gates worked closely with Casey from the very start of the director's stewardship of the CIA beginning in 1981, first as director of the executive staff in 1981, his deputy director for intelligence from 1982–1986, and then his deputy director of the CIA. Few members and staffers of the Senate intelligence committee believed Gates' testimony on Iran-Contra, and there was significant laughter in the hearing room when Gates said that he would have "resigned" if there had been the creation of an "off-the-shelf" capability to run the Iran-Contra operation out of the NSC.

Gates still had not given up on his ambition to become DCI, and he spent the next several years enhancing his relationship with Boren, who guaranteed White House senior advisor Bowden Gray that the committee would approve Gates the second time around. Nevertheless, Boren called Walsh, the independent counsel, to make sure that Gates was not going to be indicted in the Iran-Contra affair. Walsh said "probably not," but reminded Boren that they were still troubling areas suggesting that Gates had falsely denied knowledge of Oliver North's Contra-support activities and had falsely postdated his first knowledge of North's diversion of arms sale proceeds to the Contras. Walsh cited the testimony of both Kerr and Allen, but noted that it was a question of their word against Gates' denial of recollection. Therefore, Walsh "doubted Gates' veracity," but the committee was "unlikely to prosecute him."[11]

Boren's guarantees notwithstanding, many members of the SSCI believed the charges of intelligence analysts that Gates and Casey had conspired to politicize intelligence on the Soviet Union, Central America, and Southwest Asia, which led to a protracted confirmation battle from May to November 1991, a period that coincided with the collapse of the Soviet Union. Gates' fortunes declined so low that White House troubleshooter Kenneth Dubberstein, who rescued such troubled candidacies as Supreme Court Justice Clarence Thomas, formed a posse to save the day. Most of the members of the Senate intelligence committee no longer wanted to deal with Iran-Contra and did not want to hold Iran-Contra against Gates. Senator Warren Rudman (R-New Hampshire), who had been the ranking Republican on the Senate select committee on Iran-Contra, openly disparaged any discussion of the issue and accused the witnesses against Gates of McCarthyism for even raising issues dealing with Gates' integrity. Thus, a nominee who was known for his incredible memory testified thirty-three times that he did not have any recollection of the facts of Iran-Contra. The day after the Senate intelligence committee approved Gates' appointment eleven to four, the legendary *Washington Post* cartoonist, Herblock, pictured the CIA headquarters with a big banner proclaiming, "Now Under Old Management." He received confirmation from the full Senate, but in the process, attracted more negative votes (thirty-one) than all directors of central intelligence combined in the history of the CIA.

Gates became the first career CIA analyst to take over the reins of the CIA, although his role in politicizing intelligence did great harm to the mission and mandate of the Agency. Gates had a thorough understanding of how intelligence was used at the White House because of his various tours of duty there under Presidents Nixon, Ford, and Bush. But his strong ideological agenda in support of Reagan and Casey often led him down the wrong road. It was remarkable, for example, that a senior CIA Kremlinologist could be so wrong about the central issues of the day (e.g., Who was Mikhail Gorbachev? Was he serious? Would he make a difference?) and still make it to the top of the intelligence ladder. As late as 1989, when Gates was deputy director of central intelligence, he told various Congressional committees that "a long, competitive struggle with the Soviet Union still lies before us" and that the "dictatorship of the Communist party remains untouched and untouchable."[12]

Gates' well-earned reputation as an anti-Soviet ideologue was well-known to the Soviet leadership. Shortly after Gates was nominated as CIA director in May 1991, Gorbachev mentioned the nominee's anti-Soviet credentials, which U.S. ambassador Jack Matlock tried to fend off by noting that "Mr. Gates is less anti-Soviet than [KBG] Chairman [Vladimir] Kryuchkov is anti-American."[13] But Gates' low regard for Gorbachev was so well-known that when he met the Soviet leader for the first time, the Soviet chief remarked, "I understand that the White House has a special cell assigned the task of discrediting Gorbachev. And I've heard that you are in charge, Mr. Gates."[14] In fact, after one of Gates' anti-Soviet speeches in 1988, he was called and reprimanded by Secretary of State Shultz, who reminded the CIA deputy director that he had no right to comment in public on policy and that such "name-calling" would be "personally offensive to Gorbachev."[15] Secretary of State Baker had to intervene with the president to stop Gates from undermining U.S. policy toward Moscow. Gates often bragged he was the only CIA director in history who a Soviet president and two secretaries of state wanted to fire.

Gates' major contribution to the demise of the CIA was expanding the Pentagon's influence in the intelligence community and surrendering important areas of military analysis, such as order-of-battle intelligence, to the Defense Intelligence Agency. This allowed the new director of DIA to forge a campaign to refer to himself as director of military intelligence. No CIA director worked harder to improve his personal and institutional relations with the secretary of defense and the chairman of the Joint Chiefs of Staff, which permitted an exaggerated role for the military in the preparation of finished intelligence and greater militarization of the intelligence process. Gates consulted closely with Cheney and Powell on a regular basis and shared with both of them every draft memorandum of changes that he planned to make not only within the community, but within the CIA as well.

Upon receiving confirmation, Gates told Secretary of Defense Cheney that he wanted to integrate the missions of the intelligence community with the Pentagon. He appointed Cheney's aide, Richard Haver, to lead the Community Management Staff, which Gates created in March 1992 to improve intelligence support to the military. Gates also wanted to appoint an Army general to become the new associate deputy director of operations for military affairs at CIA, but the Chairman of the Joint Chiefs, General Colin Powell, initially demurred. Gates persisted, however, and a two-star Army general was eventually appointed as an associate deputy director for operations for military affairs. Gates tried desperately to remain as President Clinton's CIA director but the SSCI's leader of the effort to block Gates' confirmation, Senator Bill Bradley (D-New Jersey), convinced the new president that Gates' role in the politicization of intelligence in the 1980s disqualified him from any role in a new administration that was dedicated to more openness and candor in government.

Gates was also responsible for diminishing the role and importance of the Foreign Broadcast Information Service, the Agency's oldest intelligence branch and the key to collecting and analyzing open-source information. FBIS monitored foreign broadcast stations from positions around the world and analyzed significant news events not covered by the international media and often missed by the CIA's DI. Some of this nation's outstanding Kremlinologists and China-watchers, including Myron Rush, Arnold Horelick, Harry Gelman, Sidney Ploss, and Donald Zagoria, cut their analytical teeth at FBIS. The unclassified FBIS daily reports carried more foreign news than any other news organization and regularly scooped the foreign news reporting of *The New York Times* and the *Washington Post.* The FBIS analytical weekly was arguably the most valuable compendium of political intelligence in the entire intelligence community, more insightful and trenchant than the publications of the Office of Current Intelligence and often more premonitory than the NIEs.

But FBIS was an independent voice within the CIA, and Gates wanted to end its independence. When Gates had stopped his own directorate of intelligence from discussing Moscow's interest in arms control in the 1980s, FBIS regularly cited the policies of the Soviet politburo and the Soviet Defense Ministry favoring disarmament negotiations with the United States. The timeliness of FBIS could be embarassing: it relayed the news in 1975 that Cambodia had released the crew of the *Mayaguez* before the United States began its rescue operation. It is noteworthy that one of the more important recommendations of the 9/11 Commission was the need to create a regular organization for analyzing international news, in other words, recreating FBIS. This was achieved by the first director of national intelligence, John Negroponte, in 2005.

JAMES WOOLSEY (1993–1994)

President Clinton did not help the CIA with his successive appointments of Woolsey, Deutch, and Tenet as directors of central intelligence. In addition to these directors, Clinton also nominated national security advisor Anthony Lake, who had to withdraw from the nominating process in 1996 because of overwhelming opposition. Woolsey did considerable harm to the Agency, and in view of his hard line views and close ties to the Pentagon, he was a poor fit in Clinton's national security team. Clinton knew surprisingly little about the national security arena at the time of his election, and he knew virtually nothing about Woolsey. Clinton was close to naming career ambassador Thomas Pickering to the post of DCI, but at the last minute conservative Democrats on the Hill and Admiral William Crowe, former chairman of the Joint Chiefs of Staff, intervened to lobby for a Democratic neoconservative. Crowe suggested Woolsey, and the appointment was not a good one for the president or for Woolsey for that matter. The president-elect's press secretary, Dee Dee Myers, greeted Woolsey in their first meeting as "Admiral Woolsey," quite a promotion for someone who never rose above the rank of Army captain.[16]

The Clinton team was drawn to Woolsey because of his reputation as the "Republicans' favorite Democrat." In fact, Woolsey was an unreconstructed "cold warrior," which did not hurt him in the confirmation process on Capitol Hill, where he was confirmed unanimously in 1993. Within months, however, he antagonized key members of the Senate intelligence committee, particularly chairman Dennis DeConcini (D-Arizona), as well as important players in the White House and the chairman of the Office of Management and Budget, Leon Panetta. One of Panetta's senior staff officers commented on Woolsey's approach in dealing with OMB: "I've never seen a more graceless stonewall. . . ."[17] Said DeConcini, "Woolsey felt like he knew best, and nobody could tell him otherwise."[18]

One of Woolsey's major problems at the CIA was his management style, barricading himself behind closed doors, with little access for his top managers. He had no strategic vision for a post-cold war world and no ideas for reforming the intelligence community. He could have compensated for some or all of these limits if he had developed a political relationship with President Clinton, but he had never met the president before being nominated as CIA director and never forged a relationship with the White House. In 1994, when a Cessna aircraft crashed into the White House, some pundits observed the pilot was Woolsey and he was merely trying to get an appointment with the president. Woolsey and Secretary of Defense Les Aspin often complained to each other about their lack of access to the president.

Woolsey was an unusual choice for an administration seeking a new strategic role in the post-Soviet world. Like Gates, Woolsey had no new ideas for national security and encouraged a greater role for the secretary of defense in the intelligence community, which served to advanced the militarization of the intelligence process. During Woolsey's tenure as CIA director, the DoD gained a great deal of ground in exercising control over satellite reconnaissance activities, and under Woolsey's successor, John Deutch, the DoD gained complete control over the analysis of satellite imagery. Woolsey, however, did prevent the director of the DIA from designating himself the "Director of Military Intelligence," which would have weakened Woolsey's role as director of central intelligence. Ten years later, Secretary of Defense Rumsfeld created the post of undersecretary of defense for intelligence, which certainly trumped the modest step that DoD pursued to reduce Woolsey's authority as DCI.

The espionage activities of Aldrich Ames over a ten-year period cast a long shadow over Woolsey's stewardship and eventually caused his resignation. The White House lost confidence in Woolsey, and the new chief of the Senate Select Committee on Intelligence, Senator DeConcini, called for

Woolsey's resignation in 1994. Woolsey's response to the spying of Ames was the last straw for his opponents, particularly his unwillingness to fire or demote any of the eleven senior officers who were responsible for allowing such an incompetent alcoholic to not only move, but rise, through the CIA bureaucracy. Woolsey's response to the worst act of treachery in the history of the CIA was to give letters of reprimand to those individuals responsible for Ames' career, which meant that some of the retired officers were barred from taking on lucrative consulting contracts after they retired. These letters went to the major players in the CIA's operational culture over a period of three decades, including Clair George, the legendary director of covert operations; Gus Hathaway, the first chief of the Counterintelligence Center; and Burton Gerber, the former Soviet division chief who was considered one of the best DO spymasters. It was unbelievable that it took nearly a decade for the DO to identify an agent as slothful and careless as Ames, and that Woolsey would be so inept in handling the worst espionage scandal in the history of the CIA.

Woolsey's defense for not doing more than issuing bureaucratic reprimands was, "Sorry. That's not my way. And in my judgment, that's not the American way and it's not the CIA's way."[19] The chairman of the House intelligence committee, Dan Glickman (D-Kansas), remarked, "The question is whether the CIA has become no different from any other bureaucracy, if it has lost the vibrancy of its unique mission." The chairman of the Senate intelligence committee, DeConcini, was more harsh: "It's a very inadequate response to negligence in the biggest espionage case in the CIA's history." He concluded that it would take "dramatic reorganization to change the culture, the good old boys'club that protected this guy, promoted him, and gave him sensitive positions."[20] Ten years later, the same kinds of things could be said about Porter Goss, who covered up the CIA's accountability report on the Agency's failings prior to the 9/11 attacks. Like Goss a decade later, Woolsey saw the writing on the wall. On the day after Christmas, 1994, he called President Clinton, wrote a limp letter of resignation, and went sailing in the Caribbean. Woolsey remained angry about being dispatched, and in 1996, endorsed Senator Robert Dole for president.

JOHN DEUTCH (1995–1996)

Deutch became the first foreign-born director of the CIA, although it was not a job he pursued or even wanted. Deutch wanted to be secretary of defense, and failing that, to return to MIT and become its president. He feared correctly that serving as CIA director would end any chance to become a college president, particularly at an institution as prestigious as MIT. When Senator William

Cohen (R-Michigan) was selected to replace William Perry as secretary of defense in 1996, a disappointed Deutch immediately resigned from the CIA and returned to MIT. The fact that his resignation was surrounded by scandal, including the possible compromise of the CIA's most sensitive operational intelligence, ended any opportunity for a major position at MIT, completing his self-fulfilling prophecy.

Deutch's major contribution to the decline of the CIA and the weakening of the intelligence community was his decision in 1996 to establish the National Imagery and Mapping Agency (NIMA), which became the National Geospatial Intelligence Agency (NGA) in 2003. Mapping had always been done by the Pentagon's Defense Mapping Agency, but imagery had belonged to the CIA because of the sensitive nature of satellite imagery and the need for analysis of such imagery outside the policy bureaus of the U.S. government. In creating NIMA, Deutch abolished the Agency's Office of Imagery Analysis (OIA), which had done excellent monitoring of the various strategic arms control agreements, and the joint CIA–Pentagon's National Photographic Interpretation Center (NPIC), which had started as an Agency center in the 1950s, but became a joint activity in 1961. In losing both OIA and NPIC, the Agency lost imagery analysis as an agency function, despite its proud history during the Cuban missile crisis.

Former CIA director Helms wrote a letter to Deputy Secretary of State Strobe Talbott in 1996, warning the State Department that it had an important policy interest in questioning the move of imagery analysis to the DoD. "That big gorilla [DoD] controls enough assets," Helms wrote, "and needs no addition to its large Intelligence Community holdings. I watched for several years as the secretary of defense outgunned the secretary of state in White House meetings because he had more information sooner and in greater depth and I think State's position would be sounder if the CIA performed the service of 'common concern' as indicated in the National Security Act of 1947."[21] Helms was extremely sensitive to the need for objective intelligence analysis outside the policy community and was a participant in Agency efforts to challenge the worst-case analysis of the Pentagon's DIA, particularly during the Vietnam War. He recognized the risks in allowing the Pentagon sole authority in analyzing sensitive satellite photography central to decision making on military budgets and procurement, the likelihood of conflict, and the Soviet–American relationship. At a press conference in 1995, a skeptical questioner asked Deutch whether NIMA might not be the "next lemon of the decade, like the hide-bound NSA?"[22] Deutch tried to deflect the question by saying he thought it would be the "lemonade of the decade," but NIMA's failure to anticipate and monitor India's nuclear tests in 1998 and its role in supporting the bombing of the Chinese embassy in Belgrade in 1999 pointed to lemons, not lemonade.

Deutch was arguably the most irascible and unpopular DCI in the history of the Agency, with the possible exception of James Schlesinger, who lasted only several months. Since Deutch didn't want to be CIA director and refused Clinton's initial recruitment efforts, he sensed his strong bargaining position and demanded a position in the Cabinet in return for accepting Clinton's second offer. The president relented despite the unfortunate precedent of Casey's policy role on the Cabinet, where he pretended to be speaking for the Agency when he was actually speaking for himself.

Deutch's move from the Pentagon to the CIA was demoralizing to CIA leadership, and it opened the door to greater military influence at the Agency. He brought with him Nora Slatkin, an assistant secretary of the Navy, who immediately acquired the nickname of "Tora, Tora, Nora" because of her erratic and worst-case views on a variety of intelligence issues. Deutch brought other military aides with him to the CIA and even created the new position of associate director of central intelligence for military support, confirming the notion that the CIA's major task would be intelligence support to the warfighter. The increasingly inadequate job that the CIA did on terrorism and arms control can be ascribed in part to the preoccupation with support for the Pentagon, which lacked interest in both of these key strategic issues. Washington decision makers do not understand that military issues should not automatically trump all other issues in the intelligence community. Deutch inserted more high-level aides from outside the intelligence community than all previous CIA directors, which made for extremely bad blood between the office of the CIA director and the top managers of the directorates of intelligence and operations. They were glad to see him go, and there was much *shadenfreude* over the investigation of Deutch's security breeches that involved compromising the most sensitive black operations of the directorate of operations. Deutch had introduced sensitive intelligence to a home computer that had been used for accessing a variety of pornographic sites, but he blamed others in the household for the compromise, although he and his new wife were empty-nesters.

GEORGE TENET (1997–2004)

The most extroverted CIA director in the history of the Agency, George Tenet was the most popular. Open-faced and affable, he would slap backs and clutch arms; he liked off-color humor and laced his conversation with "good ol' boy" profanity. Tenet had health issues and a weight problem, but he liked good food and drink, and although a heart condition kept him from smoking, he often had one of his favorite cigars unlit in his mouth. He often ate in the CIA cafeteria and, like a good politician, he never seemed to forget a name. I attend few Georgetown University basketball games at the Verizon Center in Washington, but I never attended one where Tenet was not at courtside with no sign of the director's usual security detail, one arm around the president of the university and the other arm gesticulating about the outstanding play of one Hoya or another. His unusual seven-year tenure at the CIA (only Allen Dulles served longer) ended the revolving door at the CIA headquarters building in Langley, Virginia, that saw four directors in seven years. At the outset, he ended a period of genuine bureaucratic turbulence, but he left the Agency in the worst condition of its existence, and he opened the door to a successor, Representative Porter Goss (R-Florida), who tried to make the CIA the personal intelligence agency of the White House and the Pentagon. Now, it is up to a four-star general officer, Michael Hayden, who broke laws at the NSA in authorizing warrantless eavesdropping of American citizens, to right this terribly slacken ship.

It probably didn't hurt Tenet's image with rank-and-file employees that his role model for the position of DCI was Richard Helms, who had been a career officer in the DO and a smooth dog who was at ease in the halls of Congress and on the tennis courts of the old-line Columbia Country Club. On his first day at work, Tenet moved the oil portrait of Helms in the main floor lobby to his plush wood-paneled office on the seventh floor: it was Helms who described Tenet's "outgoingness" as a "genuine gift."[23] But Helms was also known to many as one who manipulated intelligence on the North Vietnamese and the Viet Cong in order not to wear out his welcome in the White House of President Johnson and was fined for lying to Congress about the CIA's role in the coup in Chile, which led to the death of a democratically elected leader, Salvador Allende. In an obvious political gesture to gain leverage with a Republican administration, Tenet (a registered Democrat) renamed the headquarters building the Bush Intelligence Center, after the former director, George H. W. Bush, who headed the Marble Palace for less than a year but left no lasting footprints. It didn't hurt Tenet to follow one of the most disliked directors in CIA's history—John Deutch—and precede arguably the most incompetent—Porter Goss.

Tenet did more harm to the CIA than any director in its history with the possible exception of Bill Casey. He was the CIA's boss during a series of major intelligence failures: the failure to anticipate and monitor Indian nuclear testing in 1998; the failure to anticipate al Qaeda terrorist attacks on the U.S. homeland on 9/11; and the architect of tailored intelligence used to justify a costly and unnecessary war against Iraq in 2003. After the Indian failure, Tenet told the chairman of the Senate intelligence committee, Senator Shelby (R-Alabama) the CIA could no longer verify the Comprehensive Test Ban Treaty, which angered the scientists and technicians who created the CIA's excellent monitoring system for strategic weapons. This led to the defeat of the CTBT in the Senate's ratification process. After the 9/11 failure that took more lives than the 1941 Japanese attacks on Pearl Harbor, he denied any failure. And in response to President Bush's demand for intelligence to support the case for war in Iraq, Tenet responded that it would be a "slam dunk" to provide the White House with intelligence making the case for war. He had developed a close personal relationship with the president and was thankful for Bush's decision to stick with President Clinton's intelligence chief. As a result, Tenet seemed determined to respond to every presidential demand, even if it meant the corruption of the intelligence process.

Tenet's popularity demonstrated the importance of personality and style over substance and integrity. He roamed the halls of the CIA headquarters without the security officials who were always beside Bob Gates; many employees were seduced by his charm. He also tried to charm the senior members of the national security bureaucracy with insider tales of espionage and overseas operations, but was far less successful. Secretary of Defense Rumsfeld and Secretary of State Powell were simply uninterested and never took Tenet seriously. He pandered to the policy whims of the Bush administration and was unwilling to tell truth to power, which remains the major mission of the CIA chief. His unwillingness to document the Bush administration's lack of interest in intelligence warnings on terrorism and his politicization of intelligence on Iraqi WMD led directly to the President's Freedom Award, the highest honor that can be bestowed on a civilian in the federal government. General Tommy Franks and Ambassador Paul Bremer, who share much of the responsibility for the Iraqi failure, were Tenet's corecipients that shameful day in the White House. As for Tenet, his two-word epitaph will always remain "slam dunk," promising that intelligence would be politicized to suit the policy whims of the Bush administration.

Tenet and McLaughlin also actively participated in drafting the speech Secretary of State Powell gave to the UN that contained dozens of false assertions about Iraqi WMD and the so-called "sinister nexus" between Iraq and the al Qaeda organization. The speech was designed as the official and authoritative case for war, and it was written over a three-day period at the CIA. The CIA was directly responsible for the most ludicrous materials and charges in a speech that was designed to scare the international community in supporting U.S. use of force in Iraq. The major European intelligence services were appalled by the distortions in the speech, although the *Washington Post* and many major U.S. newspapers fell for it. Never in the history of the CIA had senior Agency leaders taken part in the drafting of a major statement on such a sensitive issue involving war and peace. "Sham dunk" was closer to the truth for this exercise.

Tenet's role in providing misinformation to the White House on Iraqi WMD has been comprehensively and authoritatively recorded in the reports of the Robb-Silberman Committee, the House Permanent Select Committee on Intelligence, and the Senate Select Committee for Intelligence. His memoir conceded that the October 2002 NIE on Iraqi WMD was flawed, which was a classic understatement, but a far cry from his defense of the NIE at Georgetown University in 2004. The Congressional reports led directly to Tenet's decision to resign in June 2004 because he preferred not to spend his days explaining his actions to a series of Congressional committees. Like most defeated bureaucrats, he cited family reasons for his departure on July 11, which marked his seventh anniversary as CIA director.

Hans Blix, the chief UN inspector for WMD in Iraq, was referring to Tenet when he recounted that he had never seen a situation where the United States had 100 percent certainty there were WMD in Iraq and 0 percent knowledge about such weapons. Blix's UN commission and Mohamed El Baradei's IAEA had inspected thirteen major "facilities of concern" from various US and British reports and found no signs of weapons or weapons-making. The IAEA also publicly exposed the Niger fabrications and found the aluminum tubes poor candidates for centrifuges. Checking supposed sites for manufacturing mobile labs, Blix's teams debunked Curveball's tall tale that was a major item in Powell's UN speech. Following the war, Tenet sent David Kay to Iraq with more than 1,500 weapons technicians and intelligence experts (the Iraq Survey Group) to locate WMD. Kay, who fully expected to find significant caches of WMD, soon realized that there was nothing to find. When he tried to inform the CIA and official Washington, he ran into roadblocks, describing an "absolutely closed mind" in the Bush administration.[24] In December 2003, he flew back to Washington and met with Tenet and McLaughlin. "I couldn't budge John, and so I couldn't budge George," Kay concluded; he resigned and told the Congress there had been no WMD threat.

Tenet named Charles Duelfer, like Kay a senior UN inspector from the 1990s, to take over the hunt for arms. Duelfer arrived in Iraq in February 2004 and was in Baghdad when Tenet made a secret trip there to address the Iraq Survey Group at its headquarters on the lakeside Perfume Palace. According to veteran inspector Rod Barton, an Australian biologist, Tenet sounded more like a football coach than a spymaster. "Are we 85 percent done?" the CIA chief demanded.[25] The arms hunters knew what the boss wanted and shouted, "No!" Tenet responded, "Let me hear it again," and they shouted "No!" once again. Duelfer, like Kay, ignored the pressure from Washington and London and concluded weapons did not exist.

Unlike Kay, however, Duelfer was careful not to offend his CIA boss before presenting his final report. CIA members of the Iraq Survey Group pressured Duelfer not to discredit Curveball's clandestine reporting on the so-called mobile biological weapons laboratories. Therefore, in March 2004, when Duelfer presented his interim report to the U.S. Congress, there was no mention of the mobile labs and the issue of the aluminum tubes was said to be still under study. The White House and the CIA didn't want any statements from the Iraq Survey Group to undermine the president's case for war during the election campaign, and President Bush stuck to WMD as the case for war against Iraq in his debate appearances with Senator Kerry (D-Massachusetts). Duelfer's 1,000-page final report concluded that Saddam Hussein had disarmed soon after Desert Storm in 1991.

Prior to the Iraq War, Tenet played another role in misusing intelligence for policy purposes. In January 1997, when Tenet was serving as acting director, he denied that the CIA withheld relevant information regarding chemical exposures to U.S. forces during Desert Storm in 1991. In fact, the CIA had conclusive intelligence in 1986 that chemical weapons were routinely stored at the Khamisiyah weapons depot, which was destroyed by American forces during the Gulf War. NSC counterterrorist specialist Richard Clarke told me Tenet guaranteed, to the White House in 1998, that there was unambiguous intelligence proving that a pharmaceutical plant in Sudan was making lethal chemicals. But the CIA's clandestine corps knew its search of the Al Shifa plant was inconclusive and wanted additional inquiries. Moreover, subsequent imagery of the plant, which was released by the Pentagon, showed no evidence of special security measures associated with chemical weapons production facilities.

Just as Gates had surrendered important areas of military intelligence collection and analysis to the Pentagon, Tenet allowed Secretary of Defense Rumsfeld to enhance the authority of the Pentagon in conducting covert actions abroad. Although Executive Order 12333 of December 1981 assigns primacy to the CIA in the area of covert action, Tenet agreed to Rumsfeld's assignment of special operations forces to covert action in the global war on terrorism. Tenet also made no attempt to block Rumsfeld's creation in 2003 of an undersecretary of defense for intelligence, which gave the Pentagon leadership over all intelligence agencies housed in the DoD. Deutch tried to get his former deputy to fight this maneuver on the Hill, but Tenet did not want to deal with Rumsfeld's bureaucratic clout. Deutch believed that Tenet would have had important allies to block Rumsfeld's maneuver in view of the Aspin-Brown study of 1996 and the Scowcroft Commission draft report of 2001 that urged greater authority for the DCI over major "national" intelligence agencies. Nor did Tenet try to stop Rumsfeld's creation of the Office of Special Plans that produced disinformation to support the case for war. Finally, Tenet ignored the laws of the land and stopped declassification of intelligence materials needed by the State Department for its authoritative series on "Foreign Relations of the United States." He also reversed the successes of his immediate predecessor, Deutch, in declassifying historic information on covert action.

PORTER GOSS (2004–2006)

Goss will be known as the last director of central intelligence and the first director of the CIA in the postreform era. Like Casey, he was far too partisan to be taken seriously as a CIA director. Goss surrounded himself at CIA headquarters with four members of his congressional staff who were primarily interested in conducting a witch hunt of CIA officials unwilling to do the dirty business of politicization for the Bush administration. Goss' last official act in this regard was orchestrating the leak investigation within the Agency to find the source or sources for the *Washington Post's* Pulitzer-prize winning pieces on CIA's secret prisons in Eastern Europe and the outrageous rendition of a German citizen, Khalid al-Masri, to Afghanistan. He finally frogmarched Mary McCarthy out of the building in April 2006, although she had no knowledge of the special collection that dealt with the secret prisons. Her greatest offense may have been modest campaign contributions to Senator Kerry.

There were no limits to Goss' partisanship, which should have disqualified him from consideration for the CIA position and led to seventeen votes against him in the confirmation process, the second most votes against any CIA director. Only Gates attracted more opposition from the Senate intelligence committee. Goss was particularly critical of Senator Kerry's campaign for the presidency in 2004, citing Kerry's support for cutting the intelligence budget in the 1990s. Goss never mentioned his own cosponsorship of a measure in 1995 that called for cutting CIA personnel by 20 percent over a five-year period. Former CIA director Turner branded Goss the worst appointment ever made to the position of CIA director, although Casey shouldn't be tossed aside so easily.[26] Before being named to head the CIA, Goss served for eight terms in the House of Representatives and eventually became chairman of the House intelligence committee, where he branded himself as an "advocate" for the CIA. As "advocate," he made no attempt to learn anything about the intelligence failures that preceded the 9/11 intelligence failures and the run-up to the Iraq War. He demonstrated no interest whatsoever in the White House's outing of Valerie Plame, although from 1962 to 1971, he too worked as a clandestine officer at the CIA, occupying several low-ranking DO positions in Latin America.

Before he was named CIA director, Goss indicated he wanted to lead the Agency in a Republican administration; after he was named director, he informed the employees of his Agency of the importance of serving the president and his policies. He took no actions after his appointment to disappoint his Republican supporters, including the cover-up of the Inspector General's 9/11 accountability report and the suppression of unclassified information that would embarrass the CIA in any way. Just as Woolsey moved to cover-up the senior officials who allowed Ames to spy for the Soviets and the Russians for nearly a decade, Goss refused to establish an accountability board, as recommended by the CIA's Inspector General (IG), to judge the poor performances singled out in the IG's inspection of the 9/11 intelligence failure. Goss would not even permit an unclassified version of the report to be issued, despite calls from the Congress and the families of the 9/11 victims for such an accounting.

In addition to the cover-up of the IG's 9/11 accountability report, Goss reversed himself on the important issue of whistle-blower protection for members of the intelligence community. In 1998, as the chairman of the House intelligence committee, Goss was a leading advocate for passage of the Intelligence Community Whistle-blower Protection Act. The bill was largely gutted by members of the committee, including the right of the CIA director to counsel CIA whistle-blowers on how to contact the intelligence committees "in accordance with appropriate security practices." Thus, the CIA director was given veto power over the ability of CIA employees to contact the oversight committees, which probably explains why active and retired CIA officers must leak evidence of CIA secret prisons and extraordinary renditions to journalists, rather than take such information to Congressional oversight committees.

Like Woolsey, Goss barricaded himself in his seventh-floor executive suite, surrounded by four former staffers from the House intelligence committee, who were known as the "Gosslings" or, far less benign, "Hitler youth."[27] Goss typically worked a congressman's schedule, arriving at the CIA late Monday or early Tuesday and leaving for his farm in Virginia late Thursday or early Friday. The CIA's public affairs office evolved from a rather open office under Deutch to a closed operation run by a political apparatchik from the Bush-Cheney campaign staff, Jennifer Millerwise Dyck, who worked for Goss on the House intelligence committee. Senior CIA analysts, who were not undercover, lost the ability to present papers to academic meetings, and retired operatives had their manuscripts gutted by a politicized public affairs office reviewing them for clearance. Goss returned the Agency to the bad old days of the cold war when the CIA believed that it was not accountable to the country in any way. Goss gave no interviews; the Freedom of Information Act was ignored; and the security office conducted leak investigations that were witch hunts, never finding anyone actually responsible for leaks of information on secret prisons and the conduct of torture and abuse.

Goss' handpicked executive secretary, Kyle "Dusty" Foggo, a CIA logistical expert who had no professional background for the third highest position at the CIA, had to resign for steering millions of dollars in Agency contracts to a lifelong friend, Brent Wilkes, one of the individuals who bribed former congressman Randall "Duke" Cunningham. Cunningham is currently serving an eight-year sentence on corruption charges. Foggo was reminiscent of Milo Minderbender in Joseph Heller's "Catch 22." Minderbender turned a black market sideline into a global corporation. Since the FBI arrived at CIA headquarters and padlocked Foggo's office, we must assume that the government now holds a wealth of incriminating documents on Agency contracts for operatives in Iraq and elsewhere. With the exception of the FBI's role in the Ames spy scandal, there is no other example of an FBI presence in the CIA for a criminal investigation. Foggo was indicted in May 2007 for providing sensitive intelligence documents to Wilkes in order to garner Agency contracts, and both men face numerous charges of fraud, bribery, and money laundering. Foggo would have been indicted even earlier, but the U.S. attorney, who was investigating the matter, Carol Lam, was abruptly fired by the Bush administration in February 2007, several days after trying to indict Foggo.

Goss had a mandate to bring the CIA under his control and to make sure that a few heads rolled in the process. To his credit, he did remove some of the key Tenet appointments responsible for the flawed intelligence in the run-up to the Iraq War. The deputy director for CIA, McLaughlin, was the first to go, and this was a step in the right direction. McLaughlin was a careerist who helped to cover up the politicization of intelligence in the 1980s for Gates, and ignored the warnings about flawed intelligence on Iraq that found their way into Powell's UN speech. David Kay, the chief U.S. weapons inspector in Iraq, considered McLaughlin the "real villain at CIA" regarding politicized intelligence, clinging stubbornly to the belief that Iraq had mobile biological weapons labs and that the disputed aluminum tubes could only be for the manufacture of nuclear weapons. When Kay reported to McLaughlin that Saddam Hussein had no chemical or biological weapons, McLaughlin replied, "Don't tell anyone this. This could be upsetting. Be very careful. We can't let this out until we're sure."[28]

Several additional Tenet cronies, particularly John Moseman and Mark Lowenthal, saw the writing on the wall and voluntarily left the Agency. The cronies who would not budge, such as the executive director Buzzy Krongard, who had no background or understanding of intelligence issues, were pushed out, and the deputy director of intelligence, Jami A. Miscik, who was incompetent, was also dispatched. Miscik was responsible for distributing flawed intelligence to the policy community, although the senior analysts of the intelligence directorate knew that it was tainted or unsubstantiated or both. Unfortunately, Goss removed Miscik for not moving quickly enough in politicizing the intelligence on Iraq, and not for her incompetence.

There were many resignations and forced retirements for individuals who were needed at the CIA and whose only flaw was that they had served under Tenet. There was extreme turbulence in the directorate of operations, which already lacked the seniority and expertise to train and mentor the unprecedentedly large number of new recruits. The top two members of the DO, Steve Kappes and Michael Sulick, both highly respected, resigned over the arrogance of the "Gosslings" and Kappes' replacement, Robert Richer, lasted less than a year before bidding goodbye. (Kappes soon returned to become CIA deputy director under General Hayden and Sulick returned to lead the Nation Clandestine Service.) Richer told the members of the Senate intelligence committee that he simply lost confidence in Goss' leadership.[29] Senior counterterrorism officials also left, including the veteran Mary Margaret Graham, who immediately received a high-level position for the intelligence czar Negroponte. A former director of operations, John MacGaffin, argued that Goss lacked "a clear view for the future" and, as a result, senior leadership of the clandestine corps "does not believe the Agency is organized and heading in a direction, let alone the right direction."[30] The Agency's official response is that it is attracting record high numbers of applicants for the CIA, but this merely points to the greater problem of the lack of senior officials to train and monitor the new recruits. The overwhelming majority of Agency operatives and intelligence analysts have less than five years' experience in their particular areas of expertise.

Many senior DO officers left the CIA in Goss's first several months at the Agency, representing a prima facie case for Goss' dismissal from the outset. After all, if he was responsible for much of the turbulence in the National Clandestine Service, then how can it be said that he was capable of bringing stability and coherence to an agency that is crucial to the so-called war against terrorism? Some of the senior DO officers who left were actually promoted by Goss in the director's first year. The ranking Democratic member of the House intelligence committee, Jane Harman, observed that "hundreds of years of leadership and experience have walked out the door in the last year, and more senior people are making critical career decisions as we speak."[31] Seniority and experience are particularly crucial at an intelligence agency because there are no manuals or guidebooks to train new operators and analysts; there is simply a folk tradition of the grayer members of the corps inducting and training the rookies.

The creation of a DNI in December 2004 responsible for the entire intelligence community meant that Goss' only responsibility was directing the CIA. Goss was never known for having a heavy workload as a representative on the Hill, and he didn't reveal much energy as director of the CIA. He was uncomfortable with foreign liaison representatives and held few meetings with the very individuals who provide the United States with the most important intelligence on terrorist operations overseas. He was not comfortable dealing with his own senior staff and relied on his former Hill staffers, who accompanied him from his Hill office, and resigned en masse when Goss left. There was bad blood from the beginning when Agency sources leaked information from the personnel records of one of these staffers, dealing with a shoplifting charge near Agency headquarters, that prevented his appointment as Executive Officer on the director's staff.

GENERAL MICHAEL HAYDEN (2006-PRESENT)

General Michael Hayden was named in May 2006 to replace Goss and he is clearly following in the footsteps of his predecessor to politicize the CIA. In September 2007, he began an unprecedented investigation of the Office of the Inspector General, which has been critical of the CIA's renditions and interrogations programs. Whereas Goss targeted and fired an IG officer, Mary McCarthy, who was working on renditions issues, Hayden has targeted the IG himself, John Helgerson, who has recommended the creation of "accountability boards" for CIA officers involved in 9/11 intelligence failures, torture and abuse, and illegal renditions. Helgerson was appointed by the president in 2002 and cannot be fired by the CIA director, but at the very least Hayden is trying to get the office of the IG to pull its punches on these damaging investigations. Unless the congressional oversight chairmen come to Helgerson's defense, it will be very difficult for the IG's office to do its job.

Hayden is the third general officer to serve as director of the CIA in the past fifty-five years, and the first since President Carter named Rear Admiral Stansfield Turner in 1977. The former director of the NSA and the former deputy director of national intelligence, Hayden immediately charmed the employees of the CIA by telling them soon after his confirmation that "amateur hour" at the CIA was over. But Hayden entered the CIA under a cloud, because as NSA director he approved the warrantless eavesdropping campaign that began after 9/11. This campaign violated the FISA Act of 1978 and the Fourth Amendment of the Constitution that prohibits unlawful seizures and searches. At the National Press Club in January 2006, Hayden's defense of warrantless eavesdropping revealed a stunning lack of understanding of the Fourth Amendment that protects all Americans against "unreasonable searches and seizures." He strongly argued that the amendment did not stipulate the importance of "probable cause," which of course it does.[32] He also conceded that he relied on advice from White House lawyers and never considered consulting the legal staff of NSA. Nevertheless, Hayden convinced many Democratic members of the Senate that the eavesdropping campaign would have been even worse if he had not been the head of the NSA during the period. Democrats and Republicans alike took his remarks at face value.

In taking over a thoroughly demoralized CIA, Hayden symbolizes the steady militarization of the intelligence community where general officers now direct those agencies that account for nearly 90 percent of the intelligence budget. Although his career has not been associated with Secretary of Defense Gates, it will be difficult for a general officer to ignore the demands and perhaps the dictates of a strong-willed secretary of defense and a bureaucratically powerful undersecretary of defense for intelligence. Most of the wrangling over the intelligence reorganization act of December 2004 was to make sure that the Pentagon did not lose any of its considerable influence over the intelligence community. Hayden's appointment is one more indication that the Pentagon has very little to worry about. Moreover, his defense of warrantless eavesdropping at NSA and the right of torture and abuse for CIA interrogators should give great pause to political conservatives and civil libertarians. Hayden was so confident of the lack of genuine Congressional oversight that he named John Rizzo as the CIA's general counsel. Rizzo had been the Agency's leading lawyer in pursuing legal justification for torture and abuse of terrorist suspects, and the policy of extraordinary renditions. Fortunately, Senator Wyden blocked the confirmation of Rizzo, who withdrew his nomination in September 2007. Hayden's lack of experience in strategic intelligence and clandestine collection of human intelligence should also give pause to members of the Congressional intelligence committees. Finally, Hayden's multibillion-dollar modernization program at NSA, known as Trailblazer, which ran huge cost overruns and is widely considered to be a huge failure, should have attracted attention during his confirmation process, but it inexplicably failed to do so.

In any event, Hayden promises to be a much weaker CIA director than his predecessors. He is the first CIA director who enters the headquarters building without the title of director of central intelligence since Rear Admiral Roscoe Hillenkoetter in 1947. He will have to share authority over clandestine collection of intelligence and even covert actions with the Pentagon, where Rumsfeld restructured the intelligence bureaucracy and carved out a significant role for clandestine operations. Under the authority to "prepare the battlefield," the Pentagon now conducts counterterrorism operations in Iraq,

Afghanistan, Iran, Somalia, and other foreign countries without the scrutiny of the intelligence oversight committees. The undersecretary of defense for intelligence has veto power over the ability of the DNI to transfer personnel from individual intelligence agencies into joint centers or other agencies in order to advance the integration of the military and civilian intelligence agencies. This power grab will make it more difficult for both the DNI and CIA director Hayden to advance the integration of the intelligence community and to make intelligence more responsive to the changing needs of policymakers.

The key to managing the CIA is based on the integrity and competence of the director and his senior management. CIA director Helms once testified the United States had to trust that "honorable men" were working inside America's intelligence services. He uttered that remark during his testimony in 1973 to the Senate on the CIA's involvement in Chile, when he perjured himself regarding the CIA's role in subverting the Chilean government. He paid a fine of $2,000; so much for honorable men! It would suffice if individual integrity was enough, but of course it isn't. An intelligence chief and the Agency's senior leaders must be tough, candid, and honest; they must be willing to tell truth to power or step aside. One of the first CIA directors, Walter Bedell Smith, had these qualities; John McCone and William Colby were also willing to stick their necks out to defend unpopular positions. Admiral Turner wanted to clean up the Agency on behalf of President Jimmy Carter. They would not have lent themselves to the kind of politicization of intelligence that occurred with Soviet issues in the 1980s or the run-up to the Iraq War.

Too many CIA directors, particularly in the recent past, have not had these qualities, and as a result, the Agency has been in the hands of careerists and syncophants. Helms and Tenet were unwilling to contradict the policy interests of the White House; both lied to the Congress. Casey and Gates were dedicated to providing the Reagan administration with the intelligence needed to support presidential policy and to defeat the détente policies of Secretaries of State Shultz and Baker. Webster didn't have the energy to manage the Agency, let alone the intelligence community; Woolsey didn't know the first thing about taking disciplinary actions to clean up a corrupt Agency. Deutch wanted to be secretary of defense and not director of central intelligence. Goss, a former Agency operative who had chaired the House intelligence committee, was responsible for a stewardship of the Agency that had witnessed the greatest personnel turbulence in its history. His executive secretary was forced to resign, and the FBI searched his office for evidence of criminal transgression. General Hayden broke the Fourth Amendment against illegal searches and seizures during his tenure at NSA, and actively lobbied on the Hill to permit CIA interrogators to torture and abuse suspected terrorists. Record numbers of senior officers are resigning and retiring, and many of them have told members of the Senate intelligence committee they have lost confidence in the CIA's leadership.

The Congressional oversight committees have never examined the dearth of talent among the stewards of the CIA over the past twenty-five years. Two of these directors have come from Capitol Hill (Goss and Tenet), and both were major players in the politicization of intelligence. The political processes of the Hill are probably not the best training ground for senior CIA positions. The Hill is an institution of compromise and even caprice; the CIA relies on principled positions and the ability to tell truth to power. Two more directors (Casey and Gates) had professional intelligence backgrounds, but they were prone to politicize intelligence. Two directors had excellent experience in the policy community (Woolsey and Deutch), but seemed uninterested in the professional problems of the CIA and the intelligence community and were extremely unpopular in the CIA headquarters building and the corridors of the Congress. Judge Webster seemed to have the judicious personality and the professional experience to lead the Agency, but lacked the stamina and focus that the job demands. The current director, General Hayden, remains difficult to judge, but his military background is not suited to the strategic and analytical demands of the intelligence community. Moreover, his release of the so-called "family jewels" is a reminder that the CIA's current policies of secret prisons and extraordinary renditions points to an Agency that still cannot find its moral compass. There probably is no perfect resume to suggest suitability for the role of CIA director, but perhaps if George Kennan had accepted the DCI position he was offered in the 1950s, or if President Clinton had followed up on his instincts to name Ambassador Thomas Pickering to the position in the early 1990s, the CIA would have had the strategic and analytical leader that it requires.

It is particularly unfortunate that the CIA is bleeding such talent at a time when intelligence collection and analysis are the strategic keys to dealing with the problem of terrorism. The loss of experienced personnel presents a prima facie case for starting over at the CIA. It appears that the "culture of secrecy" has blurred the judgment of many CIA leaders and the tainted intelligence of the run-up to the Iraq War is only the latest example of the institutional misuse of intelligence. As long as the intelligence oversight committees remain in the hands of timid chairmen who are trying to protect the reputation of the president and his administration and are unwilling to roil political waters, there will be no major change at the CIA. The Agency can be organized and reorganized as many times as the deck chairs on the *Titanic* can be rearranged, but without a stable and senior leadership it will continue to flounder.

13

What Needs To Be Done?

What the CIA should be, what it should do, and what it should prepare to do are less clear than at any time since the beginning of the cold war. Throughout the cold war, the need to count and characterize Soviet weapons systems and to find indications of a surprise Soviet attack focused the efforts of the CIA. These issues disappeared with the collapse of the Berlin Wall in 1989, the Warsaw Pact in 1990, and the Soviet Union in 1991. Now, the CIA must deal with the motivation and mindset of terrorist organizations that have left the Agency in an operational quandary and an analytical void. The lack of strategic warning for the 9/11 terrorist attacks and the misuse of intelligence to provide the Bush administration with its case to go to war against Iraq exposed serious systemic problems that the 9/11 Commission and the Intelligence Reform Act of 2004 failed to solve.

There should have been major reform of the intelligence community with the end of the cold war, but there was none. Senator David Boren and Representative David McCurdy, both Democrats from Oklahoma, made attempts in 1992 and 1994 to reform the Agency, but there was great resistance from Republicans who were under the influence of the Pentagon, and there was no support from their Democratic colleagues. The intelligence failures that contributed to the 9/11 attacks created another opportunity for reform, but the flawed thinking of the 9/11 Commission, the Congressional rush to judgment, and unwise pressures from the families of the 9/11 victims led to changes that made a bad situation worse. The creation of a new bureaucracy under a DNI beholden to the White House led to a more centralized system of intelligence that stifles creative thinking and runs the risk of more politicized intelligence. The appointment of a national intelligence czar, John Negroponte, who covered up sensitive intelligence in Central America in the 1980s and was unwilling to tell the truth to power, was a step in the wrong direction. Replacing Negroponte in 2006 with a retired general officer does not augur well for rebuilding strategic intelligence and guaranteeing independent intelligence.

In the wake of the CIA failure to even imagine a terrorist attack in the United States, Tim Weiner of *The New York Times* asked, "What will the nation's intelligence services have to change to fight this war? The short answer is: almost everything."[1] But the congressional and political critics outside the intelligence community simply have no idea of the decline and despair within the CIA that has led to a major deterioration in the ability to prepare strategic intelligence and to inform the policy community. There is no consensus whatsoever on what is needed to reform the world of intelligence. No one has taken on the need to demilitarize the intelligence community and to reform covert operations; no one has undertaken the need to resolve key turf issues and ensure the sharing of intelligence. The Congress is an unlikely source for conducting such a revolution; its modus operandi calls for throwing money at problems, but the needed reforms have nothing to do with additional funds. There has never been a time in the nation's history when so much money has been spent on intelligence with so little accountability and so few results.

Although the 9/11 Commission had a straightforward vision—the creation of a DNI to enforce bureaucratic cooperation and to attract skilled personnel to the community—it had a limited understanding of the hows and whys of the community, and gave too much attention to the organization of the community as opposed to the personnel problems. One of the lessons of my own experience at the CIA and INR is that people make the intelligence system work and the structure itself has much less to do with providing strategic intelligence. The Commission lobbied for a lean structure for the office of the DNI, but the Intelligence Reform Act of December 2004 permitted the creation of a new office that has a principal deputy director, four deputy directors, three associate directors, and no fewer than nineteen assistant deputy directors. Moreover, the DNI lacked the bureaucratic clout to challenge the Pentagon's ontrol of key intelligence agencies. At the same time, the failure of the Department of Homeland Security to create a central repository to fill the collection gaps between domestic and international terrorist threats leaves the major problem exposed by 9/11—the lack of centralized collection and competitive analysis for international and domestic terrorism.

The position of the DNI was fundamentally weakened from the outset when the first director, Negroponte, lobbied to become the daily briefer of the president. Thus, Negroponte ensured that he would have little time to conceptualize and implement the strategic reforms that were needed. The focus on providing current intelligence to the White House works against providing strategic intelligence to policymakers. Preoccupying the DNI with current intelligence will drive out all of the more important problems that he should confront, including demilitarization of the intelligence community, intelligence sharing, and creating an elite corps of strategic analysts. The enormous time devoted to briefings of the president would be better spent informing high-level staff members of the NSC, as well as assistant secretaries at State and Defense, who are best positioned to insert timely and trenchant intelligence into the policy machinery of the national security system. Negroponte left the position of DNI after two years on the job, without effecting any real change. The current DNI, Admiral Mike McConnell, has less understanding of strategic intelligence than Negroponte, and will need even greater time to prepare for daily briefings at the White House. He has already complained publicly about his 16-hour days dominated by the briefing process. His appointment of Steve Kaplan to be director of the National Intelligence Council suggests business as usual. Kaplan was a leading politicizer of intelligence for Casey and Gates in the 1980s.

The challenge of intelligence reform would have been better served if the various reports that addressed the flaws of the CIA had been blended at some stage to make a coherent case for change. The 9/11 Commission (that addressed the mistakes of the intelligence community prior to 9/11), the Commission on the Intelligence Capabilities of the United States Regarding Weapons of Mass Destruction (that outlined the poor "tradecraft" of CIA's directorate of intelligence), and the CIA Inspector General's report on 9/11 (that recorded the issue of responsibility and accountability for 9/11) went about their tasks separately and failed to pool their knowledge and to connect the dots.

THE CENTRAL PROBLEMS FACING THE CIA AND THE INTELLIGENCE COMMUNITY

The serious problems that need to be addressed include the militarization of the intelligence community, which must be reversed; the absence of congressional oversight over a flawed intelligence product, which must be ended; the illegal actions of the National Clandestine Service, which must be stopped; and the seeming inability of the CIA to tell truth to power, which finds the Agency without a moral compass.

Demilitarizing the Intelligence Community

The Bush administration boasted of a "marriage" between the Pentagon and the CIA, which indicates its support for an intelligence community subordinated to Pentagon priorities. After all, the Department of Defense is the chief operating officer of the $50 billion intelligence industry. The Pentagon controls more than 80 percent of the intelligence budget and more than 85 percent of all intelligence personnel. Most collection requirements flow from the Pentagon, and deference within the policy and Congressional communities for "support for the warfighter" has evevated tactical military considerations over strategic geopolitical considerations. The Pentagon has moved into the fields of clandestine collection and covert operations, without the constraints of oversight that limit the undercover activities of the intelligence community. Former secretary of defense Rumsfeld dispatched intelligence teams overseas, often without the knowledge of U.S. ambassadors and CIA station chiefs, to gather intelligence for military and counterterrorist operations. Special operations forces are active in Iran without any oversight constraints from the Congress. Finally, there are major risks in the military domination of the important field of satellite imagery that is used to critique the defense budget, to gauge the likelihood of military conflict in the Third World, and to verify and monitor arms control agreements.

In the past, CIA analysis served to contradict the worst-case analysis of the Pentagon. CIA imagery analysis determined there was no bomber gap between the Soviet Union and the United States in the 1950s and no missile gap in the 1960s. President Eisenhower wisely accepted CIA analysis and avoided an unnecessary round of increased defense spending in the 1950s, but President Kennedy ignored the CIA analysis in the 1960s for political reasons and initiated an unnecessary round in the strategic arms race. In the late 1960s, CIA analysts battled policy agencies on other sensitive issues related to arms control and disarmament. When they demonstrated that Soviet surface-to-air missiles could not be upgraded to an antiballistic missile defense, the result was the ABM treaty of 1972. In the same period, CIA analysts also maintained correctly that the Soviet SS-9 ICBM was not MIRVed and therefore could not threaten America's ICBM force. This analysis, which contradicted the assessment of Nixon's secretary of defense, Melvin Laird, opened the way to the first strategic arms treaty, SALT I, in 1972.

One of the best examples of the dangers of entrusting satellite collection and imagery analysis to the Pentagon took place during the Persian Gulf War in 1991. Colin L. Powell's memoir, *An American Journey*, revealed that during Operation Desert Storm, General Norman Schwarzkopf claimed a smart bomb destroyed four Iraqi Scud missile launchers. Intelligence imagery showed that it had actually destroyed four Jordanian fuel tanks. General Schwarzkopf's intelligence officers would not tell him he was wrong, nor would General Powell, who concluded that preserving General Schwarzkopf's "equanimity" was more important than the truth. This type of excessive military bias and respect for the chain of command was one of the primary reasons for creating an independent CIA in 1947 outside of the policy process, removed from the Pentagon's emphasis on worst-case analysis and exaggeration of the threat. The military's willingness to suppress sensitive intelligence is a threat to American national security policy.

Another example of the Pentagon's lack of interest in strategic intelligence, particularly dealing with arms control and disarmament, occurred in 1998, when the National Geospatial Intelligence Agency failed to monitor five Indian nuclear tests. This intelligence failure led CIA director Tenet to tell Congress the CIA could not monitor the Comprehensive Test Ban Treaty and, as a result, the Senate failed to ratify the treaty. In piecing together the reasons for the intelligence failure, it was learned that the Pentagon had placed a low priority on satellite collection of intelligence against India because the military was not concerned with threats from South Asia and issues that would support an arms control agreement.

The major technical collection agencies, the NSA (which intercepts signals and communications and is essential to strategic warning), the NRO (which designs and launches spy satellites), and the NGIA (which interprets satellite imagery) must be taken from the Pentagon and transferred to a new office that reports to the DNI. The Senate Select Committee on Intelligence and the Senate Armed Forces Committee must abolish the position of undersecretary of defense for intelligence, which was created by Rumsfeld to solidify the Pentagon's control over the intelligence community. The Senate Armed Forces Committee routinely approved the position without any vetting from the SSCI. Unfortunately, the DNI has had no support from the Congress in trying to obtain control over the Pentagon's resources on these key intelligence agencies.

The Pentagon's intelligence agency, the DIA, has received authorization to allow their personnel to hide the fact that they work for the government when they seek domestic intelligence sources. DIA has gained access to FBI intelligence and has shared this intelligence with the Northern Command, established in the wake of 9/11 to provide security in the continental United States. Each of the military services has begun a post-9/11 collection of intelligence information relating to terrorist threats to military facilities. The Pentagon is seeking an exception from the Privacy Act in order to gain access to FBI intelligence on American citizens, which would provide access to information on U.S. citizens that has nothing to do with terrorism. Bert Tussig, director of Homeland Defense and Security Issues at the U.S. Army War College and a former Marine, says "There is very little that could justify the collection of domestic intelligence by the U.S. military. If we start going down this slippery slope, it would be too easy to go back to a place we never want to see again."[2] The extent of this slippery slope became even more obvious in December 2005 when we learned that, several months after the 9/11 attacks,

President Bush ordered the NSA to eavesdrop on the conversations of Americans inside the United States without court-approved warrants as part of the war against terrorism.[3] More recently, we learned that the Department of Homeland Security requested $300 million to establish a new office to conduct a domestic satellite surveillance program.

The military command has wrenched control of the three most important positions in the intelligence community from the civilian leadership: the DNI is retired three-star naval admiral Mike McConnell, the director of the CIA is four-star Air Force General Michael Hayden, and the undersecretary of defense for intelligence is retired three-star Air Force General James Clapper. They have an excellent background in the technical aspects of intelligence, but lack an understanding of the strategic and geopolitical context of intelligence. The top positions at the National Counterterrorism Center are occupied by flag officers without any background in strategic intelligence. The militarization of intelligence leadership is a blatant reversal of the kind of intelligence community that President Truman created sixty years ago, and will complicate efforts to rebuild the nation's strategic intelligence capabilities. The absence of independent civilian control over the power of military intelligence threatens civilian control over decisions to use military power and risks tailoring intelligence to suit the purposes of the Pentagon. The military domination of the intelligence cycle will also make it more difficult to rebuild strategic intelligence, which plays a major role in the development of national security policy.

Retired General Brent Scowcroft, the head of the President's Foreign Intelligence Advisory Board, conducted a comprehensive review of the intelligence community for President Bush and favored transferring budgetary and collection authority from the Pentagon to a new office that reports directly to the DCI.[4] Scowcroft recommended placing three of the key technical and analytical collection agencies (NSA, NRO, and NGA) under the authority of the DCI. The NRO, one of the largest enterprises in the intelligence community with a budget of more than $8 billion, began as a joint venture with the CIA; the NGA's responsibility for analysis was once a joint CIA-military operation, which allowed civilian intelligence analysts to provide a check on the work of military analysts. The Pentagon opposes any transfer of responsibility for the agencies to the DNI, and Congressional intelligence committees have been negligent in proposing reforms for the community or reversing the Pentagon's corporate control over the process.

Demilitarizing National Security Policy

The appointment of general officers (Hayden, McConnell, and Clapper) to the three most important positions in the intelligence community points to the militarization of overall national security policy. The trend toward militarization began in the Clinton administration, when the president's lack of military service and wartime experience led to great deference toward the military. His three appointments to the CIA, Woolsey, Deutch, and Tenet, were particularly weak, and the role of strategic intelligence declined during Clinton's presidency. The Bush administration continued the trend of militarization, including an end to arms control and disarmament and the creation of the position of an undersecretary of defense for intelligence with more influence over the intelligence community than that of the DNI or the CIA director.

One of the greatest threats to civil liberties in this country is the enhanced role of the DoD to gather and analyze intelligence within the United States. The department has created new agencies, added personnel, and sought greater legal authority to conduct domestic security activities in the name of post-9/11 surveillance.[5] The Pentagon is accumulating reporting from intelligence, law enforcement, counterintelligence, and security activities in violation of the U.S. Privacy Act of 1974 that orders the purge of all information after ninety days if not part of an ongoing investigation.[6] In 2003, the department created a little-known agency, Counterintelligence Field Activity (CIFA), to establish and "maintain a domestic law enforcement database that includes information related to potential terrorist threats." CIFA is seeking authority to investigate crimes within the United States such as treason, foreign sabotage, and economic espionage. CIFA has more than a thousand employees and a secret budget. Then Deputy Secretary Wolfowitz established a new reporting mechanism known as TALON. Threat and Local Observation Notice (TALON) reports are maintained in the CIFA database. CIFA, in turn, awarded $33 million in contracts to Lockheed Martin, Unisys Corporation, and Northrop Grumman to develop databases that comb through classified government data, commercial information, and even Internet chatter to collect information on so-called terrorists.[7] Thus, we have essentially deputized the military to spy on law-abiding American citizens, with military officers attending antiwar and peace rallies, and staff sergeants engaged in NSA's warrantless eavesdropping.

The Justice Department's Inspector General, Glenn Fine, prepared a scathing report in March 2007 criticizing the expansion of FBI administrative subpoenas to obtain telephone, business, and financial records of Americans without judicial approval. Since the passage of the Patriot Act in 2001, the FBI and the Department of Homeland Security (DHS) have issued more than twenty thousand national security letters annually to Americans who are not believed to have any connection to terrorist activity. The recipients of these letters are not permitted to discuss the contents of these letters to anyone. There is no evidence these letters have led to any useful intelligence regarding terrorist activity, let alone to arrests. The FBI's counterterrorism officials ignored the concerns of FBI lawyers and managers about this activity, and there is no evidence that members of Congress have a full understanding of the FBI program.

In addition to the use of military techniques in the implementation of domestic security policy, there has been an unusual introduction of intelligence surveillance on the local level. Since 2003, the New York City police department (NYPD) has conducted covert surveillance of people protesting the Iraq War, even bicycle riders taking part in mass rallies, and mourners at a street vigil for a cyclist killed in an accident.[8] The covert surveillance has been conducted throughout the United States, Canada, and Europe, with New York police officers attending meetings of political groups, posing as sympathizers or fellow activists. The police department's Intelligence Division created files on members of street theater companies, church groups, and antiwar organizations, as well as environmentalists and people opposed to the death penalty. The information from this activity was shared with other police departments. Once again, there is no evidence that Congress has not been briefed on the extent of the NYPD's efforts.

New York's deputy policy commissioner for intelligence, David Cohen, the former deputy director for operations at the CIA, initiated police surveillance of public events. In September 2002, Cohen wrote in an affidavit that the police department should not be required to have a "specific indication" of a crime before investigating.[9] "In the case of terrorism," Cohen wrote, "to wait for an indication of crime before investigating is to wait for too long." Cohen was thinking like the intelligence officer he used to be, and not like a policy official with respect for law and civil liberty. In granting the city's surveillance requests, a federal judge in Manhattan ruled that the dangers of terrorism were "perils sufficient to outweigh any First Amendment cost." As a result, the police department was authorized to conduct investigations of political, social, and religious groups.

Organizing for Operational Activity

There has never been an official examination of the role of the CIA's secret wars in the 1980s during the Casey era to assess the impact of these wars on future violence and even terrorism against the United States. Former national security advisor Brzezinski conceded in an interview in 1998 that clandestine U.S. involvement began in Afghanistan before the Soviet invasion, and he predicted "this aid was going to induce a Soviet military intervention."[10] The Reagan administration increased assistance to the anti-Soviet insurgency in Afghanistan and also armed Pakistan's intelligence service. The United States could have prevented the emergence of a Taliban regime in Afghanistan by assisting the Soviets in creating a coalition government in Afghanistan, but the hard-liners in the Reagan administration were opposed to such a step. The Clinton administration did not respond aggressively to terrorist actions aimed at the United States in the wake of CIA's covert actions in Africa and Southwest Asia, including the bombing of the World Trade Center in 1993, the attacks on U.S. embassies on the Horn of Africa in 1998, and the strike on the USS *Cole* in 2000. CIA secret prisons, extraordinary renditions, and torture and abuse violate both domestic and international law, and will inspire additional terrorist attacks against U.S. interests.

Virtually all CIA covert actions have been counterproductive in terms of larger U.S. strategic interests, and CIA use of force has led to serious problems for U.S. policy in the Third World. Policymakers and intelligence officers were wrong to authorize "force for force's sake" at the Bay of Pigs in 1961, the mining of Nicaraguan harbors in 1984, and support for the Contra war against the Sandinista government and for the National Union for the Total Independence of Angola (UNITA) in Angola in the 1980s, which raised the level of violence in both countries. The introduction of U.S. assistance to UNITA in 1975 encouraged Zairian strongman Mobutu to commit his own paramilitary forces to Angola, which marked the first introduction of third-country combat troops into the Angolan civil war. South Africa also began to supply arms to UNITA and the FNLA, ending any Soviet hopes of finding a truce between the MPLA and UNITA. As a result, Cuba sent several hundred additional Cuban military specialists and advisers by air, along with the first seven hundred Cuban troops. When the United States challenged Cuba's overflight rights, the Soviet Union provided longer range IL-62 airlift and began the direct airlift of Cuban troops. The Soviets did not send their own advisors until 1976, when Angola declared its independence, although CIA disinformation alleged the presence of Soviet military advisers as early as September 1975.

President Truman concluded the creation of the CIA was a mistake because "those fellows in the CIA don't just report on wars and the like, they go out and make their own, and there's nobody to keep track of what they're up to."[11] Truman pointed to the problem of a secret agency within a democracy, and the need for the concept of openness and even a "housecleaning every now and then. I don't care what branch of government is involved. *Somebody* has to keep an eye on things." Truman certainly understood that the Founding Fathers were leery of secrecy and understood that "secrecy and a free, democratic government don't mix." He and his White House counsel, Clark Clifford, wanted a CIA as a depository of information and intentionally kept the role of covert action out of the National Security Act. Later, Clifford explained that they expected covert action as part of the CIA's functions, but "expected them to be limited in scope and purpose."[12]

Revive Congressional Oversight

The decline of the CIA over the past decade coincides with the reduced role of oversight of the intelligence community by the Senate and House intelligence committees. These committees were established as elite, bipartisan committees and behaved that way for the most part from the mid-1970s to the early 1990s. But the Gingrich revolution in the Congress had a partisan impact on the intelligence committees, particularly when the Senate and House intelligence committees were in the hands of such extreme partisans as Senator Roberts, the chairman of the SSCI, and Representative Goss, chairman of the HPSCI. The term limits on members of the intelligence committees and the increased power of the Senate and House armed services committees on intelligence issues have contributed to the decline of the oversight responsibility. Roberts kept the Senate committee from conducting a counterintelligence investigation of the forged documents on Niger used in the president's State of the Union address in January 2003. He also blocked an investigation of the CIA's role in the abuse and torture of detainees in the wake of the Iraq War, as well as the Agency's policy of extraordinary renditions, which violate international covenants the United States has endorsed.

The Senate and House intelligence committees have become advocates for the CIA—particularly for the clandestine world of spies and covert operations. In doing so, Congress has failed to make the CIA accountable for its transgressions. Iran-Contra demonstrated that far more rigorous and experienced accountability was needed to monitor ideological zealots in the CIA and the National Security Council. A presidential pardon in 1992 for key CIA operatives involved in Iran-Contra meant we would never learn the extent of CIA perfidy in presidential maneuverings related to that scandal. Congressional confirmation of Gates as CIA director in 1991 sent the signal that the Senate intelligence committee was no longer interested in a senior CIA official who previously lied to Congress about his knowledge of Iran-Contra. Congressional confirmation of three flag officers for the highest positions in the intelligence community without raising the issue of military influence pointed to Congressional dereliction.

In defending his decision to go to war against Iraq, President Bush claimed that Congress supported his decision and that it had access to the same intelligence available to the White House. Actually, the president and his senior advisors have a great deal of information that is not available to the intelligence committees, and Congress is insufficiently zealous in trying to gather the intelligence it needs and notably complacent about perusing the intelligence that it receives. The president's national security team (including the national security advisor, the vice president, the secretaries of state and defense, and several key deputy secretaries) has access to the CIA's PDB, which contains sensitive intelligence that is not seen in the policy community or on Capitol Hill. Most of this intelligence is of the compartmented variety that isn't available to all intelligence analysts working on a particular problem.

Every agency or department in the intelligence community has special compartmented intelligence that is not shared with the oversight committees. The CIA's directorate of operations, for example, has what is known as "red-border" or "blue-border" clandestine reports that can be carried to the White House or the NSC, but receive very limited distribution elsewhere. Special compartmented intelligence would not be seen by members of Congress. The NSA has sensitive collections that rarely get into publications other than the PDB and are distributed by hand to only one or two members of other intelligence agencies. The State Department has sensitive cables from embassies that are marked "eyes only" or "nodis," for no distribution, which are seen by only a few outside the department.

In the context of the Iraq War, congressmen are not receiving the intelligence most useful to the vetting of a particular decision, such as the use of force in Iraq or the lack of postwar planning. The vote on the use of force in October 2002 should have been delayed to allow sufficient scrutiny of the specious NIE that arrived on the Hill several days before the vote. Incredibly, only six Senators even bothered to go to the special vaulted area to read the estimate. And the only senator who proclaimed that the document was fraudulent, Senator Bob Graham (D-Florida), was ignored. If Congress was hoodwinked by the administration, then it helped to apply its own blinders. The Congressional oversight committees have to be more aggressive in getting sensitive intelligence information that has a bearing on policy decisions, and committee staffers must be more zealous in scrutinizing the intelligence for signs of politicization.

In addition to bolstering the capabilities and missions of the intelligence committees in the field of oversight, it is necessary to revive and strengthen the President's Foreign Intelligence Advisory Board and the Intelligence Oversight Board, both weakened during the Bush era. The executive and legislative branches must radically increase their surveillance and oversight of intelligence in order to make sure that the United States maintains an intelligence community that is both effective and reflective of our democratic values. The CIA system of secret prisons, abuse and torture, and extraordinary renditions, as well as the Pentagon's domestic surveillance and collection of intelligence strongly suggest that our Fourth Amendment rights are being observed in the breach. Public accountability must be reestablished in order to restore the integrity and credibility of the entire intelligence community.

The oversight committees must take the lead in amending whistle-blower laws in order to include protection to intelligence personnel so that illegal activity can be brought to the attention of these committees. Former FBI officials Coleen Rowley and Sibel Edmonds were hit with gag orders for trying to report abuses of power at the FBI, and were forced to resign. In the 1980s, the CIA harassed the two analysts, Richard Barlow and Peter Dixon, who discovered Pakistan's program to develop nuclear weapons. In the 1990s, the CIA misused polygraph examinations to intimidate senior officials who filed signed affidavits with the Senate intelligence committee during the nomination hearings for Gates. I reported this activity to the staff of the Senate intelligence committee, but their silence was deafening. Conversely, the White House outing of a covert CIA operative in 2003 brought no sign of concern from the committees, although it violated the Intelligence Identities Protection Act of 1982.

Reform of Clandestine Operations and Covert Action

Before there can be a genuine reform of the CIA's National Clandestine Service (formerly the directorate for operations), it will be necessary to expose and end the mythology of the clandestine services that has existed since the creation of the CIA in 1947. Every reform movement on CIA operations has started with the need for greater human intelligence (HUMINT), particularly greater assets and personnel for the NCS.[13] This consensus is ignorant of the limits and myths of clandestine collection and the value of human intelligence. The report of the 9/11 Commission accepted these myths, and recent congressional testimony has repeated misinformation about the CIA and HUMINT. Previous CIA directors, particularly Goss, a former operative in the directorate of operations, and Tenet, endorsed this mythology, blocking genuine change and reform. The current CIA director, a general officer, has been captured by the clandestine culture and cadre, and is unlikely to lead a reform movement.

Myth 1: The CIA has become risk averse. Nonsense! The CIA has been risk averse since its creation in 1947. CIA operatives work under diplomatic cover, for example, so that their lives cannot be threatened and that, if captured, their worst punishment is declaration of persona non grata. This cover arrangement was adequate during the worst days of the cold war with the Soviet Union, but it limits contacts with the most unsavory communities in the Third World, let alone with nihilistic terrorist organizations. American policymakers and opinion leaders would not have it any other way, however.

Myth 2: The Church Committee in the mid-1970s and various Democratic administrations weakened the CIA, particularly the work of covert action. More nonsense! Covert action has rarely served the strategic interests of the United States and the various exercises in regime change (e.g., Chile, Congo, Cuba, Dominican Republic, Iran, and Vietnam) did great harm.

Myth 3: HUMINT is the key to operating against the forces of terrorism. The key myth of HUMINT is that the United States needs to return to the era of greater clandestine recruitment of foreign assets or spies because of the importance of human intelligence. There was no such era. Like most areas, the key to intelligence gathering and analysis is underutilized open sources and misunderstood technical collection, including signals intelligence, communications intelligence, and overhead reconnaissance. It is very difficult to collect against the so-called "hard targets" with CIA operatives; the collection of such assets are a very small part of the intelligence pie and are the most unreliable. Whenever President Nixon referred to "reliable clandestine sources," National Security Advisor Kissinger always reminded him that they "were not altogether reliable."

Myth 4: The CIA successfully recruits foreign assets. The clandestine services of the CIA rely on walk-ins and rarely recruit major espionage assets. These walk-ins, such as Colonel Penkovsky, often had great difficulty in getting CIA operatives to accept them. CIA directors and their congressional supporters believe additional clandestine operatives will permit the CIA to penetrate terrorist organizations overseas or to develop assets to do so. The NCS has had virtually no success in recruiting assets in the closed world of terrorism or such closed societies as China or North Korea. Moreover, agents recruited from Cuba, East Germany, and the Soviet Union after the Ames affair were double agents reporting to their host governments. The NCS has recruited thousands of Third-World politicians and European businessmen whose reporting did not justify the work of the directorate and whose knowledge could often be obtained gratis by State Department foreign service officers.

Myth 5: The CIA relies too heavily on foreign intelligence liaison and needs to develop its own sources. The 9/11 Commission is particularly responsible for this myth; it had support from the former chairman of the SSCI, Senator Roberts, who should have known better. The United States is particularly dependent on liaisons in dealing with nonstate terrorists and tribal societies in Southwest Asia and the Middle East. There is virtually no al Qaeda operative who has been killed or captured without the assistance of foreign liaison, particularly the Pakistani intelligence service.

Myth 6: The CIA needs more analysts and operatives. The CIA in fact, lacks the senior officers to train and mentor the analysts and operatives they have. The intelligence failures of 9/11 and the Iraq War had nothing to do with a dearth of officers; it had everything to do with an inability to tell truth to power and a failure of imagination. Additional junior officers will make this problem worse. INR, an extremely small department, outperformed the CIA on every aspect of terrorism and the Iraq War.

Myth 7: A new intelligence czar, serving in the president's cabinet, will better serve the interests of the White House. This is the most harmful myth of all.

The placing of a czar in the executive branch will increase the chances for politicized intelligence, which was a problem during the Vietnam War, various arms control negotiations, and of course Iraq. Tenet's reference to a "slam dunk" regarding a public case for Iraqi WMD is the sort of advice we can commonly expect when the intelligence backboard is placed inside the White House.

Myth 8: Intelligence analysis should be centralized under the intelligence czar. In fact, we need more redundancy and competition in intelligence analysis. Redundancy in the military budget is expensive, but it is designed to save lives. Redundancy in the intelligence budget is also expensive, but it is designed to ensure that objective and balanced analysis reaches busy policymakers. The CIA is already overly centralized, and provides insufficient attention to strategic analysis. The DNI's centralized control over the PDB and national intelligence estimates has not strengthened the production of strategic intelligence.

If the cold war and the Soviet threat generated the rules that governed the use of covert action, then the end of the cold war and the dissolution of the Soviet Union demand a reexamination of every aspect of such operations, creating new requirements and perhaps the need for fewer operations. It is not enough to suggest—as defenders of covert action have suggested—that the world remains a dangerous place and that the president needs an option short of military action when diplomacy alone cannot do the job. Many problems that could be considered candidates for covert action could be addressed openly by unilateral means or cooperatively through international measures, such as sanctions or embargoes. Proliferation problems created by missile programs in North Korea has been addressed by international diplomacy and negotiation with the United States playing a leading role. Covert action would be destabilizing in both Iran and North Korea, creating regional problems, as well as a greater risk of military force. President Bush's so-called commitment to democratizing Iran, which experienced covert action in the name of democracy in 1953, has worsened relations with Tehran. Covert action in Cuba created greater support for Fidel Castro; presumably, it is doing the same for hard-line leaders in Iran, North Korea, and Venezuela. Covert action in Somalia has worsened the national security situation for U.S. interests.

Much CIA clandestine activity could be reduced or even stopped without hurting U.S. national security. CIA propaganda has had little effect on foreign audiences and should end immediately. The recent clumsy attempt by the U.S. military to place "black propaganda" in the Iraqi press backfired and undermined the U.S. emphasis on creating democracy in the Middle East. Covert efforts to influence foreign elections or political parties should stop immediately. The United States had far better success encouraging democratic reform in such places as Georgia and Ukraine by working openly through nongovernmental organizations and international monitoring groups.

Covert actions devoted to regime change have been a particular failure. The "successful" coup in Iran in 1953 overthrew the democratically elected government of Mossadegh and introduced the corrupt and incompetent Shah of Iran to power. U.S.–Iranian relations have not recovered from this act. The CIA's attempt to assassinate Patrice Lumumba in the Congo led to the emergence of Mobutu Sese Seku, the most evil tyrant in modern African history. The various attempts by the Eisenhower and Kennedy administrations to assassinate Castro merely strengthened the Cuban leader's political standing at home and throughout the entire Western Hemisphere. CIA covert action in Chile led to the death of the democratically elected Salvador Allende and the emergence of Pinochet, another unconscionable act. The overthrow and ultimate death of President Ngo Dinh Diem marked a turning point in Vietnam, with the United States never again having the cooperation of a viable Vietnamese leader. Regime change in Iraq was not covert, but it clearly worsened the situation in Iraq and the entire Middle East.

The Brown-Aspin Commission on intelligence reform in 1996 recommended that covert operations should take place only when "essential" and where the reason for secrecy is "compelling." Most covert operations are "operations for operations' sake," however, and are undertaken with inadequate consideration of results and implications. There is no absolute political and ethical test for covert action, but former secretary of state Cyrus Vance articulated a good standard in the 1970s when he recommended covert intervention only when "absolutely essential to the national security" of the United States and when "no other means" would do.[14]

Instead of providing increased funding for more clandestine operatives and greater covert action, the congressional oversight process needs to address the criminal activities of the National Clandestine Service, which are operating on a dangerous mandate from the Bush administration. In the wake of 9/11, President Bush gave the CIA sweeping new powers to create secret prisons, conduct extraordinary renditions without policy review, and engage in torture and abuse. In February 2002, the president signed an order declaring that "none of the provisions of Geneva apply to our conflict with al Qaeda in Afghanistan or elsewhere throughout the world," which set the nation on the slippery slope to torture and abuse at Abu Ghraib and other U.S.-run prisons.

End Torture and Abuse

Senator Frank Church (D-Idaho) misstated the problem of monitoring the CIA in the 1970s, when he chaired the Church Commission's investigation of the CIA and termed the Agency a "rogue elephant out of control," and he understated the problems associated with a secret agency operating abroad without sufficient monitoring and oversight. Church insinuated that the CIA seized powers it was never granted and, as a result, had placed itself above the law." In fact, the problem is far more serious because the CIA has carefully campaigned for and benefited from White House and Justice Department memoranda that sanction the conduct of abuse and terror, in the creation of secret prisons, and the policy of renditions. The problem would be easier to solve if, indeed, the CIA was a rogue institution out of control instead of a key player in the national security bureaucracy that takes its lead from policies of the White House. The Military Commissions Act of September 2006 will make it more difficult to ensure that the White House and the CIA follow international and domestic laws against torture and abuse. CIA references to "enhanced interrogation techniques" are a euphemism for torture.

At the very least, the congressional oversight committees must guarantee that the comprehensive legal framework prohibiting abuse and torture is followed. Senator Kerry made a key start in this direction by adding a measure to the Intelligence Authorization Act for 2005–2006 to compel the CIA to provide a thorough list of its practices and techniques to the Senate intelligence committee, but the Republican majority carefully removed his amendment. In addition to the Geneva Conventions of 1949 and the UN Convention Against Torture, numerous international treaties prohibit the use of torture under any circumstance. These treaties include the UN's Universal Declaration of Human Rights of 1948, the Military Code of Justice, and the Hague Convention Respecting the Laws and Customs of War. Even when Congress passed a law banning torture, the White House issued a statement insisting that Article II—the power of the Commander in Chief—trumps any act of Congress. But the Constitution also states the president "shall take care that the laws be faithfully executed."

Tell Truth to Power

The Iraq War revealed the moral bankruptcy at the CIA, where there is a biblical inscription at the entrance to the CIA building in Langley, Virginia, that "the truth will set you free." The director, the deputy director, several NIOs, and senior intelligence and operations officials demonstrated no interest in the truth, and contributed to the politicization of intelligence supporting the phony case to go to war. Tenet said the public case for war would be a "slam dunk," and McLaughlin ignored Agency officers who had doubts about the veracity of CIA intelligence. NIO Walpole managed the production of a specious NIE that falsified Iraqi holdings of WMD, NIO Pillar directed an unclassified white paper that took the argument on WMD to the Congress and the American people, Alan Foley did not block the White House's use of a fabricated intelligence report in the State of the Union speech in 2003, and numerous Agency officials took part in preparing Powell's UN speech. The speech had a profound impact on the editorial writers in major American newspapers and even liberals such as the late Mary McCarthy wrote a column entitled, "I'm Persuaded," following Powell's speech.

The CIA requires a director and senior management that are capable of instilling integrity into the Agency from top to bottom. CIA directors Goss and Hayden failed that major test because of their roles in blocking the distribution and declassification of the CIA Inspector General's report on the Agency's performance on issues related to the 9/11 intelligence failure. Ironically, Goss was one of the four congressional leaders who requested the CIA accountability report on 9/11 as part of his stewardship of the House intelligence committee in 2002. At that time, the joint Senate-House inquiry requested that the IG of the CIA (along with the IGs of the DoS, DoD, and DoJ) prepare an accountability report of those personnel who may have been responsible for the failures that led to the 9/11 attacks. By the time the CIA completed its report, the CIA director was none other than Goss, who delayed the distribution of the report to the intelligence committees and then heavily restricted the distribution of the report on the Hill. Hayden tried to continue Goss' policy, although all other agencies and departments have declassified or sanitized these reports for public distribution. Finally, the Congress forced Hayden to release an unclassified version of the executive summary of the report in August 2007.

The Abuse of Secrecy and the Need for Glasnost

One of the greatest scandals within the intelligence community is the overclassification of government documents in order to keep important information out of the hands of the American people. It costs billions of dollars for government and industry to classify documents, with several million individuals in the government and private industry having the right to classify information.[15] Government vaults hold over 1.5 billion pages of classified information that are more than twenty-five years old and, thus, unavailable to scholars and researchers, let alone the general public. Senator Kerry, when he served on the Select Committee on POW/MIA Affairs, learned what all of us who served in the intelligence community always understood: documents are often classified to hide embarrassing political information, not secrets. Since the 9/11 attacks, more than one million pages of historical government documents have been removed from public view.

Classification is typically a political decision and not a technical action. More than half of the classified documents year in and year out belong to the DoD, with another 30 percent emanating from the CIA, representing tens of thousands of pages every year. These classified pages represent actions, plans, and proposals that should be made available to the American public, after their original sensitivity disappears, so that citizens can make reasonable decisions about the policies of their government. In 1996, the CIA had more than 165 million pages of classified materials, but had declassified less than 20,000 by 1997. The report of the Commission on Secrecy told a typical story of a journalist who used the Freedom of Information Act in 1984 to gain information on Saudi oil production during the 1970s. Nine years later, he received a one-page chart that took five years to clear at the Department of Energy and another four years at the CIA, with half of the numbers deleted.

The Bush administration has gone to unusual lengths to limit access to information, particularly after the 9/11 terrorist attacks. These policies have harmed the public debate on national security, diminished government accountability, and compromised the international standing of the United States. Greater respect for openness might have prevented the policies that led to the abuse and torture at Abu Ghraib prison, the network of secret prisons, and the policy of extraordinary renditions. Greater openness and debate might also prevent counterproductive covert actions. American policymakers should ask the simple question, "How do we explain a covert action after the United States becomes explicitly connected to such actions?" If such a covert action could not be explained in a way that is understandable to American and international audiences, perhaps it should be reconsidered, refined, or withdrawn.

Staunching the Exodus

Whenever there has been politicization of intelligence or an abuse of the CIA's power, there has been personnel turbulence at the CIA. This happened in the 1980s and early 1990s, when the politicization of intelligence on the Soviet Union led to a loss of many senior Soviet and Eastern European analysts. A combination of bad morale, opposition to the leadership of Casey and Gates, and intelligence failures led to a period of disarray. And this was certainly the case during the stewardship of Goss, who directed the Agency to support the policies of the Bush administration. As a result, we witnessed a wholesale departure of senior operational officers, whose experience was invaluable.

The NCS has become additionally demoralized by the failure of Agency leaders to support pessimistic reporting from senior operatives in Baghdad, which countered the optimism of the Pentagon and the NSC in support of the Bush administration. When the president received one of these reports in July 2004, he reportedly asked, "What is he, some kind of defeatist?"[16] Once again, with senior intelligence positions in the hands of active or retired general officers, it will be far more difficult for civilian officials to file objective and balanced assessments of the chaos in Iraq and Afghanistan, particularly when the Bush administration is trying to defend its policies there.

During Goss' first year as director of the CIA, there was a virtual turnover of the clandestine services' senior leadership, including the director and deputy director of the service, the directors of the CTC and the Counterproliferation Center, many of the regional chiefs, and other senior cadre. Many of these clandestine officers left the CIA only to take senior positions with the office of the DNI, the National Counterterrorism Center, and the Department of Homeland Security. The clandestine service's director and deputy director, Stephen Kappes and Michael Sulick, left soon after Goss' arrival, and Sulick's replacement, Robert Richer, lasted less than a year. The vast turnover created a prima facie case for the removal of Goss, who was appointed by the White House to stabilize the CIA operation and not to add to the discontinuity there. When Goss was forced to resign, Kappes and Sulick returned to the CIA in an effort to boost morale in NCS.

Organizing for Intelligence Analysis

The centralization of intelligence analysis creates insufficient opportunity for providing alternative judgments and estimates to decision makers. Currently, the uniformed military dominates the collection and analysis of sensitive intelligence, which means that the CIA is no longer a check on the military bureaucracy as it was during the cold war, particularly during the Vietnam War and arms control decision making in the 1960s and 1970s. In these years, civilian analysts were a more objective and balanced source of intelligence than their military counterparts in assessing threats to the United States and the military capabilities of state and nonstate actors. Since the 1991 Gulf War, the CIA has not played a major role in military intelligence. According to a former CIA analyst, Richard Russell, "the absence of an independent civilian analytic check on military intelligence threatens American civilian control of the military instrument for political purposes."[17]

Over the past three decades, the CIA has gradually deemphasized strategic and long-term intelligence and placed too much emphasis on short-term, tactical intelligence and so-called "operational intelligence." CIA director Schlesinger, who had a background that included research at the Rand Corporation and should have recognized the importance of strategic intelligence, was primarily responsible for the demise of the historical staff and the estimates staff. The historical staff (Senior Research Staff) consisted of a small group of political, military, and economic analysts who did long-term analysis on such strategic issues as the Sino–Soviet dispute, Soviet domestic politics, and Chinese political economics. The estimates staff (Office of National Estimates) had a small cadre trained to write NIEs, the most important corporate product of the intelligence community. When these offices were abolished in 1973, their expertise was folded into larger offices and left unprotected. The failure to track the decline of the Soviet Union was due in part to the absence of long-term thinking. Academicians, such as Martin Malia, Tony Judt, and Timothy Garten Ash, were far ahead of the CIA on such issues as the collapse of communist regimes from 1989–1991, although they had limited resources and no access to classified information. The economic analysis of the CIA lagged behind such experts outside the intelligence community as Ed Hewitt of the Brookings Institution, Robert Campbell of Indiana University, and James Millar of George Washington University.

The CIA is insular and parochial and, as a result, fails to take full advantage of outside experts. The CIA's mentality is driven by a counterintelligence orientation, which puts too much emphasis on security clearances, polygraph tests, and the need-to-know. The military culture is even worse in this respect. The intelligence community is going to have to risk the occasional leak and even the compromise of information in order to attract outside expertise. No one expects the community to put sources and methods at risk, but there needs to be a freer and more open exchange of information to the people who can offer the most substantive critiques. The current analytic community is extremely young and very inexperienced, another reason for drawing from the outside community of experts.

The CIA relies heavily on so-called fusion centers, such as the CTC and the Counterintelligence Center, which combine intelligence analysts and clandestine operatives. These groups have produced mediocre work in their areas of expertise, providing no strategic warning on terrorist problems that confronted the United States in the 1990s. The Centers often sponsored the kind of clandestine collection that was favored by policymakers and used to politicize CIA intelligence or prepare worst-case assessments. The analysts for these centers come from the directorate of intelligence, which has become weaker and less effective over recent years in dealing with important strategic issues. The Centers have become more or less service centers for policymakers, answering specific questions and preparing requested briefings, but not exploring new ideas and not sponsoring competitive analysis. They justify themselves by citing the numbers of briefings given to policymakers or staffers. The emphasis is on quantitative evaluation and rarely on qualitative assessment or lessons learned.

The first DNI, John Negroponte, had little authority to realign the community, and made no attempt to create a corporate analytical community. He was powerless to use the intelligence budgets and personnel of the sixteen intelligence agencies to create an environment for genuine reform. He failed to form an elite analytical cadre from the key analytical and collection institutions (CIA, INR, DIA, NSA, NGA), and could not select the directors of these agencies. The DNI has failed to open the analytic community to the larger academic and think-tank community outside the intelligence arena. In such areas as ethnic politics and ethnic violence, where the CIA lacks expertise in linguistic and cultural studies, it is essential to gain greater exposure to outside experts.

The CIA has also done a poor job in incorporating open-source unclassified information, relying on clandestine sources that have uneven reliability and authority. Early on in the history of the CIA, the Agency took advantage of its Foreign Broadcast and Information Service (FBIS), which did an outstanding job of integrating open sources into the body of intelligence knowledge and published a weekly analysis of international news that had a better record of anticipating change than the classified publications of the DI. But in 1992, CIA director Gates, who opposed the independence of FBIS and his inability to control its analysis, weakened the department and virtually ended its analytical mission. Fortunately, Negroponte resurrected FBIS as the Open Source Center; it is located at CIA headquarters, but it reports to the DNI.[18]

Even DNI McConnell has concluded that, in view of the intelligence that the United States had collected prior to 9/11, the terrorist attacks were "preventable."[19] Nevertheless, he has not addressed the linguistic skills of the intelligence community that are particularly lacking. Few CIA analysts have an understanding of Arabic. The FBI lacked the means to translate documents found in the wake of the murder of Rabbi Meir Kahane that could have provided significant intelligence on the role of al Qaeda. A vigorous pursuit of the Kahane case might not have prevented the attacks on the World Trade Center in 1993 and 2001, but it would have alerted the FBI and CIA to al Qaeda and possible terrorist acts in the United States. The NSA lacked the means to translate important messages that were intercepted on the eve of September 11 stating, "Tomorrow is zero hour." The U.S. embassy in Baghdad, the largest U.S. embassy in the world with over one thousand officers, has only a handful of officers fluent in Arabic, and Ambassador Ryan Crocker has encountered resistance from Secretary of State Rice in posting more seasoned officers to the largest and most important U.S. embassy in the world.

The Problem of Prediction

Prediction is a key measure of the success of any intelligence organization, particularly the CIA, which often finds its predictions subject to public scrutiny. The simple fact of expertise does not necessarily translate into the ability to make predictions. So-called Soviet experts inside and outside government failed to predict the collapse of the Soviet Union; the only expert to do so was British political scientist Bernard Levin. The CIA has a particularly poor record in the field of tactical intelligence, missing the initial testing of Soviet atomic weapons; the North Korean invasion of the South, as well as China's entry into the war; the Soviet invasion of Hungary in 1956 and Czechoslovakia in 1968; the October War in the Middle East in 1973; the collapse of the Shah of Iran and the emergence of the Ayatollah in 1979; the Iraqi invasion of Kuwait in 1990; the collapse of the Berlin Wall, the Eastern European communist regimes, and even the Soviet Union itself in the period from 1989–1991; Indian nuclear tests in 1998; the 9/11 attacks in Washington and New York; and the issue of Iraqi WMD prior to the U.S. invasion in 2003. CIA's experts did not believe Chinese forces would fire their weapons against Chinese protesters in Tiananmen Square in 1989; they were wrong. Its Eastern European experts, despite access to sensitive Polish documents on martial law, predicted that Polish forces would not turn their weapons on their own people, and thereby missed the onset of martial law in 1981. The fact of the matter is that experts, and there is a great deal of "expertise" in the intelligence community, often don't have the best track record in their particular areas of specialization, and their confidence is often due to personal self-confidence rather than confidence in their sources or their methodology.

A psychologist at the University of California in Berkeley, Philip Tetlock, studied the phenomena of expert predictions and concluded that the accuracy of an expert's predictions has an inverse relationship to the self-confidence and depth of knowledge of the expert.[20] The greater the knowledge and the self-confidence, the more likely that the opinion will be wrong; furthermore, regular readers of daily newspapers have prediction rates that rival the success of experts that are regularly quoted in these papers. Tetlock discovered something that is well-known to CIA managers in the DI: experts tend to be passionately enamored with their own predictions and do a poor job of evaluating new information that does not support their point of view. Similarly, experts are quick to credit those sources that support their views and are unlikely to credit those sources that disagree with their views or undercut their assumptions. CIA analysts rarely look for evidence to prove that they are wrong. If they were inclined to do so, then they would have come up with ample evidence that their assumptions prior to the 9/11 terrorist attacks (that the terrorists would strike vulnerable targets abroad and not more difficult targets in the United States) and the run-up to the Iraq War (that Iraq had large stocks of WMD) would have been challenged. Just as flawed thinking can set off a cascade of cognitive errors in the field of medicine, flawed assumptions can complicate the intelligence process in dealing with clandestine intelligence.

In other words, experts are no different than human beings in general—they simply do not change their minds or opinions very easily. The CIA intelligence failures on the October War in 1973, the Polish crisis and martial law in 1981, and Tiananmen Square in 1989 could be attributed to the inability to deal with new evidence that did not support old assumptions. Tetlock also concluded (and my experience at CIA confirmed) that experts underplayed the degree of probability they assigned to an event after it came to pass. The hawks on the Vietnam War, for example, forgot their certainty about victory in Southeast Asia; the hawks on the Iraq War forgot their predictions about the unlikelihood of an organized insurgency against the U.S. military presence. More than three years after a steady drumroll of confidence about the democratization of the region and the terrible nightmare that is unfolding there, *New York Times* columnist Thomas Friedman refuses to concede that his confidence in democratization may have been misplaced.[21] Instead, he now argues that democracy was "kidnapped" and blames the Europeans for "dithering" and the moderate Arabs for failing to "come together and make a fist." CIA analysts on the Middle East, however, were adamant in arguing there was very little chance for democracy to take root in such unstable ground as the Islamic world. The proponents of democratization were the policymakers within the Bush administration without any experience in the Middle East.

The Importance of Sharing Intelligence

A major failing of the office of the DNI, a bureaucratic behemoth superimposed upon the sixteen intelligence agencies and departments, has been the inability to generate genuine sharing of sensitive intelligence. Even if there is intent to share, there is still an absence of common information systems, no strategic direction for collection and analysis of intelligence, and chaotic security practices that prevent intelligence from getting to the right people and to the most critical missions. The intelligence culture is dominated by the severe need-to-know principles of the military and operational cultures, which works against sharing, as well as innovative intelligence analysis.

The inability to share intelligence was a major factor in the Pearl Harbor failure in 1941, and played a lesser role in the 9/11 failure sixty years later. The 9/11 failure had more to do with unimaginative and incomplete intelligence analysis, but the CIA's failure to share sensitive intelligence with the FBI and the NSA's unwillingness to share with the CIA compromised the corporate effort to monitor the terrorist threat. At the very least, sensitive intelligence information in the hands of military planners would have diminished the strategic losses at Pearl Harbor; sensitive data in the hands of various government agencies could have led to counteractions that may have persuaded bin Laden to at least postpone the 9/11 attacks. Unfortunately, the major intelligence agencies place too much emphasis on counterintelligence, the compartmentation of intelligence, and a strict "need-to-know," which are obstacles to intelligence sharing.

Sensitive intelligence moves vertically within each of the sixteen intelligence agencies instead of horizontally across them. In addition to the traditional problems between the CIA and the FBI and the CIA and the Pentagon, such key agencies as the Immigration and Naturalization Service, the Federal Aviation Administration, the Border Guards, and the Coast Guard, which are on the front line in the war against terrorism, have great difficulty in obtaining sensitive data from the larger intelligence agencies. And there are serious distribution problems for the DHS, which has difficulty getting significant intelligence from the community. One of the greatest lessons of the 9/11 attacks was the absence of any central depository for foreign and domestic intelligence on terrorism, but the DHS has not filled the void.

Even if the various agencies and departments of the intelligence community were willing to share information, their various computer systems would not allow the rapid transfer of information. The FBI computer system is particularly unable to move and recall data, and the FBI still has not recovered from the harm done by former director Louis Freeh, who believed computer technology was overrated and too expensive. Now the FBI is throwing millions of dollars at the problem, but the response has been too little and too late and, five years after 9/11, FBI director Robert Mueller conceded that the problem has not been solved. In the wake of 9/11, Mueller had to travel to CIA headquarters in Langley, Virginia, for terrorism briefings because his own agency could not collate relevant materials.

Failure Without Reform

For many policymakers, there is already too much intelligence and information to absorb. As Lady Astor said on the sinking *Titantic*, "I asked for ice water, but this is ridiculous." The intelligence reorganization of 2004 did nothing to improve strategic and long-term intelligence. Instead, it merely created a new layer of bureaucracy that will lead to a greater paper flow across policymakers' desks without improving the clarity and authoritativeness of the finished product. In addition to the CIA's Counterterrorism Center (CTC), there is now a National Counterterrorism Center (NCTC); both centers see the same intelligence collection and prepare similar briefing materials for policymakers. The interim director of the NCTC, John O. Brennan, resigned in July 2005 and noted that the Bush administration was "still struggling" with the redesign of the intelligence community.[22] The chief of the CTC, Robert

Grenier, was forced to resign in February 2006, when he opposed CIA director Goss' increased reliance on secret prisons and extraordinary renditions. As a result, the CTC had to accept its fourth director since 2002.

The CTC and the NCTC will have to rely in part on intelligence collected in secret prisons, from rendered suspects who often have been tortured, or what Tenet terms "enhanced interrogation techniques." Many senior officers have left the Agency because of the morale problems created by the use of torture and rendition. Hundreds of suspected terrorists have been held at facilities, such as Guantanamo, for more than five years, although the half-life of intelligence from such individuals can be counted in months, and never in years. The UN and other international organizations, as well as the secretaries of state and defense, have called for the closing of Guantanamo because of the torture and abuse that take place there. In the final analysis, torture is typically not about obtaining useful intelligence; torture is more often about power, dominance, hatred, humiliation, and fear.

The 9/11 and Iraq War intelligence failures, marked by bureaucratic corruption and incompetence at the CIA, have not been accompanied by a reform effort to correct flawed processes. The CIA corruption of the 1960s and 1970s during the Vietnam War led to the creation of the congressional oversight committees, as well as a congressional review function for covert action. The Iran-Contra scandal of 1987–1987 led to the creation of a statutory or "independent" Inspector General at the CIA, appointed by the president with the advice and consent of the Senate. A more powerful and independent IG at the CIA was required because Agency investigations of its role in the sale of arms to Iran were inadequate in comparison with the investigations of the congressional and independent counsels.

The CIA has had an Inspector General (IG) since 1952, but the IGs were appointed by the director of central intelligence, had limited access to sensitive information, and rarely had more than a handful of professionals on its staff. Even worse, the oversight committees were not given full access to IG reports until the 1990s. Not even the Justice Department was receiving all IG reports that recorded suspected illegalities. CIA director Casey was notorious for making sure that such illegalities were not reported to the Attorney General. As a result, Senator Arlen Spector (R-Pennsylvania) sponsored a bill to create an independent statutory IG at the CIA, with the eventual bipartisan support of the Democratic chairman of the Senate intelligence committee, David Boren, and the vice chairman and ranking minority member, William Cohen. This represented the last example of the bipartisan spirit that once existed within the oversight committees.

Statutory IGs were created in 1978 at most government agencies and departments as part of a post-Vietnam reform process, but the CIA was exempted from the law. The Church Committee favored a statutory IG for the CIA, but the Carter administration failed to support the proposal. The Pike Committee recommended the creation of an IG for the entire intelligence community, including the CIA, but this proposal was considered too radical at the time. The major opponent of the creation of the statutory IG in the late 1980s was CIA director Webster, who believed an independent IG would interfere with operational activities. Webster opposed an independent IG that the CIA director could not control, and he joined with Boren, who was concerned that an independent IG would be a rival to his intelligence committee on issues of oversight. Webster tried to convince the Senate intelligence committee an independent IG could also become a source of leaks and that, as a result, potential sources might be reluctant to work with the CIA.[23] There were no examples of leaks from the offices of statutory IGs at the DoS and the DoD, but Webster insisted there would be compromises of sources and methods. Fortunately for Spector, the office of the IG had prepared reports that were analytically shoddy, failing to pursue key lines of inquiry, and failing to interview key witnesses.[24] As a result, key members of the Senate intelligence committee, including Senator John Glenn (D-Ohio), were convinced that the office of the IG at the CIA lacked the professionalism to do the job. Boren realized that a bipartisan effort by Spector and Glenn could very well produce a piece of legislation that would be even less acceptable, so he agreed to compromise.

Since Glenn and Boren were close friends and allies, a deal was cut between them and they prepared to do battle with President Bush and CIA director Webster who opposed an independent IG. Boren also had become friendly with Bob Gates, who at that time was deputy to national security advisor Brent Scowcroft; Gates assured the chairman of the Senate intelligence committee that the president would not veto a bill that contained a provision for a statutory IG. Boren returned the favor three years later when he guaranteed to the Bush administration that Gates could be confirmed by the Senate intelligence committee if he were to be nominated as a CIA director for a second time. Boren then used his close friendship with Senator Nunn, an influential member of the committee and a severe critic of the past shenanigans of Gates during Iran-Contra, to make sure Nunn would not oppose Gates' nomination.

As a result of these senatorial maneuverings, which is typical of the legislative process, President Bush signed the statutory IG provisions into law in 1990. Bush, a former CIA director, objected to the possibility of an IG that would be "out of control," and used the signing ceremony to warn against any compromise of sensitive intelligence as a result of the new office. The Bush administration also waited nearly a year before appointing an independent IG, Frederick P. Hitz, a lawyer and a former member of the CIA's DO. Hitz occupied the position for eight years, and he surprisingly turned out to be just the kind of junkyard dog that the position of a statutory IG demanded.

THE CIA'S REPORT CARD

The 9/11 attacks on the WTC and the Pentagon exposed the fundamental weakness of America's intelligence community, particularly the CIA and the FBI. The absence of any terrorist attacks against the United States since 9/11 suggests that the reorganizations and reforms of the past five years have made this nation safer. We are certainly more vigilant as a nation, but the intelligence picture is complicated and much work needs to be done to limit our vulnerability to terrorism.

There have been several notable achievements, starting with the operational success of the CIA against the Taliban and al Qaeda in 2001. Too much attention has been devoted to the failure to capture bin Laden, and not enough attention has been given to the logistical and financial disruption to his organization that has limited bin Laden's ability to plan follow-up operations in the United States. The CIA and the FBI, along with foreign intelligence liaison services, have operated effectively in capturing and killing top al Qaeda leaders. When FBI director Mueller claimed to know that "al Qaeda maintains the ability and the intent to inflict significant casualties in the U.S. with little warning," the Congressional intelligence committees should have demanded his evidence.

The creation of the National Counterterrorism Center in January 2005 has led to the beginning of a central repository for terrorism information and greater connectivity between all sixteen intelligence agencies and their databases. Senior military officers still dominate the top positions at the Center, although the representation of all agencies should lead to greater sharing of information, at least with the sponsoring agencies. There has been greater consolidation of information, particularly a more comprehensive watchlist system that could have prevented 9/11 terrorists al-Mihdhar and al-Hazmi from falling through the cracks of the system. There is still an inadequate flow of information between federal and state or local intelligence agencies, and the military leadership of NCTC cannot cope with the need for strategic intelligence on terrorism. The nation lacks one central depository for all information on national and international terrorism; the DHS should be the home of this depository. The FBI lacks an effective computer system to coordinate intelligence information, which is central to preventing another terrorist attack.

The CIA's fundamental flaws, which contributed to the 9/11 failure, have gone largely uncorrected. There is far too much attention given to current and tactical intelligence and insufficient attention to the big picture needs of strategic intelligence. The CIA worries about the intelligence needs of the warfighter, and devotes insufficient attention to the geopolitical interests of the policymaker. The appointment of a four-star general, Michael Hayden, will not correct this problem, and the fact that Hayden was director of the NSA and defended the policy of warrantless eavesdropping does not augur well for the credibility of the CIA. The CIA's extra-legal activities, particularly renditions and secret prisons, have complicated the task of maintaining credible relations with our allies in the battle against terrorism. Italian and German courts have demanded the extradition of twenty-five CIA operatives, whose clumsy tradecraft left Agency fingerprints over their rendition efforts, but the Bush administration has refused to cooperate.

The greatest setback to U.S. efforts, however, has been the profligate military campaign in Iraq, which created a new base for terrorists, thus weakening the national security of the United States, the campaign against terrorism, and the collection efforts of the CIA. The war has led to CIA secret prisons, which must be closed, as well as the odious practice of secretly flying foreign suspects to foreign countries where they are routinely tortured. The CIA's use of torture and abuse, even in the case of Khalid Sheikh Mohammed, must be stopped. All of these practices speak to the moral corruption of the CIA, as well as the entire nation. Overall, the post-9/11 changes have made us safer at home, but as long as terrorists can operate the world over, we must demand better management of our $50 billion intelligence industry.

Notes

CHAPTER 1

1. Harold P. Ford, *Estimative Intelligence: The Purposes and Problems of National Intelligence Estimating* (Washington, DC: University Press of America, 1993), pp. 5–6.

2. Rhodri Jeffreys-Jones, "Why Was the CIA Established in 1947?" in *Eternal Vigilance: Fifty Years of the CIA*, eds. Rhodri Jeffreys-Jones and Christopher Andrew (London: Frank Cass, 1997), p. 21.

3. See *CIA's Analysis of the Soviet Union 1947–1991*, eds. Gerald K. Haines and Robert E. Leggett (Washington, DC: CIA's Center for the Study of Intelligence, 2001). The Center has produced useful historical studies of the CIA, but its work has been one-sided and rarely deals with intelligence and operational failures and never mentions the individual failures of various CIA directors.

4. U.S. Congress, Senate Select Committee to Study Governmental Operations with Respect to Intelligence Activities, *Supplementary Detailed Staff Reports on Foreign and Military Intelligence, Book IV* (Washington, DC: U.S. Government Printing Office, 1983), p. 7.

5. Dean Acheson, *Present at the Creation* (New York: W. W. Norton, 1969), p. 118.

6. Raymond L. Garthoff, *Assessing the Adversary: Estimates by the Eisenhower Administration of Soviet Intentions and Capabilities* (Washington, DC: The Brookings Institution, 1991), p. 20.

7. Michael Warner, ed., *The CIA Under Harry Truman* (Washington, DC: Center for the Study of Intelligence, 1994).

8. Evan Thomas, *The Very Best Men: Four Who Dared: The Early Years of the CIA* (New York: Simon and Schuster, 1995), pp. 29–30.

9. Ibid., p. 35.

10. We have little official information about the CIA-sponsored coup in Iran because the Agency illegally destroyed the official records, leaving Kermit Roosevelt's memoir (*Countercoup: The Struggle for the Control of Iran*, New York: McGraw-Hill, 1981). See Tim Weiner, "CIA Destroyed Files on 1953 Iran Coup," *The New York Times,* May 29, 1997, p. 19.

11. Gerald K. Haines, *CIA and Guatemala Assassination Proposals, 1952–1954* (Washington, DC: CIA Historical Staff); and Nicholas Cullather, *Operation PBSUCCESS: The United States and Guatemala 1952–1954,* (Washington, DC: Center for the Study of Intelligence).

357

12. Derek Leebaert, *The Fifty-Year Wound: The True Price of America's Cold War Victory* (New York: Little, Brown and Company, 2002), p. 173.

13. "Report of the Special Study Group (Doolittle Committee) on the Covert Activities of the Central Intelligence Agency" (September 30, 1954), in *The Central Intelligence Agency: History and Documents,* William M. Leary, ed. (Tuscaloosa: University of Alabama Press, 1984), p. 144.

14. *The New York Times,* January 24, 2007, p. 19.

15. Walter Pincus, "An Admonition on Intelligence," *Washington Post,* February 26, 2006, p. 18.

16. Raymond L. Garthoff, *A Journey Through the Cold War: A Memoir of Containment and Coexistence* (Washington, DC: Brookings Institution Press, 2001), pp. 43–44.

17. CIA Memorandum, "The Caesar, Polo, and Esau Paper," June 2007, p. 2.

18. Gerald K. Haines and Robert E. Leggett, eds., *CIA's Analysis of the Soviet Union 1947–1991* (Washington, DC: CIA's Center for the Study of Intelligence, 2001), p. 9.

19. Sibel Edmonds and William Weaver, "To Tell the Truth," *Bulletin of the Atomic Scientists* (January/February 2006): 72.

20. Stephen Barr, "Fast-Changing CIA Puts New Emphasis on Recruiting," *Washington Post,* February 19, 2007, p. D-1.

CHAPTER 2

1. U.S. Government Printing Office, *Hearings Before the Select Committee on Intelligence of the United States Senate: Nomination of Robert M. Gates* (Washington, DC: Government Printing Office, 1991), p. 38.

2. "Report of the Special Study Group (Doolittle Committee) on the Covert Activities of the Central Intelligence Agency" (September 30, 1954), in *The Central Intelligence Agency: History and Documents,* William M. Leary, ed. (Tuscaloosa: University of Alabama Press, 1984), p. 144.

3. Derek Leebaert, *The Fifty-Year Wound: The True Price of America's Cold War Victory* (New York: Little, Brown and Company, 2002), p. 234.

4. Robert M. Gates, *From the Shadows: The Ultimate Insider's Story of Five Presidents and How They Won the Cold War* (New York: Simon and Schuster, 1996), p. 32.

5. *The Need to Know: The Report of the Twentieth Century Fund Task Force on Covert Action and American Democracy* (New York: Twentieth Century Fund Press, 1992), pp. 21–23.

6. House Permanent Select Committee on Intelligence, *IC 21: The Intelligence Community in the 21st Century* (Washington, DC: Government Printing Office, April 9, 1996), p. 205.

7. Commission on the Roles and Capabilities of the United State Intelligence Community, *Preparing for the 21st Century: An Appraisal of U.S. Intelligence* (Washington, DC: Government Printing Office, March 1, 1996); Council on Foreign Relations, *Making Intelligence Smarter: The Future of U.S. Intelligence* (New York: Council on Foreign Relations, 1996), p. 21.

8. See Melvin A. Goodman, "Ending the CIA's Cold War Legacy," *Foreign Policy 106* (Spring 1997).

9. See Evan Thomas, *The Very Best Men: Four Who Dared: The Early Years of the CIA* (New York: Simon and Schuster, 1995).

10. "Report of the Special Study Group (Doolittle Committee) on the Covert Activities of the Central Intelligence Agency" (September 30, 1954), in *The Central Intelligence Agency: History and Documents,* William M. Leary, ed. (Tuscaloosa: University of Alabama Press, 1984), p. 144.

11. See Nicholas Cullather, *The CIA's Secret History of Its Guatemalan Coup* (Stanford: Stanford University Press, 1998), which benefited from access to CIA files on the Arbenz coup, code-named *Operation PBSUCCESS*.

12. Raymond Garthoff, *The Great Transition: American-Soviet Relations and the End of the Cold War* (Washington, DC: The Brookings Institution, 1994), pp. 32–33.

13. Bob Woodward, "CIA Favors Khomeini, Exiles; Sources Say Agency Gave Them List of KGB Agents," *Washington Post*, November 19, 1986, p. 1, 28.

14. Mark Perry, *Eclipse: The Last Days of the CIA* (New York: William Morrow, 1992), p. 486.

15. John Prados, *Presidents' Secret Wars: CIA and Pentagon Covert Operations from World War II Through the Persian Gulf War* (Chicago: Elephant Papers, 1996), p. 486.

16. See Gary C. Schroen, *First In: An Insider's Account of How the CIA Spearheaded the War on Terror in Afghanistan* (New York: Ballantine Books, 2005).

17. See Gary Berntsen, "Jawbreaker: The Attack on bin Laden and Al-Qaeda: A Personal Account by the CIA's Key Field Commander" (New York: Crown Publishers, 2005), p. 173.

18. George Tenet, *At the Center of the Storm: My Years at the CIA* (New York: Harper-Collins, 2007).

19. *The New York Times*, September 13, 1998, p. 7; February 26, 1999, p. 9.

20. *The New York Times*, February 22, 1998, p. 6.

21. Gary Cohn and Ginger Thompson, "Unearthed: Fatal Secrets," *The Baltimore Sun*, Special Report, June 11–18, 1995.

22. Gates, *From the Shadows*, p. 51.

23. See Diego Condovez and Selig S. Harrison, *Out of Afghanistan: The Inside Story of the Soviet Withdrawal* (New York: Oxford University Press, 1995); Georgy Korniyenko and Sergei Akhromeyev, *Through the Eyes of a Marshal and a Diplomat: A Critical Look at the Foreign Policy of the USSR Before and After 1985* (Moscow: International Relations Publishing House, 1985); Carolyn M. Ekedahl and Melvin A. Goodman, *The Wars of Eduard Shevardnadze* (University Park, PA: Penn State Press, 1997).

24. Prados, *Presidents' Secret Wars*, p. 48.

25. Pat M. Holt, *Secret Intelligence and Public Policy: A Dilemma of Democracy* (Washington, DC: Congressional Quarterly Press, 1995), p. 162.

26. Tim Weiner, "CIA Bares its Bungling in Report on Bay of Pigs Invasion," *The New York Times*, February 22, 1998, p. 6.

27. Gates, *From the Shadows*, p. 310.

28. Gregory F. Treverton, *Covert Action* (New York: Basic Books, 1987), p. 11.

29. Walter Isaacson, *Kissinger: A Biography* (New York: Simon and Schuster, 1992), p. 290.

30. James Risen, "CIA Says It Used Nicaraguan Rebels Accused of Drug Tie," *The New York Times*, July 17, 1998, p. 1.

31. See Mahmood Mamdani, *Good Muslim, Bad Muslim: America, the Cold War and the Roots of Terror* (New York: Pantheon, 2004).

32. Scott Ritter, *War on Iraq* (New York: Context Books, 2002), p. 55–56

33. See *The Torture Papers: The Road to Abu Ghraib*, eds. Karen J. Greenberg and Joshua L. Dratel (London: Cambridge University Press, 2004) and Mark Danner, *Torture and Truth: America, Abu Ghraib, and the War on Terror* (New York: New York Review Books, 2004).

34. Thom Shanker, "Abu Ghraib Called Incubator for Terrorists," *The New York Times*, February 15, 2006, p. 14.

35. Jennifer Harbury, *Truth, Torture, and the American Way: The History and Consequences of U.S. Involvement in Torture* (Boston: Beacon Press, 2005), p. 46.

36. Intelligence Oversight Board (IOB), *Report on Guatemala*, June 28, 1996, p. 22.

37. Harbury, *Truth, Torture, and the American Way*, p. 52.

38. The Fourth Hague Convention of 1907 prohibited the torture of captured combatants or civilians, and the Geneva Conventions of 1949 strengthened the prohibitions against abuse and torture. White House Executive Orders in 1978 and 1981 specifically prohibited CIA actions either directly or through proxy that would be unlawful in the United States or would violate civil liberties. A series of CIA internal directives prohibited abuse and torture as well.

39. Walter Pincus, "Waterboarding Historically Controversial," *Washington Post,* October 5, 2006, p. 17.

40. Anthony Shadid, "America Prepares the War on Terror," *Boston Globe,* October 7, 2001, p. 1.

41. Rajiv Chandrasekaran, "U.S. Behind Secret Transfer of Terror Suspects," *Washington Post,* March 11, 2002, p. 1.

42. Ibid.

43. Craig Whitlock, "A Secret Deportation of Terror Suspects," *Washington Post,* July 25, 2004, p. 1.

44. Chandrasekaran, "Secret Transfer," *Washington Post,* March 11, 2002, p. 1.

45. Dana Priest, "Deported Terror Suspect Details Torture in Syria," *Washington Post,* November 5, 2003, p. 1

46. Guy Dinmore, "US Tries to Assure Allies that Extraordinary Renditions are Over," *Financial Times,* December 27, 2006, p. 5.

47. Michael Scheuer, "A Fine Rendition," *The New York Times,* October 25, 2006, p. 27.

48. *Washington Post,* December 6, 2005, p. 11.

49. Bradley Graham and Josh White, "General Cites Hidden Detainees," *Washington Post,* September 10, 2004, p. 24.

50. Letter from Clark Kent Ervin, Inspector General, U.S. Department of Homeland Security, to Congressman John Conyers, Jr, January 9, 2004.

51. Press Release, American Civil Liberties Union, "The Public Should Know of our Government's Treatment of Individuals Captured and Held Abroad" (September 15, 2004).

52. Dana Priest, *Washington Post,* November 2005, p. 1.

53. Deutsche Welle, Radio Broadcast, December 2, 2005.

54. Dana Priest, "Wrongful Imprisonment: Anatomy of a CIA Mistake," *Washington Post,* December 4, 2005, p. 1.

55. Priest, "Wrongful Imprisonment," p. 25.

56. Dana Priest, "Covert CIA Program Withstands New Furor," *Washington Post,* December 30, 2005, p. 1.

57. *Washington Post,* November 23, 2005, p. 18.

58. R. Jeffrey Smith, "Worried CIA Officers Buy Legal Insurance," *Washington Post,* September 11, 2006, p. 1.

59. Mark Mazzetti, "Questions Raised about Bush's Primary Clains in Defense of Secret Detention Systems, *The New York Times,* September 8, 2006, p. 12.

60. *Secrecy and Government Bulletin 56* (March 1996), p. 2.

61. Thom Shanker and Scott Shane, "Elite Troops Get Expanded Role on Intelligence," *The New York Times,* March 8, 2006, p. 1.

62. Shanker and Shane, "Elite Troops," p. 6.

63. Stephen Rickard, "Interrogators Beware," *Washington Post,* October 17, 2006, p. 21.

CHAPTER 3

1. Tim Weiner, *Legacy of Ashes: The History of the CIA* (New York: Doubleday, 2007), p. 367.

2. Richard Helms with William Hood, *A Look Over My Shoulder: A Life in the Central Intelligence Agency* (New York: Ballantine Books, 2003), p. 299.

3. See Harold P. Ford, *CIA and the Vietnam Policymakers: Three Episodes 1962–1968* (Washington, DC: Center for the Study of Intelligence, Central Intelligence Agency, 1998).

4. *The Pentagon Papers* (Vol. IV), p. 222; David Halberstam, *The Best and the Brightest*, p. 644.

5. Ford, *CIA and the Vietnam Policymakers*, p. 109.

6. Christopher Andrew, *For the President's Eyes Only* (New York: HarperCollins, 1995), p. 350.

7. Richard Helms with William Hood, *A Look Over My Shoulder: A Life in the Central Intelligence Agency* (New York: Ballantine Books, 2003), p. 423.

8. Stanley Karnow, *Vietnam: A History* (New York: The Viking Press, 1983), p. 405.

9. *The Indochina Wars*, pp. 299–300.

10. Ford, *CIA and the Vietnam Policymakers*, p. 119.

11. Ibid., pp. 119–20.

12. In addition to National Intelligence Officers (NIOs) Robert Walpole and Paul Pillar, who did the Bush administration's bidding on Iraq with a politicized National Intelligence Estimate (NIE) and an unclassified white paper, Graham Fuller provided the Reagan administration with an estimate that provided justification for the initiative with Iran in the mid-1980s that became the intelligence justification for Iran-Contra. A long-time NIO for strategic matters, Larry Gershwin, directed a series of politicized estimates on Soviet strategic capabilities to justify radical increases in U.S. defense spending at a time of Soviet strategic decline. Gershwin and NIO John Landry were reprimanded for their work on the October 2002 NIE on Iraqi weapons of mass destruction (WMD).

13. Ibid., p. 121.

14. Lyndon B. Johnson, *The Vantage Point: Perspectives of the Presidency, 1963–1969*, pp. 371–72. Walt Rostow wrote much of the president's memoir.

15. Walt Rostow, *The Diffusion of Power: An Essay in Recent History* (New York: MacMillan, 1972), pp. 464–65.

16. *Washington Post*, February 6, 1968, p. C3.

17. Ford, *CIA and the Vietnam Policymakers*, p. 88.

18. See Sam Adams, *War of Numbers: An Intelligence Memoir* (South Royalton, VT: Steerforth Press, 1994).

19. Ford, *CIA and the Vietnam Policymakers*, p. 93.

20. Ibid., p. 93.

21. See Sam Adams, *The War of Numbers* (South Royalton, VT: Steerforth Press, 1994).

22. Richard Helms with William Hood, *A Look over My Shoulder: A Life in the Central Intelligence Agency* (New York: Ballantine Books, 2003), p. 311.

23. Mark Perry, *Eclipse: The Last Days of the CIA* (New York: William Morrow and Company, 1992), pp. 313–14.

24. Richard Reeves, *President Nixon* (New York: Simon & Schuster, 2001), p. 483.

25. Ibid.

26. Helms and Hood, *A Look Over my Shoulder*, p. 410.

27. See Ford, *CIA and the Vietnam Policymakers*.

28. William Taubman, "Khrushchev vs. Mao: A Preliminary Sketch of the Role of Personality in the Sino-Soviet Split," *Wilson Center Issues 8–9* (Winter 1996–1997): 243.

29. The *Esau* collection on Communist nations and policies included several papers on the Sino–Soviet dispute that was first identified in 1960, when the U.S. academic community was writing about a Sino–Soviet alliance. Most of the papers in the collection were declassified and placed on the CIA website in June 2007. See www.foia.cia.gov/cpe.asp.

30. See Harold P. Ford, *Calling the Sino–Soviet Split* (Washington, DC: Center for Study of Intelligence, Winter 1998–1999).

31. Ibid., p. 19, fn 71.

32. See Philip Taubman, *Secret Empire: Eisenhower, the CIA, and the Hidden Story of America's Space Espionage* (New York: Simon & Schuster, 2003). An excellent study of the CIA's contribution to the development of spy planes and reconnaissance satellites in the 1950s and 1960s.

33. Taubman, *Secret Empire*, p. 326.

34. "Intelligence Forecasts of Soviet Intercontinental Attack Forces: An Evaluation of the Record," CIA Directorate of Intelligence Research Paper (April 1989, declassified in October 1993), p. 5.

35. Ibid., p. iii.

CHAPTER 4

1. Michael Getler, "Intelligence Was Slow to Respond," *Washington Post*, February 11, 1984, p. 1.

2. George Shultz, *Triumph and Turmoil: My Years as Secretary of State* (New York: Scribner, 1993), p. 861.

3. Colin Powell, *My American Journey* (New York: Random House, 1995), p. 419.

4. October 6, 1973 was the tenth day of Ramadan and the anniversary of the Prophet Muhammad's victory at the Battle of Badr near Medina in 624. The Battle of Badr established the Prophet Muhammad as both a political and religious leader.

5. Pat M. Holt, *Secret Intelligence and Public Policy: A Dilemma of Democracy* (Washington, DC: Congressional Quarterly Press, 1995), p. 99.

6. James Carter, *Keeping Faith* (London: Collins, 1982), p. 438; Stansfield Turner, *Secrecy and Democracy: The CIA in Transition* (Boston: Houghton Mifflin Company, 1985), p. 115.

7. Gary Sick, *All Fall Down: America's Fateful Encounter with Iran* (London: Tauris, 1985), p. 30.

8. Stansfield Turner, *Secrecy and Democracy: The CIA in Transition* (Boston: Houghton Mifflin Company, 1985), p. 113.

9. "Iran: Evaluation of U.S. Intelligence Performance Prior to November 1978," House Permanent Select Committee on Intelligence, Staff Report (January 1979), pp. 6–7.

10. *Iran: Evaluation of U.S. Intelligence Performance Prior to November 1978*, Staff Report of the Subcommittee on Evaluation of the Permanent Select Committee on Intelligence in the U.S. House of Representatives (Washington, DC: U.S. Government Printing Office, 1979), p. 6.

11. *Iran: Evaluation*, p. 8.

12. Ambassador Anatoly Dobrynin, *In Confidence: Moscow's Ambassador to America's Six Cold War Presidents* (New York: Random House, 1995), p. 429.

13. David Newsome, *The Soviet Brigade in Cuba: A Study in Political Diplomacy* (Bloomington: Indiana University Press, 1987), p. 34.

14. "Intelligence Forecasts of Soviet Intercontinental Attack Forces: An Evaluation of the Record," CIA Directorate of Intelligence Research Paper (April 1989, declassified in October 1993), p. 5.

15. "Intelligence Forecasts," CIA Research Paper, p. 5.

16. Frederick P. Hitz, *The Great Game: The Myths and Reality of Espionage* (New York: Vintage Books, 2004), p. 21.

17. Duane R. Clarridge, *A Spy for All Seasons: My Life in the CIA* (New York: Scribner, 1997), pp. 269–72.

18. Robert V. Keeley, "CIA-Foreign Service Relations," in *National Insecurity: U.S. Intelligence After the Cold War*, Craig Eisendrath (Philadelphia: Temple University Press, 2000), p. 63.

19. Les Aspin, "Debate over U.S. Strategic Forecasts: A Mixed Record," *Strategic Review 8* (Summer 1980): 29–43.

20. "Trends in Global Terrorism: Implications for the United States," National Intelligence Estimate, Key Judgments (April 2006), p. 1.

21. "Trends in Global Terrorism," p. 3.

22. Thomas E. Ricks, *Fiasco: The American Military Adventure in Iraq* (New York: The Penguin Press, 2006), p. 213.

23. Michael R. Gordon and General Bernard E. Trainor, *Cobra II: The Inside Story of the Invasion and Occupation of Iraq* (New York: Pantheon Books, 2006), p. 498.

CHAPTER 5

1. Douglas Jehl, "Chief of CIA Tells His Staff to Back Bush," *The New York Times*, November 17, 2004, p. 15.

2. Louis G. Sarris, "McNamara's War on the Facts," *The New York Times*, September 8, 1995, p. 11.

3. Daniel Ellsberg, *Secret* (New York: Viking, 2002), p. 434.

4. Scott Shane, "Doubts Cast on Vietnam Incident, But Secret Study Stays Classified," *The New York Times*, October 31, 2005, p. 1.

5. Robert M. Gates, "The CIA and American Foreign Policy," *Foreign Affairs 66* (Winter 1987–1988), p. 227.

6. See Craig Eisendrath, Melvin A. Goodman, Gerald E. Marsh, *The Phantom Defense: America's Pursuit of the Star Wars Illusion* (London: Praeger, 1999), pp. 68–69.

7. Robert E. White, "Renewal in El Salvador," *Washington Post*, January 16, 1992, p. 17.

8. Peter Kornbluh and Malcolm Byrne, eds., *The Iran-Contra Scandal: The Declassified History* (New York: New Press, 1993), pp. 45–49.

9. George Shultz, *Turmoil and Triumph: My Years as Secretary of State* (Scribner, 1993); Chester Crocker, *High Noon in Southern Africa: Making Peace in a Tough Neighborhood* (New York: W.W. Norton and Company, 1992).

10. Crocker, *High Noon in Southern Africa*, pp. 294–95.

11. Frances Fitzgerald, *Way Out There in the Blue: Reagan, Star Wars and the End of the Cold War* (New York: Simon and Schuster, 2000), p. 330.

12. Ibid., p. 330.

13. Noel E. Firth and James Noren, *Soviet Defense Spending: A History of CIA Estimates, 1950–1990* (College Station: Texas A&M University Press, 1998), p. 94.

14. Senate Foreign Relations Committee, "Estimating the Size and Growth of the Soviet Economy," Senate Hearing 101–1112, 101st Congress, 2nd session, 1990, p. 4.

15. Pat M. Holt, *Secret Intelligence and Public Policy: A Dilemma of Democracy* (Washington, DC: CQ Press, 1995), p. 90.

16. Shultz, *Triumph and Turmoil*, pp. 1087–88.

17. Craig R. Whitney, "Does Tumult Imperil Gorbachev's Goals? Some U.S. Views," *The New York Times*, March 2, 1988, p. 12.

18. Peter W. Dickson, "Power Speaks to the Truth: Politicized Intelligence and the Challenge of Nuclear Proliferation," Unpublished Paper, April, 2006.

19. Walter Pincus, *Washington Post*, May 23, 2006, p. 11.

20. Seymour Hersh, *The New Yorker*, March 29, 1993.

21. Warren Strobel, "Kremlin Has Spent $150 Billion on its 'Star Wars,' CIA Estimates," *Washington Times*, November 26, 1986, p. 1.

22. CIA director George Tenet letter to Senate intelligence committee chairman Bob Graham (D-Florida), October 2002, *The New York Times,* October 9, 2002, p. 17.

23. CIA Memorandum for the Record, "Iranian Support for Terrorism—An Abrupt Change in Line in CIA Publications, Late 1985-early 1986," October 5, 1991 (Submitted to the Senate Select Committee for Intelligence as part of the documentary materials in the Gates confirmation hearings.)

24. Ibid., p. 2.

25. *Washington Post*, Outlook Section, November 29, 1987, p. 1.

26. Stephen Engelberg, "Doubts on Intelligence Data: Iran Affair Renews the Issue," *The New York Times*, August 31, 1987, p. 6.

27. Mark Danner of *The New Yorker*, Raymond Bonner of *The New York Times*, and Alma Guillermoprieto of the *Washington Post* were credited with the forensic investigations and interviews that described the role of Salvadoran soldiers in the massacre of eight hundred men, women, and children in December 1981. The massacre was conducted by the Atlacatl Battalion, the first U.S.-trained Salvadoran army unit. In response to pressure from the Reagan administration, *New York Times* executive editor Abe Rosenthal cut back Bonner's work in the *Times'* South American bureau.

28. Robert Parry, *Secrecy and Privilege: Rise of the Bush Dynasty from Watergate to Iraq* (Arlington, VA: The Media Consortium Inc., 2004).

29. Letter from CIA director George Tenet to Senate intelligence committee chairman Bob Graham (D-Florida), October 2002, *The New York Times*, October 9, 2002.

30. See Senate Hearings regarding Gates Confirmation.

31. Conversation with Ross Cowey, November 17, 2006.

32. Carolyn McGiffert Ekedahl, "The Gates Hearing: A Biased Account," *Studies in Intelligence* (Washington, DC: Central Intelligence Agency, 1994), p. 76. *(Studies in Intelligence* has been an in-house classified CIA journal since 1955, with the publication of unclassified articles since 1990.)

33. James Worthen, "The Gates Hearings: Politicization and Soviet Analysis at CIA," *Studies in Intelligence* (Washington, DC: Central Intelligence Agency, 1994).

34. *Hearings Before the Select Committee on Intelligence of the U.S. Senate,* 1991.

35. Parry, *Secrecy and Privilege*, p. 197.

36. See U.S. Senate Select Committee on Intelligence, "Hearings: Nomination of Robert M. Gates" (Senate Hearing 102–799, volumes I-III), September-October 1991. U.S. Senate Select Committee on Intelligence, "Report: Nomination of Robert M. Gates To Be Director of Central Intelligence," (Executive Report, 102–19), October 24, 1991.

37. "Report of the DCI Task Force on Politicization," Edward Proctor, Chairman of the Task Force on Politicization, January 15, 1992.

38. "The Integrity and Objectivity of National Foreign Intelligence Estimates," Richard J. Kerr, Deputy Director for Intelligence, April 28, 1987.

39. Paul Pillar, "Intelligence, Policy, and the War in Iraq," *Foreign Affairs 85* (March/April 2006): 15–27.

40. Ibid., p. 24.

41. George Tenet, *At the Center of the Storm: My Years at the CIA* (New York: Harper-Collins, 2007)

42. Lowell Bergman, Eric Lichtblau, Scott Shane, and Don Van Natta, Jr., "Spy Agency Data after Sept. 11 Led FBI to Dead Ends," *The New York Times,* January 17, 2006, p. 1.

43. David Cole, "Are We Safer?" *The New York Review of Books,* Volume LIII, Number 4, March 9, 2006, p. 17.

44. Dan Eggen and Julie Tate, "US Campaign Produces Few Convictions on Terrorism Charges," *Washington Post,* June 12, 2005, p. 1.

45. Michael Isikoff, "The Other Big Brother," *Newsweek,* January 22, 2006, p. 15.

CHAPTER 6

1. See Philip Taubman, *Secret Empire: Eisenhower, the CIA, and the Hidden Story of America's Space Espionage* (New York: Simon and Schuster, 2003), p. 283.

2. Col. A. Tsvetkov, "The United States—Placing its Stake on Strengthening Espionage," *Zaubezhnoye voyennoye obozreniye* [*Foreign Military Review 8*] (August 1981): 4. Quoted in Garthoff, *Great Transition,* p. 62fn.

3. Robert M. Gates, *From the Shadows: The Ultimate Insider's Story of Five Presidents and How They Won the Cold War* (New York: Simon & Schuster, 1996), p. 273.

4. *At Cold War's End: US Intelligence on the Soviet Union and Eastern Europe, 1989–1991* (CIA's Center for the Study of Intelligence, 1999), pp. vii-viii.

5. See Melvin A. Goodman, *Gorbachev's Retreat: The Third World* (New York: Praeger Publishers, 1992); and Carolyn Ekedahl and Raymond Duncan's *Moscow in the Third World Under Gorbachev* (Boulder, CO: Westview Press, 1990), based on papers written at the CIA in the 1980s that DDI Gates refused to release to the intelligence and policy communities.

6. R. Jeffrey Smith, "Aspin: U.S. Suppressing Data on Cuts," *Washington Post*, November 17, 1989, p. 14.

7. Jack F. Matlock, Jr., *Autopsy on an Empire: The American Ambassador's Account of the Collapse of the Soviet Union* (New York: Random House, 1995), p. 545.

8. Matlock, *Autopsy on an Empire,* p. 545.

9. Stansfield Turner, "Intelligence for a New World Order," *Foreign Affairs* (Fall 1991): 162.

10. "CIA Briefing Paper entitled 'USSR: Economic Trends, and Policy Developments,'" in *Allocation of Resources in the Soviet Union and China—1983.* Hearings before the Subcommittee on International Trade, Finance, and Security Economics of the Joint Economic Committee, 98th Congress, 1st session. (Washington, DC: GPO, 1983), p. 306.

11. Raymond L. Garthoff, *Détente and Confrontation: American-Soviet Relations from Nixon to Reagan* (Washington, DC: The Brookings Institution, 1985), p. 798.

12. Garthoff, *Détente and Confrontation*, p. 602.

13. Secretary of State Henry Kissinger, "America's Permanent Interests," *Department of State Bulletin 74* (April 5, 1976): 427.

14. Shultz, *Turmoil and Triumph*, p. 1003.

15. "Powell Calls His U.N. Speech a Lasting Blot on His Record," *The New York Times,* September 9, 2005, p. 10.

CHAPTER 7

1. Michael Eisenstadt, "Understanding Saddam," *The National Interest* (Fall 2005): 121.

2. Daniel Benjamin and Steven Simon, *The Age of Sacred Terror: Radical Islam's War Against America* (New York: Random House Trade Paperback, 2003), p. 242; Robin Wright, "Islam in the '90s: A Study of Diversity: Despite Pervasive Stereotypes, Major Islamist Groups Differ Widely in Tactics and Tenets," *Los Angeles Times*, February 7, 1995, p. 1.

3. Benjamin and Simon, *Age of Sacred Terror*, pp. 242–43.

4. Quoted in John Ranelagh, *The Agency: The Rise and Decline of the CIA* (New York: Simon and Schuster, 1986), p. 336.

5. *Washington Star*, August 19, 1980, p. 3.

6. See Raymond Garthoff, "The Great Transition," p. 94 fn, and Bernard Gwertzman, "Papal Plot May Hurt U.S.-Soviet Ties," *New York Times*, October 312, 1984, p. 3.

7. Bob Woodward, *Veil: The Secret Wars of the CIA, 1981–1987* (New York: Simon & Schuster, 1987), p. 128.

8. Joseph E. Persico, *Casey: The Lives and Secrets of William J. Casey: From the OSS to the CIA* (New York: Viking, 1990), p. 286. Persico's biography was spectacularly misinformed on the subject of the CIA and the Papal Plot. He concluded that Casey could not get the conclusions he wanted from the special assessment and that he told the president that there was "insufficient evidence" to make the case. In fact, the three coauthors of the CIA memorandum made the case Casey and Gates wanted; the assessment was delivered to the president and vice president, and the three authors received rapid promotions within the system.

9. Ibid., p. 287.

10. Clair Sterling disavowed any access to the CIA in writing her books, but she admitted to discussions with Michael Ledeen and Italian intelligence chief General Giuseppe Santovito on subjects of international terrorism and the Papal Plot. If she wasn't a witting agent for CIA propaganda, then she certainly was an unwitting one on the subject of Soviet links to terrorism, according to several clandestine service officers who met with Bill Casey in 1981. See Philip Jenkins, "The Assassins Revisited: Claire Sterling and the Politics of Intelligence," *Intelligence and National Security 1* (September 1986): 459–71.

11. Admiral Stansfield Turner, *Burn Before Reading: Presidents, CIA Directors, and Secret Intelligence* (New York: Hyperion, 2005), p. 220.

12. Richard A. Clarke, *Against All Enemies: Inside America's War on Terror* (New York: Free Press, 2004), p. 96.

13. Staff Statement No. 6, "The Military," National Commission on Terrorist Strikes.

14. Karen DeYoung, "Spy Agencies Say Iraq War Hurting U.S. Terror Fight," *Washington Post*, September 24, 2006, p. 1.

15. Michael Isikoff and David Corn, *Hubris: The Inside Story of Spin, Scandal, and the Selling of the Iraq War* (New York: Crown Publishers, 2006), pp. 314–15.

16. Clarke, *Against All Enemies*, p. 223.

17. National Commission on Terrorist Attacks Upon the United States, Staff Statement No. 8, "National Policy Coordination, March 24, 2004, p. 3.

18. Clarke, *Against All Enemies*, p. 209–10.

19. See Bob Woodward, *Bush at War* (New York: Simon and Schuster, 2002).

20. Ibid., p. 7.

21. Clarke, *Against All Enemies*, p. 224.

22. Staff Statement No. 6, p. 11.

23. George Tenet, *At the Center of the Storm: My Years at the CIA* (New York: Harper-Collins, 2007), pp. 153–54.

24. "National Policy Coordination," Staff Statement No. 8," March 24, 2004, p. 11.

25. "Intelligence Policy," Staff Reports of the 9/11 Commission, Staff Statement No. 7, pp. 137–38.

26. "Trends in Global Terrorism: Implications for the United States," National Intelligence Estimate, April 2006, Key Judgments, p. 3.

CHAPTER 8

1. James Risen, "White House Drags its Feet on Testifying at 9/11 Panel," *New York Times*, 13 September 2002, p. 10.

2. Joint Inquiry Staff Statement, Part I, Joint Inquiry Staff, 18 September 2002.

3. *Wall Street Journal*, May 13, 1998, p. 22.

4. Ronald E. Powaski, *Return to Armageddon: The United States and the Nuclear Arms Race, 1981–1999* (New York: Oxford University Press, 2000), p. 226.

5. "OIG Report on CIA Accountablity with Respect to the 9/11 Attacks," p. xii.

6. Josh White, "Alleged Architect of 9/11 Confesses to Many Attacks," *Washington Post*. March 15, 2007, p. 1.

7. Lawrence Wright, *The Looming Tower: Al-Qaeda and the Road to 9/11* (New York: Alfred A. Knopf, 2006), p. 307.

8. "OIG Report on CIA Accountability with Respect to the 9/11 Attacks," p. xiii.

9. Wright, *The Looming Tower*, p. 312.

10. *The New York Times*, 23 September 2002, p. 11.

11. Joint Inquiry, Final Report, Part 1, December 10, 2002, p. 1.

12. Richard A. Clarke, *Against All Enemies: Inside America's War on Terror* (New York: Free Press, 2004), p. 91.

13. The 9/11 Investigations, Staff Reports of the 9/11 Commission, Staff Statement No. 7, "Intelligence Policy," p. 133, cited in *The 9/11 Investigations*, ed. Steven Strasser (New York: Public Affairs, 2004).

14. James Bamford, *A Pretext for War: 9/11, Iraq, and the Abuse of America's Intelligence Agencies* (New York: Doubleday, 2004), p. 211.

15. The 9/11 Investigations, Staff Studies of the 9/11 Commission, Staff Statement No. 7: "Intelligence Policy," p. 140.

16. *Washington Post*, May 19, 2002, p. 9.

17. Letter from Rex A. Hudson, June 29, 2004.

18. Walter Lippmann, *Public Opinion* (New Brunswick, NJ: Transaction Publishers, 1997), p. 386.

19. Wright, *The Looming Tower*, p. 283.

20. Lawrence Wright, *The Looming Tower: Al Qaeda and the Road to 9/11* (New York: Alfred A. Knopf, 2006), p. 352. The most informative and the best written of all the books on 9/11.

21. "OIG Report on CIA Accountability with Respect to the 9/11 Attacks," p. x.

22. James Risen, "Spy's Notes on Iraqi Aims Were Shelved, Suit Says," *The New York Times*, August 1, 2005, p. 8.

23. Guillaume Dasquie, "September 11, 2001: The French Knew Much About It," *Le Monde*, April 16, 2007, p. 1.

24. The 9/11 Commission, "The Performance of the Intelligence Community," Staff Statement No. 11, p. 7.

25. Mark Danner, "Taking Stock of the Forever War," *The New York Times Magazine*, September 11, 2005, p. 46.

26. Ibid., p. 47.

27. Peter Baker and Karen DeYoung, "Nominee to Coordinate War Offers Grim Forecast on Iraq," *Washington Post*, June 8, 2007, p. 1

28. "Challenging the Red Line between Intelligence and Policy," Conference at the Institute for the Study of Diplomacy, Edmund A. Walsh School of Foreign Service (Washington, DC: Georgetown University, Spring 2004).

CHAPTER 9

1. Elisabeth Bumiller, "Traces of Terror: The Strategy," *The New York Times*, September 7, 2002, p. 1.

2. See George Bush and Brent Scowcroft, *A World Transformed: The Collapse of the Soviet Empire, The Unification of Germany, and The Gulf War* (New York: Knopf, 1998).

3. *The New Yorker*, October 17, 2005, p. 36.

4. Elisabeth Bumiller, "Bush Aides Set Strategy to Sell Policy on Iraq," *The New York Times,* September 7, 2002, p. 1.

5. The British established their own ad hoc group of officials under Cabinet Office Chairmanship to develop an information campaign similar to the U.S. group. Bumiller, "Bush Aides Set Strategy," p. 1.

6. Barton Gellman and Walter Pincus, "Depiction of Threat Outgrew Supporting Evidence," *Washington Post*, August 10, 2003, p. 1.

7. Jason Leopold, "DoD Report Appears to Confirm Downing Street Memo," *Truthout* (February 9, 2007): 1–2.

8. CNN, September 8, 2002; *The New York Times*, September 8, 2002, p. 1.

9. Prior to the Iraq War, but following the successful Afghan adventure in 2001, Laura Bush told the press, "Only the terrorist and the Taliban threaten to pull out women's fingernails for wearing nail polish." Three days later, Cherie Blair, the wife of the prime minister, told the press, "In Afghanistan if you wear nail polish, you could have your nails torn out." Is it possible U.S.-British coordination included the wives of the heads of state?

10. Don Van Natta, Jr., "Bush Was Set on Path to War, Memo by British Adviser Says," *The New York Times,* March 27, 2006, p. 1.

11. Thomas E. Ricks, *Fiasco: The American Military Adventure in Iraq* (New York: The Penguin Press, 2006), p. 3.

12. Paul Pillar, "An Oversight Hearing on Pre-War Intelligence Relating to Iraq," Senate Democratic Policy Committee Hearing, June 26, 2006.

13. Peter Eisner and Knut Royce, *The Italian Letter: How the Bush Administration Used a Fake Letter to Build the Case for War in Iraq* (New York: Rodale Inc., 2007), p. 56.

14. Walter Pincus and Jeffrey Smith, "Official's Key Report on Iraq is Faulted," *Washington Post*, February 9, 2007, p. 1.

15. Matt Renner, "Pentagon Officer Created Phony Intelligence on Iraq/al Qaeda Link," *Truthout* (April 6, 2007): 2.

16. See Central Intelligence Agency, National Intelligence Estimate on Iraq's Continuing WMD Programs, October 2, 2002.

17. Central Intelligence Agency, "Iraqi Support for Terrorism," January 29, 2003.

18. Thomas Powers, "What Tenet Knew," *New York Review of Books 54(12)* (July 19, 2007): 37.

19. Peter Eisner, "How Bogus Letter Became a Case for War," *Washington Post*, April 3, 2007, p. 16.

20. Ambassador Joseph Wilson, "What I Didn't Find in Africa," *The New York Times*, July 6, 2003, p. 27.

21. Craig Unger, "The War They Wanted, the Lies They Needed," *Vanity Fair*, p. 173.

22. Eisner and Royce, *The Italian Letter*, p. 76.

23. Jason Leopold and Marc Ash, "Cheney's Handwritten Notes Implicate Bush in Plame Affair," *Truthout/Report* (January 31, 2007): 1.

24. Dafna Linzer, "Prosecutor in CIA Leak Case Corrects Part of Court Filing," *Washington Post*, April 12, 2006, p. 8.

25. Bob Drogin and John Goetz, "How US Fell under the Spell of 'Curveball,'" *The Los Angeles Times*, November 20, 2005, p. 1.

26. Drogin and Goetz, "The Spell of 'Curveball,'" p. 1.

27. Karen DeYoung, *Soldier: The Life of Colin Power* (New York: Knopf: 2006), p. 317.

28. Douglas Jehl, "Report Warned Bush Team About Intelligence Doubts," *The New York Times*, November 6, 2005, p. 16.

29. President George Bush, Remarks in Meeting with President Alvaro Uribe of Colombia, September 25, 2002, see www.whitehouse.gov/news/releases/2002/09/20020925-1.html; *Washington Post*, December 22, 2005, p. 17.

30. Eric Schmitt, "Rumsfeld Says U.S. Has 'Bulletproof' Evidence of Iraq's Links to al Qaeda, *The New York Times*, September 28, 2002, p. 9; John B. Judis and Spencer Ackerman, "The First Casualty," *The New Republic* (June 30, 2003): 24.

31. President Bush, Statement after Cabinet Meeting, June 17, 2004.

32. Secretary of State Colin Powell, Speech to the UN Security Council, February 5, 2003.

33. Secretary of Defense Donald Rumsfeld, Defense Department Briefings, February 4, 2003.

34. National Security Advisor Condoleezza Rice, Interviews on "Face the Nation" and "Fox News Sunday," March 9, 2003 and September 7, 2003.

35. When Shinseki had his retirement ceremony in 2003, Secretary of Defense Rumsfeld was too busy to attend, which caused more anger among the Pentagon's general officers than the secretary's callous disregard for the inadequate force sent to Iraq.

36. Lori Montgomery, "The Cost of War, Unnoticed," *Washington Post*, May 8, 2007, p. D-1.

37. Hans Blix, *Disarming Iraq* (New York: Pantheon, 2004).

38. Bob Woodward, *State of Denial* (New York: Simon & Schuster, 2006) p. 297.

39. Jay Solomon and Gabriel Kahn, "The Italian Job: How Fake Iraq Memos Tripped up Ex-Spy," *The Wall Street Journal,* February 24, 2006, p. 1.

40. Colonel Lawrence B. Wilkerson (ret.), "Pre-War Intelligence Relating to Iraq," Senate Democratic Policy Committee Hearing, June 26, 2006.

41. Ken Adelman, "Cakewalk Revisited," *Washington Post*, April 10, 2003, p. 27.

42. Bob Woodward, *Plan of Attack* (New York: Simon & Schuster, 2004), p. 411.

43. George Tenet, *At the Center of the Storm: My Years at the CIA* (New York: Harper-Collins, 2007), pp. 2–79.

44. Murray Waas, "Cheney, Libby Blocked Papers to Senate Intelligence Panel," *National Journal*, October 27, 2005.

45. Op. cit.

46. Paul Pillar, *Foreign Affairs* 85(2) (March/April 2006): 71

47. Scot Lehigh, "Revealing the Road to 'The Dark Side,'" *Boston.com*, July 13, 2006.

48. Joby Warrick, "Lacking Biolabs, Trailers Carried Cast for War," *Washington Post*, April 12, 2006, p. 1.

49. Joseph Cirincione, "Gold Medal Inspector," Carnegie Endowment for International Peace, October 20, 2005.

50. Jeff Stein, Congressional Quarterly.com, October 23, 2006, p. 3.

51. Walter Pincus, "Senator Outlines Plans for Intelligence Panel," *Washington Post*, November 16, 2006, p. 4.

52. "Decoding Mr. Bush's Denials," editorial, *New York Times*, November 15, 2005, p. 28.

53. Richard Kerr, Thomas Wolfe, Rebecca Donegan, and Aris Pappas, "Issues for the U.S. Intelligence Community," *Studies in Intelligence* 49(3) (2005): 53.

54. Lou Dubose and Jake Bernstein, *Vice: Dick Cheney and the Hijacking of the American Presidency* (New York: Random House, 2006), p. 211.

55. Dana Millbank and Mike Allen, "Bush Skirts Queries on Iraq Nuclear Negotiations," *Washington Post*, July 10, 2003, p. 18.

CHAPTER 10

1. Paul Pillar, "An Oversight Hearing on Pre-War Intelligence Relating to Iraq," Senate Democratic Policy Committee Hearing, June 26, 2006.

2. Michael R. Gordon and General Bernard E. Trainor, *Cobra II: The Inside Story of the Invasion and Occupation of Iraq* (New York: Pantheon Books, 2006), p. 125.

3. Report of the Select Committee on Intelligence on the U.S. Intelligence Community's Pre-War Intelligence Assessments on Iraq, Together with Additional Views, July 7, 2004.

4. Commission on the Intelligence Capabilities of the United States Regarding Weapons of Mass Destruction, March 31, 2005, p. 520, cited in *The WMD Mirage: Iraq's Decade of Deception and America's False Premise for War,* ed. Craig R. Whitney (New York: Public Affairs, 2005).

5. Report of the Select Committee on Intelligence on The Use By the Intelligence Community of Information Provided by the Iraqi National Congress, September 8, 2006, p. 113.

6. Ibid., pp. 113–114.

7. Tim Phelps and Knut Royce, *Long Island Newsday*, July 22, 2003 and David Ensor, CNN, July 13, 2004 as cited in Larry Johnson, "An Updated Plamegate Timeline," www .noquarter..typepad.com, April 11, 2006.

8. SICR, p. 55, cited in Johnson, "Plamegate Timeline."

9. SICR, p. 56, cited in Johnson, "Plamegate Timeline."

10. Craig Unger, "The War They Wanted, the Lies They Needed," *Vanity Fair* (February 2007): 117.

11. Ron Suskind, *The One Percent Doctrine: Deep Inside America's Pursuit of Its Enemies Since 9/11* (New York: Simon and Schuster, 2006), p. 168.

12. In 1980, the chief of the French CIA, the External Documentation and Counterespionage Service, or SDECE, convinced Ronald Reagan and Bill Casey that the Soviets were going to test the mettle of the new president in Central America, which could have been the beginning of Casey's preoccupation with Iran-Contra.

13. Bob Drogin and John Goetz, "How the United States Fell Under the Spell of 'Curveball'," *The Los Angeles Times*, August 1, 2005. p. 8.

14. Drogin and Goetz, "Spell of 'Curveball,'" p. 1.

15. In November 2000, Congress doubled funding for Iraqi opposition groups to more than $25 million and earmarked $18 million of this money to Chalabi's Iraqi National Congress, which then paid defectors for anti-Iraq information.

16. *The New York Times*, November 8, 2001, p. 17.

17. Peter Eisner and Knut Royce, *The Italian Letter* (New York: Rodale Books, 2007), p. 117.

18. Joby Warrick, "Warnings on WMD 'Fabricator' Were Ignored, Ex-CIA Aide Says," *Washington Post*, June 25, 2006, p. 18.

19. Drogin and Goetz, "The Spell of 'Curveball,'" p. 1.

20. Ibid., p. 18.

21. Ibid., p. 8.

22. *The New York Times*, May 22, 2003, p. 16.

23. Joby Warrick, "Lacking Biolabs: Trailers Carried Cast for War," *Washington Post*, April 12, 2006, p. 22.

24. Walter Pincus, "Tenet Defends Iraq Intelligence," *Washington Post*, May 31, 2003, p. 1.

25. National Intelligence Council, "Iraq's Continuing Program for Weapons of Mass Destruction: Key Judgments," October 2002 (declassified July 2003).

26. Walter Pincus, "CIA Learned in 2002 That Bin Laden Had No Iraq Ties, Report Says," *Washington Post,* September 15, 2006, p. 11.

27. S. Rep. NO. 108–301, at 332 (2004); "Report of Select Committee on Intelligence Provided by Iraqi National Congress," p. 197.

28. Christina Shelton, "Iraq, al-Qaeda and Tenet's Equivocation," *Washington Post*, June 27, 2007, p. 23.

29. Richard Clarke, *Against All Enemies* (New York: Free Press, 2004), p. 59.

30. Central Intelligence Agency, "Iraq and al-Qa'ida: Interpreting a Murky Relationship," June 21, 2002.

31. Central Intelligence Agency, "National Intelligence Estimate on Iraq's Continuing WMD Programs," October 2, 2002.

32. Central Intelligence Agency, "Iraqi Support for Terrorism," January 29, 2003.

33. Douglas Jehl, "Report Warned Bush Team about Intelligence Suspicions," *The New York Times*, November 6, 2005, p. 14.

34. CIA, "Murky Relationship," June 21, 2002.

35. CIA, "Iraqi Support for Terrorism," January 29, 2003.

36. Ron Suskind, *The One Percent Doctrine: Deep Inside America's Pursuit of Its Enemies Since 9/11*, (New York: Simon and Schuster, 2006), pp. 190–91.

37. Thomas L. Hughes, *The Fate of Facts in a World of Men: Foreign Policy and Intelligence-Making* (New York: Foreign Policy Association, 1976), p. 24.

38. The presentation of the Nobel Peace Prize to the International Atomic Energy Agency and its director, Mohammed el-Baradei, served as an international reminder that el-Baradei and the IAEA had outperformed the CIA and the intelligence community on the key issues of Iraq's weapons of mass destruction and the possibility that Saddam Hussein was trying to obtain uranium from Niger to reconstitute his nuclear weapons program.

39. Richard Kerr, Thomas Wolfe, Rebecca Donegan, and Aris Pappas, "Collection and Analysis on Iraq: Issues for the US Intelligence Community," *Studies In Intelligence* 49(3) (2005): 48.

40. Joseph Cirincione, "Gold Medal Inspector," Carnegie Endowment for International Peace, October 20, 2005.

41. James Risen, "Spy's Notes on Iraqi Aims Were Shelved, Suit Says," *The New York Times*, February 21, 2006, p. 15.

42. Ibid., p. 8.

43. Commission, pp. 517–18 in Whitney, *The WMD Mirage*.

44. The CIA presence in U.S. embassies is essential to clandestine collection. Without an embassy presence, it would be extremely difficult for potential spies to actually locate the CIA presence in their particular countries.

45. "Iraq's Continuing Programs for Weapons of Mass Destruction," NIE, October 2002, p. 21; *The WMD Mirage*, ed. Craig Whitney.

46. "Iraq's Continuing Program for Weapons of Mass Destruction," National Intelligence Council, Washington, DC, October 2002.

47. "Iraq's Continuing Program for WMD," NIC, 2002.

48. Jessica T. Matthews and Jeff Miller, "A Tale of Two Intelligence Estimates," Washington, DC: Carnegie Endowment for International Peace, 2004.

49. Greg Miller, "CIA Corrects Itself on Arms," *The Los Angeles Times*, February 1, 2005, p. 1.

50. Scot Lehigh, "Revealing the Road to 'The Dark Side,'" *Boston.com*, July 13, 2006.

51. Kerr, Wolfe, Donegan, and Pappas, "Collection and Analysis on Iraq," p. 53.

52. Ibid., p. 53.

53. Ibid., p. 53.

54. Ibid., p. 51.

55. Thomas Powers, "The Biggest Secret," in *The New York Review of Books*, February 23, 2006, p. 11. See James Risen, *State of War: The Secret History of the CIA and the Bush Administration* (New York: Free Press, 2006).

56. John Prados, *Hoodwinked: The Documents That Reveal How Bush Sold Us a War* (New York: The New Press, 2004).

57. Risen, *State of War*, p. 175.

58. John Aloysius Farrell, "Memos: US Knew by '85 about Iraqi Diversions," *The Boston Globe*, July 4, 1992, p. 1.

59. The diversion scheme was a classic: Iraq secured loans for commodities purchases at prices far above prevailing market rates. By paying commodities suppliers less than the amount borrowed, Iraq was left with millions of dollars in excess profits. At least some this money was used to finance weapons research and purchases from German engineering firms to enhance the range of Iraqi Scud missiles and from the genius weapons designer Gerald Bull for his huge "superguns" that were capable of launching a satellite into space.

60. Douglas Jehl, "Report Warned Bush Team about Intelligence Doubts," *The New York Times,* November 6, 2005, p. 16.

CHAPTER 11

1. Pat M. Holt, "Congress Partly to Blame for Bush's Warrantless Wiretaps," *Christian Science Monitor*, January 5, 2006, p. 15.

2. John Stuart Mill, *Considerations on Representative Government* (London: Parker, Son, and Bourn, 1861), p. 104.

3. Mark M. Lowenthal, *Intelligence: From Secrets to Policy* (Washington, DC: CQ Press, 2000), pp. 141–42.

4. Marvin Ott, "The Rise and Fall of Intelligence Oversight," unpublished manuscript, p. 23.

5. Gates, "From the Shadows," p. 549.

6. Marvin Ott, "The Rise and Fall of Intelligence Oversight," unpublished draft study, p. 23.

7. Elaine Sciolino, "Senate Approves Gates by 64-31, to Head the CIA," *The New York Times*, November 6, 1991, p. 23. Sciolino offered fair and balanced coverage of the hearings until it became clear that Gates was going to receive confirmation despite the unprecedented opposition. In a conversation with the author after the hearings, Sciolino conceded that, when it became obvious that Gates would be victorious, she had to protect her access to the director of central intelligence and thus ignore the contrarian views of a former CIA analyst who had taken a pedestrian position as a faculty member at the National War College in Washington, D.C.

8. Interview with Richard Combs, Monterey, California, March 5, 1996.

9. See *The Final Report of the National Commission on Terrorist Attacks upon the United States* (Washington, DC: U.S. Government Printing Office, 2004).

10. "Advise and Assent," editorial, *The Los Angeles Times*, February 19, 2006, p. 6.

11. Lowell Bergman, Eric Lichtblau, Scott Shane, and Don Van Natta, Jr., "Spy Agency Data after Sept. 11 Led FBI to Dead Ends," *The New York Times,* January 17, 2006.

12. Louis Fisher, *House Resolutions of Inquiry* (Washington, DC: Congressional Research Service, May 12, 2003).

13. Fisher, *Resolutions of Inquiry*, p. 17.

14. Scott Shane, "U.S. Reclassifies Many Documents in Secret Review," *The New York Times,* February 21, 2006, p. 1.

15. John Harris, "Conservatives Sound Refrain: It's Clinton's Fault," *Washington Post*, October 7, 2002, p. 16.

CHAPTER 12

1. Admiral Stansfield Turner, *Burn Before Reading: Presidents, CIA Directors, and Secret Intelligence* (New York, Hyperion, 2005), p. 206.

2. Ibid., p. 190.

3. Christopher Andrew, *For the President's Eyes Only: Secret Intelligence and the American Presidency from Washington to Bush* (New York: HarperCollins Publishers, 1995), p. 460.

4. Joseph E. Persico, *Casey: The Lives and Secrets of William J. Casey: From the OSS to the CIA* (New York: Viking, 1990), pp. 372–80.

5. *The New York Times,* September 20, 1991, p. 14.

6. Lawrence C. Walsh, *Firewall: The Iran-Contra Conspiracy and Cover-Up* (New York: W.W. Norton and Company, 1997), p. 293.

7. Bob Woodward, *Veil: The Secret Wars of the CIA, 1981–1987* (New York: Simon & Schuster, 1987), p. 333.

8. Douglas F. Garthoff, *Directors of the Central Intelligence as Leaders of the U.S. Intelligence Community, 1946–2005* (Washington, DC: Central Intelligence Agency, 2005), p. 188.

9. Walsh, *Firewall,* pp. 297–98.

10. Ibid., p. 297.

11. Ibid., pp. 281–82.

12. Michael R. Beschloss and Strobe Talbott, *At the Highest Levels: The Inside Story of the End of the Cold War* (Boston: Little, Brown and Co., 1993), p. 48.

13. Ibid., p. 381.

14. Turner, *Burn Before Reading,* p. 219.

15. Beschloss and Talbott, "At the Highest Levels," p. 48.

16. Turner, *Burn Before Reading,* p. 225.

17. Douglas Garthoff, *Directors of Central Intelligence as Leaders of the U.S. Intelligence Community, 1946–2005* (Washington, DC: Center for the Study of Intelligence, Central Intelligence Agency), p. 225.

18. Turner, *Burn Before Reading,* p. 227.

19. Tim Weiner, David Johnston, and Neil A. Lewis, *Betrayal: The Story of Aldrich Ames, an American Spy* (New York: Random House, 1995), p. 284.

20. Wiener, *Betrayal,* p. 285.

21. Douglas F. Garthoff, *Directors of Central Intelligence as Leaders of the U.S. Intelligence Community 1946–2005* (Washington, DC: Center for the Study of Intelligence, Central Intelligence Agency, 2005), p. 245. Garthoff's hagiography argues against the CIA's practice of publishing so-called official history, and certainly points to the need for outside review of such works.

22. Ibid.

23. Thomas Powers, "The Trouble with the CIA," *The New York Review of Books,* January 17, 2002, p. 31.

24. Charles J. Hanley, "Mystery Unfolds Over Hunt for WMD in Iraq," AP, September 2, 2005.

25. Ibid.

26. Chalmers Johnson, "Porter Goss' WIA—Worthless Intelligence Agency," Tomdispatch .com, November 29, 2004.

27. Robert Dreyfuss, "The Yes-Man," *The American Prospect,* November, 2005, p. 17.

28. Wolf Blitzer, "The Situation Room," CNN, September 29, 2006, Interview with John McLaughlin.

29. Dafna Linzer, "A Year Later, Goss's CIA Is Still in Turmoil," *Washington Post,* October 19, 2005, p. 1.

30. Jackie Northam, "Goss, CIA Confront Leadership Exodus," NPR *Morning Edition* (NPR.org), March 1, 2006.

31. Linzer, "A Year Later," p. 1.

32. National Press Club, Washington, D.C., January 23, 2006, Hayden's response to question from Jonathan Landay of Knight Ridder. See www.globalsecurity.org/intell/library/news/2006.

CHAPTER 13

1. Tim Weiner, *The New York Times,* October 7, 2001, p. 17.

2. Op. cit.

3. James Risen and Eric Lichtblau, "Bush Lets U.S. Spy on Callers Without Courts," *The New York Times*, December 15, 2005, p. 1.

4. *Washington Post*, September 9, 2002, p. 17.

5. Walter Pincus, "Pentagon Expanding its Domestic Surveillance Activity," *Washington Post*, November 27, 2005, p. 1.

6. William Arkin, "The Pentagon Breaks the Law," *Washington Post*, December 22, 2005, p.

7. Op. Cit.

8. Jim Dwyer, "New York Police Covertly Join In at Protest Rallies," *The New York Times,* December 22, 2005, p. 1.

9. Ibid., p. 28.

10. "Le Nouvel Observateur," October 11, 1998, p. 5.

11. Merle Miller, *Plain Speaking: An Oral Biography of Harry S. Truman* (New York: G.P. Putnam's Sons, 1973), pp. 391–392.

12. Clark Clifford with Richard Holbrooke, *Counsel to the President: A Memoir* (New York, Random House, 1991), p. 170.

13. Richard K. Betts, "Fixing Intelligence," *Foreign Affairs 81(1)* (January/February 2002): 46.

14. Testimony Before the Senate Select Committee on Intelligence Activities, December 5, 1975; Executive Order 12036, Washington, DC: Government Printing Office, 1978.

15. Daniel Patrick Moynihan, *Secrecy* (New Haven: Yale University Press, 1998).

16. Linda Robinson and Kevin Whitelaw, "Seeking Spies," *US News and World Report,* February 13, 2006, p. 17.

17. Richard Russell, "CIA's Strategic Intelligence in Iraq," *Political Science Quarterly 117/2* (2002): 207.

18. See www.cia.gov/cia/public_affairs/press_release/2005/pr11082005.html.

19. Jeff Dufour and Patrick Gavin, Examiner.com, July 5, 2007.

20. Philip Tetlock, *Expert Political Judgment: How Good Is It? How Can We Know?* (Princeton, New Jersey: Princeton University Press, 2005).

21. Thomas Freedman, "The Kidnapping of Democracy," *The New York Times*, July 14, 2006, p. 25.

22. Scott Shane, "Year Into Revamped Spying; Troubles and Some Progress," *The New York Times*, February 28, 2006, p. 12.

23. L. Britt Snider, "Creating a Statutory Inspector General at the CIA," *Studies in Intelligence* (Washington, DC: Central Intelligence Agency), p. 17.

24. Ibid., p. 18.

Index

About the Author

Melvin A. Goodman is a senior fellow at the Center for International Policy in Washington, D.C., and an adjunct professor of government at Johns Hopkins University. He has more than forty years of experience in the CIA, the State Department's Bureau of Intelligence and Research, and the Department of Defense. He is the coauthor of six books, including *Bush League Diplomacy: How the Neoconservatives are Putting the World at Risk* (2004) and *The Phantom Defense: The Case Against National Missile Defense* (2001).